Immigration and the Family

Research and Policy on U.S. Immigrants

IMMIGRATION AND THE FAMILY

Research and Policy on U.S. Immigrants

Edited by

Alan Booth
Ann C. Crouter
Nancy Landale
The Pennsylvania State University

 LAWRENCE ERLBAUM ASSOCIATES, PUBLISHERS
1997   Mahwah, New Jersey

Lawrence Erlbaum Associates, Inc., Publishers
10 Industrial Avenue
Mahwah, New Jersey 07430

Cover design by Kathryn Houghtaling

LIBRARY OF CONGRESS CATALOGING-IN-PUBLICATION DATA

Immigration and the family : research and policy on U.S. immigrants / edited by Alan Booth,
    Ann C. Crouter, Nancy Landale.
        p.   cm.
    Includes bibliographical references and index.
    ISBN 0-8058-2153-8
    1. Immigrants—United States—Family relationships.   2. Children of immigrants—
United States.   3. United States—Emigration and immigration—Social aspects.   I. Booth,
Alan, 1935– . II. Crouter, Ann C.   III. Landale, Nancy.
HQ536.I49   1996
306.85—dc20
                                                                        96–15490
                                                                        CIP

Books published by Lawrence Erlbaum Associates are printed on acid-free paper,
and their bindings are chosen for strength and durability.

Printed in the United States of America
10 9 8 7 6 5 4 3 2 1

Contents

v

PART III: HOW DO FAMILY STRUCTURE AND PROCESS CHANGE ACROSS SUCCEEDING GENERATIONS?

PART IV: WHAT POLICIES ENHANCE OR IMPEDE IMMIGRANT FAMILY LINKS TO U.S. INSTITUTIONS?

Preface

THE NUMBER of first-generation, documented and undocumented immigrant individuals in the United States is 19.8 million, up 106% from 1970. Although much is known about their numbers and origin, very little is known about immigrant families even though their experience in the process of assimilation and adaptation is vital.

Several questions are central to understanding the migrant experience and family outcomes. Who migrates, and how does it affect family outcomes? How does the migration experience affect child and adolescent development? How do family structure and process change across succeeding generations? What policies enhance or impede immigrant family links to U.S. institutions? The chapters in this book address these questions and related issues. The chapters are based on the presentations and discussion from a national symposium on international migration and family change held at the Pennsylvania State University, November 2–3, 1995, as the third in a series of annual symposia focused on family issues.

ACKNOWLEDGMENTS

There are many to thank for assistance with the symposium. We are indebted to the Pennsylvania State University Population Research Institute, Center for the Study of Child and Adolescent Development, Department of Sociology, Department of Psychology, Department of Human Development and

Family Studies, and the College of the Liberal Arts for funding the symposium. We appreciate the advice and encouragement of members of the Population Research Institute and the Center for the Study of Child and Adolescent Development throughout the process of planning and conducting the symposium. The contributions of Michelle Gingery, Debra Huber, Kris Emigh, Sheri Miller, Sondra Morrison, Pat Thomas, Sherry Yocum, and Chuck Herd in assisting with the administration of the symposium were invaluable. Special thanks to professors Gordon DeJong, Kathy Fennelly, Michael Shanahan, and Sal Oropesa for their excellent work in presiding over the four sessions, and for their contributions to the flow of ideas during the sessions.

PART I

WHO MIGRATES, AND HOW DOES IT AFFECT FAMILY OUTCOMES?

1

Ties That Bind:
Immigration and Immigrant Families
in the United States

Rubén G. Rumbaut
Michigan State University

Family unity has and continues to be the cornerstone of immigration policy for the United States. A point of debate about generous family unity policies is a concern that family immigrants take rather than contribute economically. Family-based immigration is alleged to be an inefficient means of selecting workers that contributes to a decline in the skill levels of the workforce. Much of this argument misjudges the character of family-based immigration. Family-connection immigrants are also workers. Immigrants are typically admitted under family reunification provisions who could also qualify in virtually all professional and technical occupations specified in immigration laws. Indirectly, family reunification also admits workers with skills. . . . More important, however, is the economic and social role the family plays in immigrant adaptation. Families ease the considerable social and cultural dislocations caused by immigration and, by serving as intermediaries to the host society, enable the newcomer to adapt. Family and household structures are also primary factors in promoting high economic achievement. They are crucial resources in the formation of immigrant businesses, which often revitalize urban neighborhoods and specialized economic sectors. These successful social and economic transitions lay the foundations that are needed if the children of immigrants are to be effective citizen-workers of the next generation.
—Meissner, Hormats, Walker, and Ogata, 1993, pp. 13–14.

There are two families in the world, as one of my grandmothers used to say, the Haves and the Have-nots.
—Miguel de Cervantes Saavedra, *Don Quijote,* (1605–1615: II, 20)

IMMIGRATION and "family values" are in the news these days—indeed, they are hot-button political issues in the presidential campaigns now under way. It is said that there is too much of the former and too little of the latter, but (with rare exceptions) no connection is made between the two. That disconnection reflects in part the relative lack of attention given to children and family in immigration studies; they are topics that belong to the realm of what David Riesman once called *underprivileged reality*. And yet, the family is perhaps *the* strategic research site (cf. Merton, 1987) for understanding the dynamics of immigration flows (legal and illegal) and of immigrant adaptation processes as well as long-term consequences for sending and especially for receiving countries, such as the United States. Kinship is also central to understanding U.S. immigration policies and their intended and unintended consequences. Marriage and close family ties, as Meissner et al. (1993) underscored, are the basis for longstanding selection criteria built into U.S. immigration law.

Consider the 904,292 immigrants legally admitted in fiscal 1993, the second year in which the provisions of the Immigration Act of 1990 were fully in effect. Table 1.1 summarizes the main types of categories and sponsorships for all immigrant admissions, including employment-based and diversity transition visas, refugees and asylees, and IRCA (Immigration Reform and Control Act) legalizations and dependents. At the risk of oversimplifying what is a highly complex process, gaining immigrant status generally requires a sponsor who may be a U.S. citizen or legal resident, a U.S. employer, or (especially in the case of refugees) the U.S. government. Of these, the principal route to legal immigration—in over 75% of all cases in 1993—involved a close family tie, a figure that actually understates the pervasiveness of family connections because many of the principals who entered as refugees or through nonfamily preferences already had relatives in the United States. As usual, the largest single mode of legal admission involved a marriage to a U.S. citizen. The 145,843 spouses of U.S. citizens who were admitted as immigrants in 1993 was the highest total ever recorded, tripling the number of spouses admitted in 1970. Trend data over the past quarter century clearly show as well that immigration via marriage to a U.S. citizen has been growing much more rapidly than that of parents or children of U.S. citizens (INS, 1994). Indeed, despite the variety of qualitative and quantitative restrictions placed on immigrants by dozens of U.S. laws since the late 19th century, the wives (and minor children) of U.S. citizens have never been restricted from immigrating, nor have husbands from Western Hemisphere countries.[1] Under current law (the Immi-

---

[1] Of course, the operative word here is *citizen*. The right of an immigrant to become a U.S. citizen through naturalization was restricted on racial grounds until 1952. The first federal naturalization law of 1790 gave that right only to "free white persons," and a revised law in 1870 extended it to persons of African descent or nativity, including Arabs and Hindus. Most Asian immigrants were excluded from access to American citizenship until the McCarran-Walter Act of 1952. Asian

TABLE 1.1
Family Connections: Immigrants Admitted by Type of Admission and Sponsorship, 1993

Immigrants	Family-Sponsored		IRCA	Employment-Based	U.S. Government-Sponsored		Totals	
	U.S. Citizen	U.S. Resident	Legalization[1]	U.S. Employer[2]	Refugee, Other[3]	Diversity, Other[4]	N	%
Principals	—		24,278	78,685	91,487	26,061	220,511	24.4
Family members	353,527	128,308	55,344	68,327	63,770	14,505	683,781	75.6
Spouses	145,843	43,033	17,145	32,247	21,656	6,896	266,820	29.5
Children[5]	82,992	85,275	38,199	36,080	35,401	7,609	285,556	31.6
Parents	62,428	—	—	—	6,713	—	69,141	7.6
Siblings	62,264	—	—	—	—	—	62,264	6.9
Totals	353,527	128,308	79,622	147,012	155,257	40,566	904,292	100.0

[1]In 1993, only 24,278 immigrants adjusted their status under the legalization provisions of the Immigration Reform and Control Act of 1986, virtually completing the amnesty process through which about 2.7 million persons have attained permanent resident status since 1989. Under the Immigration Act of 1990, approximately 55,000 spouses and minor children of IRCA legalizees were allowed to immigrate annually during 1992, 1993, and 1994.

[2]Most immigrants admitted based on employment-based preferences are sponsored by a U.S. employer, although some qualify without a job offer. In 1993, the 26,852 principals admitted under the Chinese Student Protection Act under the employment 3rd preference were not required to have a job offer.

[3]Total includes 127,343 refugees and asylees; 11,116 Amerasians and their close family; Indochinese and Soviet parolees.

[4]Total includes 33,468 "diversity transition" immigrants, receiving visas under provisions of the 1990 Act allocated to nationals of certain countries said to have been "adversely affected" by the 1965 amendments; up to 40,000 visas annually were allocated during 1992–94, with 40% reserved for natives of Ireland.

[5]The total for children sponsored by U.S. citizens and legal permanent residents includes both minor and adult (married or unmarried) sons and daughters.

Source: Adapted from U.S. Immigration and Naturalization Service, *1993 Statistical Yearbook* (Washington, DC: U.S. Government Printing Office, 1994), Table 5.

gration Act of 1990), as has been the case for three decades, immediate relatives of adult U.S. citizens (i.e., spouses, children, and parents) may enter without any limitation. (The best quantitative analysis of marriage and family ties
in U.S. legal immigration flows remains that of Jasso & Rosenzweig, 1990; on
marriage and kinship networks among undocumented immigrants from Mexico and Central America, see Chavez, 1992; Massey & Espinosa, 1995.)

Immigration to the United States is largely a family affair and probably will
remain so for the future, regardless of the reforms and restrictions that are
currently making their way through the legislative process in Congress and
may soon become U.S. law. In the late 1980s the backlog for immigrant visas
was such that, for some preference categories, the waiting line for applicants
from main sending countries like Mexico and the Philippines extended to 10,
15, and even 20 years (cf. Rumbaut, 1991b). Susan Forbes Martin of the U.S.
Commission on Immigration Reform recently estimated that if someone applies from the Philippines today, it could take, preposterously, up to 43 years
to obtain a visa! Simply eliminating the legal eligibility of close family members to immigrate may have the unintended result of creating new pressures
and motives for illegal immigration. As Massey and Espinosa (1995) showed
in a compelling analysis of determinants of migration from Mexico to the
United States, reducing the supply of legal visas does not affect the volume of
the migrant stream but simply channels a larger proportion of it into undocumented status.

To varying degrees of closeness, the more than 22 million immigrants in
the United States today, to which can be added an even larger number of their
U.S.-born offspring, are embedded in often intricate webs of family ties, both
here and abroad. Such ties form extraordinary transnational linkages and networks that can, by reducing the costs and risks of migration, expand and serve
as a conduit to additional and thus potentially self-perpetuating migration.
Massey and his colleagues (1994) recently pointed to a stunning statistic (reported in Camp, 1993): By the end of the 1980s, national surveys in Mexico
found that about half of adult Mexicans were related to someone living in the
United States and that one third of all Mexicans had been to the United States
at some point in their lives. By the same token, despite 35 years of hostile relations, it is my guess that perhaps a third of Cuba's population of 11 million
have relatives in the United States and Puerto Rico. The proportion of immigrants in the United States in 1990 who hail from countries in the English-
speaking Caribbean, notably from Jamaica, Barbados, Trinidad and Tobago,
Belize, and Guyana, already constituted between 10% and 20% of the 1990

Indians had been able to naturalize on the grounds that they were Caucasians until the U.S.
Supreme Court, in a 1923 case, decided that they would no longer be considered white persons.
The Chinese were removed from the classes of "aliens ineligible for citizenship" upon the repeal
of the Chinese Exclusion Act in 1943, when China and the United States were World War II al-
lies. See Ueda (1981) and Hing (1993).

populations of their respective countries—a double-digit group to which can also now be added El Salvador (Rumbaut, 1992). Family connections in turn enhance the potential for further "chain" migration, both legal and extralegal. (On the family-reunification immigration multiplier among legal immigrants, see Jasso & Rosenzweig, 1986, 1989, 1990; Arnold, Cariño, Fawcett, & Park, 1989.) A recent report in *The New York Times* told about the tragic fate of a Chinese family from Chang Le, a town of 650,000 in Fujian Province that is the source of most illegal Chinese immigration to the United States (which often involves incurring family debts of as much as $30,000 to pay "snake-heads" [smugglers] for passage to New York City). According to the report, "nearly everyone in Chang Le . . . seems to have a relative or acquaintance who made the journey in the last five years" (Faison & Lii, 1995).

Such chaining processes often lead to remarkably dense ethnic concentrations in U.S. cities, consisting of entire community segments from places of origin and including extended families and friends, not just compatriots. In some cities in California and elsewhere, the links with particular towns or villages in Mexico go back generations and can be traced to the 1942–1964 Bracero Program or to earlier migration chains (see Alvarez, 1987; Massey, Alarcón, Durand, & González, 1987). However, the process can take place very quickly. For instance, when Saigon fell in 1975, there were very few Vietnamese and virtually no Cambodians and Laotians residing in the United States, and in the absence of preexisting family ties, U.S. resettlement policy succeeded initially in its aim to disperse the Indochinese refugee population to all 50 states ("to avoid another Miami," as one planner put it, referring to the huge concentration of Cuban refugees there). By the early 1980s about a third of arriving refugees already had close relatives in the United States who could serve as sponsors, and another third had more distant relatives, leaving only the remaining third without kinship ties subject to the dispersal policy (Hein, 1995; Rumbaut, 1995b). By 1985, 20% of the small Salvadoran town of Intipucá was already living in the Adams-Morgan section of Washington, DC, and had formed a Club of Intipucá City to assist new arrivals (Schoultz, 1992). Such spatial concentrations of kin and kith serve to provide newcomers with manifold sources of moral, social, cultural, and economic support that are unavailable to immigrants who are more dispersed and help to explain the gravitational pull exerted by places where family and friends of immigrants are concentrated (Portes & Rumbaut, 1996; Rumbaut, 1994b). In the process, as Tilly put it, immigrants create "migration machines: sending networks . . . articulated with particular receiving networks in which new migrants could find jobs, housing, and sociability" (1990, p. 90).

The import of immigrant family connections goes far beyond their functions for chain (or circular) migration and local support. Remittances ("migradollars") sent by immigrants to family members back home (which, worldwide, according to a United Nations estimate, amounted to $71 billion in

1991, second only to oil sales) link communities across national borders and are vital to the economies of many sending countries.[2] Remarkably, the survey of formerly undocumented immigrants who had resided in the United States since 1982 and who applied for legalization under IRCA found that the families of legalized aliens remitted about $1.2 billion to family members and friends outside the U.S. in 1987 alone. This figure represented about 7% of the family income, earned largely from low-wage jobs (INS, 1992). Across the border, one town of only 3,500 in rural Mexico received over $1 million in U.S. remittances and savings in the year prior to a recent survey there (Massey & Parrado, 1994). Or consider the role of family ties in this other example: a decade and a half ago in Vietnam, ethnic Chinese and Vietnamese refugees were paying 5 to 10 gold pieces ($2,000 to $4,000) per adult to cross the South China Sea in flimsy fishing boats—a price well beyond the means of the average Vietnamese. To afford this often required ingenious exchange schemes through kinship networks. For instance, a family in Vietnam planning to escape by boat contacted another that had decided to stay to obtain the necessary gold for the passage; they in turn arranged with family members already in the United States (usually "first wave" refugees) for the relatives of the escaping family to pay an equivalent amount in dollars to the second family's relatives (Rumbaut, 1991b). Similar exchange arrangements via family branches were developed by Soviet Jewish émigres who had been forbidden to take anything of value with them upon leaving the Soviet Union (Orleck, 1987).

That embeddedness in family, in a web of primary ties of affection, trust, and obligation—or what Bodnar described as "the ligaments of responsibility among kin" (1987, p. 72)—is at once a rich resource and a potential vulnerability. The family is, in Lasch's (1977) memorable phrase, a "Haven in a Heartless World," but it can sometimes be its headquarters. Family ties are a source of both positive and negative social capital (Portes & Sensenbrenner, 1993; see also Bertaux-Wiame, 1993; Coleman, 1988; Fernández-Kelly & Schauffler, 1994; McLanahan & Sandefur, 1994; Tienda, 1980), that is, a resource that inheres not in the individual but in social (familial) relationships that can cut both ways, enabling as well as constraining particular outcomes. Family ties bind—and band, and bond, and bundle. The family is home, a place where, as Elizabeth Stone put it in her engaging study of family stories, "when you have to go there, they have to take you in" (1988, p. 21). It is the crucible of self and socialization, of character, conscience, authority and discipline, of our very names, linking us in a chain of being and meaning. But the family can also become the site for intense, deep-seated conflicts between spouses, siblings, par-

---

[2]Suro (1994), focusing on Mexican kinship networks, put it this way: "Families are the brokerage houses of migration. They raise capital and spread risk. They vouchsafe the investment's legitimacy, and when it produces a profit in the form of remittances sent home by the migrant, the family distributes dividends" (p. 36).

ents, and children. Especially among immigrant families moving from one sociocultural environment to another, gender and generational role dissonance in rapidly changing marital and parent–child relationships can amplify and intensify conflicts and lead to family breakdown (Addams, 1910; Antin, 1912; Berrol, 1995; Child, 1943; Glenn & Yap, 1994; Grasmuck & Pessar, 1991; Handlin, 1951; Hein, 1995; Hondagneu-Sotelo, 1994; Kibria, 1993, 1994; Menjívar, 1996; Min, 1995; Rubin, 1994; Sung, 1987; Thomas & Znaniecki, 1958; Vigil, 1988; Wheeler, 1972). In given circumstances, however, because families are nested in and shaped by larger structural, cultural, and historical contexts, the shared adversity of the migration and subsequent adaptation experiences can motivate the family to close ranks cohesively and productively, honing in social solidarity an adaptive ethos of effort and efficacy and providing fertile soil for often remarkable achievement in the new country (Rumbaut & Rumbaut, 1976; see also Bodnar, 1987; Caplan, Choy, & Whitmore, 1991; Johnson, 1982; Suárez-Orozco, 1989; Suárez-Orozco & Suárez-Orozco, 1995).

International migration entails more often than not a radical, engulfing, transformative process that profoundly affects and changes all who attempt it, including individuals, families, and societies. It is no mere coincidence that the words *travel* and *travail* share a common etymology (Furnham & Bochner, 1986, p. 63). The shock of such a journey depends to a large extent on the social distance traveled from origin to destination. At one end of the spectrum of migration contexts are the preliterate Hmong peasants from the Laotian highlands, who fled on foot in the aftermath of the Indochina War, crossed a jungle and the Mekong river, and were penned for years in Thai refugee camps before eventually resettling in megalopolitan California or Minnesota. A well-connected cosmopolitan English professional, job offer and visa in hand, who flies business class with her American husband from London to Boston to pursue an enticing career opportunity with a multinational conglomerate headquartered in New England, is quite at the other end. Both of these, and tens of thousands of others located between these poles in widely divergent contexts of exit and reception, of choice and fate, immigrate to the United States each month, with or without permission, by foot, boat, or jumbo jet. Haves and have-nots alike, immigrant families come in all shapes and must confront dramatically different contexts of adaptation, a fact that should be obvious upon a moment's reflection were it not largely lost in the aggregate statistics, the policy agendas, the Procrustean debates, the 30-second soundbites, the sheer complexity of the flows. Indeed, to make sense of the diversity of immigrant families we need to begin with the recognition that it makes no sense to speak of a singular immigrant family experience. Often the most insightful statements on what goes on within such families, whose class origins range from manual laborers to professionals to entrepreneurs to once well-heeled exiles, are found in both fictional and nonfictional autobiographical tracts written with a perspicaciously nuanced mastery of the new language by children of immigrants, such as Mary Antin (1912), Henry Roth (1992/1934), Eva Hoffman (1989), Maxine Hong Kingston (1976), Amy Tan (1989), Chang Rae Lee (1995), Richard Rodriguez (1982), Julia Alvarez (1991), Cristina García (1992), and Gustavo Pérez Firmat (1994, 1995), who have variously come of age between two worlds.[3]

Historically, much of the literature on the experience of immigrant families has oscillated between the poles of unmitigated stories of woe and "social disorganization" on the one hand, and idealized, sepia-tinted nostalgia on the other. Whatever our concerns as scholars or policymakers or service providers dealing with some aspect of contemporary immigration to the United States —to assess the modes of entry and incorporation of today's immigrant groups, the divergent trajectories of a new second generation coming of age in American cities, or the impact of migration that ensues—the centrality of the family is indisputable. Migration and adaptation are highly complex social processes, amd family outcomes ultimately need to be grasped and measured not only in the first years after arrival (or in transnational jaunts or sojourns) but across generations. The issue then is to take stock of the evidence on immigrant families and see what we can learn from the extraordinary complexity and diversity of the new immigration and what light can be shed on its outcomes.[4] To this end, I contextualize the discussion by sketching a profile of the new immigration, looking comparatively if briefly at historical contexts and contemporary flows, main types, and issues of human capital, political capital, and social capital among families from principal immigrant nationalities. I also discuss some effects of migration on family outcomes over time, looking selectively at contemporary patterns of immigrant family structure, change, and conflict and at the effect of family characteristics and contexts on the educational attainment and aspirations of their children, both those who came at an early

---

[3] Pérez Firmat (1995) wrote in his absorbing memoir of exile and of his "troubled family that I love and loathe so dearly," that "no family survives exile intact. . . . Exile is a heavy weight. The family is a muscle that grows stronger by lifting heavy weights, or tears in the attempt. In our family, but I'm certain that it's not just our family, the muscle has torn. . . . Exile pushes us to the limit. There, at the limit, we find our best and worst selves. . . . Moving to the United States made it more difficult for my father to be a good father and for us to be good brothers and sons. Instead of sticking together and helping each other cope, we flew off in separate directions" (pp. 168–172).

[4] For comparative historical evidence on Southern and Eastern European immigrant families in the early years of this century, see, for example, Bodnar, 1987; Brown, 1994; Hareven and Modell, 1981; Miller, Morgan, and McDaniel, 1994; Pozzetta, 1991; U.S. Immigration [Dillingham] Commission, 1911. There is a wide-ranging literature on immigrant and ethnic minority families focused on specific ethnic groups, past and present; for other examples of case studies that depict the diversity of migration and family experiences, see Agbayani-Siewert and Revilla, 1995; Baca Zinn, 1994; Carrasquillo, 1994; Diner, 1995; Espiritu, 1995; Glenn, 1986; Gold and Phillips, 1995; Griswold del Castillo, 1984; Laguerre, 1994; Leonard, 1992; Min, 1995; Nishi, 1995; Pérez, 1986, 1994; Rumbaut and Ima, 1988; Sheth, 1995; Takagi, 1994; Waters, 1994; Wong, 1995; Yans-McLaughlin, 1977.

age and those who were born in the United States. For the former I rely on national-level Immigration and Naturalization Service (INS) and census data; for the latter I draw mainly on a new data set from a large-scale study of children of immigrants in Southern California and South Florida.

WHO MIGRATES? PERSPECTIVES ON THE "NEW" IMMIGRATION

A century ago another massive wave of immigration to the United States from Southern and Eastern Europe was dubbed the "new" immigration by the U.S. Immigration [Dillingham] Commission (1911) to distinguish it from the "old" immigration from Northwest Europe. It became a pejorative appellation, for the Commission's 42-volume report to the Congress consisted largely of a statistical compendium of the negative traits of the new relative to the old. INS data show that 8.8 million immigrants were admitted during the 1900–1910 decade, the largest on record (an official figure certain to be surpassed in the 1990s). Much of this flow was initiated by active recruitment on the part of American employers, and many immigrants returned home after a few years in the United States (fully a third overall, according to the Commission, ranging from less than 10% for the "Hebrew" [Eastern European Jews] to some 60% for the Italians). Those "birds of passage" were predominantly young single men, whose movements tended to follow the ups and downs of the American business cycle (Piore, 1979).[5] After World War I broke out, immigration began an uneven and then precipitous decline with the passage of restrictive national-origins quota laws in the 1920s (the Act of 1924 did not go fully into effect until 1929) and especially as a result of the Great Depression, until the trend reversed itself immediately after World War II.

In the post-World War II period, legal immigration flows have been sustained more by family preferences in the allocation of immigrant visas and by kinship networks developed over time (Jasso & Rosenzweig, 1990) than by economic cycles and deliberate recruitment; thus, whereas in the first four decades of the century 67% of all immigrants were men, since 1941 the majority, 55%, have been women (INS, 1994). Since 1970, moreover, the great majority of immigrants legally admitted to permanent residency have come not from Europe and Canada but from Asia and Latin America and the Caribbean. Contemporary flows have also notably included sizable and increasing proportions of three distinct types of immigrants: *political refugees and*

---

[5] Indeed, observing that "family immigration is naturally more permanent," the Commission noted that "the fact that more than three-fourths of the newer immigration, Hebrews excepted, is composed of males suggests that there are relatively fewer families than among immigrants of the older class. . . . It is well known that Hebrew immigration is essentially a movement of families" (p. 24).

asylees, beginning with the 1948 Displaced Persons Act, which first recognized refugees in U.S. law; *highly skilled professionals, executives, and managers*, who have entered variously under employment-based visa preferences, in the first waves of refugee exoduses, or under student or other temporary statuses (who may then later adjust their status via marriage to a U.S. citizen or connections with U.S. employers); and *undocumented laborers*, whose numbers began to swell after the termination in 1964 of the Bracero Program (begun to meet labor shortages in the southwest during World War II but maintained during the postwar years of rapid expansion of the U.S. economy) and also ironically after passage of the 1965 law (and its sequels in 1976 and 1978) which placed for the first time numerical limits on legal immigration from the independent countries of the Western Hemisphere even as it abolished the national-origins quota system that had governed admissions from the Eastern Hemisphere. Once forged and set in motion, family networks can sustain the expansion of each of these types of flows through chain migration.

To be sure, this threefold classification of contemporary immigrants is not exhaustive of their diverse origins and modes of incorporation, but it will help to organize our analysis by focusing attention on the most salient types. Each of these immigrant types is represented by several nationalities, and conversely, within a single nationality individuals who represent different types may be found (Portes & Rumbaut, 1990). Each type is generally characterized by distinct sets of resources and vulnerabilities in distinct contexts of exit and of reception that are likely to shape their adaptation process. The social class resources (i.e., financial and human capital), the legal status at entry (i.e., political capital), and the social networks and family structure and cohesiveness (i.e., social capital) of these salient types of immigrants combine in ways that produce cumulative social advantages or disadvantages as they make their way in America. All three of these factors can be expected to have substantial impact on virtually all subsequent individual and family outcomes (including their psychological and cultural dimensions).

For example, the undocumented tend to consist disproportionately of manual laborers (more so for those who enter illegally by crossing the border than those who overstay a temporary visa). They are politically disenfranchised by definition, and their legal vulnerability makes them in turn more economically exploitable. Because intact family unit migration, especially when it involves young children, involves greater costs and resources, undocumented labor flows tend to be disproportionately composed of males and of separated, split, or transnational families (cf. Chavez, 1992; Hondagneu-Sotelo, 1994). Professionals are more typically found among pioneer immigrants who come under the occupational preferences of U.S. law, often in nuclear family units whereupon, once established as permanent residents or naturalized U.S. citizens, they can sponsor the immigration of other immediate family members, and also among the more elite first waves of refugee flows. Immigrant professionals are also more likely to be geographically dispersed because they tend to rely more on their qualifications and job offers than on preexisting kinship networks and ethnic communities, as do working-class immigrants and entrepreneurs. Refugees, by contrast, especially escapees from war-torn countries such as Indochina, are often distinguished from other types of immigrants by harsh contexts of exit, less planning and preparation, blocked return options, and the psychological ramifications of exile and coerced homelessness (cf. Rumbaut, 1989, 1991a). However, the legal status of refugee or asylee (which, among other things, allows means-tested access to public assistance and social services that other equally poor legal or illegal immigrants do not have) is conferred or not by the U.S. government largely for foreign policy reasons that are independent of the harshness of the conditions that may have motivated a particular migration. These factors interact in complex ways with external contexts of reception such as the extent of racial discrimination and nativist prejudice, government policies, the state of the economy and employer preferences in local labor markets, and the strength of existing co-ethnic communities in areas of immigrant settlement to mold the diverse fates of immigrant groups. Origins shape destinies.[6]

---

[6]Although it is beyond the scope of this chapter to elaborate the point, it might be added that immigrant family formations are shaped within historically specific contexts of migration and reception. For example, the Cuban migration saw an exodus of intact families as well as of some 15,000 "Peter Pan" children who were sent without their parents during the first waves of 1959–1962; the tens of thousands who came annually during the 1965–1973 freedom flights brought a disproportionate number of elderly (i.e., the Castro government did not allow young people of military age to leave), with a result today that there are more three-generation Cuban households in Miami with resident grandparents than almost any other ethnic group in the country, a fact that has played a significant role in their family economic success story; and the *Marielitos* of 1980 and the thousands of *balseros* in the 1990s disproportionately involved young men, single or separated from their families left behind in Cuba (see Olson & Olson, 1995; Pérez 1986, 1994; Rumbaut & Rumbaut, 1976). There is thus no single "Cuban family type" in the United States; but rather, family outcomes have shaped and have been shaped by immigrants' reactions to specific contexts and contingencies. The same can be said about all other immigrant families, past and present. Thus, Wong (1995) and others have noted how exclusionary policies and vastly disparate sex ratios among Chinese immigrants through the early 20th century formed bizarre family structures referred to variously as split household and mutilated family, which later evolved transitional forms (especially after the 1943 repeal of the Chinese Exclusion Act began to make family reunification possible) and, in the wake of large-scale post-1965 immigration waves, bimodal family types ("dual worker," "ghetto" or "downtown" vs. "uptown" and "semi-extended" families). Koreans, Filipinos, and Asian Indians also were marked early on by disparate male ratios, and in California many of the latter married Mexican wives (see Leonard, 1992). Japanese family formation reflected a far more balanced population sex ratio than other Asian groups (in part because the "Gentlemen's Agreement" of 1908 between the two governments allowed wives and children to enter, plus the impact of "picture brides" and "Kandodan brides") but also confronted the generation-defining experience of internment during World War II (Glenn, 1986; Hing, 1993; Nishi, 1995). War orphans by the thousands were adopted during and after the Korean War by U.S. servicemen, and by the 1970s and 1980s over 3,000 Korean children annually were adopted by U.S. citizens and admitted to the United States—accounting for about 60% of all foreign-born children

The National Origins of the New Immigration

Changes in U.S. immigration laws and in particular the amendments passed in 1965 (fully implemented in 1968), which abolished the national-origins quota system and changed the preference system to give greater priority to family reunification over occupational skills, have often been singled out as the principal reason for the new immigration and the change in the national origins of its composition, which is documented by the trend data presented in Table 1.2. However, the causal effects of the Hart-Celler Act of 1965 have been exaggerated and misinterpreted by this *legal determinist* position, especially with regard to Latin American immigration and the large-scale entry of Cold War refugees (to say nothing of illegal immigration). It bears emphasizing that until this law was passed, Western Hemisphere immigration had been unrestricted, largely at the behest of American agribusiness; in fact, as Zolberg (1995) has pointed out, the legislative history of the 1965 Act "indicates very clearly that the objective was to deter the growth of black and brown immigration" (p. 155) from Latin America and the Caribbean while increasing that from Southern and Eastern Europe (see also Díaz-Briquets, 1995; Rumbaut, 1991b). For that matter, the 1965 law had nothing to do with determining, say, the huge Cuban exile flows of the early 1960s or the even larger Indochinese refugee flows that followed in the aftermath of the Vietnam War. What is more, the most important consequences of the 1965 Act, notably the removal of barriers to immigrants from Asian and African countries (Hing, 1993; Reimers, 1985), were largely unintended. The law does matter, of course: It influences migration decisions and constitutes a key context of reception shaping the incorporation of newcomers, especially their right to full membership and future citizenship, and thereby provides a source of political capital unavailable to residents without legal status. Yet it cannot control historical forces or determine the size or source of migration flows. Indeed, the very existence of large flows of undocumented migration underscores the limits of immigration policies, particularly when what is sought is nothing less than to control a world on the move, with the United States as a main destination.

Migration patterns, rather, are rooted in historical relationships established between the United States and the principal sending countries (Portes & Rumbaut, 1990, 1996; Zolberg, 1995). The size and source of new immigrant

---

adopted by U.S. citizens (Min, 1995). By 1994, over 100,000 Amerasians (i.e., children of Vietnamese mothers and American fathers who served in Vietnam during the war) and their immediate relatives had been resettled in the United States under a special law enacted in 1987. Indeed, Vietnamese and Cambodian families and sex ratios today reflect fundamentally different contexts of exit and processes of family fission and fusion in the course of flight, resettlement from refugee camps to third countries, and later reunification through secondary migrations over time to join family members elsewhere (Hein, 1995; Rumbaut, 1995b). These are but illustrative pieces of complex histories that are irreducible to a single form or cultural ethos.

TABLE 1.2

Trends in Legal Immigration to the United States, by Region and Principal
Sending Countries, in Rank Order of Total Admissions From 1960 to 1993

Region/Country of Birth	Period of Immigrant Admission to U.S. Permanent Resident Status				
	1960–1969	1970–1979	1980–1989[1]	1990–1993[2]	Total
Worldwide	3,213,749	4,336,001	6,332,218	5,241,919	18,645,073
Latin America and Caribbean	1,222,797	1,760,918	2,626,039	3,066,271	8,676,025
Asia	372,800	1,492,584	2,714,942	1,412,116	5,992,442
Europe and Canada	1,569,943	960,278	697,112	613,958	3,841,291
Africa	33,466	85,627	170,300	126,941	416,334
More Developed Countries					
Canada	303,853	115,040	116,001	62,677	597,571
United Kingdom	240,937	122,219	141,680	68,587	573,423
Italy	196,610	149,638	35,074	10,985	392,307
Germany	222,064	69,081	67,749	31,097	389,991
U.S.S.R.*	17,240	33,581	69,100	184,689	304,610
Poland*	77,650	42,446	81,578	93,086	294,760
Japan	50,129	42,612	41,739	28,719	163,229
Less Developed Countries					
Mexico	431,516	624,952	1,030,862	1,965,598	4,052,928
Cuba*	248,718	278,068	163,666	46,451	736,903
Dominican Republic	84,065	141,578	226,853	170,989	623,485
Jamaica	57,318	138,058	207,762	84,997	488,135
El Salvador	14,381	29,964	140,502	180,533	365,380
Colombia	66,592	72,991	111,536	69,911	321,030
Haiti	31,536	59,097	126,379	88,947	305,959
Philippines	73,316	349,103	473,831	251,831	1,148,081
China[3]	86,290	188,964	369,371	228,423	873,048
Vietnam*	3,167	137,648	396,110	241,448	778,373
Korea	27,990	248,950	338,891	96,204	712,035
India	21,491	164,265	253,781	152,607	592,144
Laos*	NA	8,596	149,238	36,377	194,211
Cambodia*	NA	5,625	113,893	12,642	132,160

[1] Data include 478,814 persons whose status was legalized in FY 1989 under the Immigration Reform and Control Act (IRCA).

[2] Data include 2,191,154 persons whose status was legalized in FY 1990–1993 under the Immigration Reform and Control Act (IRCA).

[3] Includes Mainland China and Taiwan.

*Denotes country from which the majority of immigrants to the United States have been admitted as refugees.

Source: U.S. Immigration and Naturalization Service, *Annual Reports*, 1960–1977, and *Statistical Yearbooks*, 1978–1993.

communities in the United States today are directly if variously related to the history of American military, political, economic and, pervasively, cultural involvement and intervention in the major sending countries and to the linkages that are formed in the process that often unintentionally open a surprising variety of legal and illegal migration pathways.[7] Thus, ironically, at a macrostructural level, immigration to the United States can be understood as a dialectical consequence of the expansion of the nation to its post-World War II position of global hegemony. As the United States has become more deeply involved in the world, the world has become more deeply involved in America—indeed, in diverse ways, it has come to America (Rumbaut, 1991b, 1992, 1994b, 1995b). When it does, at a microstructural level, legal as well as undocumented immigrant flows are sustained through social networks, especially via family connections (Grasmuck & Pessar, 1991; Massey et al., 1987).

Although today's immigrants come from over 140 different countries, some regions and nations send many more than others, despite the equitable numerical quotas provided to each country by U.S. law since 1965. One pattern, a continuation of trends already underway in the 1950s, is made quite clear in Table 1.2: Immigration from the more developed countries has declined over time, whereas that from less developed countries has accelerated. Among the more developed countries, this is clearest for Canada and most European countries. About half of all Europeans and Canadians came before 1960; many British, German, and other European scientists and professionals journeyed to America in the aftermath of World War II to pursue opportunities not then available in their countries, but by the 1960s prosperous postwar economies had dampened the relative attraction of America. The Japanese, who had accounted for most postwar Asian immigrants until the early 1960s (overwhelmingly entering as war brides), also declined proportionately thereafter, despite the removal of barriers by the 1965 law. The immigrant flow from Japan has since remained small and stable over time, with roughly half consisting of marriages to U.S. citizens. Among the less developed countries, the major countries of legal immigration are located either in the Caribbean Basin in the immediate periphery of the United States or in a handful of Asian nations also characterized by significant historical, economic, political, and military ties to the United States.

The INS data in Table 1.2 show that from 1960 to 1993 Mexico was by far the largest source of legal immigration, accounting for over 4 million admissions; the Philippines ranked second, with well over one million. These two countries share the deepest structural linkages with the United States, dating

---

[7]Two recent examples of such unintended consequences involve the thousands of former Iraqi soldiers and prisoners of war from the 1991 Persian Gulf War who resettled in the United States as refugees (many going to the Detroit area, where the largest Arab communities in North America are found) and of Somalis in the wake of the U.S. involvement in Somalia in the early 1990s (leading already to the formation of a "Little Mogadishu" in the San Diego area).

to the Mexican and Spanish-American Wars in the last century, and a long history of dependency relationships, external intervention, and in the Philippines direct colonization. As well, decades of active agricultural labor recruitment of Mexicans to the Southwest and Filipinos to plantations in Hawaii and California preceded the establishment of family networks and chain migrations. The extensive U.S. military presence in the Philippines has also fueled immigration through marriages with U.S. citizens stationed there through unique arrangements granting U.S. citizenship to Filipinos who served in the armed forces during World War II and through direct recruitment of Filipinos into the U.S. Navy. Tellingly, in their analysis of spouse-immigrant flows, Jasso and Rosenzweig (1990) found that the most powerful determinant of the number of immigrants admitted as wives of U.S. citizens was the presence of a U.S. military base in the country of origin.[8] Geopolitical factors thus shape the marriage market in immigrant visas, a vivid example of the connection between macro and micro social structures.

American foreign policy in the transformed post-World War II world, especially the doctrine and practice of global communist containment, is of key importance in explaining several of the other sizable migrations from different world regions—indeed, one might add, in effectively helping to create the conditions that produced the flows in the first place. During the Cold War this included direct U.S. involvement in "hot" wars in Korea, Vietnam, and Central America and interventions in Guatemala, Iran, Cuba, the Dominican Republic, and elsewhere. Among the leading countries of recent immigration, linkages unwittingly structured by American foreign policy and military intervention are most salient in the exodus of the Koreans in the aftermath of the Korean War and the subsequent U.S. economic and political involvement and permanent military presence in South Korea. Vietnamese, Cambodians, and Laotians have been admitted as political refugees, a dialectical legacy of the U.S. role in the Indochina War. The largest and most recent European arrivals have been former Soviet Jews and Poles, who also have been admitted mainly as refugees, like other groups from communist countries. Ironically,

---

[8]These authors also found that not only are women from a country with a U.S. military base more than twice as likely to have immigrated as wives of U.S. citizens, but they are also 20% more likely to be divorced or separated after entry as women from countries otherwise identical. Also, among ever-married women, recent immigrants were much less likely to have been divorced than their native-born counterparts, although over time in the United States both immigrants and natives experienced similar increases in divorce rates and although among immigrant women marital instability varied by country of origin and visa category. Among U.S. citizens, men are more likely than women to sponsor foreign spouses, especially from Eastern Hemisphere countries which host U.S. military installations. This explains why the large majority of immigrants from West Germany and South Korea and Japan and the Philippines have been women (Jasso & Rosenzweig, 1990). On sources of marital conflict and value incongruence in recent international inmarriage among Koreans (i.e., marriage between a Korean American and a partner from Korea), see Min (1995).

these people have come in increasing numbers since the end of the Cold War in 1989 and of the Soviet Union in 1991. From Latin America the most recent arrivals have been the Salvadorans, Guatemalans, and Nicaraguans who fled civil wars and deteriorating economic conditions in Central America in the 1980s in a context long shaped by American foreign policy. Salvadorans and Guatemalans, like Haitians, were denied refugee status and entered mostly without documents, although the Immigration Act of 1990 granted temporary protected status to many Salvadorans. Cubans entered primarily in the 1960s, despite the subsequent freedom flights that extended into the 1970s, the chaotic flotilla of 125,000 *Marielitos* that began the decade of the 1980s, and the *balseros* of the 1990s. With the exception of the Mariel entrants and until the reversal of U.S. policy after the dramatic events on the high seas in 1994, Cubans had been the classic example of U.S. use of refugee policy as foreign policy. In fact, it was to "prevent another Cuba" that a variety of U.S. interventions throughout the Caribbean Basin were justified, such as in the Dominican Republic after the assassination of Trujillo in 1961 and the U.S. military occupation in 1965, which opened key immigration pathways that over time have led to the large Dominican population in the United States (see Grasmuck & Pessar, 1991; Mitchell, 1992). Emigration connections forged by U.S. intervention and foreign and immigration policies were also a common denominator in the exodus of the Chinese after the 1949 revolution and most recently in the issuance of immigrant visas to tens of thousands of Chinese students in the United States after the events of Tienanmen Square in 1989 and of the Iranians after the 1978 revolution. In short, contemporary immigration to the United States and the creation and consolidation of social networks that serve as bridges of passage to America have taken place within this larger historical context and cannot be adequately understood outside of it, nor reduced to the cost–benefit calculus of individual migrants or to the immigration policies of particular states.

Mexico is far and away the main source of both legal as well as unauthorized immigration. It alone accounted for over one fourth of the 22.6 million immigrants estimated from the 1994 Current Population Survey and over two thirds of the nearly 3 million formerly undocumented immigrants whose status has been legalized to date under the amnesty provisions of IRCA. As a result, no scholarly or policy study of immigrant families in the United States can neglect to examine the nature and implications of the Mexican case. An analysis by Massey and Espinosa (1995) of a large-scale data set drawn from 25 Mexican communities provides an illuminating empirical test of theories of international migration (i.e., neoclassical economics, new economics of migration, social capital theory, segmented labor markets, and world systems) to predict the course of post-1965 migration from Mexico to the United States. They analyze the process by which migration (legal or illegal) is initiated and perpetuated and look at the determinants of return migration to Mexico as well. In a nutshell, the findings underscore the crucial role of social capital, especially family networks, in predicting the odds of initial, repeat, and return migration.

Several points merit highlighting. Most first trips to the United States were made by people without documents and with ties to migrant family members, especially parents and siblings from households where someone was legalized under IRCA. The odds of a first trip fall with marriage, age, and, more weakly, education, suggesting that undocumented migrants are negatively selected with respect to human capital variables such as education. The typical first-time legal migrant was the son and to a lesser extent the brother of someone who was legalized earlier, with the father most commonly being the sponsor; a family tie rather than job skills was the main mode of legal entry. Repeat undocumented migration was related to changes and needs in the family life cycle, so that its likelihood increased for young unmarried men, decreased with marriage, and increased again as the number of dependent children rose. The odds of taking additional trips to the United States, with or without documents, were most strongly raised by migration-specific social capital: the migration of wives and children and the birth of children in the United States (Donato, 1993). Those same family ties also promoted the settlement process, strongly lowering the odds of returning to Mexico, especially among those with legal papers. The key is legalization, and once it occurs, wives and children (generally the last family members to migrate) strongly deter the return option. By contrast, marriage had the opposite effect for undocumented immigrants, increasing the probability of return to Mexico. Not surprisingly, net of family considerations, the odds of return migration fall as education rises, especially for legal immigrants. The undocumented with education have less incentive to stay in the United States, where an illegal status is a significant block to economic mobility beyond menial jobs, and more incentive to return to Mexico—a result that paints a strong pattern of migrant selectivity by legal status (Massey & Espinosa, 1995). Although this study was concerned with the process of migration rather than incorporation and its outcomes, we can infer that long-term Mexican settlement in the United States is a function of cumulative and self-reinforcing advantages of human capital, social capital, and political capital that accrue to immigrant family units with legal residency status. The undocumented who remain are less likely than their compatriots to be educated and in intact family units and more apt to become increasingly marginalized.

The Social Class Origins of the New Immigration

A widespread point of view in the contentious debate about the new immigration is that it constitutes, relative to those who came in earlier decades, a declining stock of less educated and more welfare-dependent populations, partly because of its national origins and partly because of putatively nepotistic family reunification preferences in U.S. law. This latter contention has been rebutted by recent research that shows that immigrants who are admitted through family ties are as successful in their economic contributions as those who come under employment preferences. As Meissner, Hormats, Walker, and Ogata (1993) observed, family-preference immigrants are also workers, and all of them join economic units. Sorensen and her colleagues (1992) found that family-sponsored immigrants showed no negative effects on the earnings or employment opportunities of native workers; the employment-preferred immigrants were actually the most likely to compete with natives in the labor market. Jasso and Rosenzweig (1995) more recently documented a narrowing of the differential in long-term occupational outcomes between the two types.

The fact that most legal immigration to the United States since the 1960s has come from comparatively poorer nations—notably the 14 less affluent countries listed in Table 1.2—does not mean that the immigrants themselves are drawn from the uneducated, unskilled, or unemployed sectors of their countries of origin. Available occupational data from the INS, including the percentage of professionals, executives, and managers at the time of immigrant admission, are summarized in Table 1.3 and indicate just the opposite. Over the past 3 decades, more than 2 million immigrant engineers, scientists, university professors, physicians, nurses, and other professionals and executives and their immediate families have been admitted into the United States. As the quinquennial trends in Table 1.3 show, from the late 1960s to the early 1980s, worldwide about one third of all legal immigrants to the United States (excluding dependents) were high-status professionals, executives, or managers in their countries of origin. The proportion of these so-called "brain drain" immigrants declined somewhat to 26.5% by the late 1980s, still a higher percentage than that of the native-born American population, but then rebounded again to 34% by 1993, despite the fact that the overwhelming majority of immigrants have been admitted under family preferences over this period. In part these data suggest that although many "pioneer" immigrants entered with formal credentials under the occupational preferences of U.S. law, their close kin who joined them later are drawn from the same social classes. This accounts for both the relative stability and similarity of their flows over time, if with a gradually diminishing upper-crust occupational profile as family chain migration processes evolve and expand.

However, the data presented in Table 1.3 reveal very sharp differences in the class character of contemporary legal immigration to the United States. Regionally, the flows from Asia, Africa, and Europe had achieved rough parity by the 1980s, with close to half (44% to 48%) of all occupationally active immigrants from these regions in 1993 consisting of professionals and managers, in sharp contrast to the less than 10% from Latin America and the Caribbean. Among the principal sending countries there are huge differences in the occupational backgrounds of immigrants. Highly skilled immigrants have domi-

TABLE 1.3
Trends in Occupational Backgrounds of Legal Immigrants, 1967–1993,
by Region and Main Sending Countries: Percentage of Immigrant
Professionals, Executives, and Managers, in Regional Rank Order

	Reported Occupation of Immigrants Prior to Admission to Permanent Resident Status[1] Percentage Professional Specialty, Executives and Managers					
Region/Country of Birth	1967	1972	1977	1982	1987	1993[3]
Worldwide	32.4	36.0	33.0	31.9	26.5	33.7
Asia	59.3	67.3	53.2	39.9	39.5	47.9
Africa	53.7	67.3	60.7	45.8	39.4	43.9
Europe and Canada	29.7	26.6	41.5	44.4	40.7	44.7
Latin America and Caribbean	22.3	13.8	15.4	15.8	11.3	9.5
More Developed Countries						
Japan	57.6	50.1	44.6	48.5	42.2	59.9
Canada	48.7	51.6	61.3	57.9	55.0	67.2
United Kingdom	43.3	51.5	58.3	60.8	52.9	59.0
U.S.S.R.*	40.9	41.0	42.0	39.1	47.0	32.0
Poland*	32.3	27.1	30.6	32.1	26.9	38.9
Germany	30.5	43.5	37.2	40.9	35.7	44.7
Italy	8.4	8.5	21.0	30.8	33.6	51.4
Less Developed Countries						
India	90.6	91.6	79.1	73.7	61.7	72.9
Korea	80.5	72.9	49.6	42.9	44.0	57.7
Philippines	60.2	71.6	46.8	44.9	45.9	51.9
China[2]	48.6	52.5	53.9	47.3	34.3	58.1
Vietnam*	71.6	56.9	36.6	11.4	7.7	3.9
Cambodia*	NA	NA	NA	7.1	2.0	8.1
Laos*	NA	NA	NA	4.7	2.1	4.0
Cuba*	33.1	13.9	14.4	22.3	5.1	9.3
Colombia	32.5	27.5	17.4	20.2	20.6	20.0
Haiti	23.3	26.8	14.1	17.4	8.1	19.8
Jamaica	19.1	15.9	33.4	21.6	18.6	15.8
Dominican Republic	14.5	15.3	13.1	13.8	12.2	18.7
El Salvador	15.2	16.0	10.0	13.0	7.1	1.9
Mexico[3]	8.5	5.1	6.6	7.0	5.9	3.9

[1] Between 50% and 66% of immigrants admitted as permanent residents report no prior occupation to the INS; they are mainly homemakers, children, retired persons, and other dependents. Data are based on 152,925 immigrants who reported an occupation in 1967; 157,241 in 1972; 189,378 in 1977; 203,440 in 1982; 247,072 in 1987; and 325,611 in 1993.

[2] Includes Mainland China and Taiwan. In 1993, the percentage for Taiwan was 77.7, compared to 53.5 for Mainland China.

[3] In 1993, the total for Mexico is based on 126,561 persons reporting an occupation, of whom 17,534 (14%) were mostly "special agricultural workers" whose status was legalized under the amnesty provisions of IRCA. No other country in 1993 had a significant proportion of IRCA legalizees among its admissions. Most IRCA legalizations took place during 1989-1992, substantially lowering the overall occupational status profiles for immigrants admitted in those years, particularly for Mexico, El Salvador, and Haiti. In 1992, when 57% of Mexican immigrants reporting an occupation were IRCA legalizees, only 1.7% of the total were professionals or managers.

*Denotes country from which the majority of immigrants to the United States have been admitted as refugees.

Source: U.S. Immigration and Naturalization Service, Annual Reports, 1967, 1972, 1977; and Statistical Yearbooks, 1982, 1987, 1993.

nated the flows of Indians, Koreans, Filipinos, and Chinese (including especially the Taiwanese) since the 1960s, and their proportions have increased noticeably since the passage of the 1990 Immigration Act, which nearly tripled the number of such employment-based visas. High proportions are also in evidence among the Japanese, Canadian, and British groups, although their immigration flows are smaller, as well as among Soviet Jews and the more sizable first waves of refugees from Vietnam and Cuba. By contrast, legal immigration from Mexico, El Salvador, the Dominican Republic, and until recently Italy has consisted predominantly of manual laborers and low-wage service workers; this has also been the case among refugees from Laos and Cambodia and the more recent waves of Vietnamese, Cubans, and Haitians. Over time, the drop in the proportion of highly skilled immigrants within particular national groups is mostly apparent among certain non-European refugees. This finding is consistent with a general pattern that characterizes refugee flows: Initial waves tend to come from the more resourceful and better connected higher socioeconomic strata, followed later by heterogeneous working-class waves more representative of the society of origin. As Table 1.3 shows, rapid declines are seen among refugees who come from poor countries such as Vietnam where only a small proportion of the population is well educated (Portes & Rumbaut, 1990; Rumbaut, 1991b, 1995b).

The information provided in Table 1.3, although useful as a first step to sort out the diverse class origins of the new immigration, is limited in several ways. The INS does not collect data on the educational backgrounds of legal immigrants, nor on the characteristics of undocumented immigrants or of emigrants (i.e., those who leave the United States after a period of time, estimated at well over 200,000 annually). A more precise picture can be drawn from the last available census, which counted a foreign-born population of 19.8 million persons in 1990. Census data on several relevant indicators for the largest immigrant groups in the United States as of 1990 are presented in Table 1.4, rank-ordered by their proportions of college graduates, which may serve as a proxy for social class of origin. The table focuses first on two measures of family structure, the proportions of female householders with no husband present and of children under 18 living with two parents, and then on education and labor force participation, poverty and welfare use rates, length of residence in the United States, citizenship, English proficiency, age, and gender. The picture that emerges shows clearly that in all of these respects the foreign-born are not a homogeneous population; instead, to borrow Gordon's (1964) term, the formation of different "ethclasses" is apparent. Less apparent is the fact that within particular nationalities there is often also considerable social and economic diversity.[9]

---

[9]Within particular groups there are often also many class differences that reflect different waves and immigration histories. For example, although 31% of adult immigrants from China have college degrees, 16% have less than a fifth grade education. This bimodal distribution in part

Taken as a whole, despite their many modes of exit, migration, and entry into the United States (i.e., legal arrivals, entries without inspection, visa adjusters and overstayers, unaccompanied minors and orphans, refugees and asylees), the foreign-born are slightly less likely to have single-parent households, and their children are more likely to reside with both parents. Immigrants overall have the same proportion of college graduates (20%) as does the native-born population, as well as an equivalent rate of labor force participation. They are, however, more likely than natives to be poor and to work in low-status jobs. However, decontextualized data at this level of analysis conceal far more than they reveal. In fact, by far the most educated and the least educated groups in the United States today are immigrants, as are the groups with the lowest and the highest rates of poverty, welfare dependency, and fertility—a reflection of polar-opposite types of migration embedded in very different historical and structural contexts. Disaggregated by region and country of birth, the very wide differences between immigrants become apparent.

One point that stands out in Table 1.4 is the very high degree of educational attainment among some immigrant groups, especially from the developing countries of Africa and Asia: 47% and 38%, respectively, are college graduates. An upper stratum is composed of sizable foreign-born groups whose educational and occupational attainments significantly exceed the average for the native-born American population. Without exception, all of them are of Asian origin, from India, Taiwan, Iran, the Philippines, Japan, Korea, and China, with recently immigrated groups reflecting the highest levels of attainment.[10] These immigrants are perhaps the most skilled ever to come to the United States. Their class origins help explain the popularization of Asians as a "model minority" and to debunk nativist calls for restricting immigrants to those perceived to be more assimilable on the basis of color, language, and culture. In addition, the social capital of these groups is reflected in the fact that

---

reflects different patterns of Chinese immigration and enterprise between the pre-1965 "old overseas Chinese" and the post-1965 "new immigrants." Desperate Haitian boat people arriving by the thousands in the 1980s and 1990s masked an upper-middle-class flow of escapees from the Duvalier regime in the early 1960s; by 1972 the number of Haitian physicians in the United States represented an incredible 95% of Haiti's stock (see Rumbaut, 1991b). Similarly, the post-1980 waves of Cuban Mariel refugees and Vietnamese boat people from modest social class backgrounds differed sharply from the elite first waves of the 1959–1962 Cubans and the 1975 Vietnamese, underscoring the internal diversification of particular national flows over time.

[10] Also in this upper stratum were several other smaller immigrant groups (of less than 100,000 each, not shown in Table 1.4), notably those from Nigeria, Egypt, South Africa, Kenya, Israel, Lebanon, Ghana, Hong Kong, and Argentina. By the mid-1970s, one fifth of all U.S. physicians were immigrants, and there were already more foreign medical graduates from India and the Philippines in the United States than African American physicians. By the mid-1980s, over half of all doctoral degrees in engineering awarded by U.S. universities were earned by foreign-born students, with one fifth of all engineering doctorates going to students from Taiwan, India, and South Korea, and one third of all engineers with a doctorate working in U.S. industry were immigrants (Rumbaut, 1994b).

TABLE 1.4
Family Contexts and Socioeconomic Characteristics of Principal Immigrant Groups in the United States in 1990, by Percentage of College Graduates[1]

Country of Birth	Family Contexts				Socioeconomic Status			U.S. Citizenship and English			Age and Gender	
	Persons (N)	Female H'holder	Children <18 with 2 parents	College Graduates	In Labor Force	Poverty Rate	Public Assistance	Immigrated Post-1970	Not a Citizen	English Poor	Median Age (yrs)	Female
Well below U.S. average												
Mexico	4,298,014	14.1	73	3.5	69.7	29.7	11.3	81	77	49	30	45
El Salvador	485,433	21.4	61	4.6	76.3	24.9	7.1	95	85	49	29	46
Laos*	171,577	11.9	81	5.1	49.7	40.3	45.5	100	83	43	27	48
Cambodia*	118,833	24.3	71	5.5	48.4	38.4	49.5	100	80	43	29	52
Guatemala	225,739	19.5	66	5.8	75.7	25.8	8.3	91	83	45	30	49
Dominican Republic	347,858	41.3	47	7.5	63.8	30.0	27.8	80	72	45	34	55
Italy	580,592	9.8	85	8.6	46.4	8.0	5.5	19	24	16	59	52
Haiti	225,393	27.6	56	11.8	77.7	21.7	9.3	87	73	23	35	50
Near U.S. average												
Jamaica	334,140	34.6	53	14.9	77.4	12.1	7.8	80	62	0	36	55
Colombia	286,124	21.5	65	15.5	73.7	15.3	7.5	79	71	34	35	54
Cuba*	736,971	16.2	72	15.6	64.1	14.7	16.2	45	49	40	49	52
Vietnam*	543,262	15.3	73	15.9	64.4	25.5	26.2	99	57	31	30	47
Poland*	388,328	11.1	83	16.3	50.4	9.7	5.4	44	38	20	57	53
Germany	711,929	16.4	75	19.1	54.7	7.7	4.3	19	28	2	53	65
Canada	744,830	12.3	86	22.1	52.1	7.8	4.8	29	46	1	53	59
United Kingdom	640,145	13.9	85	23.1	57.3	6.6	3.7	40	50	0	50	60
Soviet Union*	333,725	10.8	88	27.1	39.7	25.0	16.7	51	41	24	55	55

Table 1.4
(Continued)

Country of Birth	Persons (N)	Family Contexts			Socioeconomic Status			U.S. Citizenship and English			Age and Gender	
		Female H'holder	Children <18 with 2 parents	College Graduates	In Labor Force	Poverty Rate	Public Assistance	Immigrated Post-1970	Not a Citizen	English Poor	Median Age (yrs)	Female
Well above U.S. average												
China	529,837	8.2	87	30.9	62.3	15.7	10.6	76	56	44	45	51
Korea	568,397	11.1	87	34.4	63.9	15.6	7.9	92	59	30	35	57
Japan	290,128	14.7	95	35.0	54.2	12.8	2.2	69	72	25	38	63
Philippines	912,674	15.1	78	43.0	76.3	5.9	10.4	82	46	7	39	57
Iran	210,941	7.6	86	50.6	67.9	15.7	7.7	91	73	12	35	42
Taiwan	244,102	10.2	81	62.2	64.9	16.7	3.7	92	61	17	33	53
India	450,406	3.3	92	64.9	74.6	8.1	3.4	88	65	9	36	45
Total foreign-born	19,767,316	14.8	74	20.4	64.3	18.2	9.1	69	59	26	37	51
Total native-born	228,942,557	16.1	73	20.3	65.4	12.7	7.4	—	—	1	33	51

[1]Percentage of family households headed by a female householder with no husband present and of children under 18 years old living with two parents. Educational attainment for persons aged 25 years or older. Labor force participation for persons 16 years or older. Percentage of persons below the federal poverty line and percentage of households receiving public assistance income. Percentage of persons aged 5 years or older who speak English not well or at all.

*Denotes country from which most recent migrants to the United States have been officially admitted as refugees.

Source: U.S. Bureau of the Census, The Foreign Born Population in the United States, CP-3-1, July 1993; and 5% Public Use Microdata Sample (PUMS) of the 1990 Census.

they also generally have the highest proportions of two-parent families and of dependent children who reside with both parents among ethnic groups in the United States. The Filipinos are a curious exception to this pattern; they exhibit very high levels of English proficiency and the lowest poverty rate in the country but have slightly elevated rates of single-parent households (i.e., the non-Hispanic White rate was 12%) and welfare receipt at the same time.

By contrast, the lower socioeconomic stratum includes recent immigrants from Mexico, El Salvador, and Guatemala, many or most of whom were also undocumented, as well as disproportionately male and younger; a somewhat smaller number of such immigrants arrive from the Dominican Republic and Haiti. They had higher rates of labor force participation but much lower levels of educational attainment, were concentrated in low-wage unskilled jobs, and had poverty rates as high as those of native minority groups (i.e., 30% among African Americans, 32% among mainland Puerto Ricans), but they also had much lower proportions of households on welfare, with the signal exception of the Dominicans. Here also are less educated but less visible European immigrants, of whom Italians comprised the largest group. Two Asian-origin groups, Laotian and Cambodian refugees, exhibited by far the highest rates of poverty and welfare dependency in the United States. Southeast Asians and to a lesser extent Chinese and Korean workers are much in evidence, along with undocumented Mexican and Central American immigrants, in a vast underground sweatshop economy that expanded during the 1980s and 1990s in Southern California. These data debunk the stereotypes that have been propounded in the mass media as explanations of Asian success and point instead to the contextual diversity of recent immigration and to the class advantages and disadvantages of particular groups.

However, among these low-SES groups there was no equally direct correspondence between poverty and father-absent family structures. Four groups are very high on both forms of vulnerability: the Dominicans (with 30% and 41% rates of poverty and female-headed one-parent households, respectively), Haitians (with 22% and 28%), Salvadorans (25% and 21%), and Cambodians (38% and 24%). Among these, the Dominicans have by far the highest proportion of female householders (41%) of any immigrant group, about the level of Puerto Ricans (37%) and African Americans (43%), reflecting levels of marital disruption that are associated with very high poverty rates and that are highest (as with Puerto Ricans) in the same New York area where they are densely concentrated (cf. Grasmuck & Pessar, 1995; Landale & Ogena, 1995). The prevalence of single-parent families among Cambodian refugees reflects not so much divorce or separation as extremely high proportions of widows, a consequence of the "killing fields" of the late 1970s in Cambodia (see Rumbaut, 1989).

In sharp contrast, however, are four other groups with equally high or higher poverty rates but remarkably low rates of maritally disrupted family structures: the Mexicans (30% in poverty vs. 14% female householders), Vietnamese (26% vs. 15%), Laotians (40% vs. 12%), and Soviet (mostly Jewish) refugees (25% vs. 11%). Significantly, three of those four are refugee groups who receive substantial welfare state support for their resettlement, and the fourth, the Mexicans, exhibit dense, deeply rooted kinship networks and evidence of cohesive families and conjugal bonds during the first (immigrant) generation in the United States.[11] A comparative study of Salvadoran, Mexican, and Vietnamese immigrant kinship networks in the San Francisco area (Menjívar, 1996) showed that although all rely heavily on their relatives in the United States prior to and upon arrival, the Vietnamese and Mexicans continued to receive support from their family ties, whereas the Salvadoran networks tended to weaken under multiple burdens and break down. The author pointed to contextual factors that sustained the former two, such as state and community support, but were unavailable to the Salvadorans (Menjívar, 1996; cf. Kibria, 1993).

Indeed, census and other data are consistently indicating patterns of low rates of divorce and of single-parent families in the first (immigrant) generation but striking increases in the prevalence of marital disruption over time in the United States and particularly in succeeding generations, for some groups much more than for others. Generational analyses of a unique 1990 Census PUMS child data file by Landale and Oropesa (1995) and Jensen and Chitose (1994) have recently underscored such patterns, especially between the first and third generations. For instance, Jensen and Chitose (1994) found that children of immigrants overall are more likely to be in married-couple families than are the children of natives. However, U.S.-born parents are more likely to be divorced, separated, or never married than are immigrant parents, among foreign-born heads of households with children under 18, but their rates of both divorce and separation increase over time in the United States. Landale and Oropesa (1995) found sharply higher proportions of single-parent families in the third as compared to the first generation for Dominicans and Puerto Ricans, then for Cubans, Mexicans, and Filipinos, and least so for the Chinese—although for all groups the generational trend was toward greater maritally disrupted family structures.

---

[11] From the 1990 census I calculated that among Mexican-origin males 15 years and older (excluding widows and the never married), the level of marital disruption (i.e., divorce and separation) for immigrants who had come between 1980 and 1990 was 7.1%. For immigrants who came before 1980 the rate was 8.7%, but for the U.S.-born, the rate was 24.1%. Among Mexican-origin women 15 years and older, the rates were 10.4%, 14.8%, and 21.9% for recent immigrants, long-term immigrants, and natives, respectively. An analysis based on the PUMS further suggests that marital disruption among Mexican-origin men and women increases not only over time and generation in the United States but also as education increases. Similar patterns of results have been observed for a wide range of other outcomes, including infant health and mortality, mental health, diet, and alcohol and drug abuse. For a review of that evidence, see Rumbaut and Weeks (1996).

Such findings carry particularly significant implications about the potential deterioration of familial social capital (see McLanahan & Sandefur, 1994) as it bears on the future socioeconomic prospects of the second generation coming of age in American cities (Gans, 1992; Portes, 1994; Portes & Zhou, 1993). Especially for immigrant groups with little human capital trying to adapt under often discriminatory conditions of extreme economic, cultural, and social disadvantage, the likelihood of success will hinge to a large extent on the availability of strong family solidarity, centered on a cohesive conjugal and parental bond, and ethnic community support. Where the cohesiveness of the marital bond breaks down, the family's social capital begins to evaporate; adaptive gaps, role reversals, and generational conflicts between parents and children become more consequential as parental authority is dissipated and undermined. This is, of course, nothing new in the American immigrant experience (Antin, 1912; Portes & Rumbaut, 1996); indeed, that a house divided cannot long stand is ancient wisdom. However, whether and why some immigrant groups seem to be more adept than others at generating and sustaining positive familial social capital under often intensely conflictual, dissonant, and stressful circumstances are important empirical questions that await further comparative research (but see Fernández-Kelly & García, 1990; Hondagneu-Sotelo, 1994; on patterns of marital disruption among Hispanics in recent decades, see also Bean & Tienda, 1987).

CHILDREN OF IMMIGRANTS AND FAMILY OUTCOMES: SOME NEW EVIDENCE

In this section I explore a related question by looking at some aspects of the educational progress and prospects of over 5,000 children of immigrants surveyed in two key areas of immigrant settlement: Southern California and South Florida. Recent publications have focused on a range of other results from the first phase of this ongoing study (e.g., Portes, 1994, 1995; Rumbaut, 1994a, 1995a; Fernández-Kelly & Schauffler, 1994). The students surveyed were in the eighth and ninth grades, a level at which dropout rates are still relatively rare, to avoid the potential bias of differential dropout rates between ethnic groups at the senior high school level. To be eligible for inclusion in the study, a student had to be either foreign-born or U.S.-born with at least one foreign-born parent. Because the schools do not collect information on the nativity of parents, a brief initial survey of all eighth and ninth graders in the district was first done to determine their eligibility. Eligible students representing 77 nationalities were then administered the survey at school during the Spring 1992 semester.

The final sample in San Diego included over 2,400 Mexican, Filipino, Vietnamese, Cambodian, Laotian, and other Asian and Latin American students;

in the Miami and Fort Lauderdale areas, the sample totaled about 2,800 Cuban, Haitian, Nicaraguan, Jamaican, and other Latin American and West Indian students. Most of the respondents were 14 or 15 years old. The sample is evenly split by gender and grade level. By generation, 44% are U.S.-born children of immigrant parents (i.e., the second generation), and 56% are foreign-born youths who immigrated to the United States before age 12 (i.e., the "1.5" generation).[12] Among the foreign-born, the sample is evenly split by age at arrival: About half had lived in the United States for 10 years or more and were preschool-age at arrival, whereas the other half had lived in the United States 9 years or less (i.e., they had reached elementary school age in their native country but arrived in the United States before adolescence). In this sense, time in the United States for immigrant children is not only a measure of length of exposure to American life but an indicator of different developmental stages at the time of migration.

The survey included questions on respondents' demographic characteristics, family, socioeconomic status, ethnic self-identity, peers, language, hours spent on homework and television, educational and occupational aspirations, perceptions of discrimination, self-esteem, and depression (see the Appendix for further details on some of the measures used; also Rosenberg, 1979; Rumbaut, 1994a). In addition, school data on grade point averages, Stanford reading and math achievement test scores, LEP/FEP classification, gifted status, and related variables were obtained from the respective school systems for all the students in the sample. Some selected results describing the main national origin groups are displayed in Table 1.5.

In line with 1990 census and annual INS information, the survey data show that the Indochinese and the Nicaraguans were the most recent arrivals, most coming during the 1980s, and few teenagers in those populations were U.S.-born (the relatively small number of U.S.-born Vietnamese are children of the elite first wave of 1975 refugees). The Cubans, on the other hand, had been in the United States the longest, and over 70% of them were born in the United States, a higher proportion by far than any other. The large size of the Cuban sample (1,227) accurately reflects their preponderance in Dade County schools; indeed, the Cubans were the only ethnic group in the sample who constituted a majority of the population in their community. Levels of

---

[12]I had coined the terms "one-and-a-half" or "1.5" generation in the 1970s with reference to Cuban youth and the dynamics of identity formation in adolescence. The idea for the term came from Thomas and Znaniecki's (1958) *The Polish Peasant in Europe and America*, where they referred in passing to the "half-second generation" (p. 1776). The concept applies best to the situation of children who immigrate after reaching school age in the country of origin but before reaching puberty (i.e., roughly ages 6–12). Teenagers and preschool children are at different developmental stages and seem closer to the experience, respectively, of the first and second generations and might even be termed, pursuing the decimal system, 1.25ers and 1.75ers (Rumbaut, 1991a; Rumbaut & Ima, 1988; see also Cropley, 1983; Pérez Firmat, 1994; Piore, 1979, pp. 65–68).

TABLE 1.5

Characteristics of Children of Immigrants in Southern California and South Florida, 1992, by National Origin of Parents[1]

Social Characteristics: (N=)	Latin America and Caribbean								Asia						Total
	Mexico (757)	Cuba (1,227)	Nica-ragua (344)	Colombia (227)	Latin America (478)	Haiti (178)	Jamaica (155)	West Indies (106)	Philip-pines (818)	Vietnam (371)	Lao (155)	Hmong (53)	Cambodia (96)	Other Asia (162)	Total (5,127)
Nativity and time in U.S.															
U.S.-born	60.2	71.1	7.6	53.7	50.6	43.3	40.0	67.0	55.0	15.6	1.3	5.7	3.1	53.1	49.4
Less than 10 years in U.S.	28.4	9.0	57.9	26.9	30.2	28.8	36.1	20.7	28.7	42.4	44.5	33.9	48.0	27.7	27.8
One parent is U.S.-born	17.3	10.1	1.5	11.9	19.0	5.6	11.6	23.6	19.6	3.2	0.6	0	0	27.2	12.6
Socioeconomic status															
Father is college graduate	7.3	25.4	38.4	24.2	28.0	10.1	23.9	17.9	29.0	15.1	10.3	1.9	5.2	42.0	22.3
Mother is college graduate	4.2	20.9	28.5	19.4	22.0	11.2	30.3	23.6	38.1	8.6	3.9	0	4.2	25.9	20.0
Own home	32.5	67.2	33.4	53.3	57.3	64.6	63.9	58.5	73.7	34.5	24.5	1.9	11.5	71.0	53.7
English															
Speaks English only	2.4	0.7	0.6	1.3	4.2	4.5	47.1	56.6	18.0	1.6	0	0	0	19.1	7.3
Prefers English	45.2	82.3	74.4	70.5	73.6	80.9	71.0	85.9	88.3	51.5	52.3	64.2	65.6	75.3	71.7
Speaks English with parents	19.3	36.8	11.1	19.8	33.1	44.4	74.8	88.7	84.4	9.7	7.7	1.9	12.5	53.1	38.3
English Proficiency Index (1-4)	3.47	3.85	3.69	3.82	3.79	3.80	3.91	3.93	3.84	3.35	3.27	3.13	3.37	3.70	3.70
Homework/Television															
Hours daily on homework (0-5)	1.16	1.21	1.28	1.24	1.21	1.82	1.90	1.46	1.87	2.00	1.84	2.32	1.73	1.96	1.48
Hours-of-homework-to-TV ratio	0.88	0.81	0.82	0.89	0.87	0.88	1.06	0.87	1.02	1.31	1.24	1.53	1.29	1.29	0.96

Table 1.5
(Continued)

Social Characteristics (N=)	Latin America and Caribbean								Asia						Total
	Mexico (757)	Cuba (1,227)	Nicaragua (344)	Colombia (227)	Latin America (478)	Haiti (178)	Jamaica (155)	West Indies (106)	Philippines (818)	Vietnam (371)	Laos Lao (155)	Laos Hmong (53)	Cambodia (96)	Other Asia (162)	(5,127)
Educational achievement															
Grade point average (GPA)	2.24	2.28	2.32	2.33	2.31	2.28	2.58	2.45	2.93	3.04	2.86	2.95	2.72	3.24	2.52
Stanford Reading test (percentile)	26.6	47.5	38.0	44.7	42.9	30.4	47.8	43.0	51.1	37.6	22.3	15.2	14.0	62.0	41.2
Stanford Math test (percentile)	31.9	58.5	55.4	58.4	55.3	45.0	55.5	49.8	59.1	60.4	42.1	29.7	35.7	74.3	52.9
Educational aspirations															
Educational aspirations (1-5)	3.90	4.42	4.41	4.42	4.36	4.44	4.51	4.41	4.40	4.18	3.70	3.52	3.93	4.51	4.29
Family structure and attitudes															
Family household size	4.8	3.4	4.5	3.7	3.7	5.0	3.8	3.9	4.5	5.3	5.7	6.9	5.4	3.5	4.3
Both natural parents at home	59.3	58.7	62.8	58.6	57.3	44.9	39.4	46.2	79.5	73.1	71.6	77.4	68.8	77.8	63.3
Father absent from home	35.3	34.7	29.4	33.5	37.7	44.9	51.0	51.9	14.9	19.1	16.8	18.9	25.0	16.1	30.1
Grandparent present in home	8.2	20.6	15.5	12.1	13.4	15.7	11.3	10.5	23.6	14.9	20.3	11.3	12.5	14.3	16.3
Aunt/uncle present in home	10.6	4.8	16.4	9.9	7.9	16.3	10.0	11.4	13.2	18.9	11.8	7.5	11.5	6.8	10.4
Embarrassed by parents	8.1	16.5	16.9	16.3	12.1	25.3	6.5	13.2	17.2	25.9	20.7	35.9	31.3	33.3	16.7
Parent–child conflict scale (1-4)	1.69	1.63	1.63	1.67	1.67	1.91	1.71	1.76	1.76	1.85	1.80	1.96	1.94	1.72	1.71
Familism attitudes scale (1-4)	2.07	1.79	1.83	1.81	1.83	1.79	1.77	1.77	1.87	2.09	2.15	2.12	2.11	1.77	1.89

[1]Sample N = 5,127 eighth and ninth grade students surveyed in the San Diego, Dade, and Broward County School Districts, with at least one foreign-born parent. All differences between national origin groups are significant beyond the .0001 level for all variables shown.

parental education were lowest for the Mexicans, the Haitians, and the Indochinese, especially the Laotians and the Cambodians; the Indochinese also
had the highest proportions of parents who were not in the labor force, a reflection of their high rates of poverty and welfare dependency in the United
States. The Filipinos and the other Asians (i.e., Chinese, Japanese, Koreans,
and Indians) showed the highest proportions of college graduates among
mothers and fathers, and their families were much more likely to own rather
than rent their homes.

Table 1.5 also presents information on their patterns of English use and
proficiency. With the obvious exception of immigrants from the English-
speaking Caribbean and a nontrivial number of Filipinos and other Asians,
very few of the respondents spoke English only (7.3% of the total sample).
However, nearly three fourths of the total sample *preferred* English, including
substantial majorities in every group and nearly 9 out of 10 Filipinos. The
single exception was the Mexicans, who were the most loyal to their mother
tongue and who, in San Diego, also live within a few miles of the Mexican border, although even among them 45% preferred English. Already more than a
third spoke mostly in English with their parents. Longer-resident Cuban parents, along with English-speaking Jamaican and other West Indian parents,
were most often reported by their 8th and 9th grade children to be the principal source of school-related help to them. By contrast, virtually no Hmong
parent spoke in English with their children, and their households were the
most linguistically isolated, according to the 1990 census. The Laotians and
the Cambodians also had the lowest scores in both the 4-item self-reported
English Language Proficiency Index (see Appendix) and in the standardized
Stanford reading achievement test, which they are given each year in school
(the test scores in Table 1.5 reflect national percentiles).

Several other key indicators of educational attainment and aspirations are
provided in Table 1.5. The other Asians group, including Chinese, Japanese,
Koreans, and Indians, showed a level of ability in the Stanford math achievement test that is well above national norms—around the 75th percentile—
followed by the Vietnamese, Filipinos, Cubans, and Colombians, all of whom
were well above the 50th percentile. The Hmong, Mexicans, and Cambodians
tested well below national math norms, followed by the Lao and the Haitians.
The students' rankings in math test scores generally reflect the socioeconomic
status of their parents. However, the association between social class and educational attainment outcomes does not similarly extend to academic grade
point averages (GPAs). For example, despite their poor performance on
achievement tests and the fact that they come from the poorest families, the
Hmong had earned the highest academic GPAs of almost all the groups except
for the high-achieving Vietnamese and other Asians. One measure of effort
provides a main reason: The Hmong devoted far more hours per day to homework and less time watching television than any other group. In general,

Asian-origin students put in the most homework time and Latin American students the least, with those from the Afro-Caribbean in between. The highest GPAs were found for students with the highest ratios of homework-to-television-watching hours; this group included all the Asian-origin groups and the Jamaicans.

In fact, as measured by GPA, immigrant students as a whole outperform the native-born, including majority non-Hispanic white students of native parentage (Rumbaut, 1995a). Significantly, over time and generation in the United States, reading achievement test scores go up, as does the amount of time spent watching television, but the number of hours spent on homework goes down, as does GPA—a finding that confirms similar findings among immigrant students in California and elsewhere (Rumbaut, 1995a; see also Caplan, Choy, & Whitmore, 1991; Kao, 1995; Kao & Tienda, 1995; Olsen, 1988; Rumbaut & Ima, 1988; Suárez-Orozco, 1989; Suárez-Orozco & Suárez-Orozco, 1989; Sung, 1987). Most of the national origins groups reported very high educational aspirations, led by the Jamaicans and other Asians. The Laotians, Cambodians, and Mexicans, on the other hand, exhibited notably lower aspirations than all other groups; they were the only groups with average aspirations scores under 4 on a 5-point scale, where 4 indicates an expectation of finishing a college education (see the Appendix for details on the wording and scoring of the 2-item measure of educational aspirations).

Of particular interest to our focus here are the data on family-household size and composition, on the quality of parent–child relationships, and on a measure of attitudinal familism (see the Appendix for items composing these scales). There was a notable contrast between all Asian-origin groups and the rest of the sample in their higher proportion of families with both natural parents at home; the somewhat higher incidence of father absence among the Hmong and especially the Cambodians is, again, due not to divorce but to the death of the father prior to arrival in the United States, a reflection of extraordinarily harsh contexts of exit (Rumbaut, 1991a) but nonetheless a telling measure of family loss: The loss of family ties reduces children's social capital. About half of all families from the Afro-Caribbean had no father present at home (cf. Foner, 1987). A high percentage of Cuban as well as Filipino families had grandparents living at home; Vietnamese, Haitians, and Filipinos had a high percentage of aunts and uncles coresiding at home. These data are reflections of vertical and horizontal extensions of the family household as the parents and siblings of the youth's parents are incorporated into the home. Indochinese children were the most likely by far to report feeling embarrassed by their parents (including 36% of the Hmong, who experience the greatest contextual dissonance between the world of their parents and the Southern California world in which they are growing up), and, along with Haitian children, to exhibit the highest levels of parent–child conflict as measured by our scale. Mexican and Jamaican youths were the least likely to feel embarrassed

TABLE 1.6

Characteristics of Children of Immigrants in Southern California and South Florida, 1992, by Type of Family Structure and Level of Parent–Child Conflict[1]

Characteristics (N=)	Family Structure/Headship				Level of Parent–Child Conflict				
	Two Natural Parents (3,247)	Two Parents/ One Stepparent (674)	Single Parent (1,206)	p²	Low (985)	Low-Middle (1,280)	High-Middle (1,719)	High (1,060)	p²
Socioeconomic status									
Father is college graduate	25.0	21.4	15.8	**	26.5	23.4	21.9	18.5	**
Mother is college graduate	22.5	13.1	17.1	**	22.8	22.1	19.4	16.1	**
Own home	60.6	48.4	37.9	**	57.9	50.7	53.7	53.9	*
Attends inner-city school	26.7	26.7	38.4	**	45.2	39.7	41.0	40.0	**
Household size and composition									
Household size (persons in home)	4.51	4.27	3.56	**	4.03	4.22	4.31	4.40	**
Grandparent present in home	15.5	13.3	20.2	**	16.4	16.4	16.7	16.0	NS
Aunt/uncle present in home	9.2	8.6	14.8	**	8.4	9.4	11.5	11.9	*
Homework/school help									
Hours daily on homework (0–5)	1.55	1.36	1.35	**	1.66	1.52	1.44	1.32	**
No one helps with school	21.2	27.6	28.9	**	16.8	19.1	26.9	31.1	**
Psychological well-being[3]									
Self-esteem scale (1–4)	3.32	3.29	3.22	**	3.55	3.41	3.25	2.99	**
Depressive affect scale (1–4)	1.59	1.75	1.76	**	1.40	1.53	1.69	2.00	**
Educational achievement									
Grade point average (GPA)	2.64	2.34	2.29	**	2.71	2.55	2.50	2.37	**
Stanford Reading test (percentile)	43.0	39.6	36.8	**	45.2	39.7	41.0	40.0	**
Stanford Math test (percentile)	55.5	48.1	47.9	**	57.1	53.0	52.3	50.2	**
Educational aspirations									
Educational aspirations (1–5)	4.31	4.25	4.22	*	4.47	4.33	4.25	4.13	**

[1] N = 5,127 eighth and ninth graders surveyed in the San Diego, Dade, and Broward County School Districts, with at least one foreign-born parent.

[2] Significance of difference between means: ** = p < .001; * = p < .05; NS = not significant.

[3] Rosenberg 10-item self-esteem scale (mean of 10 items, scored 1 to 4; higher scores indicate higher self-esteem); and Center for Epidemiological Studies-Depression (CES-D) 4-item depression subscale (mean of 4 items, scored 1 to 4; higher scores indicate more depressive symptomatology).

by their parents, and Cubans and Nicaraguans reported the lowest levels of parent–child conflict.[13]

The research literature has pointed to high levels of familism—a deeply ingrained sense of obligation and orientation to the family—among Mexican immigrants in particular (cf. Suárez-Orozco & Suárez-Orozco, 1995). A high score in this measure of felt collectivistic obligations to the family contrasts with the pull of individualistic values in the American milieu. Our data here confirm that Mexican respondents exhibit significantly higher scores on the familism attitudes scale than any other group, with one major exception: All of the Indochinese groups, who also have the largest family households, score even higher on that scale. Bivariate analyses of these familism scores showed that for all groups except the Haitians, Jamaicans, and West Indians, familism declined significantly over time in the United States, and also with parents' higher socioeconomic status. In a multiple regression analysis (not shown here) of a wide array of likely determinants of familistic attitudes, the strongest effects were observed for more recently arrived teenage boys (who were much more likely than girls to endorse the items comprising the familism scale) with poorer English proficiency, who did not prefer English nor spoke with their parents in English, who resided in large family households, and who reported that their parents and siblings were their major source of help with school-work. Even after controlling for multiple predictors, several ethnicity dummy variables remained significantly associated with higher familism scores: Mexicans, Filipinos, Vietnamese, and the other Indochinese groups. All other Latin American and Afro-Caribbean nationalities washed out of the analysis.

What is the relationship between family contexts and other variables portrayed herein? Table 1.6 presents a breakdown of selected characteristics by two measures of family-household contexts: a structural variable (i.e., whether the home is headed by both natural parents, by a stepparent and a natural parent, or by a single parent—typically the mother), and a psychosocial variable (i.e., the level of parent–child conflict, ranging from low to high). Looking at objective structural contexts first, the results show that highly educated fathers and mothers who own their homes are significantly more likely to be found in

---

[13] Parent–child conflict, as measured by the 3-item scale, had the most powerful effect, controlling for a wide range of other expected predictors, on our two outcome variables measuring psychological well-being: self-esteem (i.e., Rosenberg scale) and depressive symptoms (i.e., CES-D subscale). In turn, the strongest determinants of greater parent–child conflict among the more than 5,000 children of immigrants in our study included female gender (i.e., conflict was significantly greater among teenage girls), experiences and expectations of discrimination, acculturative gaps (i.e., preference for English coupled with poor command of the parent's language), and low-SES one-parent family structures. Greater conflict with parents was also associated with fewer hours spent by the youths on homework, more hours spent watching television, and lower GPAs and educational aspirations (results which need to be interpreted within the limitations of cross-sectional data). For an analysis of determinants of parent-child conflict, self-esteem, depressive affect, and ethnic self-identification for the sample as a whole, see Rumbaut, 1994a.

immigrant families with both natural parents at home, compared to stepfamilies and single-parent households. Single-parent families in particular are much more likely to rent their homes, and children in those family circumstances are more likely to attend inner-city schools; their households are smaller but more likely to include a grandparent or aunts and uncles. In homes with both natural parents present, children do more daily homework and have significantly higher GPAs, math and English achievement test scores, self-esteem, and aspirations. Children in single-parent homes are at the opposite end on each of these outcome measures, with stepfamilies occupying an intermediate position except with respect to depressive affect and the perception that there is no one to help with their schoolwork, which are equally likely to be higher in both stepfamilies and single-parent households.

Looking alternatively at the subjective climate in the home and the quality of parent-child relationships, Table 1.6 shows that cohesive families with low levels of parent–child conflict and disparagement are significantly advantaged with respect to virtually all the variables under consideration. That is, the lower the level of such friction, the higher the youths' educational achievement and aspirations, as well as their level of effort, social support, and psychological well-being; conversely, the more conflictual the parent–child relationship, the poorer the youths' profiles of school achievement and ambition, self-esteem, and depression. Furthermore, the evidence points to a connection between subjective and objective factors: Lower parent–child conflict is associated with higher parental education in smaller and more economically stable two-parent households. Put another way, the human capital of parents and the social capital of family relationships appear to combine to yield cumulative and self-reinforcing advantages in the process of adaptation, much as this also seems to be the case in the process of migration itself.

An Analysis of Educational Achievement and Aspirations in Immigrant Families

The observed differences between national origin groups in patterns of educational achievement and aspirations during adolescence offer significant if tentative clues of their generation's future school-to-work transitions and passages to adulthood. We have already seen that family contexts are associated with such outcomes in various ways. To explore in more detail likely determinants of educational achievement and expectations among these children of immigrants, I carried out a series of least-squares multiple linear regression analyses of four key outcomes: academic GPA, math and reading achievement test scores, and educational aspirations. The results are presented in Table 1.7. Because the results are based on cross-sectional data, we cannot unambiguously untangle the causal or temporal sequence of effects in these associations, and it may be that reciprocal effects are involved, especially with respect to subjective measures. Data collected in 1995 add a longitudinal dimension to our

TABLE 1.7
Predictors of Educational Achievement and Aspirations Among Children of Immigrants:
Least-Squares Multiple Regressions for Southern California and South Florida Sample, 1992[1]

Predictor Variables	Academic GPA (Mean = 2.54)		Math Scores (Mean = 53.3)		Reading Scores (Mean = 41.1)		Educational Aspirations (Mean = 4.31)	
Age and Gender								
Gender (1 = male, 0 = female)	−.25	(−10.01) ***	NS		NS		−.16	(−6.73) ***
Age	−.14	(−7.37) ***	−5.4	(−8.52) ***	−3.3	(−5.89) ***	−.05	(−3.11) **
Oldest sibling in family	.05	(1.90) *	2.1	(2.40) *	3.1	(4.00) ***	NS	
Grade in school	.06	(1.99) *	4.7	(4.53) ***	2.4	(2.64) **	NS	
Acculturation and Effort								
Length of residence in U.S.[2]	−.09	(−5.27) ***	NS		1.8	(3.73) ***	−.04	(−2.69) **
Knowledge of English	.16	(4.55) ***	8.2	(6.95) ***	16.7	(16.15) ***	.28	(8.70) ***
Friends are co-ethnics	.06	(2.29) *	4.4	(5.15) ***	2.5	(3.26) **	.06	(2.38) *
Homework (daily hours)	.14	(15.13) ***	2.0	(6.45) ***	1.5	(5.24) ***	.10	(11.74) ***
TV watching (daily hours)	−.04	(−5.20) ***	−1.1	(−4.37) ***	−1.0	(−4.53) ***	−.03	(−4.46) ***
Socioeconomic Status								
Education of parents	.02	(3.83) **	0.8	(4.67) ***	0.9	(6.19) ***	.04	(9.16) ***
Parents are professionals	.13	(5.29) ***	2.7	(3.23) **	3.4	(4.63) ***	.05	(2.31) *
Own home (1 = own, 0 = rent)	.13	(4.52) ***	5.3	(5.65) ***	4.3	(5.19) ***	.07	(2.99) **
Family Structure and Attitudes								
2 natural parents at home	.15	(5.45) ***	3.1	(3.49) ***	NS		NS	
1 parent is U.S.-born	−.07	(−1.93) *	NS		NS		−.09	(−2.67) **
Parent–child conflict scale	−.16	(−8.09) ***	−1.7	(−2.48) *	NS		−.10	(−5.39) ***
Familism scale	−.09	(−4.37) ***	−5.8	(−8.80) ***	−6.6	(−11.42) ***	−.07	(−4.10) ***
Ethnicity								
Vietnamese	.65	(11.97) ***	8.2	(4.50) ***	NS		NS	
Lao/Hmong/Cambodian	.58	(9.56) ***	−8.7	(−4.34) ***	−8.1	(−4.57) ***	−.31	(−5.62) ***
Filipino	.33	(8.41) ***	−3.6	(−2.79) **	NS		−.12	(−3.28) **
Mexican	NS		−17.9	(−12.28) ***	−9.0	(−7.03) ***	−.26	(−6.35) ***
Cuban	−.14	(−4.04) ***	NS		NS		NS	
Haitian	NS		−8.5	(−3.54) **	−11.2	(−5.33) ***	.15	(2.25) *
Jamaican	NS		NS		NS		NS	
(Constant)	3.52	(12.04) ***	63.28	(6.50) ***	NS		3.84	(14.32) ***
Adjusted R²	.273		.241		.322		.217	

[1]Unstandardized regression coefficients (b), with T-ratios in parentheses. See text and appendix for details of measurement. ***$p < .0001$; **$p < .01$; *$p < .05$; NS = not significant. Sample $N = 5,127$ eighth and ninth grade students.

[2]A 3-point variable, where 1 = 5 to 9 years in U.S., 2 = 10 years or more in U.S., 3 = born in U.S.

study and help address those concerns; the entire student sample was reinter-
viewed at ages 17 and 18. These interviews include students who have trans-
ferred to other school districts or dropped out since the original survey, and
interviews with their parents were included also. For our purposes, the multivariate results in Table 1.7 should be construed not as direct causal influences
but as relationships between educational outcomes and likely predictor variables selected for their theoretical and policy relevance.

Beginning with students' individual characteristics, we note first the effect
of gender and age on educational outcomes. It is clear that girls have a significant edge over boys when it comes to academic GPA and also have greater aspirations, although gender had no effect on math scores or reading skills.
Controlling for grade level, (older) age was strongly and negatively associated
with all outcomes across the board. Both of these are familiar results in the literature on educational attainment. In addition, sibling rank order made a difference in outcomes: Being the oldest child in a family was positively (if more
weakly) associated with higher achievement, in GPA as well as test scores, although it was not significantly associated with aspirations.

An important finding, supporting our earlier reported research, is the negative association of length of residence in the United States with both GPA and
aspirations. Time in the United States is, to be sure, strongly predictive of improved English reading skills, but despite that seeming advantage, longer residence in the United States and second generation status (i.e., being born in
the United States) is connected to declining academic achievement and aspirations, net of other factors. That finding does not support a linear assimilation hypothesis. What is more, as Table 1.6 shows, having a parent who is
also U.S.-born is associated with lower GPAs and lower aspirations; students
whose parents both are immigrants outperform their counterparts whose
mother or father is native-born. A similar finding has recently been reported
by Kao and Tienda (1995) with national data from the NELS:88, again indicative of deterioration in outcomes over generations in the United States
(Matute-Bianchi, 1986). However, English language proficiency itself was
positively associated with GPA, both test scores, and aspirations, net of everything else. Also, having a peer group made up of co-ethnic friends who are also
children of immigrants had a positive effect on GPA, and the positive influence of peers who may also be oriented toward an achievement ideology of
hard work extends to math and reading scores and to higher aspirations as well
(on the implications of this point, particularly with respect to the import of the
structure of the larger immigrant community on the adaptation process of the
second generation, see Portes, 1995). Clearly, moreover, the effort invested in
daily homework pays off handsomely across the board in higher grades, test
scores, and aspirations for the future; in fact, time spent on homework
emerged as the strongest predictor of higher GPA and higher educational aspirations. By contrast, the hours spent daily watching television were signifi-

Q: attitudinal familism (handwritten note)

cantly but negatively associated with all outcomes across the board.[14] Those factors and the mix of motivated effort and family discipline implied by those daily activities varied greatly by ethnic group and by family characteristics.

Regarding family variables, family socioeconomic status has strongly positive effects on all outcomes. Parental education, occupational status, and home ownership have positive independent effects on GPA and achievement test scores as well as on educational aspirations. Of particular interest to our analysis was the independent effect of family social capital variables on educational outcomes, with all other variables controlled. With respect to family structure, the results show that students living in a home with both natural parents were significantly more likely to have higher GPAs and math scores, net of all other factors. However, the presence of grandparents or aunts and uncles in the household did not show significant effects in these analyses.[15] With respect to family cohesiveness, higher parent–child conflict was strongly associated with lower GPAs, lower aspirations, and lower math scores. Moreover, higher attitudinal familism scores were significantly and negatively associated with all outcomes across the board, net of all other predictor variables. Without dwelling on the implications of this intriguing latter finding, I repeat a point raised at the outset: Family ties bind, but sometimes those bonds may constrain rather than facilitate particular outcomes.

Finally, it is of particular interest to note that with all those variables controlled for in these models, most of the ethnicity dummy variables nonetheless retain strong and significant effects on virtually all outcomes, although the direction of the effect differs between them, as shown in detail in Table 1.7. All the Asian ethnic groups were strongly associated with higher GPAs, above all the Vietnamese, even after controlling for all other predictors in these equations. This is so even though the Lao, Hmong, Cambodians, and Filipinos were also associated with lower math scores and educational aspirations. Mexican ethnicity was strongly related to lower achievement test scores and aspirations. Curiously, the Haitians were associated with higher aspirations but

---

[14]A recent comparative study of the math and science achievement of 24,000 13-year-olds in the United States, Canada, Great Britain, Ireland, South Korea, and Spain, prepared for the U.S. Department of Education, found that the more time students spent watching television, the poorer their performance. The American students watched the most television and got the worst math scores. For a discussion in the popular media, see Butterfield, 1990.

[15]In a separate study of Southeast Asian refugee families, we found that among objective family characteristics, the size of the household had a significant and positive effect on students' GPAs. This result goes against the grain of conventional wisdom, which presupposes that the larger the household, the fewer resources parents have to invest in their children. Field work in the Vietnamese community, however, suggested an opposite social capital explanation: The largest families were organized as mini school systems, with older siblings tutoring the younger ones and giving them harder practice tests than the ones they got at school, even in the absence of any direct parental involvement in the school or in homework (see Rumbaut 1995a; Rumbaut & Ima, 1988; cf. Caplan et al., 1991).

lower math and reading skills. Further, although not shown in Table 1.7, respondents' reported experiences and expectations of racial–ethnic discrimination were not significantly associated with these four particular outcomes. Thus, despite the richness of the data set and the wide array of variables controlled for in the analyses, the influence of ethnicity on educational achievement and aspirations was not eliminated, raising questions as to why this might be so (cf. Portes, 1995; Rumbaut, 1995a). What does "Mexican" or "Vietnamese" or "Filipino" or "Haitian" mean or stand as a proxy for in a statistical analysis of this nature? It might serve as an empirical indicator of the local ethnic community or of the distinct contexts of exit and reception of particular nationalities or perhaps as a proxy for nothing less than the culture, history, and collective memory of an entire group as embedded in the American context. The persistence of significant ethnic differences suggests the need for much more intensive, comparative ethnographic research.

Still, these results point to the association of achievement outcomes with an immigrant ethos that seems to be affirmed within the context of intact immigrant families and cohesive family ties as well as co-ethnic immigrant peer groups and communities, yet that appears to erode with increasing exposure and assimilation to native norms and contexts in different sectors of American society. That paradox of assimilation in American life belies conventional wisdom and orthodoxy and is an issue well worth further investigation.

ACKNOWLEDGMENTS

The author gratefully acknowledges the financial support provided by research grants from the Andrew W. Mellon Foundation, the Russell Sage Foundation, the Spencer Foundation, and the National Science Foundation, for the project "Children of Immigrants: The Adaptation Process of the Second Generation," being carried out in collaboration with Alejandro Portes of The Johns Hopkins University and Lisandro Pérez of Florida International University. Some results from this ongoing study are reported in this chapter.

REFERENCES

Addams, J. (1910). Immigrants and their children. In *Twenty years at Hull House*, chapter 11. New York: Macmillan.

Agbayani-Siewert, P., & Revilla, L. (1995). Filipino Americans. In P. G. Min (Ed.), *Asian Americans: Contemporary trends and issues* (pp. 134–168). Thousand Oaks, CA: Sage.

Alvarez, J. (1991). *How the García girls lost their accents.* Chapel Hill, NC: Algonquin Books.

Alvarez, R. R., Jr. (1987). *Familia: Migration and adaptation in Baja and Alta California, 1800–1975.* Berkeley: University of California Press.

Antin, M. (1912). *The promised land.* Boston: Houghton Mifflin.

Arnold, F., Cariño, B. V., Fawcett, J. T., & Park, I. H. (1989). Estimating the immigration multiplier: An analysis of recent Korean and Filipino immigration to the United States. *International Migration Review, 23*, 813–838.

Baca Zinn, M. (1994). Adaptation and continuity in Mexican-origin families. In R. L. Taylor (Ed.), *Minority families in the United States* (pp. 64–81). Englewood Cliffs, NJ: Prentice-Hall.

Bean, F. D., & Tienda, M. (1987). *The Hispanic population of the United States*. New York: Russell Sage Foundation.

Berrol, S. C. (1995). *Growing up American: Immigrant children in America, then and now*. New York: Twayne.

Bertaux-Wiame, I. (1993). The pull of family ties: Intergenerational relationships and life paths. In D. Bertaux & P. Thompson (Eds.), *Between generations: Family models, myths, and memories* (pp. 39–50). New York: Oxford University Press.

Bodnar, J. (1987). *The transplanted: A history of immigrants in urban America*. Bloomington: Indiana University Press.

Brown, M. E. (1994). Parents and children: Fundamental questions about immigrant family life. In T. Walch (Ed.), *Immigrant America: European ethnicity in the United States* (pp. 89–102). New York: Garland.

Butterfield, F. (1990, January 21). Why they excel. *Parade Magazine*, 4–6.

Camp, R. (1993). *Politics in Mexico*. New York: Oxford University Press.

Caplan, N., Choy, M. H., & Whitmore, J. K. (1991). *Children of the boat people: A study of educational success*. Ann Arbor: University of Michigan Press.

Carrasquillo, H. (1994). The Puerto Rican family. In R. L. Taylor (Ed.), *Minority families in the United States* (pp. 82–94). Englewood Cliffs, NJ: Prentice-Hall.

Chavez, L. R. (1992). *Shadowed lives: Undocumented immigrants in American society*. San Diego: Harcourt Brace.

Child, I. L. (1943). *Italian or American? The second generation in conflict*. New Haven: Yale University Press.

Coleman, J. S. (1988). Social capital in the creation of human capital. *American Journal of Sociology, 94*, S95–S120.

Cropley, A. J. (1983). *The education of immigrant children: A social-psychological introduction*. London: Croom Helm.

Díaz-Briquets, S. (1995). Relationships between U.S. foreign policies and U.S. immigration policies. In M. S. Teitelbaum & M. Weiner (Eds.), *Threatened peoples, threatened borders: World migration and U.S. policy* (pp. 160–189). New York: Norton.

Diner, H. (1995). Erin's children in America: Three centuries of Irish immigration to the United States. In S. Pedraza & R. G. Rumbaut (Eds.), *Origins and destinies: Immigration, race, and ethnicity in America* (pp. 161–171). Belmont, CA: Wadsworth.

Donato, K. M. (1993). Current trends and patterns of female migration: Evidence from Mexico. *International Migration Review, 27*, 748–771.

Espiritu, Y. L. (1995). *Filipino American lives*. Philadelphia: Temple University Press.

Faison, S. & Lii, J. H. (1995, October 5). Brutal end to an immigrant's voyage of hope. *The New York Times*, p. A-1.

Fernández-Kelly, M. P., & García, A. (1990). Power surrendered, power restored: The politics of home and work among Hispanic women in Southern California and South Florida. In L. Tilly & P. Guerin (Eds.), *Women and politics in America* (pp. 130–149). New York: Russell Sage Foundation.

Fernández-Kelly, M. P., & Schauffler, R. (1994). Divided fates: Immigrant children in a restructured U.S. economy. *International Migration Review, 28*, 662–689.

Foner, N. (Ed.). (1987). *New immigrants in New York*. New York: Columbia University Press.

Furnham, A. & Bochner, S. (1986). *Culture shock: Psychological reactions to unfamiliar environments*. New York: Methuen.

Gans, H. J. (1992). Second-generation decline: Scenarios for the economic and ethnic futures of the post-1965 American immigrants. *Ethnic and Racial Studies, 15*, 173–192.

García, C. (1992). *Dreaming in Cuban*. New York: Ballantine.

Glenn, E. N. (1986). *Issei, Nisei, war bride: Three generations of Japanese women in domestic service*. Philadelphia: Temple University Press.

Glenn, E. N., & Yap, S. G. H. (1994). Chinese American families. In R. L. Taylor (Ed.), *Minority families in the United States* (pp.115–145). Englewood Cliffs, NJ: Prentice-Hall.

Gold, S. J., & Phillips, B. (1995). Mobility and continuity among Eastern European Jews. In S. Pedraza & R. G. Rumbaut (Eds.), *Origins and destinies: Immigration, race, and ethnicity in America* (pp. 182–194). Belmont, CA: Wadsworth.

Gordon, M. M. (1964). *Assimilation in American life: The role of race, religion, and national origins*. New York: Oxford University Press.

Grasmuck, S. & Pessar, P. (1991). *Between two islands: Dominican international migration*. Berkeley: University of California Press.

Grasmuck, S. & Pessar, P. (1995). Dominicans in the United States: First- and second-generation settlement. In S. Pedraza & R. G. Rumbaut (Eds.), *Origins and destinies: Immigration, race, and ethnicity in America* (pp. 280–292). Belmont, CA: Wadsworth.

Griswold del Castillo, R. (1984). *La Familia: Chicano families in the urban Southwest, 1848 to the present*. Notre Dame, IN: University of Notre Dame Press.

Handlin, O. (1951). *The uprooted*. Boston: Little, Brown.

Hareven, T. K., & Modell, J. (1981). Family patterns. In S. Thernstrom (Ed.), *Harvard encyclopedia of American ethnic groups* (pp. 345–354). Cambridge, MA: Harvard University Press.

Hein, J. (1995). *From Vietnam, Laos, and Cambodia: A refugee experience in the United States*. New York: Twayne.

Hing, B. O. (1993). *Making and remaking Asian America through immigration policy, 1850–1990*. Stanford: Stanford University Press.

Hoffman, E. (1989). *Lost in translation: A life in a new language*. New York: Penguin.

Hondagneu-Sotelo, P. (1994). *Gendered transitions: Mexican experiences of immigration*. Berkeley: University of California Press.

Immigration and Naturalization Service (INS), U.S. Department of Justice. (1992). *Immigration reform and control act: Report on the legalized alien population*. Washington, DC: U.S. Government Printing Office.

Immigration and Naturalization Service (INS), U.S. Department of Justice. (1994). *1993 Statistical Yearbook*. Washington, DC: U.S. Government Printing Office.

Jasso, G. & Rosenzweig, M. R. (1986). Family reunification and the immigration multiplier: U.S. immigration law, origin-country conditions, and the reproduction of immigrants. *Demography, 23*, 291–311.

Jasso, G. & Rosenzweig, M. R. (1989). Sponsors, sponsorship rates, and the immigration multiplier. *International Migration Review, 23*, 856–888.

Jasso, G. & Rosenzweig, M. R. (1990). *The new chosen people: Immigrants in the United States*. New York: Russell Sage Foundation.

Jasso, G. & Rosenzweig, M. R. (1995). Do immigrants screened for skills do better than family reunification immigrants? *International Migration Review, 29*, 85–111.

Jensen, L. & Chitose, Y. (1994). Today's second generation: Evidence from the 1990 U.S. Census. *International Migration Review, 28*, 714–735.

Johnson, C. L. (1982). Sibling solidarity: Its origin and functioning in Italian-American families. *Journal of Marriage and the Family, 44*, 155–167.

Kao, G. (1995). Asian Americans as model minorities? A look at their academic performance. *American Journal of Education, 103*, 121–159.

Kao, G. & Tienda, M. (1995). Optimism and achievement: The educational performance of immigrant youth. *Social Science Quarterly, 76*, 1–19.

Kibria, N. (1993). *Family tightrope: The changing lives of Vietnamese Americans*. Princeton: Princeton University Press.

Kibria, N. (1994). Vietnamese American families. In R. L. Taylor (Ed.), *Minority families in the United States* (pp. 164–176). Englewood Cliffs, NJ: Prentice-Hall.

Kingston, M. H. (1976). *The woman warrior: Memoirs of a girlhood among ghosts.* New York: Knopf.

Laguerre, M. S. (1994). Headquarters and subsidiaries: Haitian immigrant family households in New York City. In R. L. Taylor (Ed.), *Minority families in the United States* (pp. 47–61). Englewood Cliffs, NJ: Prentice-Hall.

Landale, N. S., & Ogena, N. (1995). Migration and union dissolution among Puerto Rican women. *International Migration Review, 29,* 671–692.

Landale, N. S., & Oropesa, R. S. (1995). *Immigrant children and the children of immigrants: Inter- and intra-ethnic group differences in the United States.* Population Research Group (PRG) Research Paper 95–2. East Lansing: Institute for Public Policy and Social Research, Michigan State University.

Lasch, C. (1977). *Haven in a heartless world: The family besieged.* New York: Basic Books.

Lee, C. R. (1995). *Native speaker.* New York: Putnam.

Leonard, K. (1992). *Ethnic choices: California's Punjabi-Mexican-Americans, 1910–1980.* Philadelphia: Temple University Press.

Massey, D. S., Alarcón, R., Durand, J., & González, H. (1987). *Return to Aztlán: The social process of international migration from Western Mexico.* Berkeley: University of California Press.

Massey, D. S., Arango, J., Hugo, G., Kouaouci, A., Pellegrino, A., & Taylor, J. E. (1994). An evaluation of international migration theory: The North American case. *Population and Development Review, 20,* 699–752.

Massey, D. S., & Espinosa, K. E. (1995). *What's driving Mexico–U.S. migration? A theoretical, empirical, and policy analysis.* Manuscript submitted for publication.

Massey, D. S., & Parrado, E. (1994). Migradollars: The remittances and savings of Mexican migrants to the United States. *Population Research and Policy Review, 13,* 3–30.

Matute-Bianchi, M. E. (1986). Ethnic identities and patterns of school success and failure among Mexican-descent and Japanese-American students in a California high school: An ethnographic analysis. *American Journal of Education, 95,* 233–255.

McLanahan, S. & Sandefur, G. (1994). *Growing up with a single parent: What hurts, what helps.* Cambridge, MA: Harvard University Press.

Meissner, D. M., Hormats, R. D., Walker, A. G., & Ogata, S. (1993). *International migration challenges in a new era: Policy perspectives and priorities for Europe, Japan, North America and the international community.* New York: Trilateral Commission.

Menjívar, C. (1996). Immigrant kinship networks: Vietnamese, Salvadorans, and Mexicans in comparative perspective. *Journal of Comparative Family Studies.*

Merton, R. K. (1987). Three fragments from a sociologist's notebooks: Establishing the phenomena, specified ignorance, and strategic research materials. *Annual Review of Sociology 13,* 1–28.

Miller, A. T., Morgan, S. P., & McDaniel, A. (1994). Under the same roof: Family and household structure. In S. C. Watkins (Ed.), *After Ellis Island: Newcomers and natives in the 1910 Census* (pp. 125–173). New York: Russell Sage Foundation.

Min, P. G. (1995). Korean Americans. In P. G. Min (Ed.), *Asian Americans: Contemporary trends and issues* (pp. 199–231). Thousand Oaks, CA: Sage.

Mitchell, C. (Ed.). (1992). *Western Hemisphere immigration and United States foreign policy.* University Park, PA: Pennsylvania State University Press.

Nishi, S. M. (1995). Japanese Americans. In P. G. Min (Ed.), *Asian Americans: Contemporary trends and issues* (pp. 95–133). Thousand Oaks, CA: Sage.

Olsen, L. (1988). *Crossing the schoolhouse border: Immigrant students and the California public schools.* San Francisco: California Tomorrow.

Olson, J. S., & Olson, J. E. (1995). *Cuban Americans: From trauma to triumph.* New York: Twayne.

Orleck, A. (1987). The Soviet Jews: Life in Brighton Beach, Brooklyn. In N. Foner (Ed.), *New immigrants in New York* (pp. 273–304). New York: Columbia University Press.

Pérez, L. (1986). Immigrant economic adjustment and family organization: The Cuban success story reexamined. *International Migration Review, 20,* 4–20.

Pérez, L. (1994). Cuban families in the United States. In R. L. Taylor (Ed.), *Minority families in the United States* (pp. 95–112). Englewood Cliffs, NJ: Prentice-Hall.

Pérez Firmat, G. (1994). *Life on the hyphen: The Cuban-American way.* Austin: University of Texas Press.

Pérez Firmat, G. (1995). *Next year in Cuba: A Cubano's Coming of Age in America.* New York: Anchor.

Piore, M. J. (1979). *Birds of passage: Migrant labor and industrial societies.* Cambridge: Cambridge University Press.

Portes, A. (1994). Introduction: Immigration and its aftermath. *International Migration Review, 28,* 632–639.

Portes, A. (1995). Children of immigrants: Segmented assimilation and its determinants. In A. Portes (Ed.), *The economic sociology of immigration: Essays on networks, ethnicity, and entrepreneurship* (pp. 248–279). New York: Russell Sage Foundation.

Portes, A., & Rumbaut, R. G. (1990). *Immigrant America: A portrait.* Berkeley: University of California Press.

Portes, A., & Rumbaut, R. G. (1996). *Immigrant America: A portrait* (2nd ed.). Berkeley: University of California Press.

Portes, A., & Sensenbrenner, J. (1993). Embeddedness and immigration: Notes on the social determinants of economic action. *American Journal of Sociology, 98,* 1320–1350.

Portes, A., & Zhou, M. (1993). The new second generation: Segmented assimilation and its variants. *The Annals of the American Academy of Political and Social Science, 530,* 74–96.

Pozzetta, G. E. (Ed.). (1991). *Immigrant family patterns: Demography, fertility, housing, kinship, and urban life.* New York: Garland.

Reimers, D. M. (1985). *Still the golden door: The third world comes to America.* New York: Columbia University Press.

Rodriguez, R. (1982). *Hunger of memory.* Boston: David R. Godine.

Rosenberg, M. (1979). *Conceiving the self.* New York: Basic Books.

Roth, H. (1992). *Call it sleep.* New York: Farrar, Straus & Giroux. (Original work published 1934)

Rubin, L. (1994). *Families on the fault line.* New York: HarperCollins.

Rumbaut, R. D., & Rumbaut, R. G. (1976). The family in exile: Cuban expatriates in the United States. *American Journal of Psychiatry, 133,* 395–399.

Rumbaut, R. G. (1989). The structure of refuge: Southeast Asian refugees in the United States, 1975–1985. *International Review of Comparative Public Policy, 1,* 97–129.

Rumbaut, R. G. (1991a). The agony of exile: A study of Indochinese refugee adults and children. In F. L. Ahearn, Jr. & J. L. Athey (Eds.), *Refugee children: Theory, research, and services* (pp. 53–91). Baltimore: Johns Hopkins University Press.

Rumbaut, R. G. (1991b). Passages to America: Perspectives on the new immigration. In Alan Wolfe (Ed.), *America at century's end* (pp. 208–244). Berkeley: University of California Press.

Rumbaut, R. G. (1992). The Americans: Latin American and Caribbean peoples in the United States. In A. Stefan (Ed.), *Americas: New interpretive essays* (pp. 275–307). New York: Oxford University Press.

Rumbaut, R. G. (1994a). The crucible within: Ethnic identity, self-esteem, and segmented assimilation among children of immigrants. *International Migration Review, 28,* 748–794.

Rumbaut, R. G. (1994b). Origins and destinies: Immigration to the United States since World War II. *Sociological Forum, 9,* 583–621.

Rumbaut, R. G. (1995a). The New Californians: Comparative research findings on the educational progress of immigrant children. In R. G. Rumbaut & W. A. Cornelius (Eds.), *California's Immigrant children: Theory, research, and implications for educational policy* (pp. 17–70). La Jolla: Center for U.S.–Mexican Studies, University of California, San Diego.

Rumbaut, R. G. (1995b). Vietnamese, Laotian, and Cambodian Americans. In P. G. Min (Ed.), *Asian Americans: Contemporary trends and issues* (pp. 232–270). Thousand Oaks, CA: Sage.

Rumbaut, R. G., & Ima, K. (1988). *The adaptation of Southeast Asian refugee youth: A comparative study.* Washington, DC: U.S. Office of Refugee Resettlement.

Rumbaut, R. G., & Weeks, J. R. (1996). Unraveling a public health enigma: Why do immigrants experience superior perinatal health outcomes? *Research in the Sociology of Health Care, 13,* 337–391.

Schoultz, L. (1992). Central America and the politicization of U.S. immigration policy. In C. Mitchell (Ed.), *Western hemisphere immigration and United States foreign policy* (pp. 157–220). University Park, PA: Pennsylvania State University Press.

Sheth, M. (1995). Asian Indian Americans. In P. G. Min (Ed.), *Asian Americans: Contemporary trends and issues* (pp. 169–198). Thousand Oaks, CA: Sage.

Sorensen, E., Bean, F. D., Ku, L., & Zimmerman, W. (1992). *Immigrant categories and the U.S. job market.* Washington, DC: Urban Institute.

Stone, E. (1988). *Black sheep and kissing cousins: How our family stories shape us.* New York: Penguin.

Suárez-Orozco, M. M. (1989). *Central American refugees and U.S. high schools: A psychosocial study of motivation and achievement.* Stanford: Stanford University Press.

Suárez-Orozco, M. M., & Suárez-Orozco, C. (1995). The cultural patterning of achievement motivation: A comparative study of Mexican, Mexican immigrant, and non-Latino White American youths in schools. In R. G. Rumbaut & W. A. Cornelius (Eds.), *California's immigrant children: Theory, research, and implications for educational policy* (pp. 161–190). La Jolla: Center for U.S.–Mexican Studies, University of California, San Diego.

Sung, B. L. (1987). *The adjustment experience of Chinese immigrant children in New York City.* New York: Center for Migration Studies.

Suro, R. (1994). *Remembering the American dream: Hispanic immigration and national policy.* New York: Twentieth Century Fund.

Takagi, D. Y. (1994). Japanese American families. In R. L. Taylor (Ed.), *Minority families in the United States* (pp. 146–163). Englewood Cliffs, NJ: Prentice-Hall.

Tan, A. (1989). *The Joy Luck Club.* New York: Putnam.

Thomas, W. I., & Znaniecki, F. (1958 [1918–20]). *The Polish peasant in Europe and America.* New York: Dover.

Tienda, M. (1980). Familism and structural assimilation of Mexican immigrants in the United States. *International Migration Review, 14,* 383–408.

Tilly, C. (1990). Transplanted networks. In V. Yans-McLaughlin (Ed.), *Immigration reconsidered: History, sociology, and politics* (pp. 79–95). New York: Oxford University Press.

Ueda, R. (1981). Naturalization and citizenship. In S. Thernstrom (Ed.), *Harvard encyclopedia of American ethnic groups* (pp. 734–748). Cambridge, MA: Harvard University Press.

U.S. Immigration [Dillingham] Commission. (1911). *Reports of the Immigration Commission, Vol. 4: Emigration Conditions in Europe.* Washington, DC: U.S. Government Printing Office.

Vigil, J. D. (1988). *Barrio gangs: Street life and identity in Southern California.* Austin: University of Texas Press.

Waters, M. (1994). Ethnic and racial identities among second-generation Black immigrants in New York City. *International Migration Review, 28,* 795–820.

Wheeler, T. C. (Ed.). (1972). *The immigrant experience: The anguish of becoming American.* New York: Penguin.

Wong, M. G. (1995). Chinese Americans. In P. G. Min (Ed.), *Asian Americans: Contemporary trends and issues* (pp. 58–94). Thousand Oaks, CA: Sage.

Yans-McLaughlin, V. (1977). *Family and community: Italian immigrants in Buffalo, 1880-1930.* Ithaca, NY: Cornell University Press.

Zolberg, A. R. (1995). From invitation to interdiction: U.S. foreign policy and immigration since 1945. In M. S. Teitelbaum & M. Weiner (Eds.), *Threatened peoples, threatened borders: World migration and U.S. policy* (pp. 117–159). New York: Norton.

APPENDIX

Composition and Reliability of Scales

Scale and Scoring	Cronbach's Alpha	Items and Measures
English Proficiency Index (4 items: scored 1 to 4)	.92	How well do you (speak, understand, read, write) English? 1 = Not at all 2 = Not well 3 = Well 4 = Very well
Educational Aspirations (2 items: scored 1 to 5)	.80	What is highest level of education you would like to achieve? And *realistically* speaking, what is the highest level of education that you think you will get? 1 = Less than high school 2 = High school 3 = Some college 4 = Finish college 5 = Finish a graduate degree
Parent–Child Conflict (3 items: scored 1 to 4)	.56	In trouble with parents because of different way of doing things. My parents are usually not very interested in what I have to say. My parents do not like me very much. 1 = Not true at all 2 = Not very true 3 = Partly true 4 = Very true
Familism Scale (3 items: scored 1 to 4)	.57	One should find a job near his/her parents even if it means losing a better job somewhere else. When someone has a serious problem, only relatives can help. In helping a person get a job, it is always better to choose a relative rather than a friend. 1 = Disagree a lot 2 = Disagree 3 = Agree 4 = Agree a lot

2

Immigrant Generations

Leif Jensen
Yoshimi Chitose
The Pennsylvania State University

RUBÉN RUMBAUT effectively draws together a rich blend of qualitative and quantitative evidence to accomplish his twin goals of providing a profile of the new immigration and describing some of the outcomes of migration. Evidence ranges all the way from the memoirs of immigrants in exile to 15 × 24 statistical tables, and from secondary INS data to primary data gathered by Rumbaut and colleagues in San Diego and Miami. The deep and broad list of citations stretches all the way from Amy Tan to Marta Tienda and everything in between. Presented in wonderfully textured prose, Rumbaut brings several important messages to this volume. He cautions, for example, that we should not place undue weight on the 1965 immigration legislation as a cause of the new immigration. Rather, we should view it in the broader context of geopolitical forces that have created a worldwide web of money, capital, and migrants. Rumbaut throws a spotlight on the critical nexus of family and immigration, and he dramatically underscores the great diversity in family and immigration linkages, both within and between country-of-origin groups.

Rumbaut also informs us about a number of unresolved and emerging areas of inquiry. There is a small boatload of dissertation topics embedded in his chapter that ought to keep students of immigration busy for years to come. We were intrigued, for example, about the apparently negative implications of length of residence in the United States for academic achievement and aspirations, raising the prospect that immigrants may be socialized to a society's bad habits just as easily as its good ones (Portes, 1994). Another area for future work evolved regarding the correspondence between three types of capital—

human, political and social—and how they vary across immigrant groups. More needs to be learned about the causes of and relationships between this constellation of capitals and how they interact to affect immigrant family outcomes. A salient question for immigrant families is whether deficiencies in human or political capital are compensated for by social capital endowments in the pursuit of goals. Concentrated work in this area might lead to more valid and reliable measures of social capital. We worried about a couple of passages in Rumbaut's chapter where simply being in a household headed by a married couple, as opposed to other headship configurations, was taken as a proxy for social capital. Indeed, some of Rumbaut's most intriguing findings emerge from the analyses using more direct measures of social capital. Why is it, for example, that the Indochinese are more likely to feel embarrassed by their parents and have high parent–child conflict scores but at the same time score high on a scale that measures familism, or "collectivistic obligtions to the family"? Finally, Rumbaut observes that social capital, as manifest in family ties, can actually keep individuals from seeing and seizing opportunity. More research is needed on the detrimental effects of social captial on socioeconomic outcomes.

Rumbaut's impressive chapter provides a springboard to subsequent discussions in this volume. In the same spirit of offering background information, we offer our own complementary analyses. Rumbaut writes, "migration and adaptation are highly complex social processes, and family outcomes ultimately need to be grasped and measured not only in the first years after arrival . . . but across generations" (p. 10). With that call as a point of departure we offer an analysis of recent U.S. Census Bureau data in an effort to describe the circumstances of the first, second, and third immigrant generations.

Our analysis builds on a recent study conducted for a special issue of *International Migration Review* that concerned today's second generation—the children of immigrants (Jensen & Chitose, 1994). That special issue was motivated by the fact that the circumstances and performance of the native-born offspring of immigrants were less well understood than those of their parents. We analyzed data from the public-use file of the 1990 U.S. Census to provide a statistical portrait of the second generation. However, because the 1990 Census long form did not ask about the nativity of parents, that analysis was necessarily constrained to those in the second generation who were still residing with their parents. We analyze a data set that allows us to describe the sociodemographic and economic status of the entire second generation and to draw comparisons to other immigrant generations.

DATA

We analyze the March 1994 Current Population Survey (CPS). Based on a nationally representative sample of about 55,000 households and the 150,000 individuals residing within them, the March CPS contains a wide range of socio-demographic and economic variables including employment circumstances, income receipt, and human capital characteristics of individuals. This particular March CPS also included supplementary questions about place of birth, immigrant status, and year of immigration of individuals, as well as the place of birth of the parents of individuals. This affords the unique opportunity to identify the second generation, regardless of whether they are still residing with their parents.

We use a five-category nativity breakdown in our descriptive tables. The first generation consists of individuals who are foreign born, excluding those born abroad of native parents (15,000 unweighted cases). The second generation, all of whom are native born, are those with at least one immigrant parent (16,716). This group is further subdivided into those who have only one immigrant parent (7,666) and those who have two immigrant parents (9,050). Finally, third and higher generations (which we refer to for convenience as the third generation) are identified in the tables as native-born individuals with native-born parents (119,227).

IMMIGRANT GENERATIONS: A STATISTICAL PORTRAIT

Table 2.1 shows several sociodemographic characteristics of individuals. Although the groups differ trivially in the percentage of females, there are important differences in age distribution. Compared to the first and third generations, the second generation has a bifurcated age distribution; they are disproportionately found in the oldest and youngest age categories. This is especially true for those with both parents being foreign born, 40.8% of whom are under 17 and 29.5% of whom are age 65 or over. The relative paucity of second-generation individuals who are in their prime working years likely reflects the pause in immigration during the middle part of this century. A crude generalization then is that today's second generation consists predominantly of either the offspring of the great wave of immigration ending in the 1920s or of the more recent new immigration, which began sometime during the 1960s.

This age distribution must be borne in mind when considering the overall sociodemographic and economic profiles of these groups. Clearly it helps explain variation in marital status. That the percentage who are widowed is 14.1 among the second generation generally and 18.0 among those with both parents foreign born clearly reflects their disproportionate tendency to be age 65 or more. As Rumbaut also reports, when it comes to the percentage of people who are separated and divorced, foreign-born individuals and the second generation are comparatively advantaged with respect to the third generation.

The shifting composition of immigrant flows toward Asian and Latin American countries of origin is clear in the race and ethnic composition of immi-

TABLE 2.1
Selected Sociodemographic Characteristics of Individuals
by Nativity and Nativity of Parents, 1994

| | Native-born individuals | | | | |
	Native-born Parents	At least one foreign-born parent	Only one foreign-born parent	Both parents foreign-born	Foreign-born individuals
Percentage of females	51.2	51.0	50.6	51.4	50.6
Age					
0–17	28.8	37.0	32.6	40.8	12.6
18–34	33.6	19.2	23.8	15.0	44.5
35–64	27.2	20.1	26.2	14.7	31.4
65 or more	10.4	23.8	17.4	29.5	11.6
Mean age	33.7	36.6	35.9	37.3	38.8
Marital status among those age 18 or more					
Married	57.8	55.7	56.9	54.5	62.7
Separated	2.5	1.6	3.7	1.1	2.9
Divorced	9.9	7.5	8.7	6.4	5.3
Widowed	6.3	14.1	10.7	18.0	6.4
Never married	23.5	21.1	22.2	20.0	23.1
Race/ethnicity					
Non-Hispanic White	79.5	60.2	71.6	50.2	28.1
Non-Hispanic Black	14.2	4.0	4.9	3.2	5.9
Hispanic	4.2	27.7	18.6	35.7	44.3
Non-Hispanic other	2.2	8.1	4.9	11.0	21.7
Education among those age 25 or more					
High school grad or better	83.5	78.7	83.0	73.4	64.8
College grad or better	22.1	22.2	25.8	18.6	23.2

Source: Current Population Survey, March 1994.

grant generations. Among the third generation, about 80% are non-Hispanic White, followed by 14.2% non-Hispanic Black, 4.2% Hispanic, and 2.2% non-Hispanic other (mostly Asians and Native Americans). This differs sharply from the pattern for the foreign born, only 28.1% of whom are non-Hispanic White. The second generation falls between these extremes. However, there are marked differences depending on how the second generation is defined. Those with only one foreign-born parent resemble more the pattern for the third generation, whereas those with two foreign-born parents lean toward the pattern of the first generation.

Rumbaut points out that today's immigrant streams are composed of both the very well educated and the relatively poorly educated. This is evident in the last rows in Table 2.1. Of those age 25 or more who have at least graduated from high school, the first generation is at a distinct disadvantage, though almost two thirds of the foreign born (64.8%) have a high school degree. Within the second generation, those with two foreign-born parents are less likely to be high school graduates, by 10 percentage points, than those with only one foreign-born parent. On the other hand, proportionately as many first-generation adults as third generation adults have college degrees. Within the second generation, those with two foreign-born parents are less likely to have a college degree.

However creditable to social capital, children living with both parents are better off on average than those who are not (Eggebeen & Lichter, 1991). The data in Table 2.2 confirm that the first and second generations are advantaged in this sense. Native-born children of native-born parents are less likely to be

TABLE 2.2
Selected Household Characteristics of Individuals
by Nativity and Nativity of Parents, 1994

	Native-born individuals				
	Native-born Parents	At least one foreign-born parent	Only one foreign-born parent	Both parents foreign-born	Foreign-born individuals
Mean household size	3.4	3.5	3.4	3.6	4.0
Percentage residing in a family	85.2	84.7	84.8	84.6	85.0
Presence of parents among those under age 18 and not family heads					
Both parents present	68.9	75.1	73.0	76.6	74.4
Mother only present	24.6	20.5	21.9	19.5	17.3
Father only present	3.4	2.8	3.4	2.4	3.0
Neither parent present	3.3	1.6	1.7	1.6	5.3
Place of residence					
Metropolitan	74.9	88.9	84.9	92.5	94.2
Central City	(21.8)	(30.5)	(24.7)	(35.7)	(42.2)
Other metropolitan	(36.4)	(45.2)	(44.8)	(45.5)	(42.6)
Missing	(17.6)	(13.7)	(15.9)	(11.7)	(9.6)
Nonmetropolitan	24.2	10.7	14.6	7.2	5.6
Missing	0.9	0.4	0.6	0.3	0.3
Region of residence					
Northeast	18.4	28.0	25.5	30.2	23.8
Midwest	26.1	16.0	18.2	13.9	10.1
South	37.3	22.2	24.4	20.3	25.0
West	18.3	33.8	31.9	35.5	41.1

Source: Current Population Survey, March 1994.

living with both parents (68.9%) and more likely to be living with their mother only (24.6%) than either the second generation (at 75.1% and 20.5%) or the first generation (74.4% and 17.3%). Interestingly, at 5.3%, foreign-born children are more likely to live with relatives other than their mothers or fathers or with nonrelatives. Table 2.2 also provides some information about the residential and regional locations of immigrant generations. As Rumbaut reports, more than the third generation, first- and second-generation individuals are relatively concentrated in metropolitan locales and regionally in the Northeast and West.

At first blush, the economic characteristics of U.S. individuals, shown in Table 2.3, tell a predictable story of increasing economic well-being across the immigrant generations. For example, the third generation has the lowest official poverty rate (the percentage below 100% of the official poverty threshold), followed in order by the second and first generations. However, important differences in economic well-being emerge when the second generation itself is decomposed. Within the second generation, near poverty rates are only slightly over one fifth for those with only one immigrant parent but almost one third among those with two. In fact, the most advantaged of any of the nativity groups is the second generation with only one immigrant parent.

Table 2.3 also details income receipt across immigrant generations by showing the percentage of individuals who receive positive income from six separate sources. Across all individuals, the first and third generations are quite similar. Noteworthy among these similarities is that public assistance is as likely to be received by foreign-born individuals or their families as it is among third-generation individuals or their families. The pattern for the second generation reflects the relatively high percentage who are older, in that they are less likely to have family earnings (i.e., wages or salaries) and more likely to have social security income.

The final panel of Table 2.3 portrays the same income receipt prevalence but is restricted to the near poor. The first-generation near poor stand out as having comparatively high receipt of earnings and low receipt of social security. Moreover, both the first- and second-generation near poor have lower percentages receiving income from means-tested programs, including supplemental security income, public assistance, and food stamps. The foreign-born poor are the least likely to receive means-tested transfers. We return to this issue in a later section.

A final descriptive table captures selected labor force characteristics of immigrant generations. Table 2.4 begins with current labor force status for individuals aged 18 to 64. The second and especially the first generations are slightly disadvantaged by having lower prevalence of employment and higher prevalence in the unemployed and not in the labor force categories. Measured as mean usual hours worked per week and mean weeks worked, the labor sup-

TABLE 2.3
Selected Economic Status Characteristics of Individuals
by Nativity and Nativity of Parents, 1994

	Native-born individuals				
	Native-born Parents	At least one foreign-born parent	Only one foreign-born parent	Both parents foreign-born	Foreign-born individuals
Percentage below 150% of poverty line	23.4	27.9	21.9	33.2	37.3
Percentage below 100% of poverty line	10.2	10.7	8.6	12.6	15.0
Percentage below 50% of poverty line	6.2	5.7	4.7	6.6	8.5
Mean total family income (dollars)	42562	40530	45000	36456	36696
Percentage with family income from:					
Wages or salaries	81.7	73.0	78.4	68.2	80.5
Non-farm self-employment	12.3	10.7	13.0	8.8	9.9
Social security	19.0	30.4	25.1	35.1	15.4
Supplemental security income	3.9	3.4	2.8	4.0	5.4
Public assistance	6.9	6.5	5.9	7.1	6.9
Food stamps	10.5	10.0	8.9	11.0	11.7
Percentage of near poor with family income from:					
Wages or salaries	57.3	58.1	58.4	58.0	66.7
Non-farm self-employment	8.5	6.9	6.5	7.1	7.0
Social security	22.9	24.9	24.3	25.3	12.6
Supplemental security income	10.7	6.7	7.8	6.1	7.9
Public assistance	24.8	20.1	22.3	18.9	16.1
Food stamps	38.6	31.9	35.8	29.7	27.3

Source: Current Population Survey, March 1994.

ply among those who worked in the previous year is quite similar across the immigrant generations. The distribution of workers across very broad categories of occupation and industry reveals some expected disadvantages for the foreign born, who are less likely to be professionals and more likely to have operative and laborer positions. The second generation is more advantaged than the third generation in both respects.

TABLE 2.4
Selected Labor Force Characteristics of Individuals
by Nativity and Nativity of Parents

		Native-born individuals			
	Native-born Parents	At least one foreign-born parent	Only one foreign-born parent	Both parents foreign-born	Foreign-born individuals
Current labor force status of those age 18–64					
Employed	72.5	69.0	71.3	65.8	64.3
Unemployed	5.0	5.1	5.1	5.2	6.5
Not in the labor force	22.5	25.8	23.7	29.0	29.2
Among those employed in previous year:					
Mean hours worked per week	39.2	37.9	38.3	37.1	39.4
Mean weeks worked per year	45.2	44.7	45.2	44.0	45.2
Current occupation of those employed					
Professional	26.8	31.0	32.3	29.0	20.9
Technical	31.6	33.2	31.7	35.5	22.3
Service	24.4	22.0	22.0	22.2	31.1
Operative	17.2	13.8	14.0	13.3	25.8
Current industry of those employed					
Extractive	9.3	7.2	7.1	7.3	9.7
Manufacturing	16.7	14.3	13.5	15.6	21.4
Service	47.3	50.2	51.5	48.3	41.1
Trade	26.7	28.3	28.0	28.8	27.8

Source: Current Population Survey, March 1994.

MULTIVARIATE MODELS OF WELFARE RECEIPT

The United States has long been somewhat duplicitous when it comes to attitudes about poverty and immigration. On the one hand, we warm up to the idea of being a haven for the tired and poor of the world; on the other, we always have sought to exclude the poorest of would-be immigrants for fear they will become public charges. Worries about public service utilization among immigrants are especially acute now, in view of constrained federal and state budgets. As Rumbaut points out, the current welfare reform legislation that will soon emerge from conference committee for Congressional vote contains provisions that would severely restrict the flow of support to immigrants. For example, current legal permanent residents will be ineligible for food stamps and supplemental security income until they are citizens or have worked long enough to qualify for social security. But to what degree do immigrant families rely on welfare income when compared to natives? To answer this question, we conclude with multivariate models of welfare receipt among families. This issue is part of broader debates about whether immigrants and their families are a net benefit or detriment to public coffers and what our family and immigration policies should be.

In the literature, one dimension that separates empirical assessments of nativity differences in welfare receipt is whether or not statistical controls are included. Borjas (1994) tracked gross differences in welfare receipt and found a higher prevalence of welfare receipt among immigrants than natives and notable increases among immigrants over time, especially among recent immigrant cohorts. Another approach is to analyze welfare receipt while controlling for nativity, eligibility, and other predictors (Jensen, 1988). This tack addresses more the question of whether immigrants have a proclivity to welfare receipt, as some observers worry, and generally finds lower prevalence among immigrants than otherwise comparable natives.

We follow both approaches by estimating three sets of nested logistic regression models; one set each for receipt of public assistance (mostly aid to families with dependent children and general assistance), supplemental security income (SSI), and food stamps. We constrain this analysis to individuals who are residing in families and who are either family or subfamily heads. In the analyses of all three types of welfare income, the first model includes only dummy variables for nativity. With the third generation as the reference group, we distinguish the people in the second generation with only one versus two immigrant parents, and we further subdivide foreign-born individuals into those arriving before 1970, between 1970 and 1983, and after 1983. We then add controls for being near poor and for age in a second model and controls for other correlates of welfare receipt in a third model.

Model I in Table 2.5 shows that compared to the third generation, the second generation is less likely to receive public assistance, and despite previous tables showing them to be worse off in many respects, this negative effect is stronger among those with two immigrant parents. Among the foreign born, only those arriving after 1983 are more likely than the third generation to receive public assistance. Because these are means-tested programs, Model II adds a dummy variable for near poverty to see how public assistance receipt varies across immigrant generations among those apt to be income eligible. It also includes a control for age, given the differential age group targeting of these welfare programs. With age and poverty status controlled, all but second-generation individuals with only one immigrant parent and the for-

TABLE 2.5
Logistic Regression of Public Assistance Receipt
on Nativity and Other Predictors

	Model I		Model II		Model III	
	b	r	b	r	b	r
Nativity						
Native born of native parents (ref.)						
Native born of one foreign-born parent	−.433**	−.049	−.148	−.017	−.057	−.006
Native born of two foreign-born parents	−1.558**	−.170	−.943**	−.103	−.846**	−.092
Foreign born, immigrated before 1970	−.771**	−.074	−.263	−.025	−.278	−.027
Foreign born, immigrated 1970–1983	.005	.000	−.552**	−.062	−.504**	−.056
Foreign born, immigrated after 1983	.550**	.056	−.550**	−.056	−.395**	−.04 0
Near poor			3.484**	.787	2.586**	.584
Age						
Less than 35 (ref.)						
35–64			−1.036**	−.281	−.680**	−.184
65 and older			−3.647**	−.727	−3.105**	−.619
Female					1.705**	.428
Education						
Less than high school (ref.)						
High school graduate					−.225**	−.058
Some college or more					−.619**	−.169
Marital status						
Married (ref.)						
Never married					1.446**	.213
Other					.924**	.185
Race/ethnicity						
Non-Hispanic White (ref.)						
Non-Hispanic Black					.253**	.045
Hispanic					.349**	.055
Non-Hispanic other					.760**	.081
Metropolitan resident					.107	.025
Intercept	−2.769		−3.953		−5.284	
−2 log likelihood	18051		11769		9591	
Somers' D	.095		.802		.893	

Note: The table shows unstandardized (*b*) and standardized (*r*) logistic regression coefficients.
*Coefficient significant at .05 ≥ *p* > .01.
**Coefficient significant at *p* ≤ .01.
Source: Current Population Survey, March 1994.

eign born who arrived before 1970 are significantly less likely than the third generation to receive public assistance. Model III adds several variables known to affect economic status generally. The descriptive tables revealed that the nativity groups differ in their distributions across several of these additional predictors. Although the nativity effects generally weaken, the second generation with two foreign-born parents and the two groups of more recent foreign-born arrivals continue to be less likely than the third generation to receive public assistance.

Table 2.6 shows a parallel set of models for receipt of SSI, a means-tested program for people who are elderly, blind, or disabled. Because SSI is targeted more toward the deserving (as opposed to able-bodied) poor, the stigma associated with its receipt may be less severe. If the apparent reluctance of first- and second-generation families to receive welfare reflects avoidance of societally proscribed behaviors to facilitate assimilation, then any negative effects among more recent immigrant generations may be less strong for SSI. Table 2.6 provides some support for this possibility. Model I suggests that compared to third-generation family heads, the second generation with two foreign-born parents are less likely to receive SSI, whereas all three groups of foreign-born heads are more likely to receive this form of welfare. These nativity differences disappear in Models II and III, with the notable exception of the second generation with two immigrant parents, who remain less likely to receive SSI, other things equal. Still, not one of the immigrant generations is significantly more likely than otherwise comparable third-generation heads to receive this income source.

The final set of models is for food stamp receipt (Table 2.7). The pattern of effects across immigrant generations is quite similar to that for public assistance. With no controls, the second generation and the foreign born arriving before 1970 are significantly less likely to receive food stamps than the third generation, whereas later first-generation immigrants are significantly more likely to receive food stamps. With poverty status and age controlled, all first- and second-generation family heads are significantly less likely to receive food stamps than the third generation are (Model II). With other predictors added in Model III, this same pattern of nativity effects generally holds.

There are at least two ways to view these multivariate results. On the one hand, to be sure, all things are not equal, as Borjas (1994) and others would say. Because recently arrived foreign-born family heads are more likely to be poor and in need of assistance, they are more likely to receive that assistance. However, with the exception of SSI, among those families at greater risk of needing help, recent immigrants and the second generation with two immigrant parents appear especially averse to means-tested programs as an economic survival strategy.

TABLE 2.6
Logistic Regression of Supplemental Security Income Receipt
on Nativity and Other Predictors

	Model I		Model II		Model III	
	b	r	b	r	b	r
Nativity						
Native born of native parents (ref.)						
Native born of one foreign-born parent	−.318	−.036	−.233	−.027	-.097	−.011
Native born of two foreign-born parents	−.614**	−.067	−.750**	−.082	-.647**	−.071
Foreign born, immigrated before 1970	.470**	.045	.289	.028	.260	.025
Foreign born, immigrated 1970–1983	.375*	.042	.038	.004	−.121	−.013
Foreign born, immigrated after 1983	.418**	.043	−.055	−.006	−.091	−.009
Near poor			2.247**	.508	1.482**	.335
Age						
Less than 35 (ref.)						
35–64			.497**	.135	.634**	.172
65 and older			1.038**	.207	1.108**	.221
Female					.523**	.131
Education						
Less than high school (ref.)						
High school graduate					−.725**	−.187
Some college or more					−1.070**	−.293
Marital Status						
Married (ref.)						
Never married					.589**	.087
Other					.863**	.173
Race/ethnicity						
Non-Hispanic White (ref.)						
Non-Hispanic Black					.505**	.090
Hispanic					.260*	.041
Non-Hispanic other					.735**	.081
Metropolitan resident					−.048	−.011
Intercept	−3.903		−5.312		−5.187	
−2 log likelihood	8264		7296		6808	
Somers' D	.077		.551		.687	

Note: The table shows unstandardized (*b*) and standardized (*r*) logistic regression coefficients.
*Coefficient significant at $.05 \geq p > .01$.
**Coefficient significant at $p \leq .01$.
Source: Current Population Survey, March 1994.

TABLE 2.7
Logistic Regression of Food Stamp Receipt on Nativity and Other Predictors

	Model I		Model II		Model III	
	b	r	b	r	b	r
Nativity						
Native born of native parents (ref.)						
Native born of one foreign-born parent	−.497**	−.056	−.295**	−.034	−.217	−.025
Native born of two foreign-born parents	−.884**	−.097	−.489**	−.054	−.412**	−.045
Foreign born, immigrated before 1970	−.436**	−.042	−.255*	.025	−.328*	−.032
Foreign born, immigrated 1970–1983	.369**	.041	−.203*	−.023	−.333**	−.037
Foreign born, immigrated after 1983	.583**	.059	−.469**	−.048	−.500**	−.05 1
Near poor			3.462**	.782	2.878**	.651
Age						
Less than 35 (ref.)						
35–64			−.406**	−.110	−.264**	− .071
65 and older			−1.318**	−.263	−1.211**	−.241
Female					.467**	.117
Education						
Less than high school (ref.)						
High school graduate					−.443**	−.114
Some college or more					−.858**	−.235
Marital Status						
Married (ref.)						
Never married					.605**	.089
Other					.679**	.136
Race/ethnicity						
Non-Hispanic White (ref.)						
Non-Hispanic Black					.471**	.084
Hispanic					.308**	.049
Non-Hispanic other					.360**	.040
Metropolitan resident					.019	.004
Intercept	−2.179		−3.492		−3.448	
−2 log likelihood	27119		17950		16813	
Somers' D	.106		.741		.816	

Note: The table shows unstandardized (b) and standardized (r) logistic regression coefficients.
*Coefficient significant at .05 ≥ p > .01.
**Coefficient significant at p ≤ .01.
Source: Current Population Survey, March 1994.

DISCUSSION

Rubén Rumbaut provides compelling evidence that the family is the critical arena for the study of processes of immigration and adaptation. He stresses that a complete understanding requires an examination that looks across immigrant generations as well as a theoretical and empirical recognition of the rich diversity of immigration. Our complementary analyses echo the statistical profiles by Rumbaut and others, which show signs of both hope and stress for immigrants and their offspring. For example, immigrants themselves, and the second generation as a group, have lower incomes, higher poverty rates, and lower status occupations, and they are less likely to have a high school degree. On the other hand, compared to third and higher generations, first- and second-generation adults are less likely to be divorced, and first- and second-generation children are more likely to be living with both parents. This provides indirect corroboration for Rumbaut's observations that immigrant families are marked by strong family ties that can provide much needed "moral, social, cultural, and economic support" (p. 7). Also encouraging for the future of today's immigrants is the progressive improvement in economic status between the first and second generations. However, this optimism must be tempered by recognition that this is a cross-sectional comparison of immigrant generations. Many in today's second generation had parents from immigrant cohorts that enjoyed a rapidly expanding U.S. economy. More recent immigrants and their offspring will face a restructuring economy that offers far fewer opportunities, especially for those with limited human capital (Portes, 1994).

Data limitations have forced us to ignore much of the very diversity that Rumbaut would like to see more fully acknowledged. The sample size of the March CPS will simply not allow for in-depth study of particular country-of-origin groups, let alone pertinent social divisions within individual flows. However, we have been able to highlight a form of diversity that also is little recognized in the literature. Namely, we uncovered important differences between people from the second generation who had only one versus two immigrant parents. In many ways, second-generation people with two foreign-born parents were more likely to have the same relative disadvantages and advantages seen among the first generation. Compared to second-generation individuals with only one immigrant parent, those with two had poorer economic characteristics but were apparently more likely to reside in intact families. Moreover, our multivariate results indicated they were among the most averse to welfare receipt. The people from the second generation who had only one foreign-born parent resembled the third generation in these respects. These divergent patterns make sense considering that second-generation people with two foreign-born parents are more likely to be steeped in the immigrant experience and may have had parents who went through that experience as a couple. More research is needed to verify and explain these intriguing differences within the second generation.

Finally, Rumbaut found a negative effect of time in the United States on educational achievement and aspirations. Our analyses offer additional support for the unfortunate possibility that duration in the United States can see later generations come to emulate some of the less positive characteristics of preceding immigrant generations. Comparisons of first, second, and third generations reveal progressively greater prevalence of single parenthood as well as welfare receipt among the poor.

ACKNOWLEDGMENTS

Support for this research was provided by the Population Research Institute, Penn State, which has core support from the National Institute of Child Health and Human Development (P30 HD28263–01). The authors alone are responsible for any errors in logic or analysis.

REFERENCES

Borjas, G. J. (1994). The economics of immigration. *Journal of Economic Literature, 32,* 1667–1717.

Eggebeen, D. J., Lichter, D. T. (1991). Race, family structure, and changing poverty status among American children. *American Sociological Review, 56,* 801–817.

Jensen, L. (1988). Patterns of immigration and public assistance utilization, 1970–1980. *International Migration Review, 22,* 51–83.

Jensen, L., & Chitose, Y. (1994). Today's second generation: Evidence from the 1990 U.S. Census. *International Migration Review, 28,* 714–735.

Portes, A. (1994). Introduction: Immigration and its aftermath. *International Migration Review, 28,* 632–639.

3

Migration and the Dynamics of Family Phenomena

Guillermina Jasso
New York University

IN THIS chapter I do three things. First, I underscore some points that Rumbaut (this volume) makes and that I believe are crucial to our understanding of migration and the family. Second, I raise some points of a statistical nature, including some matters where data deficiencies impede progress in improving and increasing our knowledge. Third, I set out some propositions, variously derived from theories, conceptual models, and empirical explorations, that highlight the operation of family mechanisms and migration mechanisms in shaping both migration outcomes and family outcomes and that thus may be useful to examine systematically.

UNDERSTANDING MIGRATION AND THE FAMILY: SOME IMPORTANT POINTS IN RUMBAUT'S PAPER

Importance of the Family

The family is perhaps *the* strategic research site . . . for understanding the dynamics of immigration flows (legal and illegal) and of immigrant adaptation processes as well as long-term consequences for sending and especially for receiving countries, such as the United States. (Rumbaut, this volume, p. 4)

In my view, anyone who studies migration and neglects explicit consideration of family processes is likely to be seriously misled, and, equally, anyone who studies the family and neglects explicit consideration of migration processes

63

broadly defined—leaving town, going to war, settling in a new community—
is likely to miss core aspects of the dynamics of family phenomena.

Importance of Marriage

> The largest single mode of legal admission involve[s] a marriage to a U.S. citizen. (p. 4)

The United States is committed to the principle that its citizens may both
marry anyone they wish (excepting, of course, minors and persons of certain
very close degrees of consanguinity) and live with that person in the United
States if they so wish. This principle is unlikely to be demolished. In consequence, when other routes to immigration are blocked, marriage to a U.S. citizen becomes a singularly attractive route to a visa—attractive not only to
prospective migrants themselves but also to their families, who may through
the marriage achieve a life in the United States. It is interesting to note that
the marital immigration time series suggests that any time there is a change in
the law for visa allocation, there is a spurt of marriages to U.S. citizens. Presumably, every change in the law brings about winners and losers, and the
losers seek a new avenue. This mechanism is not the end of the marriage/
immigration story, for there are important further consequences set in motion
by these marriages. These include, among others and other things the same:

- fragility of marriages in which the visa-conferring faculty enhanced the
  American spouse's attractiveness as a mate;
- diminished propensity to naturalize among the immigrant spouses, due to
  the operation of a citizenship-portfolio diversification mechanism;
- enhanced possibilities for assimilation among the immigrant spouses;
- accelerated rates of upward occupational mobility among spouse immigrants, possibly due to superior screening by U.S. citizens marrying foreigners (relative to U.S. employers), as shown in Jasso and Rosenzweig
  (1995);
- enhanced possibilities for adaptation among the children of these international marriages; and
- the rise of a cosmopolitan group of children of international marriages who
  may grow up to play important roles in international activities, including
  trade and foreign relations.

Increasing Interconnectedness in the Modern World

> By the end of the 1980s, national surveys in Mexico found that about half of
> adult Mexicans were related to someone living in the United States. (p. 6)

As numerous travelers will attest, it is striking how many people one meets around the world who have U.S. family connections. At a dinner party in Germany, a prosperous and proper German couple tell me that their daughter is married to an American and lives in Arizona; in Rouen, France, an elderly shopkeeper tells me that his son went to study in Pittsburgh and decided to stay in the United States; in India I learn that siblings of both my hosts and their driver now reside in America; and in Mexico, people of all walks of life—importantly, not only the poor—seem to have relatives in the United States.

Numerical Restrictions on Western Hemisphere Immigration

> The 1965 law . . . placed for the first time numerical limits on legal immigration from the independent countries of the Western Hemisphere even as it abolished the national-origins quota system that had governed admissions from the Eastern Hemisphere. (p. 12)

This is a well-known fact in the history of U.S. immigration law. Yet it is surprising how often it is ignored, and how often one reads the inaccurate statement that the 1965 law increased immigration from the Western Hemisphere.

Role of the United States in the World

> Immigration to the United States can be understood as a dialectical consequence of the expansion of the nation to its post-World War II position of global hegemony. (p. 16)

The part played by the United States in the world is dramatically evident in flows of marriages to U.S. citizens, which often involve U.S. military personnel stationed abroad, and of refugees and asylees. One of the lovely features of Rumbaut's chapter appears on Table 1.1, where distinction is explicitly made between family-sponsored, employer-sponsored, and government-sponsored immigration.

Having provided a small catalog of some of the truly insightful ideas in Rumbaut's chapter, I now note that in one particular area the chapter borders on the intemperate. In general, his chapter makes the (cogent) case that many elements are involved in the migration process and that no single one can alone account for the observed phenomena. However, in making the case for the importance of a particular element, the operation of the other elements is sometimes deprecated; this is most vivid in the discussion of U.S. law and the passing comment about cost–benefit calculations (Rumbaut, this volume, pp. 17–18). Such hyperbole is unnecessary. Currently, the best framework for understanding migration is one that unabashedly incorporates all the elements and does so in a simple and parsimonious way. In this framework, individuals and families choose where to live, taking into account their endowments, skills, and tastes, subject to the constraints embodied in the laws and socioeconomic and political environments of both origin and destination countries, and attentive to present and projected returns to their endowments and skills in both countries.

OBTAINING RELIABLE KNOWLEDGE ABOUT MIGRATION AND THE FAMILY: EMPIRICAL PROCEDURES

It is a commonplace in immigration research that our understanding of migration processes is hampered by the lack of appropriate data. By now it is well known that longitudinal data are required in order to understand adaptation processes; that, due to the operation of emigration selectivity, we can be seriously misled by comparison at one point in time of immigrants of differing vintages; that cross-sectional data do no permit identification of the separate effects of age, duration, period, and cohort influences; that the use of dummy variables for origin countries masks our ignorance and cannot substitute for explicit inclusion of the operant country characteristics (Jasso & Rosenzweig, 1987, 1990). By now it is also well known that many dangers lurk in the specification and estimation of regression equations. These dangers include endogeneity bias, selection bias, errors-in-variables bias, to name only a few. Rumbaut is well aware of the empirical challenges, and based on previous discussions, I know that he intended the preliminary regressions reported in Table 1.7 only as suggestive. In his chapter, however, Rumbaut discusses the estimates reported in Table 1.7 as if they were estimates possessed of all the desirable statistical properties (e.g., unbiasedness, consistency, etc.) drawing substantive conclusions from them. It would thus be useful to examine the regression equations reported in Table 1.7, so that, in the spirit of collegially and collectively increasing our understanding, we may identify any sources of bias and take steps to mitigate any shortcomings.

To my graduate students, I suggest using a checklist—just as pilots do prior to takeoff. Here now are some items in the checklist, together with an initial assessment of the equations in Table 1.7.

Endogeneity Bias.   The equations reported in Table 1.7 are vulnerable to endogeneity bias. All five factors in the "Acculturation and Effort" group are, to varying degrees, choice-based and thus potentially jointly produced with the dependent variables of achievement and aspirations. To identify the effects of these variables, it is necessary to explicitly specify a system of equations and use instrumental-variables methods or use a fixed-effects estimator or both.

Errors-in-Variables Bias.   The equations reported in Table 1.7 are vulnerable to errors-in-variables bias. Note that there are two scales included as regressors, the parent–child conflict scale and the familism scale. Some procedure for mitigating the ensuing bias, such as the use of instrumental variables, is needed here.

Proper-Name Dummy Variables. The equations reported in Table 1.7 include binary regressors for origin countries, such as Vietnam or Mexico. The fundamental conceptual work on this topic was carried out by Przeworski and Teune (1970), who showed some 25 years ago that the challenge is to unpack the dummy variable and identify the features that are operating on the particular dependent variable of interest. And almost 10 years ago, it was shown that in equations of immigrant earnings, inclusion of characteristics of origin countries—such as GNP per capita, whether the economy is centrally planned or not, social and geographic distance to the United States—almost completely eliminates the effects of country dummies (Jasso & Rosenzweig, 1986b).

Indeed, the response of the empirical literature to the challenge of identifying and describing the migration-relevant features of origin countries—and note that this challenge falls squarely in the territory of the *migration context* emphasized by Rumbaut—may be thought of as comprising three generations of immigration research.

The early multivariate studies of the earnings attainment of immigrants, pioneered by Chiswick (1978), characterized country conditions by dummy variables representing countries. The results generally consisted of estimated regression equations in which each origin country had its own intercept. Table 1.7 exemplifies this early tradition.

The second generation of studies sought to identify the relevant country conditions by (a) characterizing the country environment by such variables as GNP per capita, literacy rates, and whether the economy is centrally planned and (b) characterizing the origin country's relation to the United States by such features as whether English is an official or dominant language, whether the country hosts a U.S. military installation, whether the United States broadcasts to the country in its native language(s), the number of its nationals who are residents in or became citizens of the United States, and its distance from the United States. This new way of capturing country conditions was implemented by Jasso and Rosenzweig (1986a, 1986b, 1988, 1990) and by Borjas (1987) and discussed by Greenwood and McDowell (1986). As noted by Greenwood and McDowell (1986), one finding from this literature was that inclusion of country-condition variables often eliminates the observed association between the proper name country dummy variables and immigrant earnings.

The third generation of empirical studies, recently initiated in the work of Donato (1989, 1993) and Sabagh, Bozorgmehr, Light, and der Martirosian (1989), goes beyond characterization of whole countries to characterization of the specific environments facing subsets of a country's residents. Those authors argue that to the extent that a country treats its residents differently by gender (Donato, 1989, 1993) or by race or ethnicity or religion (Sabagh et al., 1989), the propensity to migrate will differ by gender, race, ethnicity, and religion. To our knowledge, no other researchers have yet sought to characterize

TABLE 3.1
Trios of Exactly Linearly Dependent Variables:
Trios Whose Elements are Measured Along the Time Dimension

Age	= Date of observation	– Date of birth
Experience as Ph.D.	= Date of observation	– Date of Ph.D.
Experience as Ph.D.	= Age	– Age at receipt of Ph.D.
Duration in United States	= Date of observation	– Immigration date
Duration in United States	= Age	– Age at immigration
Marital duration	= Date of observation	– Marriage cohort
Marital duration	= Age	– Age at marriage
Labor-force experience	= Date of observation	– Date of entry into the labor force
Labor-force experience	= Age	– Age at entry into the labor force

the home-country environments faced by prospective outmigrants—or by U.S. immigrants contemplating a return home—in this more refined way. Thus, an important task that lies ahead is to augment country-characteristics data sets by including features of the subnational environments faced by subsets of the population, defined by gender, race, ethnicity, or religion.

Trios of Exactly Linearly Dependent Variables.   The equations in Table 1.7 include age and length of residence. These two variables are involved in a trio of exactly linearly related variables. The missing third variable is age at entry, as shown in Table 3.1 (which also provides other examples of trios of exactly linearly dependent variables). This means that the estimated coefficients of the two included factors confound the effects of all three factors, effects which cannot be separately identified. In fact, the negative effect of age, estimated in all four equations, could be interpreted as a negative coefficient of age at entry, because, for given duration, the greater the age, the greater the age at entry. Unfortunately, it is also the case that the negative coefficient of duration, in two of the four equations, could be interpreted as a positive effect of age at entry, because, for a given age, the greater the duration, the lower the age at entry. This is what we mean when we say that the effects cannot be identified. Fortunately, Rumbaut has collected longitudinal data, and he can use the approach based on the fixed-effects estimator to help obtain estimates of the separate effects of the variables involved in the linear dependency. The procedure is outlined in my article on marital sexual behavior (Jasso, 1985).

TOWARD A FULLER UNDERSTANDING OF MIGRATION AND THE FAMILY: SOME PROPOSITIONS IN SEARCH OF FURTHER THEORETICAL AND EMPIRICAL ANALYSIS

Children as Engines of Their Parents' Migration

It is customary to think of children as passive receivers of the environments crafted by their parents. In the context of migration, children are often regarded as "tied movers" (Mincer, 1978), not unlike the other putative tied movers, their mothers. However, a moment's reflection will persuade that sometimes children are the engine of migration. For example, a child is born musically gifted, and the parents decide to move to a musically rich environment; a child is born hyperenergetic, and the parents decide to move to a farm. So, too, it may be with international migration.

In this section I use data from the cohorts of immigrants admitted in Fiscal Years 1971 and 1977 to investigate a conjecture that repeatedly surfaces in newspapers and cocktail parties: that, *ceteris paribus*, parents who have only daughters are more likely to seek a life in the United States than are parents who have only sons or who have both sons and daughters. Variants of this conjecture address differences in the proportion female among the children of immigrants admitted under different entry criteria or from different origin countries or in different time periods.

Because family-reunification immigrants and employment immigrants may differ, we distinguish between the children of immigrants admitted as siblings, on the one hand, and the children of immigrants admitted in the two employment-based categories under the law in effect in Fiscal Years 1971 and 1977 (third and sixth), on the other hand. Of course, the Western Hemisphere was not covered by the preference-category system in 1971.

Table 3.2 reports the proportion female in the two entry-visa groups, by hemisphere and year. As shown, there is a dramatic difference in the proportion female among the children of the 1971 immigrants. Whereas sibling immigrants had more sons than daughters, employment-based immigrants had more daughters than sons; the proportion female differs by more than 12 percentage points. It would appear that in 1971, in reaching the migration decision, employment-based immigrants were more likely than sibling-based im-

TABLE 3.2
Percent Female Among First-Generation Children — The Immigrant Children of Immigrants Admitted in the Employment (3rd and 6th) and Sibling (5th) Categories, by Hemisphere, for the FY 1971 and the FY 1977 Cohorts

	Eastern Hemisphere		*Western Hemisphere*	
	Employment-Based	*Sibling-Based*	*Employment-Based*	*Sibling-Based*
FY 1971	54.9	42.5	—	—
FY 1977	47.7	47.0	48.7	48.2

Note: Figures for FY 1971 are estimates based on the FY 1971 Immigrant Cohort Sample, a one-in-one-hundred sample; figures for FY 1977 are based on the FY 1977 Immigrant-Naturalization File, which contains 459,356 usable cases out of an immigrant population of 462,315. Child immigrants are admitted on P33, P38, P53, P58, P63, and P68 visas. In FY 1971, the preference-category system of visa allocation covered only the Eastern Hemisphere.

migrants to be influenced by the sex ratio of their offspring. In 1977, however, although the proportion female among the children of employment-based immigrants exceeded that among the children of sibling immigrants, the gap had almost closed. In neither hemisphere did the difference reach a single percentage point.

What do these results mean? Alternative interpretations cannot be ruled out given these minimal data. But it is possible that a change occurred between 1971 and 1977, such that the characteristics of the offspring exerted relatively less influence on the parents' decision to migrate, compared with other causal factors such as world economic conditions. It is possible that those ubiquitous newspaper and cocktail-party accounts are the nostalgic reminiscences of (or about) immigrants who in the late 1960s and early 1970s did indeed take their cues from their children. Alternatively, it is possible that the disparity in opportunities for girls and for boys has narrowed in other countries, such that the future is brighter for little girls than it might have been 20 or 30 years ago, and hence the parents of all-girl families have less incentive to migrate. Finally, it is possible that perceptions of the climate for girls in the United States changed in the interval between 1971 and 1977, and that the United States in 1977 was seen as a more dangerous place in which to raise daughters, a place characterized by greater sexual freedom and its attendant risks (e.g., early marriage, pregnancy out of wedlock).

Before leaving the general topic of children as engines of their parents' migration, I note that a prevailing conjecture concerning the composition of the currently resident population of undocumented aliens involves exactly this mechanism. As of January, 1995, the backlogs of approved applicants for immigrant visas numbered 3,692,506, of whom a substantial proportion must be children.[1] It is well known that children adjust more smoothly to a move—any move, but *a fortiori* an international move—if the move occurs prior to puberty. Both the literatures on language acquisition and on self-esteem (Simmons & Blyth, 1987) point in this direction. It follows that parents in the visa backlogs, caring about their children's well-being, would be willing to risk life as an illegal alien in the United States—for a temporary period prior to obtaining the immigrant visa—if that would increase their children's well-being. Many immigration researchers believe that, indeed, a substantial proportion of the illegal alien population consists of approved visa applicants in the backlogs who, much like cohabiting couples, move to the United States somewhat in advance of receipt of the visa, and that many do so out of concern for their children.

---

[1]For example, in Fiscal Year 1993, over 45% of the immigrants admitted in the four family-sponsored preference categories (which in January, 1995, constituted 96.3% of the visa backlogs) were admitted on child visas (U.S. Immigration and Naturalization Service, 1993; U.S. Department of State, 1995).

The Sponsorship Behavior of Child Immigrants

Child immigrants grow up. They become naturalized citizens of the United States, and they take their place among the American people. Like native-born U.S. citizens, they have certain privileges, including that of sponsoring new immigrants. A question of both scientific and policy concern is the question of the sponsorship behavior of immigrants. How many new immigrants does a current immigrant sponsor over his or her lifetime? Although sponsorship of numerically-limited relatives (such as siblings) is by definition limited, sponsorship of numerically-exempt relatives is in principle boundless. A given naturalized immigrant might sponsor several spouses (in tandem), two parents, unlimited adopted children, and, of course, any children born abroad who are not already U.S. citizens or immigrants.

The only currently available data set that can shed some light on the sponsorship behavior of child immigrants is the GAO Fiscal Year (FY) 1985 Immediate-Relatives File, described in a report by the U.S. General Accounting Office (U.S.GAO, 1988). The GAO data set includes information on the sponsors of a probability sample of immigrants admitted as immediate relatives in FY 1985. Sample selection was stratified by 11 groups, 10 countries which represented the top origin countries for the entire class of immediate relatives in FY 1985 and a residual category. The sponsors included both native-born U.S. citizens and naturalized U.S. citizens; information on the entry visa of naturalized sponsors was obtained. Thus, this data set enables estimation of the number of immediate relatives sponsored in one year by naturalized immigrants who had entered in particular visa categories (weighting by the inverse of the sponsored immigrant's probability of selection into the sample).

By relating these estimates of sponsored relatives to the number of entrants in each (sponsor) visa category, for given period of time, it is possible to construct crude sponsorship rates. Even if one is uneasy about the estimated sponsorship rates themselves, the ratios of estimated sponsorship rates remain meaningful.

The sample is small—799 naturalized sponsors out of 2,299 sponsors— and thus I combine the third and sixth preference categories into a single employment-based category. All sponsors who gained admission to the United States as the child of an employment-based principal are included in one group; the relevant visas are P33, P38, P63, and P68. All sponsors who gained admission as the child of a sibling principal are included in the second group; the relevant visas are P53 and P58.[2]

---

[2] Visa designators ending in a "3" refer to individuals arriving in the United States in possession of the visa documents; visa designators ending in an "8" refer to persons who were in the United States on temporary papers and adjusted their status to legal permanent residence while in the United States. The GAO sample does not contain any persons who adjusted status to the rel-

TABLE 3.3

Sponsorship Behavior of the First Generation—Immigrants Admitted as
the Children of Employment-Based and Sibling-Based Principals:
Evidence from the GAO FY 1985 Immediate-Relative Immigrants File

	Spouse	Child	Parent	All Imm. Rels.
Estimated number of immediate relatives sponsored in FY 1985 by immigrants who had been admitted on child visas				
Employment-based (3rd, 6th prefs.)	336	0	0	336
Sibling-based (5th pref.)	1936	129	300	2365
Estimated ratio of child-of-sibling sponsorship rate to child-of-employee sponsorship rate				
Based on FY 1971 immigrants	2.285	—	—	2.792
Based on FY 1977 immigrants	1.496	—	—	1.827
Based on FY 1978–1980 immigrants	1.944	—	—	2.375

Note: Estimates of sponsored immigrants are obtained from the GAO FY 1985 Immediate-Relative Immigrants File; estimates are weighted to reflect the sample selection procedure. Sponsorship rates are calculated for three cohorts of immigrants admitted with child visas in the third, fifth, and sixth preference categories; those who entered, respectively, in FY 1971, FY 1977, and FY 1978–1980. Child-visa immigrant data are obtained from the INS FY 1971 Immigrant Cohort Sample File, the INS FY 1977 Immigrant-Naturalization File, and published tabulations in the *INS Annual Reports* and *Statistical Yearbooks*.

Panel A of Table 3.3 reports the estimated number of immediate relatives sponsored in FY 1985 by immigrants who had gained admission to the United States as the children of employment-based and sibling immigrants, by type of relative sponsored. As shown, children of employees are found in the sample only as the sponsors of spouses; the estimated number of spouses sponsored is 336. In contrast, children of siblings sponsored all three kinds of immediate relatives, including children (all were biological children; none were adopted), for a total of 2,365 sponsored immigrants.

To put these figures in perspective, we note the following: In FY 1985, the total number of immediate relatives was 198,143; of these, 124,093 were spouses, 38,986 were parents, and 35,064 were children. Jasso and Rosenzweig (1989, 1990) estimate that although only 20% of the sponsors of spouses (i.e., approximately 24,819) were themselves former immigrants, more than 95% of the sponsors of parents (i.e., approximately 37,037) were

---

evant child categories. Although the numbers are small, this fact may be suggestive; perhaps the longer the time spent in the United States, the less the probability of sponsoring a spouse, parent, or child from the origin country or another foreign country.

themselves former immigrants. Thus, naturalized immigrants sponsor about 1.5 parents for every spouse they sponsor.

Both child-of-worker and child-of-sibling immigrants depart from the general pattern, the children of workers by sponsoring no parents and the children of siblings by sponsoring over six spouses for every parent they sponsor. Thus, initial results suggest that, as would be expected of persons who become immigrants on child visas, they sponsor fewer parents than other immigrants.

Our main interest, however, lies in contrasting the behavior of the children of siblings and the children of employment-based immigrants. To that end I constructed sponsorship rates based on the counts of new immigrants holding the relevant child visas. A question arises as to the appropriate count to use. The sponsors immigrated over the period from 1965 to 1978. If the GAO sample were larger, and year-specific sponsoring more reliably estimated, I would construct sponsorship rates for each represented entry cohort. However, given the small numbers, I assume that all the sponsors entered in the same cohort. To represent the number of entrants in each visa category, I use the entry counts for three different periods: FY 1971, FY 1977, and the 3-year period FY 1978–1980. FY 1978 is the first year for which these counts are published; counts for FY 1971 and 1977 were obtained from the FY 1971 Immigrant Cohort Sample and the FY 1977 Immigrant-Naturalization File. I would have preferred 3-year counts for all three estimates (to smooth out any year-specific blips) but currently can provide a 3-year count only for the 1978–1980 period. Thus, for each visa category and type of sponsored immigrant, we have three estimates of the sponsorship rate.

Next, I calculated the ratios of the child-of-sibling sponsorship rate to the child-of-employee sponsorship rate for the spouses category and the all-immediate-relatives total. The results, shown in Panel B of Table 3.3, show that the children of siblings have substantially higher sponsorship rates than the children of employment-based immigrants. The children of sibling immigrants are between 1.5 and 2.3 times as likely as the children of employee immigrants to marry a foreign-born person and sponsor his or her immigration. The overall ratio ranges from 1.8 to 2.8, indicating that children of siblings sponsor more than twice as many new immigrants in the immediate-relative categories than the children of employment-based immigrants.

At first blush this result appears startling, for prima facie the children should not differ. It suggests that persons admitted to the United States as the siblings of U.S. citizens are less fully integrated than immigrants who enter the United States by dint of skills and that their diminished attachment to the United States is inherited by their children. This result is also consistent with a family-network interpretation, such that, for given intensity of self-selection, the presence of kin preserves attachments to the origin country. Finally, note that the differential sponsorship behavior could be due to systematic age differences between the two groups; that is, the children of siblings may be older, and hence more attached to the origin country, than the children of employment immigrants. Only new data can help adjudicate among these alternative interpretations.[3]

Migration and Gender Inequality

In recent theoretical work, Jasso (1992) develops a framework for studying the link between migration and societal gender inequality. The starting idea is that sex-selective spousal status disparity may be implicated in the rise and maintenance of the complex of customs, laws, and institutions known collectively as gender inequality. The framework provides a general model for investigating the distribution of spousal status disparity, and establishes that a necessary condition for the (long-run) majority of couples to exhibit sex-selective spousal status disparity, in three types of societies characterized by three idealized mating rules, is that the distribution of bride's parental wealth differ from the distribution of groom's parental wealth. Next, the framework distinguishes between natives and immigrants among the newlyweds, yielding the result that, given different mean wealth among the natives and immigrants, a necessary and sufficient condition for generating brides' and grooms' parental wealth distributions of different means is that the sex ratio among native newlyweds differ from the sex ratio among immigrant newlyweds. Jasso (1992) describes scenarios for generating a majority of couples of the same unequal type; for example, if the immigrants are wealthier than the natives and also have a sex ratio at marriage greater than unity, then the conditions are satisfied for generating a majority of groom-superior couples.

Drawing together the mathematical results obtained from the spousal status disparity and migration framework and the growing evidence that early agriculture spread by migration and intermarriage, Jasso (1992) shows that the evidence is consistent with a scenario in which intermarriage with the immigrant Neolithic farmers—wealthier than the natives and with a sex ratio greater than one—led to a majority of couples being of the groom-superior type. Thus, Jasso suggests that the early migration of Neolithic farmers is deeply implicated in the rise of gender inequality.

If spousal status disparity is an engine of societal gender inequality, then it may be possible to observe its operation at any point of space and time. It may be useful to investigate traces of this process in modern times. The modern context differs from the prehistoric context in that gender inequality is a thriv-

---

[3]New data could also establish differences between sibling immigrants and employment immigrants in completed family size and in the nativity configuration of the offspring. Note that it is possible that the children of employment immigrants sponsor as many spouses as the children of siblings, but that a higher proportion of the children of employment immigrants are born in the United States, and hence cannot be identified in the data set.

ing institution. Thus, any effect of the spousal disparity mechanism will be in the direction of intensifying or attenuating gender inequality, not in engendering it or dealing it a mortal blow.

There are two cases that appear especially useful to explore; both involve the United States. The first concerns the mass migrations of the late 19th and early 20th centuries. The second involves post-World War II immigration. Though full analysis of these cases is outside the scope of this chapter, we may outline an initial look at them.

Immigration to the United States before World War I was overwhelmingly male. In the period of largest immigration, in the first decade of this century, the sex ratio was as high as 2.28—that is, 2.28 male immigrants for every female immigrant. The immigrants were also unambiguously poorer than the natives. Thus, pre-World War I immigration to the United States, and especially immigration during the late 19th and early 20th centuries, satisfies the conditions for generating large numbers of bride-superior couples. Accordingly, we would expect to find an attenuation of gender inequality in the United States and a new impetus for full equality between the sexes. Such attenuated gender inequality caught the attention of many travelers, including de Tocqueville, and it may be no accident that the drive for female suffrage intensified in the late 19th and early 20th centuries, culminating in 1920 with ratification of the Constitutional amendment granting women the vote.

What about more recent immigration? There are several avenues to explore. First, the sex ratio among single skill-based legal immigrants is greater than one; thus, one element of the immigrant stream satisfies both conditions for generating groom-superior couples. Second, most immigrants admitted as spouses of U.S. citizens are female, reflecting in large part the U.S. military presence around the world. If this element of the migration stream is poorer than the natives and has a sex ratio smaller than one, then, again, it is conducive to groom-superior couples.

More generally, as U.S. immigration law moves toward granting a greater priority to highly skilled immigrants, then, given that most highly skilled persons in other countries are male, the immigrant stream will be wealthier than the natives and have a sex ratio greater than one. These conditions are the very conditions that we have seen generate groom-superior couples.

Accordingly, although I refrain from reaching any conclusions until a systematic and rigorous review of the evidence has been conducted, it is possible to suggest that the broad outlines of post-World War II immigration to the United States appear to support the necessary conditions for reinforcing gender inequality.

Thus, migration may be deeply implicated not only in the historic rise of gender inequality but also in reinforcing or attenuating gender inequality in the United States. The foregoing brief initial review suggests—pending systematic investigation—that pre-World War I immigration, consisting of a preponderance of poor males, favored a diminishing of gender inequality, but that post-World War II immigration, containing streams of highly skilled males and relatively poor females, has favored a reinforcing of gender inequality.

REFERENCES

Borjas, G. J. (1987). Self-selection and the earnings of immigrants. *American Economic Review, 77,* 531–533.

Chiswick, B. R. (1978). The effect of Americanization on the earnings of foreign-born men. *Journal of Political Economy, 86,* 897–921.

Donato, K. M. (1989, August). *Why so many women: Cross-national variation in the sex composition of U.S. immigrants.* Paper presented at the annual meeting of the American Sociological Association, San Francisco, California.

Donato, K. M. (1993). Current trends and patterns of female migration: Evidence from Mexico. *International Migration Review, 27,* 748–771.

Greenwood, M. J., & McDowell, J. M. (1986). The factor market consequences of U.S. immigration. *Journal of Economic Literature, 24,* 1738–1772.

Jasso, G. (1985). Marital coital frequency and the passage of time: Estimating the separate effects of spouses' ages and marital duration, birth and marriage cohorts, and period influences. *American Sociological Review, 50,* 224–241.

Jasso, G. (1992, August). *Migration and gender inequality.* Paper presented at the annual meeting of the American Sociological Association, Pittsburgh, Pennsylvania.

Jasso, G., & Rosenzweig, M. R. (1986a). Family reunification and the immigration multiplier: U.S. immigration law, origin-country conditions, and the reproduction of immigrants. *Demography, 23,* 293–311.

Jasso, G., & Rosenzweig, M. R. (1986b). What's in a name? Country-of-origin influences on the earnings of immigrants in the United States. *Research in Human Capital and Development, 4,* 75–106.

Jasso, G., & Rosenzweig, M. R. (1987). Using national recording systems for the measurement and analysis of immigration to the United States. *International Migration Review, 21,* 1212–1244.

Jasso, G., & Rosenzweig, M. R. (1988). How well do U.S. immigrants do? Vintage effects, emigration selectivity, and occupational mobility. *Research in Population Economics, 6,* 229–253.

Jasso, G., & Rosenzweig, M. R. (1989). Sponsors, sponsorship rates, and the immigration multiplier. *International Migration Review, 23,* 856–888.

Jasso, G., & Rosenzweig, M. R. (1990). *The new chosen people: Immigrants in the United States.* The Population of the United States in the 1980s: A Census Monograph Series. New York: Russell Sage.

Jasso, G., & Rosenzweig, M. R. (1995). Do immigrants screened for skills do better than family-reunification immigrants? *International Migration Review, 29,* 85–111.

Mincer, J. (1978). Family migration decisions. *Journal of Political Economy, 86,* 749–773.

Przeworski, A., & Teune, H. (1970). *The logic of comparative social inquiry.* New York: Wiley.

Sabagh, G., Bozorgmehr, M., Light, I., & der Martirosian, C. (1989, March–April). *Internal ethno-religious differentiation of immigrant groups: Iranians in Los Angeles.* Paper presented at the annual meeting of the Population Association of America, Baltimore, Maryland.

Simmons, R. G., & Blyth, D. A. (1987). *Moving into adolescence: The impact of pubertal change and school context.* New York: Aldine de Gruyter.

U.S. Department of State. (1980–1995). *Annual report of the Visa Office.* Washington, DC: U.S. Government Printing Office.

U.S. General Accounting Office. (1988). *Immigration: The future flow of legal immigration to the United States.* Washington, DC: U.S. Government Printing Office.

U.S. Immigration and Naturalization Service. (1943–1978). *Annual report of the Immigration and Naturalization Service.* Washington, DC: U.S. Government Printing Office.

U.S. Immigration and Naturalization Service. (1979–1993). *Statistical yearbook of the Immigration and Naturalization Service.* Washington, DC: U.S. Government Printing Office.

4

Immigrant Families at Risk: Factors That Undermine Chances for Success

Mary C. Waters
Harvard University

RUBÉN RUMBAUT'S wide-ranging chapter provides a number of well-supported findings worth stressing again. I concentrate on the three that I believe to be most important. First, there is no singular immigrant family experience. Rather, families differ in the amount of human, political, and social capital they bring with them and create in the United States. Second, an "immigrant ethos" of strong family ties, high aspirations among children, hard work among children (measured in terms of number of hours spent on homework), and achievement (measured in terms of GPA) all tend to erode with time in the United States and with increasing exposure to native norms. Third, even when a large number of background characteristics are controlled, ethnicity has a strong effect on the outcomes and experiences of immigrant families. Because I agree wholeheartedly with these points and believe that Rumbaut surveyed a great deal of the freshest and most well-done research on this topic to arrive at these conclusions, I do not rehash them here. Instead I outline some new research questions arising from the conclusions. I address a few of the questions using findings from my own ethnographic work with West Indian immigrant families.

Another way of describing Rumbaut's central findings is that the "old line" assimilation model of cultural and social assimilation in lockstep with socioeconomic success is not correct anymore. Class mobility for immigrants and their children is no longer associated with increasing Americanization for all groups. Different trajectories of socioeconomic incorporation, success, and cultural integration describe the experiences of different families. Given the

79

newness of the central finding that assimilation and socioeconomic success
have been decoupled, how are we to understand the how and why of this?
What are the particular social factors that dissipate the social capital of the immigrants over time? What about the migration process itself undermines or
strengthens the ties between parents and children in particular families? Why
does exposure to the United States have deleterious effects on some children,
causing their GPAs and aspirations to decline, whereas other children do spec-
tacularly well? Finally, the $64,000 question from my perspective, what is in
the "black box" we call ethnicity that has an independent effect on family outcomes, net of family background characteristics, and most other variables that
can be measured in the valuable surveys of the type Rumbaut and his colleagues have been conducting?

These are all large questions worth pursuing by scholars in the coming
years. Taking Rumbaut's first point to heart, that immigrant families have very
heterogenous backgrounds and outcomes, I describe some of the factors affecting the families I have studied, in order to outline some of the middle-
range causal mechanisms that influence the outcomes of families in the United
States. Specifically, I outline a few factors operating on the families I studied
that tend to erode the chances of socioeconomic success for their children. I
do not concentrate on the factors that tend to improve the situations of immigrant families.

In order to understand the immigration experience of families from the
Caribbean, I conducted 202 in-depth interviews in New York City in 1991 and
1992. The study includes three major case studies that examine distinct populations—low-skilled immigrant workers working for a food service company
in downtown Manhattan, second-generation adolescents at two New York City
high schools and in various other samples, and middle-class immigrants working as teachers in New York City public high schools. The entire study included interviews with 72 first-generation immigrants, 73 second-generation
immigrants, 27 Whites, and 30 native-born Black Americans. The native-
born Whites and Blacks were co-workers of the immigrants and were interviewed about their assumptions about the identities of the immigrants and
their interactions with them.

West Indians in the United States have long been a favorite topic for conservative writers because of their purported success relative to American
Blacks.[1] For instance, very few articles about possible Presidential candidate
Colin Powell fail to mention that he is a second-generation Jamaican American. That purported success, however, characterizes only some of the immigrants and their children. Very often the families who do not fare well in the

---

[1] There is a debate about how well West Indians actually fare compared to African Americans
in the United States. The scope of this debate is beyond the purview of this chapter. For a good
empirical discussion, see Kasinitz (1992), Model (1991, 1995), and Farley and Allen (1987).

United States describe themselves as African Americans and are described and labeled as such by other Americans. It is interesting to note that very few articles about the controversial leader of the Nation of Islam, Louis Farakhan, mention that he is a second-generation Barbadian American.

The arguments of conservative writers such as Thomas Sowell are that West Indians fare better than American Blacks in the United States, despite the fact that both groups have black skin. They suggest that the success of the West Indians is due to higher values of education and family values (Sowell, 1978). In fact, some of the ideas that unskilled immigrants express about the American dream, about working for what you want, about the importance of education, and about distancing from so-called ghetto underclass behavior suggest a neoconservative's dream population. Ronald Reagan could not express a better disdain for welfare or faith in the Horatio Algier myth than do many West Indian families. (Of course, as a few writers have pointed out but which never seems to make it into American mainstream discussions, most stable Black working-class people in the United States share many of these same views.) However, many of these values are systematically undermined by various assaults on Black people in the United States and not rewarded. Over the course of one generation, many changes happen in how people think about race relations, economic and social opportunity, the value of education, and the kinds of work one should accept. In effect, the immigrant ethos and the social capital of many Caribbean families are undermined by various forces in American society as well as by the immigration experience itself. The major factors that contribute include serial migration, the isolation of nuclear families, the long hours parents spend at work, conflicts between the immigrants and American norms about discipline for children, the role of racial discrimination, and the disinvestment of American society in inner-city neighborhoods and institutions, particularly schools. I examine each of these in turn.

SERIAL MIGRATION

Americans often imagine the immigration of a family as Mom, Dad, three kids, and some suitcases arriving on the boat or the plane. Many of the families I interviewed were single-headed families headed by women even before immigration; this family form is prevalent in the Caribbean. Even for the husband–wife Caribbean families I interviewed, in most cases their migration happened sequentially, often with the mother coming to the United States first under an occupational visa as a domestic or a registered nurse and sending for her children and her husband later. This process can sometimes take longer than a decade. The children are usually left behind with relatives, often a grandmother or aunt.

Sometimes leaving or sending children is intentional and not related to migration dynamics. It is a commonly held belief among the immigrants that the United States is a bad place to raise young children but a place of educational opportunity for older ones. There is a long tradition of this child fostering in the Caribbean. In a society where rural-urban, inter-island, and now island to the United States migration has been the norm for over a century, child fostering has been an accepted way of life. Because of this prevalence, child fostering is not seen as much of a variation or aberration in the Caribbean. However, the migration experience creates conditions that have effects on relations between generations.

Serial migration and intentional child fostering both lead to a situation in which the biological parent is not the primary caretaker of the child in early childhood. However, most immigrants send for their children when they reach early adolescence, either because the parent has become established enough in New York to support them or because a child is nearing high school age and can only attend secondary school in the United States (most students do not finish high school in the islands; the system does not guarantee an academic high school education for all children). Problems between the generations may occur when parents try to establish firm discipline over children with whom they have spent very little time or often have not seen for over 5 or 6 years. Parents and children encounter one another as strangers, and many of the young teens feel that their parents had abandoned them when they left the Caribbean. Many of the students reported that they learned in the United States that it is not right for a parent to leave a child behind with a grandmother and that it means that the parent does not love them. Often the parent cannot understand such an "American" idea, for the mother herself might have been raised by her grandmother. However, the taken-for-granted nature of child fostering in the islands means that it was not a stigmatized practice when it happened to the mother. For young teens in New York, it feels otherwise when they learn that this is not a common thing to do in the United States.

Often reunions of mothers and their children cause problems in the opposite direction. For instance, in one of the schools where I did fieldwork the guidance counselor showed me a letter written to her by a tenth grader who had grown up in the Jamaican countryside with a very strict and religious grandmother. The girl had recently come to live with her mother, who drank alcohol and took drugs and "slept around." This young woman was scandalized by her mother's behavior and wanted to be removed from the home. Thus, these reunions contain the trauma of children confronting Americanized parents as well as the trauma of parents confronting Americanized children. These separations and reunions put a great deal of strain on the relations between generations.

IMMIGRANTS' HARD WORK

The much-vaunted immigrant ethos of hard work and saving also can cause some difficult problems that undermine the ability of the second generation to succeed. Many of the parents work long hours at low-paying jobs. The mothers of the teens I interviewed were often home health aides who worked long shifts, often at night, or they worked cleaning houses and offices on long shifts. Fathers were security guards, maintenance men, or cab drivers. It was very common for these parents to work two or more jobs. In fact, many respondents pointed with pride to the TV show "In Living Color," which had a Jamaican character who was satirically described as having 28 jobs. The immigrants thought the description of the hard-working Jamaican was accurate and missed the satire.

When both parents or a single parent works, there is often no parent at home for the children. Even if a grandmother or other extended family member is present in this country, that person often works long hours too. This is very unlike life in the islands, where most children have an adult relative at home during the day and night. This relative was not always a parent, but most immigrants stressed that neighbors and extended family members—and even strangers in their town or neighborhood—would take responsibility for watching out for and disciplining children and teens. The nuclear family in New York City neighborhoods rarely has such social supports. The parents who are working all the time express dismay, anger, and bewilderment that the children do not appreciate or understand their sacrifices. However, the children need the social support of the parents in the home far more than they need the material goods the parents are striving for.

When the children were in the islands, the parents maintained ties by sending money and material goods. Parents are proud of the access to consumer goods that were way beyond their means in the islands, so they have a tendency to buy their children material goods. On the other hand, the dollar that went so far and the one pair of sneakers that meant so much back home are a drop in the bucket in the United States, where small paychecks do not allow the parents to give all the material things the kids want, especially fancy clothes for school. With assimilation, the children I studied expected expensive consumer goods like fashionable clothes and jewelry from parents, but the parents saw these as unreasonable expectations. The teens interpreted it as parents refusing to support them in the American way, which the parents themselves led the children to expect through the economic remittances before they sent for their children. This difference between the expectations of the children and the limited resources available for the hard-working parents leads to teens' increased susceptibility to the underground economy.

At the same time that the parents are scrimping and saving as the unskilled working poor, the easy money of drugs is all around the immigrants in the inner-city neighborhoods they inhabit in Brooklyn. Another incident from my fieldwork makes this clear. One of the math teachers told me he was teaching a remedial class for mostly immigrant teenagers from the Caribbean. He wanted to make a point in math class about interest and decided to try to make it something the students could relate to. He described how he bought his car with a loan and tried to involve the students in figuring out how to calculate the interest that would be due. The response of the class was that his students laughed at him because one of their classmates had a much fancier car that he had bought with cash he had made in the underground drug economy. This teacher told this story to emphasize the degree to which the easy money of drugs undermines the authority of the older generation in the eyes of the younger generation. Parents look like chumps when they work so hard at low-paid service sector jobs if their children are enticed by the attractions of the underground economy. Thus, both the immigrant parental generation and the adolescents associate becoming American with access to consumer goods and full participation in a materialist culture. The parents' immigrant metric of what constitutes a good job and a way to gain those material advantages is not shared by their children, many of whom come to expect an easier and simpler way to make it rich in America, a version of which is readily available to them in the local underground drug economy.

DISCIPLINE

The parents we spoke with believe that physical punishment is the best way to deal with a child who has misbehaved. They are shocked that this is unacceptable in the United States and consistently told us that it was one of the most disturbing aspects of living in the United States. That the state can dictate that a parent cannot beat a child is seen as a real threat to the parents' ability to raise their children correctly. One of the first things children learn when they arrive is that beating is considered child abuse in the United States, and they can report their parents to child welfare. Many teens do report their parents. The parents are outraged that the state can come between a parent and a child. They believe that it is their right to beat their kids. This is an enormous policy problem in the schools. Principals have to warn the teachers not to send negative notes home because often the students will return black and blue. Parents come to school and want to know why the children are not beaten in school by the teachers, an accepted and respected part of Caribbean school discipline. Alternatively, children who have been massively beaten in schools in the islands believe they have a lot of freedom in the United States to misbehave in school. Parents don't know any other way to raise children. In short, these parents believe that the state government tries to deprive them of their chosen technique for disciplining their children, but offers no other alternative to teach respect and good behavior to teenagers.

RACE AND DISCRIMINATION

These parents grew up in a situation where Blacks were the majority. They do not want to be "racial" in the United States—they do not want race to play a big part in their lives. The teens experience racism and discrimination constantly and develop perceptions of the overwhelming influence of race on their lives and life chances that differ from their parents' views. These teens experience hassles by police and store owners, rejections for jobs they apply for, and attacks on the streets if they venture into White neighborhoods. These problems make them angry and resentful. The media also projects images that tell these students that Blacks are devalued by American society. Parents tell their children to strive for upward mobility and to work harder in the face of discrimination, but the children think their chances of success are very slim.

One question about how things had changed since the civil rights movement shows striking differences in the patterns of responses between American-born, second-generation teenagers and more recently arrived immigrant teens. The vast majority of teens born in the Caribbean give answers I suspect most White Americans would give. They thought things were much better in the United States since the civil rights movement. They gave answers like, "You can ride at the front of the bus now" or "You can go to school with Whites." The irony of course is that I was sitting in an all-Black school when they gave these answers. The vast majority of teens who were born in the United States said that things were no better since the civil rights movement. Instead, many said things were worse but now the discrimination is "on the low down, covered up, more crafty." Some of these students pointed out that people had marched for integration, but we were sitting in an all-Black school.

These different interpretations of the role race plays in one's life also creates a gulf between parents and children. Parents tell their children to strive for upward mobility and have high aspirations, but often the peer group and the children's day-to-day experiences tell them the color of their skin might make it difficult or impossible to meet those aspirations.

DECLINING ECONOMIC OPPORTUNITIES AND DISINVESTMENT IN INNER-CITY SCHOOLS

The decline of midlevel manufacturing jobs means that the students need college or trade training if they are going to have any chance at a middle-class life. The New York City neighborhood schools do not have any vocational education. In the schools I visited, the drop-out rate was above 50%. Getting into a good college or even graduating high school are very difficult hurdles for these students. Three things are happening in these schools simultaneously. Racial segregation means that the Caribbean American students go to all-Black schools. They experience a great deal of pressure to be Black American. This often involves adopting an oppositional identity that associates doing well academically with "acting white." In addition, newly arrived students from rural areas or islands with bad school systems as well as children who have not been in school for a long time are barely literate, speak Patois and very little standard English, and do very poorly in school. They often lack the special attention they need to catch up to grade level. Finally, students who recently arrived from top selective schools in cities such as Kingston or from islands with strong school systems such as Barbados are invariably valedictorians and the best students in the schools because they have not had all their schooling in the New York City school system and because some come from a middle-class background. Their parents have enough cultural capital to help their children achieve in school, even when the schools themselves are not very good.

Yet the poor quality of the neighborhood schools thwarts the futures for many of these students. The schools I interviewed in were two of the five most dangerous schools in New York City. The schools showed the absolute economic disinvestment of the wider society. Because of the violence and the availability of weapons, teachers with seniority and skills opt out of these schools. The structure of the staffing is such that there are a few experienced, dedicated teachers, but the schools were filled with young inexperienced teachers or older teachers waiting for retirement. Burnt out or scared, many of the older teachers were openly racist and pined for the days when the schools used to be all White. The teens cite them often for what they perceive as racist behavior. Immigrants in these neighborhoods who know better, often the middle class, enroll their children in magnet schools, but many of the immigrant parents insist that their children go to a local school within walking distance because they believe it is safer. This is ironic because the magnet schools for academically gifted students are probably much safer and would provide a much better education.

CONCLUSION

Rumbaut found that immigrants and their children sometimes fare worse as they spend time in the United States. Although this is not true for all immigrant families, and human, political, and social capital can provide for much happier outcomes, there is some evidence that the United States can actually erode some of the strengths immigrants bring with them. Rumbaut also claimed that different ethnic backgrounds have different effects on outcomes, even when a number of individual-level characteristics are controlled. The ethnographic material I have briefly sketched here shows some social factors that put further strains on immigrant families and may contribute to decline in aspirations, academic achievement, and hard work among immigrant children. I also think the role of racial discrimination and exclusion, which is so very important for Black immigrants from the Caribbean, may play a part, but certainly not the whole part, in explaining differential outcomes across different national origin groups.

ACKNOWLEDGMENT

This research was supported by a grant from the Russell Sage Foundation and by a fellowship from the Guggenheim Foundation.

REFERENCES

Farley, R., & Allen, W. R. (1987). *The color line and the quality of life in America.* New York: Russell Sage Foundation.

Kasinitz, P. (1992). *Caribbean New York: Black immigrants and the politics of race.* Ithaca: Cornell University Press.

Model, S. (1991). Caribbean immigrants: A Black success story? *International Migration Review, 25,* 248–257.

Model, S. (1995). West Indian prosperity: Fact or fiction? *Social Problems, 42,* 535–554.

Sowell, T. (1978). *Essays and data on American ethnic groups.* Washington, DC: Urban Institute Press.

PART II

HOW DOES THE MIGRATION EXPERIENCE AFFECT CHILD AND ADOLESCENT DEVELOPMENT?

5

The Psychological Experience of Immigration: A Developmental Perspective

Cynthia García Coll
Katherine Magnuson
Brown University

OVERVIEW OF RESEARCH

FOR THE most part, past theories and research on international migration focus nearly exclusively on adults and tend to present children as appendages to their parents rather than as distinct subjects worthy of investigation (Sung, 1985). The typical immigrant is conceptualized as a young adult who was socialized in his or her homeland and then relocated to another country. In contrast, immigrant children are often thought to be the first of their families to be socialized into the receiving community's culture. Thus, immigrant children are generally thought to have an easier time adapting than adults because they are younger, more malleable, and more exposed to the new culture through the native school system (Chud, 1982).

Our inability to delineate comprehensive models and theories about the psychological and psychosocial impact of immigration on children has severely hampered our ability to work on this issue. To date, two models have been presented specifically for children, none have been supported by empirical research with children, and only one has attempted to account for the outcomes as well as the processes of international migration in all children. Chud's (1982) threshold model postulates that although the immigrant's home usually reverberates with the culture of the country of origin, there is a point at which there is "the beginning of something new" (p. 96). Chud referred to this point as the threshold. According to Chud, the threshold is wherever the host culture meets the immigrants' culture (e.g., the front door). The importance placed on this meeting point is meant to highlight how the immigrant child interacts with two cultural systems in a dynamic fashion. Chud delineated three types of thresholds: the unobstructed, the problematic, and the traumatic threshold. The distinctions between the thresholds reflect the ease with which the child can move from one culture to another.

Laosa (1989) constructed a more specific model to explain how immigration affects Hispanic children, although it is relevant to non-Hispanic immigrant children. He utilized a metaphor of lenses and filters, which intensify or moderate the effect of events, to explain the interaction of the variables that mediate the stresses of migration and the child's adaptation, adjustment, and development over time. The variables that impact the child's development include the characteristics of the sending environment, the background of the family prior to migration, the characteristics of the receiving community, the cognitive structure and coping mechanisms of both the child and the family, the school context, and the dynamic and changing nature of psychosocial and developmental processes (see Laosa, 1989). Although Laosa's model seems useful and insightful, no empirical studies have been undertaken to support his work.

An additional model has introduced age as a variable to be included in analyses. Rumbaut (1991) created a general model to explain the relationship of migration, adaptation, and psychological distress among Indochinese refugees. The model suggests that a variety of variables will affect psychological outcomes over time. Of particular interest is the way in which Rumbaut emphasized the importance of the contextual variables in the adaptation process. In his model, the context of both exit and entry interact with the characteristics of an individual's migration process (i.e., antecedent variables) and adaptation process (i.e., mediating variables) and lead to psychological distress measured by outcome variables. For example, variables that are thought to have an impact on the outcome of adaptation include an individual's motivation for migrating, socioeconomic status, social support network, sex, and age. The model was tested with longitudinal data on adult refugees collected by the Indochinese Health and Adaptation Research Project in San Diego, California. The model was able to explain a substantial amount of the variance in psychological distress outcomes. Much of the variance, however, remained unaccounted for (Rumbaut, 1991).

The children who began to be socialized and educated in their homeland and then moved to the United State with the parents, members of the 1.5 generation, are often overlooked in the discussion of immigrants and particularly in generational comparisons (Hirschman, 1994). However, the existence of such a cohort begs us to consider the impact of migration as a function not only of whether the immigrant is a child or an adult but also at what age they migrate and how long they have been in the United States. Although the literature on immigration is full of comments that a child's experience with migration depends on his or her development stage (Eisenbruch, 1988; Hirschman, 1994; Laosa, 1989), this idea has yet to be fully articulated into the theories and principles that describe these children's experiences. This is critical because the role and importance of various factors involved in the migration process are mediated and differentiated by the age of the child (Hirschman, 1994; Inbar, 1977; Schrader, 1978), a proxy variable for various developmental processes. This shift toward a developmental perspective requires the researcher to acknowledge the changing relationship between the person and the environment as well as the ongoing normative development of the child. As Laosa (1989) stated, "It is helpful to view the individual's characteristics (e.g., abilities, needs, behavioral style) and the environment (e.g., societal expectations, demands, opportunities)" (p. 27).

The research on immigrant adults is dominated by two different theories of adjustment: stress and selection. It is assumed that differences in adjustment are due either to the self-selection of migrants or to acculturative stress (i.e., stress engendered by the migration process). Most studies of children deal specifically with the acculturative stress theory because children do not self-select their migration and in some instances neither understand nor accept the reasons they are given to justify their move to a new land (Ashworth, 1982).

The emphasis placed on acculturative stress has led nearly all of the researchers concerned with immigrants to try to identify and document the negative impact of migration and acculturation through measurable indicators. Consequently, a large number of studies have focused on the comparative rates of maladjustment among young immigrants as presented in psychiatric or behavior disorders, rather than on the normative adjustment or development of these children. Ironically, studies have shown that the majority of immigrant children are not maladjusted. Rather, they are able to overcome the difficulties in immigration and acculturation and adapt readily to their surroundings, both at home and at school (Weinberg, 1979). In a review of literature that considered the majority of studies that documented immigrant children's adjustment, Aronowitz (1984) concluded, "studies of a variety of kinds in disparate settings suggest that a cohort of immigrant children may adjust better, no differently, or less well than the native populations to which they migrate" (p. 243). However, Aronowitz also remarked that when disorders appear in immigrant children, they tend to be manifested in two distinct ways: as behavior disorders and as identity disorders in adolescence. Acute psychiatric disorders are less often presented in immigrant children (Sam, 1994). Nevertheless, the way in which researchers have approached the study of immigrant children has led them to chart the adjustment of children based on measurable negative outcomes and has disposed them to overlook measurement of normative outcomes inclusive of the experiences and processes involved in acculturation and adjustment.

One reason this has happened is that many processes are involved in migration, and trying to disentangle the effects of the simultaneous and various processes is difficult. Relying on the native population to determine standards is misguided because of the sociocultural differences between immigrant children and the native population. However, different immigrant children have been exposed to all or many of the same processes; thus, determining comparison measures or standards with which to try to measure the effect of various processes is very complicated. Nicol (1971) suggested that, to reveal the effects of the process of migration, it would be helpful to compare children born to immigrant parents in the host country to those born in a foreign country who have undergone migration, but this has rarely been done. Most studies consider place of birth as an important variable indicator of one's degree of acculturation rather than as a core construct, which evokes different processes and engenders a different experience (for an exception, see Gil, Vega, & Dimas, 1994).

Furthermore, the lack of a developmental perspective combined with the emphasis of migration as a stressful experience has prevented researchers from trying to understand the ways in which immigration might serve as a growth-enhancing event. Little research or work has moved beyond discussing the ways in which children adjust or adapt and toward discussing the ways in which they might benefit psychologically from the event. Thus, what little is known about children and their rates of maladaptation leaves even less known about their subjective experiences as immigrant children, their abilities to cope and adapt, their ability to grow, and the impact that immigration has in their life (Rumbaut, 1994; Sung, 1985).

In general, most research on immigrant children not only lacks appropriate theoretical principles, but also lacks a consensus on methodological issues, such as how to choose samples and what constitutes appropriate comparison groups. The emphasis that theories have placed on the negative impact of migration and difficulties in obtaining access to informants have meant that many studies have drawn their samples from clinic-referred immigrant children rather than from the general population of immigrant children (e.g., Burke, 1980; Graham & Meadows, 1967; Lipson & Meleis, 1989). The variations in the rates of disorders found among different ethnic groups leads to the conclusion that it is erroneous to lump all immigrants together in one category for research purposes. Nevertheless, the small numbers of available subjects has led some researchers to study immigrant children as a unified group with similar behavior patterns (e.g., Ekstrand, 1976) or to combine ethnic or national groups that are considered similar (Cochrane, 1979; Derbyshire, 1970). Commenting on their own research, Touliatos and Lindholm (1980) suggested that "future studies of needs assessment should include large enough sample so that all children of immigrants are not regarded as comprising one group or children in closely related ethnic groups are not combined" (p. 31).

Whereas some studies have not differentiated between ethnic groups, other studies have looked comparatively at the outcome of adaptation across groups of immigrant children and native children (e.g., Cochrane, 1979; Rumbaut, 1994) or have looked very closely at one specific group without regard for any other groups (e.g., Kallarackal & Herbert, 1976; Sung, 1985). Very few studies have tried to look at how different ethnic groups have both similar and discrepant experiences (an exception is Rumbaut's work on the adjustment of Indochinese adolescent refugees, 1988, 1991, 1994). The way in which the sample groups have been constructed and the studies designed makes it hard to make generalizations about the psychological impact of migration and acculturation based on an aggregation of research findings on immigrant children.

Finally, research has indicated that emotions are expressed differently in different cultures; many cultural backgrounds discourage the direct expression of feelings and shape health beliefs to favor psychosomatic symptoms. However, little attention has been given to the incidence of these symptoms among immigrant children (Sam, 1994; for an exception, see Rodriguez, 1973). By not considering the effects of migration in psychosomatic outcomes we might be overlooking a very valuable source of information (Vega & Rumbaut, 1991).

In summary, the extant literature presents studies that, for the most part, used conceptual models derived from research with immigrant adults and therefore lack a developmental perspective. Moreover, the emphasis has been on problematic outcomes rather than normative experiences or processes that lead to differential outcomes. Finally, methodological issues have included the composition of samples and the definition and measurement of constructs across different immigrant groups.

CHILDREN'S REACTIONS TO STRESS

Realizing that our knowledge and conceptualizations fall short in so many areas, what can we say about how immigration psychologically affects children? Migration and acculturation require the child to deal with stress. An individual's stress response is a transaction between the environment and the individual, with the meaning and appraisal of the event intrinsic to its definition. Whether the stress has a positive or negative impact and whether the stress has repercussions beyond the immediate context depend on a large number of factors.

Some characteristics of individual children are known to affect their stress response. The sex of a child has been associated with a variation in response to stress: Young boys show more stress than girls (Rutter, 1983). It is unclear why this is, but it has been hypothesized that parents might be less supportive of boys' attempts to deal with stress.

The child's temperament also seems to be a likely factor in accounting for a child's stress response, although no direct evidence has pinpointed its specific contribution. In particular, an association has been found between the child's temperament and other people's, usually parents', reaction to the child. Therefore, the child's temperament may protect the child or put the child at risk by virtue of its effect on the parent–child interaction (Rutter, 1983). Tradd and Greenblatt (1990) suggested that emotional flexibility, affective resources to express his or her experiences, and positive emotional outlook, all of which are considered parts of a child's temperament, are important in affecting the resilience of children. Finally, the individual's cognitive appraisal of the situation, attributional style, and locus of control all affect a child's response to stress (Rutter, 1983; Tradd & Greenblatt, 1990).

Relevant to the influence of cognitive appraisal are what Laosa (1989) termed "beliefs," general ideas about oneself and the environment that influence one's appraisal of events. This notion of beliefs is especially relevant for immigrant children because some of these beliefs may stem from shared historic or sociocultural premises of their homeland (i.e., attitudes, beliefs, and values that are fundamental determinants or shared personality characteristics of a given culture).

One of the most important factors regarding children's reaction to stress is age. Maccoby (1983) pointed out that no linear increase or decrease in vulnerability to stress is associated with the development of children. However, the nature of the events and coping responses elicited changes as a child develops. Many factors that theoretically make young children more vulnerable to stress are balanced by factors that also make them less vulnerable. For instance, the unfamiliarity of a situation is an important element in an event's capacity to act as a stressor, and because a young child is essentially unfamiliar and inexperienced with the world, one would expect a child to be susceptible to large amounts of stress. On the other hand, children do not experience stress from events whose power to harm is not understood. They are not humiliated by the failure to handle problems that are not their responsibility, and they are not upset by criticism when their ego is not developed and they are not invested in appearing strong (Maccoby, 1983). Thus, although at first glance it might seem as if young children are more susceptible to stress, in many ways they are buffered by their age and their relationships with their caretakers.

Several other factors that have an impact on a child's stress response have been identified. Studies of children in institutional settings show that a stable relationship with an adult, not necessarily a parent, is associated with better social adjustment. Good relationships and family harmony also seem to be protective features. Kallarackal and Herbert (1976) attributed the low rate of deviance among immigrant Indian children in Britain to the quality of their family life, which the authors believed reduced the risk of developing disorders. The children in their sample were living with both parents, and their family relationships appeared to be warm and loving despite the parents' strict supervision and firm discipline. Likewise, Athey and Ahearn (1991) stated, "The ability of the family to provide a strong sense of safety and support to the child and to serve as a buffer against external threats plays a large role in how well the child functions and develops" (pp. 10–11). In addition, the impact of acute stress is also affected by the preexistence or concurrent background of chronic psychosocial adversity. The effect of a number of stressors is not merely cumulative. In fact, studies show that stresses potentiate each other; that is, the combined effect of the stressors can be far greater than the additive effect (Rutter, 1979).

Finally, the manner in which the child comes to cope with the stress is an important factor in the child's stress response. In fact the child's response to the stress is often inextricable from coping mechanisms (Compas, 1987). Coping refers to both intrapsychic processes and environmental manipulations that solve problems and regulate emotional distress. The coping process can include both effective and ineffective mechanisms. "A closer examination of studies of child and adolescent coping reveals that a strategy which might be adaptive for dealing with one stressor may be maladaptive when used in a different context or at a different point in time in response to the same stressor" (Compas, 1987, p. 399). Likewise, Laosa (1989) pointed out that although a child might possess a good repertoire of coping strategies and competencies in one cultural context, the child's coping skills might be ineffective, inappropriate, or even offensive after immigrating. Although it seems as if the coping process should have an outcome on the stressful event, the connection has yet to be recognized (Rutter, 1983). The measurement of the effectiveness of coping processes and the concepts involved are rather elusive.

Very little research has studied how the perceived stressfulness of events and the coping mechanisms employed vary across cultures or across subcultures. An exception is El-Sheikh and Klaczynski's study (1993) of variations in the types of stress, coping responses, and control beliefs across three different subcultures of young girls in Egypt: middle class, inner city, and rural. The researchers explained:

> Various taxonomies have been developed to characterize the strategies that children use to cope with stress; but without acknowledging the different types of stressors children encounter in different subcultural environments, these taxonomies may not capture the full complexities of children's coping efforts. . . . The context effect becomes especially important across cultures. Not only may the resources available for successful coping differ but the cultural prescriptions for using available resources may vary, as may definitions of successful coping. (pp. 80–81)

The types of stressors and beliefs about control varied by subcultural group, although no differences were reported in coping strategies.

Not all children who are exposed to stressful situations are adversely affected by their experiences. The recognition of these children has led many to study resilience, "the ability to recover from or easily adjust to misfortune or sustained life stress" (Laosa, 1989, p. 6). However, Rutter (1979) pointed out that although children who suffer and come through their experiences unscathed have overcome adversity and are often referred to as invulnerable, this is a relative term. These children have not entirely escaped damage or been unaffected by their experiences. Furthermore, Seifer and Sameroff (1987) highlighted the difficulty of defining the central constructs of risk and invulnerability. They remarked that it is hard to distinguish between a risk factor or a protective factor and a factor that is merely influential in a child's development. Nevertheless, there is a large difference between those who become reasonably well-adjusted people in spite of chronic stress and disadvantage and those who become criminal, mentally ill, or educationally retarded (Rutter, 1979).

Compas (1987), in his review of research on stress and coping in children, found that most of the studies focusing on resilient children and their environment do not look at how the invulnerable children cope with stress but instead try to identify enduring characteristics of the environment and the children "that distinguish them from others who respond maladaptively to stress" (p. 398). Three broad factors have consistently been found to characterize invulnerable children: dispositional and constitutional traits of the child, the presence of a supportive family environment, and a supportive individual or agency outside of the family. Rutter (1979) delineated a number of protective factors: temperament and sex, influences outside the home such as the school (which, given a positive atmosphere and quality as a social institution, can serve as a protective factor), the scope of opportunities, high self-esteem and scholastic attainment (the direction of association between self-esteem and scholastic attainment is unclear), cognitive structure and locus of control, one good stable relationship with an adult, and good coping skills (i.e., learning how to deal with a variety of new situations as they grow up).

In summary, a child's response to stress is best understood as an interaction between the child's characteristics and the environmental demands. The individual characteristics of a child, such as temperament, developmental stage, sex, cognitive appraisal, and repertoire of coping skills are important mediating factors. In addition, external factors such as parental reactions and the larger cultural context also have an impact on children's stress responses and the effectiveness of the responses. Finally, certain factors, or a combination of certain factors, may lead to unusual resilience in children or at least the ability to emerge relatively unscathed from particularly stressful life events.

STRESSORS OF THE MIGRATION EXPERIENCE

The process of migration and acculturation has its own unique set of stressors frequently termed acculturative stress. Berry (1990) described a set of stress behaviors in adult immigrants: lowered mental health, feelings of marginality and alienation, and heightened psychosomatic symptom levels. Berry, Kim, Minde, and Mok (1987) also identified several variables that moderated the relation between acculturation and stress: the nature of the larger society, the type of the acculturating group, the individual's attitude toward acculturation, the demographic and social characteristics of the individual, and the psychological characteristics of the individual. However, in many instances, immigrants are unaware of the stressful nature of the experience and its cumulative impact (Sluzki, 1979).

Several specific circumstances inherent to the migration process are stressful. One source of stress is the loss of the homeland. Children mourn the loss of loved objects, even if those objects have failed to provide a reasonable and safe environment (Eisenbruch, 1988). As Ashworth (1982) described, "Children can be deeply disturbed by the sudden loss of beloved relatives and friends; they may long for the familiar sights, sounds, and smells of the past" (p. 79). Baptiste (1987, 1993) argued that in the weeks immediately after the migration the family tends to obscure feelings of loss and longing but that frequently these feelings resurface months or even years later.

In addition to the more general loss of familiar surroundings, immigration frequently means the loss of significant individuals in the child's life. Graham and Meadows' (1967) study highlighted the impact of separation on a young child. The study focused on comparing West Indian children who were referred to a child guidance clinic with a control group of White British clinic-referred children. The West Indian children were found to have more antisocial disorders than the control group. Of the West Indian male children who had immigrated to England, not one had been brought to England with both parents. In the majority of instances, the children had been left in their native homeland with their maternal grandmothers before the age of three and were reunited with their parents in England after five or six years. Graham and Meadows attributed the higher rate of antisocial behavior exhibited by these boys to the separations that these children experienced. They explained that the children experienced two separations, one from their parents and one from their parental substitutes. Once reunited with their parents, the children denied recognizing their parents, professed a primary attachment to the parental substitutes, and expressed hostility at being taken away from their parent substitutes. Because the sample group consisted of clinic patients, the authors could not generalize their findings to the larger child immigrant population, but they concluded that migration that included an extended separation from parents affected children in an adverse manner.

Other studies have also pointed to the problems created when families are separated during international migration. Rodriguez (1973) found that children who had migrated with their mothers to Switzerland had adapted more easily than those who had remained behind with their maternal grandmothers and later rejoined their mothers. Burke (1980) identified what he termed the *rejected mother neurosis*, which occurred when an immigrant child reared by the maternal grandmother was reunited with the natural mother after a period of separation. Typically, the child withdrew from the mother and had problems confiding in the mother or treating the mother as a maternal figure. In response, the mothers had feelings of guilt and failure because of the children's negative reactions to the reunification.

Children's reactions to the loss of their familiar world and their significant attachments are shaped by developmental processes. For example, children have differing friendships and obedient stances toward others, depending on developmental age. A young child considers a friend someone with whom they play rather than a source of emotional support (Maccoby, 1983). Consequently, young children have fewer problems leaving their peers. Likewise, young children who have an obedient stance toward their parents harbor less resentment about the decision to migrate than adolescents who question their parents' decisions. However, a separation from the primary caretaker during the migration process can be much more stressful for a young child between the ages of 6 months and 4 years than for a slightly older child because during this period children are establishing selective attachments and beginning to maintain relationships during a period of separation. Rutter (1983) commented that children have milder and shorter grief reactions compared to adults, probably due to their cognitive level and varying ability to conceptualize death.

A change in the family's or parents' patterns of behavior after or during the migration can also produce stress for children. For example, role changes encountered during the migration can act as stressors. Sluzki (1979) noted that many families manifest a split between the instrumental and affective roles: One member, usually male, handles the activities that require engagement in the present or current environment while another member, usually female, centers on the present and past affective activities that sustain continuity with the previous environment. Although this coping mechanism is effective in the short term, it can be maladaptive if maintained too long, causing the isolation and retarded acculturation of the affective member and leading to the disruption of the family life.

Although cultures have patterns that families utilize to manage members' developmental needs, migration frequently requires a family to adopt new patterns of interaction and coping that may conflict with the well-established patterns of the homeland (Cornille & Brotherton, 1993). The normative internal pressures of developmental needs that result in modifications in the family structure and roles are confounded by the transition into the new culture. Problems arise when the transition is too slow or too fast. In other words, new problems of adjustment might be rooted in an old approach to developmental transitions, one that is no longer applicable to a new situation (Baptiste, 1987, 1993; Cornille & Brotherton, 1993).

Furthermore, the parents' individual responses to the immigration process has an effect on children's stress responses. Rutter (1983) noted that children who are entering the hospital react to the parents' anxiety, and Athey and Ahearn (1991) pointed out that parents' grieving and anxiety reactions "make it exceedingly difficult for parents to be as available and supportive to their children as they might otherwise be and as the child might need for optimum development" (p. 12).

Finally, for illegal immigrants, the fear of being deported can be extremely stressful and can interfere with a family's ability to provide emotional support for their children. Padilla, Cervantes, Maldonado, and Garcia (1988) found that undocumented status was the third most mentioned stressors of adult Mexican and Central American immigrants. Carlin (1990) pointed out that illegal immigrants' fear of being deported requires that they "endure frequent moving and hiding, little or no medical care, plus substandard housing, and no financial assistance" (p. 277). This fear of deportment is particularly stressful and salient given the recent attempts in California to limit social and educational services to illegal immigrants.

Migrating to a new country entails facing a numerous number of immediate stressors. Having left behind all that is familiar to them, children feel a sense of loss. For children who also face a separation from significant others, especially their parents, the feelings of loss and subsequent complications are particularly acute and are affected by their developmental age. Furthermore, the migration experience necessitates changes in family roles and patterns of interactions, which can be very stressful for both the family and the child. Likewise, the migration experience can cause stress and anxiety for parents, which can impact the child's reaction to the stress. Finally, living in the new country illegally can engender stress in immigrant families, youth, and children.

REFUGEE CHILDREN AND
POST-TRAUMATIC STRESS DISORDER

Individuals' adaptations to the receiving community will be affected by the type of migrant they are (i.e., voluntary or involuntary; Berry et al., 1987) and what circumstances surrounded their departure (Leslie, 1993). This is most apparent in the study of refugees because, although all migrants encounter stress, refugees frequently encounter greater stress than voluntary migrants due to the nature of their pre-departure experiences (Rumbaut, 1991). Leslie (1993) noted that for Central American refugees the most powerful predictor of immigrants' assessment of the stressfulness of the life events was their exposure to war. Indeed, 50% of the participants in the study had left their country because of ongoing warfare, and all participants had experienced some war-related trauma. Consequently, refugee children are more likely to manifest severe stress reactions such as post-traumatic stress disorder (PTSD). However, the stress responses of refugee children may be overlooked, often children cannot speak for themselves, and the problems presented by older refugees overshadow those of children (Eisenbruch, 1988).

A few studies have looked at trauma and traumatic responses in childhood, but it remains an underresearched area. Studies of traumatic stress primarily include either children in wars or children who have been the victims of devastating or violent episodes such as dam breaks and floods, terrorism, or the witness of a murder, rape, or suicide of their parents. All of these studies have found evidence of unresolved trauma: Children who are exposed to violence or live in violent environments generally show signs of PTSD (Osofsky, 1995).

Refugee children experience a variety of traumatic events such as violence, loss, and severe deprivation, which puts them at risk for PTSD (Athey & Ahearn, 1991; Rumbaut, 1991). Rumbaut (1991) noted that refugees tend to face more undesirable life changes, a greater degree of danger, and a lesser degree of control than voluntary immigrants, largely because of their flight from war-torn countries. Espino (1991) concluded her study of Central American children with this thought:

> Families from war torn areas arrive with the scars of traumas experienced in their country of origin as a result of exposure to violence and poverty. On their arrival they become part of the inner city working poor with the added anxiety of illegal status. The children, living in over-crowded, high conflict homes, experience neglect and abuse. Marked educational delays further inhibit their capacity to adapt, resulting in lower self esteem and depression. A large percentage of these children are further cognitively and emotionally handicapped and can be diagnosed as having PTSD. (p. 122)

When children are faced with a traumatic stress, their response depends on other developmental processes. Preschool children are particularly dependent on their parents and react with anxious attachment behavior. School-age children seem to change dramatically, becoming rude, irritable, argumentative, and complaining of somatic problems, and their school performance declines dramatically. Adolescents react more like adults; they engage in antisocial behavior or lose impulse control. They tend to fear being ostracized and are pessimistic about the future (for diagnostic criteria of PTSD in children over 3, see Pynoos, 1993). In a study of Central American children, Arroyo (1985, cited in Espino, 1991) found that young children also tended to withdraw and suffer from the loss of acquired skills and bedwetting, whereas school-age children suffered from learning inhibitions and adolescents displayed antisocial behavior marked by delinquency. In addition, the manifestation and severity of children's reactions also appear to be related to the degree of violence, presence or absence of personal injury, and access to family support (Athey & Ahearn, 1991).

The stress reaction and acculturation of a refugee child are mediated by several factors other than the severity of the traumatic events the child was exposed to before migrating and developmental stage. For example, whether the refugee child remains with his or her biological family, an adoptive family, or a foster family has an impact on adjustment and adaptation (Carlin, 1990; Rumbaut, 1991). A child who remains with the biological family may retain a sense of security. Studies of refugee children who have remained with their parents show that families that stay together develop stronger bonds due to the shared crisis, and subsequently the children show fewer signs of psychological disturbance (for a review, see Ressler, Boothby, & Steinbock, 1988). However, a child who remains with the biological family will probably not have access to adequate financial resources. Furthermore, the caregivers will most likely be experiencing their own problems with adjustment or depression. Because parental anxiety has a negative impact on children, children may experience additional problems. However, children placed in adoptive families and foster care families frequently face problems regarding their expectations, disenchantment, or cultural conflicts.

When refugee children are placed with foster families, the sociodemographic characteristics of the new family affect adjustment. Porte and Torney-Purta (1987) did a comparative study of Indochinese unaccompanied refugee minors in ethnic and nonethnic placements and found that children who lived in a home with an ethnic adult had substantially lower depressive scores than those who were placed in a nonethnic home. The benefits of the ethnic placement seemed to accrue beyond the depression scale. These children had higher GPAs, made more positive attributions about their academic performances, and were more likely to see their schoolwork as relatively more under their control. Likewise, they saw themselves as being successful at making friends and were more likely to turn to another person for help when feeling sad. Porte and Torney-Purta contended that the day-to-day contact with an adult who is similar to the refugee child is important because it facilitates social learning, provides a role model, and is a source of continuity in identification.

Similarly, Eisenbruch (1988) pointed out that although the Western concept remains of an uprooted individual, the concept of an *uprooted community* must also be considered to understand the acculturation of refugee children. He claimed that, often for refugees and immigrants, personal equilibrium rests on the receiving community's equilibrium and that social disintegration in this community can cause individual psychopathology. Eisenbruch's indices of community disintegration include economic inadequacy, cultural confusion, widespread secularization, high incidence of broken homes, few and weak associations, few patterns of recreations, high patterns of interpersonal hostility and crime, and a weak fragmented network of communications. In addition to the condition of the receiving ethnic community, the condition of the nonethnic receiving community affects the transition of refugee families.

Factors such as the labor market and governmental policies have an impact on the migration experiences of refugees.

However terrifying and difficult the transitional period is for the refugee, the experience can also be strengthening. Individuals may go on to be successful and contributing members of their receiving community. As Rumbaut and Rumbaut (1976) eloquently stated:

> Beyond the numerous casualties that this process inevitably produces, many of the survivors excel in their endeavors. All of their inner resources have been fully tested, their dormant qualities and potentials have been invoked, and their purposes and goals have been challenged. For those able to cope successfully with the exceptional demands, a more fulfilling and productive life may lie ahead. After all, a victory is rewarding in direct proportion to the amount of personal effort it requires. . . . The mass reception of refugees need not be a chaotic, counterproductive or alienating experience. It can be enriching, creative, and an engaging opportunity to grow while learning a poignant lesson of universal history. (pp. 397–398)

In sum, for the immigrant child who is also a refugee, numerous other sources of stress add to the already enumerated stress of migration. The bulk of these new stresses are related to the experiences that surround the often involuntary departure from the native nation. In many cases the children witness traumatic events before arriving in a new land. A child's response to the traumatic events is mediated by age, and the adjustment to the new community is influenced by a number of factors including separation from the family and the vitality of the ethnic community in the new nation. Although it may be easier to describe the deleterious effects of the refugee experience for children, it is still important for us to remember that many refugee children overcome their difficulties and become healthy and productive individuals with unique sets of strengths.

DEVELOPMENT OF A DUAL FRAME OF REFERENCE AND BICULTURALISM

After the initial stage of migration, a lifelong process of adaptation and acculturation begins. Thus, the psychological impact of immigration is not limited to the immediate sources of stress. To understand the complexity and contradictions in the impact of immigration fully, it is necessary to focus on how migration can be simultaneously a stressful and a growth-enhancing experience. This reconceptualization is facilitated by seeing the process of migration in both a narrative and a temporal manner and considering the political, economic, sociological, and political context in which it occurs (Rumbaut, 1991). By doing so, we move away from the underlying assumption that immigration has only negative psychological implications. What constitutes a stress in the initial period of immigration may or may not facilitate a longer term benefit. As the immediate strains of the immigration experience subside, a more gradual process of acculturation and adaptation begins, and the individual child is faced with both greater challenges and greater rewards. Thus, research on immigrant children should inform how the process of immigration can increase an individual's repertoire of coping skills, facilitate the acquisition of new of different skills, and broaden opportunities as well as world views. For instance, the process of learning to speak English for a child whose parents only speak Chinese might be a large source of stress. However, having learned both languages, the child is bilingual, a valuable asset in an increasingly interdependent and multicultural world.

The process of acculturation requires immigrant children to navigate their way in both the culture of their parents and mainstream culture. A survey of immigrant parents conducted in Miami and Detroit (Lambert & Taylor, 1990) showed that the respondents send a message to their children to become bicultural and bilingual. They want their children to maintain their cultural heritage and native language as well as to adopt measures that will make them more accepted and successful in their new home. This request is not without problems. As Cropley (1983) described, "the crucial problem is being simultaneously exposed to two sets of norms—those of the homeland and those of the receiving society. . . . One set of socializing influences . . . attempts to pass on to the children the norms of the motherland, while another set of socializing influences transmits the norms of the receiving community" (pp. 110–111). He explained that native children are also exposed to two sets of socializing influences but that in their case there is a high level of agreement between the norms espoused by the family and those espoused by the wider society. In the case of immigrant children, there may be clear conflict or disagreement between the two forces (Cropley, 1983). Immigrant children are therefore frequently metaphorically characterized as between two worlds or, as Zavala Martinez (1994a) described Puerto Ricans, "entremundos."

Baptiste's (1987) discussion of family therapy with Spanish-heritage immigrant families sheds further light on the difficulty that children face being between two worlds:

> The clash of values and styles places children in an impossible bind. A majority of these families migrated in search of a better life. Consequently, in order for the children to fulfill that dream and show their appreciation to their parents, they need to achieve in the new culture. In order to achieve, they need to let go of some of their native culture and make new friends, improve their English, and become acculturated. To do so, however, is to risk alienation from the family. On the other hand, rejection of the new culture assures that acculturation will not be achieved or at best will be delayed. (pp. 239–240)

Sung (1985) listed a number of areas in which young Chinese immigrants in the city of New York face bicultural conflicts. These areas included the expression of sexuality and aggressiveness, the assertion of independence and individualism, involvement in sports, and academics. Sung commented that these bicultural problems often go unrecognized by parents or teachers and that the children are censured for their behavior. The censure upsets the children and makes them feel as if they should choose between what is taught in the home and what is accepted by mainstream culture. "In his desire to be accepted and to be liked, he may want to throw off that which is second nature to him; this may cause anger and pain not only to himself but also to his parents and family" (Sung, 1985, p. 257).

One of the greatest difficulties involved in having a dual frame of reference is the transgenerational–transcultural problems it creates. Most children and their parents face generation conflicts, simply because the parents and the children are socialized into different worlds in a temporal sense. This generational conflict is even more pronounced in the children of immigrants because they are being socialized into different cultures as well. For example, Cropley (1983) saw one common source of conflict in Britain as the amount of freedom immigrant adolescent girls are allowed to have. He noted that Pakistani parents do not consider higher education a strong priority for girls but that British society socializes girls to become more independent and strive for a higher level of self-development. Baptiste outlined several areas in which parent–child conflict is manifested in Spanish-heritage immigrant families, including the lessening of parental authority to discipline children or to select their children's mates. Another illustration offered by Sung (1985) is the difficulty that children of Chinese immigrant parents face when they believe that their parents do not love them because of the distance and formality that mark their relationships. The distant upbringing that they frequently receive stands in sharp contrast with the prevalent mainstream image of warm and affectionate parents.

The sense of being caught between two worlds is also an issue when the children of immigrants serve as a cultural bridge for their parents. School-age children usually acculturate faster and become fluent in the new language faster than their parents because of their exposure to the host society in their schooling (Baptiste, 1993; Leslie, 1993). Thus, in many families, the children serve as linguistic interpreters for their parents. In such a situation the child assumes a new role in the family, generational boundaries are crossed, and the child becomes privy to information that the child would otherwise not know. This change has the potential to cause significant stress for families that are accustomed to strict generational boundaries and parental authority and can cause distress for the child, making him or her feel like a yo-yo. Baptiste (1993) explained that when children serve as interpreters to complete a job application or during a visit to the doctor, they become involved in situations that children are usually excluded from. If the child asks questions about the situation at a later point, he or she is frequently reprimanded and reminded of his or her child status (Baptiste, 1993; Koplow & Messinger, 1990). Athey and Ahearn (1991) claimed that when a child serves as a cultural translator, the situation becomes one of "status inconsistency for the child—a situation in which a person occupies two or more distinct social statuses with incompatible social expectation leading to chronic stress" (p. 12). Furthermore, parents can come to resent their dependence and the children's involvement in adult business.

It has been suggested that, when a child takes on a role as an interpreter for the family, life events involving family members become particularly stressful. Zambrana and Silva-Palacios' (1989) study to assess how a group of Mexican American adolescents ranked stressful life events revealed that the highest ranked perceived stresses were related to issues of family constancy or stability. Items such as parents getting sick or arrested generated high stress responses. Zambrana and Silva-Palacios suggest that this is normative for adolescents and might be particularly relevant to these immigrant adolescents given their role in the family as negotiator with the external world. The researchers concluded that the adolescent's need to serve as an interpreter in a difficult situation might increase the perceived stressfulness of the situation. It is also possible that the emphasis that Mexican American culture places on family relationships contributes to this heightened perception of stress. The situation might be extremely stressful for the child not simply because he or she must serve as a translator, but because the family is undergoing a series of stressful situations.

Cropley (1983) also pointed out a special conflict between competing socializing forces regarding the education of immigrant children. In general, immigrants understand that education is highly valuable and is essential for achieving success in their new community. However, schools reflect the norms and values of the dominant society, which frequently includes prejudice against the immigrants. Therefore, schools are the single most powerful agent that threatens the norms of the homeland. To succeed in school, an immigrant child must accept norms that may conflict with the norms of the parents' country of origin. Cropley (1983) termed this the double bind; as children are encouraged to succeed, they are consequently encouraged to be alienated from the ways of the homeland.

Cropley's discussion of the double bind might be too narrow a perspective on the interaction of a child and the school context. Laosa (1989) took a more comprehensive look at how the school context has an impact on a Hispanic child's adjustment in the United States. He suggested a range of factors that influence a child's adjustment and adaptation, including ESL resources, the presence or absence of cultural minority students, the school climate, the ethnolinguistic composition of both the student body and the teaching staff, and the nature and frequency of teacher–parent interactions, parental involvement, and peer tutoring. Delgado-Gaitan's (1994) case study of Mexican-American and Mexican immigrant families documented the way in which the first-generation families handled cultural and linguistic alienation and cultural discontinuities. She found that first-generation American parents tried to remake their socialization roles in order to make the home more congruent with the school culture, while also trying to maintain an ethnic identity. She also found that parent and community organizations were pivotal in empowering the parents. Organizations provided effective means to intervene in the school system, taught the parents how to build learning environments that corresponded to the schools' expectations, and helped them maintain their culture and language. Delgado-Gaitan's work illustrates the importance of community-based organizations in a child's adaptation experience. Finally, Rumbaut (1991) found that the Vietnamese and Chinese adolescent refugees in the San Diego metropolitan area had high levels of education achievement in high school, higher even than native-born Anglo students. Higher grade point averages were associated with parents' sense of ethnic resilience and solidarity as well as their intention to stay in the United States and affirm their ethnic culture and social networks. Other factors that affected school achievement included socioeconomic status and parents' psychocultural status.

The notion of a dual frame of reference necessitates a further examination of what this term means in the lives of children and adolescent immigrants. Frequently, this notion leads scholars and researchers to focus on the idea that an immigrant child or adolescent is caught between two worlds, that is, that they belong to neither. More recently, the concept of biculturalism has emerged, which emphasizes that it is possible for an individual to function effectively in two or more cultures without any deleterious impact. The notion that an immigrant child, adolescent, or adult may come to be comfortable and capable interacting in both an ethnic culture and a mainstream culture is critical to a discussion of an immigrant's adjustment. It puts forth the suggestion that from an immigrant's dual frame of reference can emerge the capability to manage two cultural realities with comfort and efficacy. That is, an immigrant can come to belong to both the culture of the homeland and the culture of his or her receiving community. However, it is important to note that biculturalism does not mandate and is not contingent upon a bicultural self-identity (Rotherham-Borus, 1993). We discuss the formation of ethnic identities and bicultural ethnic identities later in the chapter.

This ability to be bicultural does not necessarily mean that an individual switches between two cultural realms depending on the cultural context (i.e., code switching), nor does it mean that an individual blends the two cultures. Instead, across domains such as values and language, the impact of biculturalism may be different. For instance, in the language domain, a bicultural individual may engage in code switching. However, because it is difficult to code switch in the realm of values, blending may occur. We argued elsewhere that the notion of biculturalism encompasses both affective and behavioral components and that a fully bicultural individual would "be competent in both cultures, engage in typical behaviors of both cultures, would prefer to remain involved in practices and lifestyles of both cultures, and would feel a sense of belonging toward both cultural communities" (Tropp, Ekrut, Alarcon, García Coll, & Vázquez, 1994, p. 8). Nevertheless, to be bicultural in all domains requires that an individual achieve functional competence in two cultures. However, this does not imply that biculturalism is dichotomous. There is a continuum of biculturalism, and an individual's position on this continuum can change as he or she grows more or less competent in another culture and as attitudes toward the individual's culture and the mainstream culture evolve (LaFromboise, Coleman, & Gerton, 1993).

Bicultural competence has several dimensions, outlined by LaFromboise et al. (1993). Dimensions include knowledge of cultural beliefs and values, positive attitudes toward both majority and minority groups, a sense of efficacy in both cultures (i.e., the belief that one has the ability to establish and maintain effective relationships in both cultures), communication ability, role repertoire (i.e., a range of culturally appropriate behaviors), and a sense of being grounded (i.e., a well-developed social support system in or of both cultures). An individual must possess a competence in these arenas in order to manage the process of living in two cultures.

The ramifications of biculturalism are profound, especially in an increasingly multicultural society. The ability to be bicultural not only increases an individual's knowledge base, that is, cognitive content but it encourages and fosters some important skills. Ramirez (1983) suggested that for those who embrace biculturalism, adaptability and flexibility of coping and the ability to relate and empathize with a variety of people from different backgrounds are the greatest assets. Furthermore, the bicultural individual is capable of learning from many cultures because he or she is more than just sensitive to many cultures—he or she is a part of and apart from many cultural realities. This has practical and behavioral implications. For example, Ramirez (1984) found that multicultural college students placed in leadership positions had more behavioral and perspective repertoires available than did leaders who were monocultural. They were more effective in communicating with all the members of their groups and made sure that everyone was able to express opinions and that the other understood. Similarly, Szapocznik, Kurtines, and Fernandez (1981) found the bicultural Cuban adolescents who had the ability to communicate and negotiate in two cultures were able to adjust better than adolescents who overacculturated. For these adolescents, whose parents were immigrants from Cuba, "effective adjustment requires an acceptance of both worlds as well as skills to live among and interact with both cultures" (Szapocznik et al., 1981, p. 354).

Although the notion of biculturalism is particularly salient for children who are born in one country and migrate to another, biculturalism will continue to be important for the second, third, and subsequent generations of immigrants in the United States (García Coll et al., in press). Many of the developmental processes that affect immigrant children will continue to affect their children as they grow up, not as immigrant children but as minority children (for a review of the literature on the development of minority infants and children, see García Coll, 1990; García Coll et al., in press). Therefore, minority children share with immigrant children some important developmental processes and outcomes, such as biculturalism, that neither group shares with mainstream White children.

In sum, after a child arrives and the immediate stresses and strains of the migration process subside, a lifelong process of acculturation begins. The beginning of the acculturation process signifies an individual's endeavor to negotiate living in two cultures. In doing so, the two sets of socializing forces and norms to which the child is exposed may conflict, and problems may arise for families and their children. These problems may be particularly acute as immigrant parents and their children face not only a generational but also a transcultural gap. It has been suggested that the school may be an arena in which bicultural conflicts are manifested, but it is likely that the extent to which schooling creates bicultural conflicts is impacted by a large number of factors such as the ethnic composition of the student body and teaching staff, the availability of ESL resources, and the presence or absence of parent–teacher organizations. Although the notion of being between two worlds can create conflict, an individual can live effectively in more than one culture. Furthermore, by becoming bicultural an individual has gained valuable skills such as flexibility and adaptability in coping skills. Finally, acculturation and biculturalism are not just issues for recent immigrants but for all minority children.

BILINGUALISM

In order to become bicultural, the immigrant must acquire new skills in the new homeland. One of the main skills that immigrants acquire is the ability to speak the native community's language. Initially this can be stressful, because immigrants may be unfamiliar with the language or ridiculed about their accent by their peers (Zambrana & Silva-Palacios, 1989. Sung (1985) determined in her study of Chinese immigrant students in New York that "the language barrier was the problem most commonly mentioned by the immigrant Chinese. Frequently, language looms largest because it is the conduit through which we interact with other people. It is the means by which we think, learn, and express ourselves" (p. 256). Immigrants must learn how to communicate with people in a nonverbal way; children must learn how to read expressions and gestures and to understand intonations of the new language (Westermeyer, 1989).

For children of immigrants, the process of learning a new language is facilitated by enrollment in a mainstream school. Baptiste (1987, 1993) pointed out that children fearing the stigmatization of an accent are very invested in learning the language quickly. Hirschman's (1994) study of educational attainment for immigrants revealed that immigrant children had a high constant enrollment in schools regardless of the duration of their residence in the United States. He also noted an initial handicap for immigrants who had been here less than 5 years and a slightly higher rate for immigrants who had been here longer than 5 years. Some results indicated that a greater exposure to United States culture leads to poorer prospects and lower enrollment rates among Caribbean immigrants, who are more likely to be black and live in African-American-dominated neighborhoods.

Although it is frequently assumed that social and emotional adjustment are related to language proficiency, Ekstrand (1976) found that among immigrant pupils in Sweden, social adjustment was only subtly associated with language proficiency. Therefore, although the acquisition of the host language may be necessary for an immigrant child's social adjustment, it is probably not sufficient. Similarly, Rumbaut (1994) found that a higher English proficiency and educational attainment as measured by the students' GPA were associated with immigrant children's positive self-esteem and depression score. "Knowledge of English in particular showed a strong positive association with self-esteem, underscoring the psychological importance of linguistic acculturation for children of immigrants in American social contexts" (Rumbaut, 1994, pp. 783–784). However, these data did not demonstrate the direction of the associations or causality, and most likely, reciprocal effects are involved. Thus, although proficiency in the receiving community's language is associated with social adjustment, research has yet to clarify how a child's adjustment is related to language proficiency.

If children have not yet learned the language of their parents' homeland, it is important that they learn both the new language and their parents' language. Paulston (1978) concluded that children should have firm grounding in their mother language before trying to learn another language. Paulston found that children who migrated from Finland to Sweden at age 10 succeeded in mastering two languages most easily. Children who migrated at age 12 learned Swedish well but somewhat slower than the 10-year-olds. The children who migrated prior to preschool or after one year of schooling had the hardest time mastering two languages; this was attributed to the absence of a sound linguistic base in their mother tongue. If children do not become bilingual, difficulties may arise in communicating with their parents, whose affective language is different than theirs (Koplow & Messinger, 1990). Cropley (1983) noted that the mother tongue is a vital link with the norms of the immigrant's homeland, and an inadequate mastery of it represents a disruption of relationships with the original culture and parents. Accordingly, Rumbaut's (1994) survey of immigrant children revealed that children's preference for

English and poor command of their parents' native language were positively associated with high levels of parent–child conflict.

Bilingualism is different from the promotion of the majority language at the loss of the minority language. Furthermore, bilingualism can be further differentiated, by the age at which an individual acquires the second language, into either successive or simultaneous bilingualism (Padilla & Lindholm, 1984). Children who first learn one language and then acquire the second language are successive bilinguals. Children who are simultaneous or balanced bilinguals have age-appropriate abilities in two languages. The measurement of bilingualism and language proficiency has mostly been by standardized testing instruments. This tendency raises questions about how and whether instruments should be used to measure bilingualism in a naturalistic context (Padilla & Lindholm, 1984).

It is clear that more is involved with becoming bilingual than simply acquiring more linguistic knowledge. Bilingualism at an early age may have profound effects upon the process of cognitive development. Early research into the impact of bilingualism on cognition found that bilingual children showed cognitive deficits (Lambert, 1977; Padilla & Lindholm, 1984). However, the research was methodologically flawed. In particular, the comparison groups were not matched in important sociocultural and economic variables. More recent research shows that balanced bilingualism can promote cognitive development or cognitive flexibility (Padilla & Lindholm, 1984). Lambert (1977) reported that when he began his study of bilingual children in Canada, he expected to find bilingual children demonstrating cognitive deficits. However, balanced bilingual French-English children scored significantly higher than monolingual children on verbal and nonverbal measures, and the pattern of test results suggested that the children had a more diversified structure of intelligence and more flexibility in thought. Lambert's work is supported by similar research (for a review of research, see Diaz, 1985; Padilla & Lindholm, 1984) that also found a link between bilingualism and cognitive flexibility, creativity, or divergent thought. The ability of bilingual children to develop more flexible or divergent thinking may rest in part on the interrelation between language development and cognitive development. That is, children who are bilingual gain metalinguistic awareness, an objective understanding of language. Consequently, their increased awareness of the cognitive functions of language leads to an increased use, understanding, and mastery of language for cognitive functions (Diaz & Klinger, 1991).

However, the study of bilingualism and biculturalism needs to be further expanded. For example, there are varying levels of bilingualism. Research in the United States has been confounded by the fact that most educational opportunities for bilinguals do not promote a balanced knowledge of two languages but rather emphasize English at the expense of the native language. Most research outside the United States has tried to focus on balanced bilinguals. Consequently, it is unclear whether the benefits of becoming a balanced bilingual are shared by those who become successive bilinguals. Furthermore, the impact of bilingualism is hard to measure given the typically large range of other important factors that differ for bilingual and monolingual children in most study comparison groups. Whether one becomes bilingual depends on a large range of social variables, and even controlling for age, socioeconomic status, and years of schooling does not ensure that samples are equivalent on all relevant variables (Diaz, 1985). This is particularly true given that within the United States English is the sociolinguistically dominant language and its speakers benefit from higher prestige and greater communicative utility.

Discrepancies in social variables indicate that an analysis of bilingual individuals should consider contextual variables. Hakuta, Ferdman, and Diaz (1987) argued that the context in which bilingualism occurs should be included in research on the impact of bilingualism on cognition. In their framework, bilingualism is conceptualized as consisting of three levels of analysis. First, it is a characteristic of people who possess two language systems, which has implications for their cognitive development. Second, it is a psychosocial concept characteristic of people who organize the world into different groups that are associated with different languages, and it has implications for an individual's group affiliation or ethnic identity. Finally, bilingualism encompasses a societal concept that is characteristic of interactions between social groups and institutions and that corresponds to linguistic boundaries. This is the societal context in which a bilingual individual lives. These different levels take into consideration that individuals who acquire the ability to speak two languages are affected by the context of the community and society in which they reside.

Although our current knowledge base might be inadequate from which to draw any definitive answers about the effects of bilingualism and biculturalism on cognition, we know much about the effects of culture on cognition provided by cross-cultural studies of cognitive development in the past thirty years. Wagner's (1978, 1981) work on memory skills in norther Africa, Cole and Scribner's (1974) work among Liberian rice farmers, and the cross-cultural work done by many investigators on the universality of Piagetian stages (see Dasen & Heron, 1981), for example, suggest that biculturalism has important consequences on developmental processes. A major lesson from this research, which might be particularly relevant for the study of immigrant children, is that the context of learning might be as important as the acquisition of the cognitive skill per se. Thus, Liberian rice farmers demonstrate better problem-solving skills for mathematical problems involving rice than abstract symbols; the opposite is true in the case of undergraduates in Michigan. The same can be said about rug sellers in Morocco or Guatemalan children doing conservation tasks. Cognitive development is not simply a matter of acquiring a particular skill that can be applied universally because culture and context affect where, when, and how the skill is used. This needs to be studied if we hope to unravel the effects of biculturalism and acculturation on immigrant children.

In sum, it is important that immigrant children and adolescents learn the language of their new country as well as develop their knowledge of their parents' language. Although not knowing the new language may be stressful, the immigrant child is frequently invested in the learning process, and the learning process is facilitated through enrollment in native schools. Although earlier research showed that bilingual children demonstrated cognitive deficits, more recent work critiqued the methodologies of past studies and presented more promising results that suggest that balanced bilingual children develop more flexible or divergent cognitive skills than monolingual children. Unfortunately, research on bilingualism and cognition within the United States has been plagued by the facts that children are usually taught English at the expense of their native languages and that bilingual children within the United States usually differ from monolingual children on a wide range of relevant variables. Such discrepancies point to the need for a multilevel analysis of bilingualism. Finally, the knowledge that has been accumulated in the field of cross-cultural cognition suggests culture and context affect an individual's use of a particular cognitive skill; these findings may have particular bearing upon immigrant children. The impact of both bilingualism nd biculturalism on cognitive development is an important avenue of research if we are to further understand the migration experience of adolescents and children.

IDENTITY AND SELF

Migration can have a major impact on a child or adolescent's self and identity processes. Although many adolescents have a difficult time during adolescence, immigrant children have a particularly difficult time because they are trying to forge an identity in a context that may be racially and culturally dissonant. Therefore, whereas many adolescents confront insecurities about themselves, immigrant adolescents frequently find these insecurities exacerbated by their membership in a minority group (Spencer, Swanson, & Cunningham, 1991). Consequently, immigrant children and adolescents have the developmental task of constructing adequate ethnic identities as part of their more general identity development.

In the discussion of immigrants, an abundance of terms hint at the negative impact of migration on an individual's sense of self and identity: marginalized man, self-alienated, and uprooted. The underlying consensus is that arriving to settle in another culture can have negative implications for both an individual's sense of self and the way in which one understands and relates to others.

Cropley (1983) argued that exposure to two sets of conflicting norms as a child can lead to self-alienation. He distinguishes between cultural identity and personal identity:

> Cultural identity involves acceptance of the norms of a particular society; personal identity, on the other hand, derives from a sense of belonging to a particular group. If the process of adoption of values, habits, attitudes, and the like, of the receiving society is not accompanied by a feeling of belonging as an individual to some respected group, the result is self alienation. Even more difficult is the situation in which the norms of the receiving society actually conflict with those factors which actually lead to a sense of belonging. . . . Even immigrants who have achieved good adaptation in the sense of cultural identity may experience enormous difficulties in the area of personal identity. The resulting identity conflict leads, not infrequently . . . to "a sense of masked inferiority." For example West Indian pupils may describe themselves as speaking "bad" English or as coming from a "bad" family. (p. 121)

Brody (1966) echoed these thoughts: "This need to deal with multiple, conflicting and poorly perceived standards for behavior, the exclusion-produced defects on long-range planning for distant goals and the persistent reminders that one's personal worth is low, all contribute to an identity problem for the culturally excluded individual" (p. 855). Brody cited Erikson: "'Ego identity gains real strength only from wholehearted and constant recognition of . . . achievement that has meaning in the culture.' This kind of achievement appears to be out of reach for the bulk of the excluded, with a consequent lack of the rewards that assure a man of his personal worth, dignity, and importance to others" (Brody, 1966, p. 855). Mendelberg (1986) claimed that minority group members are unable to identify with the mainstream culture but that identifying with their ethnic group is "fraught with difficulties" (Mendelberg, 1986, p. 223).

What remains to be done is to move this discussion from a very vague and general discussion of the possible negative implications of migration on identity to a more concrete discussion that encompasses both the complexity of the processes and possible positive outcomes. This is necessary because it has yet to be shown that an ethnic self-identity, any particular ethnic self-identity, or minority status has a negative impact on self-concept (Rosenthal, 1987; Rotherham-Borus, 1993). Nonetheless, it would be just as misinformed to argue that immigration and minority status had no impact on identity processes. For immigrant children and adolescents, the development of ethnic identity appears to be a part of the process of forging an adequate personal identity.

To date, there is no widely agreed-on definition of ethnic identity, although most agree that ethnic identity formation is a complex, vital, and dynamic process (Zavala Martinez, 1994b). Most children know their ethnic group and its obvious characteristics, but it remains unclear how a child's knowledge evolves into attitudes about and behaviors toward oneself and others. In a review of research and literature, Phinney (1990) found that as a construct, ethnic identity had been defined to encompass differing emphasis on self-concept derived from group membership, self-identification, feelings of belonging and commitment, shared values and attitudes, or attitudes toward one's own group. The different definitions and measures of ethnic identity utilized in research with adults and adolescents have generated findings that are inconsistent, contradictory, and hard to compare (Phinney, 1990).

Examining identity formation in adolescents and children is confounded by the fact that identity formation is a dynamic process that continues over time and will likely be influenced by a variety of factors. Ethnic identification is usually considered achieved after a period of self-discovery and examination (Phinney, 1993). However, most children and adolescents have not had such an experience; thus, discussions of immigrant children's and adolescents' self-identifications frequently focus not on self-identification but on the identification of reference groups (Rotherham-Borus, 1993). Reference group identification or orientation reflects the youth's wish to be compared to a particular group (i.e., ethnic group, mainstream, or bicultural) or held to the standards of this group. That is, it reflects what and who they admire and aspire to be. Young children usually do not verbally identify their chosen reference groups; choices are inferred from their behavioral responses on forced-choice tests (Rotherham-Borus, 1993). However, as children grow they make self-determined choices that stem in part from their previous socialization patterns but also encompass greater variability and independence. The reference groups also become an organizing construct evident in self-labels, attitudes, values, social behaviors, and expectations (Rotherham-Borus, 1993).

In the United States today a variety of ethnic identities or reference groups exist from which immigrant adolescents and children can choose: ethnic, pan-ethnic, bicultural, or mainstream (Rumbaut, 1994). One identity is not more healthy or adaptive than another identity. As Rotherham-Borus (1990) explained, "being mainstream, bicultural or ethnically identified are all associated with positive outcomes" (p. 1080). However, immigrants who have "had explored ethnicity as a factor in their lives, and are clear about the meaning of their ethnicity are likely to show better overall adjustment" (Phinney, 1993, p. 75). Emphasis should be placed on the process of an adolescent's identity development or choice of reference group rather than on the particular chosen identity.

The development of an ethnic identity and the choice of a reference group are both formed by and should be understood within the framework of the contexts in which an individual is developing. A large number of contextual factors appear to influence the reference group choice of immigrant adolescents. For example, research suggest that collective identity plays an important role in the process of reference group determination. As Fernández-Kelly and Schauffler (1994) observed, "Whether youngsters sink or soar frequently depends on how they see themselves, their families, and their communities. For that reason, the immigrant life is preeminently an examined life. Iterative processes of symbolic and factual association and detachment shape immigrants' self definition" (p. 682).

Rumbaut (1994) conceptualized social identity and self-esteem as derivatives from self-comparisons with reference groups. Consequently, ethnic self-awareness is blurred or reinforced depending on the consonance or dissonance of the context. Rumbaut hypothesized that the process of identification is not a unidirectional process into the dominant group ethnicity. Rather, multiple ethnic identities may emerge corresponding to the distinct modes of immigrant adaptation and the social contexts of reception. Factors thought to have an impact on identity are experiences with racial discrimination, the location in which children live (e.g., inner-city versus rural setting), and the ethnicity of the receiving community. Rumbaut suggests that a good combination of these factors can lead to a resilient ethnic identity and that a bad combination leads to an oppositional racial attitude.

The work of Rotherham-Borus (1989, cited in Rotherham-Borus, 1993) underscores the multideterministic nature of self-identification processes and the importance of the school and peer group context. They investigated the self-identification of adolescents in two ethnically and racially integrated high schools with balanced student bodies. In each school, about 45% of the Black, Puerto Rican, and Filipino students self-identified as bicultural. The students from the integrated schools were compared with ethnic students from a school that had a less balanced student body (i.e., more Black and Puerto Rican students than White students) and greater cross-ethnic tensions. In this school, more than 70% of the Puerto Rican, Black, and White students reported an ethnic identification. This study suggests that in contexts in which race and ethnicity are particularly salient, adolescents' self-identifications vary.

The choice of a bicultural identity is common among minority adolescents (Rotherham-Borus, 1993). Rumbaut (1994), studying ethnic self-identification in children of immigrants in California and Florida, found that 27% identified with a national or ethnic origin, 40% identified as a hyphenated-American identity, 11% identified as Americans, and 21% chose pan-ethnic identifications. There were differences between the children who were native born and those who were foreign born: 43% of the foreign born selected a national origin identity, whereas only 11% of the U.S. born selected a national origin identity. Likewise, 32% of the foreign born selected a hyphenated identity, and 49% of the U.S. born selected a hyphenated identity. Only 3% of the foreign born selected an American identity, whereas 20% of the U.S. born selected such an identity. The use of pan-ethnic identity varied between ethnic groups. Less than 1% of the Asian youth surveyed identified with the Asian

American pan-ethnic identity; however, 28% of Spanish-speaking children from Latin America chose the identity of Hispanic. The one exception was the Cuban children who were the least likely to choose a pan-ethnic identity.

Four contextual factors that affect a bicultural adolescent's choice of reference group have been distinguished: the freedom of contact, the attitudes of the majority group, the strength of the majority group, and the relationship of the family to the adolescent (Rosenthal, 1987). These factors influence the adolescents' choice of labels and the relation between their self-labeling and their behavioral indices of adjustment. For example, when Rotherham-Borus (1989, cited in Rotherham-Borus, 1993) compared high schools with ethnic tensions to schools without tension, she found that the schools with less tension endorsed biculturalism more. In these schools, the students identified as bicultural had higher social competencies and performed better academically than the students identified as bicultural in the cross-ethnically tense schools (Rotherham-Borus, 1993).

The ways in which these variables influence a child's or adolescent's developmental identity processes require careful and further investigation. Knight, Bernal, Garza, Cota, and Ocampo (1993) looked at the relation between ethnic identity and socialization among 45 Mexican American children between 6 and 10 years old. They proposed a model to explain how the characteristics of the family's social ecology influences the joint socialization experiences created by family and nonfamily agents, which then influence a child's ethnic identity and lead to ethnically based behavior. The model proposes that the more recently the family migrated to the United States, the more ethnically identified and less assimilated the adults are, the more the parents teach their children about their culture, and the more sense of ethnic identity and pride the children have. A study to confirm the model was carried out with Mexican American mothers and their children. Mothers who were comfortable with their Mexican culture taught their children more about their culture and had children who were more ethnically identified. Also of interest was that a mother's comfort with her culture was influenced by the immigrant generation of the father. In other words, if the father were a recent immigrant, the mother was more likely to teach her children about Mexican culture.

Finally, the work of Waters (in press) and Rumbaut (1994) reminds us not to lose sight of the individual characteristics of the immigrant adolescents and their influence on ethnic identity processes. Waters' interviews with West Indian adolescents found that the same number of girls and boys identified themselves as American rather than with an ethnic identification. However, the importance that the boys and girls attached to their self-identifications was different. The girls discussed being Black American in terms of the freedom they desired from their parents and the restriction that their parents placed on them. They were critical of the strictness that their parents demonstrated. The boys discussed their Black American identification in terms of racial solidarity, societal exclusion, and disapproval. They felt more racial harassment than their female counterparts and were less comfortable leaving their Black neighborhoods.

Similarly, Rumbaut (1994) found that language use was closely linked to the formation and maintenance of an ethnic identity. Those who spoke English were more likely to identify as American. Those with a greater fluency in national language were more likely to pick a national identity, and bilinguals were more likely to pick hyphenated identities. The association of language use and choice of ethnic self-identity highlights the importance of individual acculturation rates and of interpersonal and social relationships. Thus, although we have emphasized the importance of contextual factors, we recognize that identity development is also strongly influenced by the characteristics of the individual.

Although the construct of ethnic identity has been conceptualized in several different ways, a consensus has emerged that immigration has an important impact on an individual's self and identity processes. Some authors have focused on the identity problems that children and adolescent immigrants face, employing such terms as "self-alienation" in their discussions. Other researchers have emphasized the multideterministic and dynamic nature of identity processes and reference group choices as well as the variety of ethnic labels and identities chosen by immigrant children and adolescents. A number of factors that affect an individual's choice of identity have been identified, yet it is still unclear how many of these factors affect self and identity processes. More research should be undertaken to understand the ways in which immigrant children develop their ethnic identities and how different contexts and variables influence this process.

COPING WITH DISCRIMINATION, RACISM, AND PREJUDICE

Another important developmental task for immigrant children and adolescents is that of coping with discrimination, racism, and prejudice. Discrimination against immigrants, and particularly immigrants of color, is widespread in America today, as evidenced by the introduction of Proposition 187 in California during the fall of 1994. However, the impact of discrimination on immigrant children is hard to measure and has not been subject to much investigation (García Coll et al., in press). This is increasingly true as overt racism becomes replaced by symbolic and subtle racism (Duckitt, 1992). As racism evolves into a more complex and covert phenomenon, its effects become harder to document and measure in some instances.

Although adolescents of color may no longer face a legally segregated society, Waters (in press) found in her interviews with West Indian adolescents both immigrant and first generation that these Black adolescents, and particularly young males, felt that they were frequently the victims of racial harassment. Commonly reported situations included "being followed in stores because they were suspected of shoplifting, people recoiling in fear in public places—on the street, on the subway, in parks, and anywhere youngsters encountered whites" (Waters, in press).

Padilla et al. (1988) found that immigrant adults found discrimination a significant source of stress. The respondents indicated that they felt discriminated against and believed they were treated unfairly because they were Latino and that Americans had negative stereotypes of them. They also felt that they could not do much about being the victims of prejudice because they feared losing their jobs or residences if they confronted those who discriminated against them and because their command of English was not good enough to articulate their grievances effectively. Therefore, they endured the prejudice of native residents without taking any consequential action.

How the increasing complex nature of discrimination and racism affects the adjustment of children immigrants in our society remains unclear. One possibility is that higher rates of behavioral disorders are seen in settings in which children experience discrimination. For example, Rutter, Yule, Berger, Yule, Morton, and Bagley (1974) studied immigrant schoolchildren in Britain and found that children who presented behavior disorders in school did not do so at home at the same rate. The authors were hesitant to pinpoint what about the school environment led these children to have greater disturbances, but they suggested that the awareness of discrimination in the school setting may be a possible root of the disturbances. Although Graham and Meadow (1967) did not focus on the effect of discrimination in the immigrant child's life, they raised the issue: "there is the question of color prejudice, and much less often, color discrimination, which many of the immigrant children attending the clinic put forward as one of the main reasons for their difficulties in school" (p. 114).

An interesting point of consideration was raised by Gil, Vega, and Dimas (1994) about variations in adolescent immigrants' perceptions of discrimination across generations. Their comparative analysis of the effects of acculturation and acculturative stress on the self-esteem of Hispanic and Latino adolescents showed that the process of adjustment was different for those who immigrated and those who were born in the United States. In particular they found that U.S. born Hispanic adolescent males who had low acculturation levels were more likely to report perceived discrimination than foreign born immigrant Hispanic adolescent males. They suggest that this was because foreign born immigrants had different expectations about American society than U.S. born immigrants. Rogler, Cortes, and Malgady (1991), in their review of studies on Hispanic's acculturation and mental health, suggested that because most migrations represent opportunity-seeking efforts, first-generation immigrants feel less deprived because immigration has improved their standards of living. However, subsequent generations have an increased sense of deprivation because of higher unmet aspirations. This is important because, according to Rogler et al. (1991), unmet expectations are a very likely contributor to psychological distress.

A further examination of immigrants' perceptions of discrimination suggests that differential experiences and expectations of discrimination can create generation gaps between first- and second-generation immigrants. Rumbaut (1994) found that parent–child conflict increased if the children experienced discrimination and believed that regardless of educational attainment the discrimination would continue. Rumbaut suggested:

> Perhaps the implicit outlook that sees discrimination as trumping education contradicts immigrant parents' folk theories of success. . . . That is, immigrant parents tend to define the situation in instrumental terms (extolling the virtues of hard work and good grades), whereas their children tend to seek to fit in socially and to experience in expressive terms the impact of disparagement within an ethnic minority status. (1994, pp. 786–787)

Although immigrants might have different expectations and experiences, facing prejudice and discrimination on a regular basis requires that immigrant children and adolescents develop behavioral or psychosocial coping skills. Belonging to an ethnic enclave is one way in which immigrants cope with prejudice (Brody, 1990; Fernández-Kelly & Schauffler, 1994). Although the ethnic enclave is frequently thought of in stigmatizing terms, it is also a "staging ground" for the movement of migrants out into the larger society (Brody, 1990). Moreover, for the immigrants who do not wish to move out into the larger society, the enclave may provide a social structure permitting success and leadership positions within a congenial cultural context. The ethnic enclave thus provides immigrants with opportunities outside of the receiving community's structure.

Rodriguez (1975) maintained that Puerto Ricans who lived in the "ghetto" were cushioned to some degree from discrimination: Everyone who lived in the segregated neighborhood was like everyone else and was treated the same. Because the discrimination was not directed at individuals as much as it was directed at the entire group and was a fact of life, it seemed to be felt less. Similarly, Beiser (1988) found that the social support within an ethnic community was instrumental in reducing the depression and facilitating the adjustment of Southeast Asian refugees. Finally, we have argued elsewhere that an ethnic enclave can be a promoting environment for the development of minority children (García Coll et al., in press).

Although earlier theories about and studies of minority status and self-esteem suggested that minorities internalized the dominant group's negative evaluation and thus had lower self-esteem, more recent studies have shown that this is not necessarily true (Gil et al., 1994). It seems as if some individuals who face racism or discrimination are able to transform harmful messages and render them harmless (García Coll et al., in press). Minority children undergo a process of racial or ethnic socialization whereby they learn to cope with the demands of living in a society that might devalue their race, culture, and heritage (García Coll et al., in press; García Coll, Meyer, & Brillon, 1995).

Jenson, White, and Galliher (1982) looked at negative self-evaluation of minorities in different sites in Arizona. They found that although African American and Chicano students perceived greater mistreatment that their White counterparts, they were no less likely to "think highly of themselves and their schoolmates as a result of the mistreatment" (p. 238). Phinney, Chavira, and Tate (1993) studied the effect of showing minority adolescents negative or threatening information about their ethnic group. The study found that the videotaped information had an effect on the subjects' overall rating of their group but not their ethnic self-identification. The group that saw a negative tape rated their group less favorably than the group that saw a neutral tape. However, the individuals were able to differentiate between themselves and the group, "recognizing that the negative traits in their group did not necessarily reflect on its members" (Phinney et al., 1993, p. 476).

Fernández-Kelly and Schauffler (1994) discussed how the ability to shift ethnic identities often provides "a defense from a stigma and an incentive to defy the leveling pressures" (p. 684). Immigrants may shift between identifying themselves as Mexican, Hispanic, or Latino depending with whom they are speaking. Moreover, the authors pointed out that Cubans who were members of a successful group resisted being brought into a broader classification of Hispanic. They also comment that one of the strongest antidotes to downward pull of gangs is a sense of membership in a group with an undamaged collective identity. In this manner, an individual's self-identification as an immigrant can protect him or her from "negative stereotypes and incorporation into more popular but less motivated groups" (Fernández-Kelly & Schauffler, 1994, p. 683).

One possible result of discrimination is the formation of cultural mistrust or an oppositional identity. *Cultural mistrust* was a term created to describe the lack of trust that Blacks exhibit toward Whites. In the early 1980s, Terrell and Terrell (1981) developed the Cultural Mistrust Inventory, which measured specific characteristics of Black individuals who reflected mistrust. It measured mistrust in four areas: educational and training settings, political and legal systems, work and business arenas, and the social and interpersonal contexts. The mistrust is thought to develop because of exposure to prejudicial or discriminatory practices of White dominant society. "Among adolescents the first elements of mistrust are thought to develop in the home, where parents and siblings provide some initial definitions, parameters, and cautions of being Black in a predominantly White society" (Biafora, Taylor, Warheit, Zimmerman, & Vega, 1993, p. 269). The educational system is also thought to play a significant role in forming cultural mistrust. The importance of the school context was demonstrated by Rotenberg and Cerda (1994). They studied Native American and White children attending 4th or 5th grade in same-race and mixed-race schools and found that the groups demonstrated higher levels of trust in members of their own race. In a same-race school, Native American children expected a White child to be less likely to keep promises and secrets or to tell the truth. However, trust patterns were different in mixed race schools, where Native American children only expressed that they did not think that White children were as likely to keep a secret.

As a reaction to discrimination, cultural mistrust can provide a positive psychological defense mechanism, despite the negative connotations of mistrust (Biafora et al., 1993). Cross (1995) suggested that a Black oppositional identity can serve several protective functions for Blacks. The protection function involves an awareness of racism as part of the American experience, the anticipation of racism regardless of one's social, educational, or economic status, ego defenses to be employed when one is faced with racism, a predisposition to find fault in one's circumstances rather than in oneself, and a religious orientation that prevents the development of bitterness or hatred of Whites. The Black identity helps the individual deal with the problems that being Black creates on a daily basis. It mitigates "the pain, imposition, and stigma that come when one is treated with disrespect, rudeness, and insensitivity" (Cross, 1995, p. 197).

Most of the research on this issue has been based on African American Blacks, and little research has determined whether the level of mistrust found in African Americans is also found in other minorities or in Blacks from other ethnic and cultural backgrounds. Biafora et al. (1993) showed that one third of the Black students in their sample expressed mistrust of Whites. Of particular interest is that the researchers found that Haitians, especially those born outside of the United States, expressed the highest levels of mistrust, with nearly 50% believing that Blacks should be suspicious of "friendly whites." However, students of Caribbean Island backgrounds, especially those born in the United States, reported the lowest levels of mistrust. Similarly, Taylor, Biafora, and Warheit (1994) found no difference in mistrust levels among Black middle-school boys of African American, Haitian, and other Caribbean Island origins.

Some evidence suggests that this mistrust of White society may be manifested to some degree in other minority populations who face discrimination. Athey and Ahearn (1991) commented that "racism in the settlement society is often an impediment to reestablishing a trustful and ordered community life. It stigmatizes and further isolates refugees" (p. 15). Rumbaut's (1994) respondents who faced discrimination were less likely to identify as Americans, and respondents who thought that people would discriminate against them no matter how well educated they became were more likely to self-identify with their nation of origin. Attending a school where the majority of students were minorities increased the identification of pan-ethnic labels. Rumbaut concluded that experiences of rejection or exclusion, based on ascribed traits, clearly undercut the process of assimilation. However, because immigrants may use their ethnic identities to shield themselves from the negative impact of racism or discrimination and to differentiate themselves from other minority groups within the United States, the relation between immigrant status and cultural mistrust or oppositional identity is complex. Immigrants who view other minority groups as the victims of their own individual and collective liabilities (Fernández-Kelly & Schauffler, 1994) might be less likely to develop cultural mistrust or an oppositional identity.

In sum, immigrant children and adolescents in the United States must learn to cope with racism, discrimination, and prejudice as it is manifested in both overt and subtle ways. Furthermore, the different expectations and experiences with discrimination that immigrants of different generations encounter can create conflict within families. The coping mechanisms that children develop include both behavioral and psychological skills. Behaviorally, immigrant families often learn to cope with discrimination by living in an ethnic enclave. Psychologically, immigrant children and adolescents do not internalize the mainstream society's negative evaluations, and some immigrants, especially Black immigrants, might form cultural mistrust or an oppositional identity. However, more research needs to be done to unravel and document the various ways in which children learn to cope with prejudice, racism, and discrimination and the factors that influence their perceptions and reactions to mainstream society.

CONCLUSIONS

The initial focus of this chapter was the psychological effects of migration on children. In the past, the guiding frameworks and research have concentrated on the negative impact of migration. More recently, we and others (Delgado-Gaitan, 1994; Diaz, 1985; Gil, Vega, & Dimas, 1994; LaFromboise, Coleman, & Gerton, 1993; Laosa, 1989; Rumbaut, 1991, 1994; and others) are trying to present a more balanced and thorough view. That is, throughout this chapter we have tried to take into account the possible positive benefits of migration, the influence of the developmental stage on the adjustment process, the complexity of the involved processes, and the crucial influence of the present historical, political, economical, and educational contexts.

Rumbaut and Rumbaut's (1976) metaphor of migration as an experience of both death and rebirth is very suitable. Although created to describe refugees in particular, this metaphor suggests that all immigrants face a range of experiences in migration and subsequent adaptation. The metaphor recognizes a certain amount of loss involved in the migration experience; it also recognizes a certain amount of rebirth as well. Just as older ways of life and familiar people and places are often lost, new places, opportunities, people, and experiences are found.

As developmentalists we argue that the impact and process of migration and subsequent acculturation will be largely dependent on a person's developmental needs and issues. It has been suggested many times that children acculturate faster, thereby implying easier, than others, thus making the age of contact important. However, we propose that the relation between age and speed and ease of acculturation is in most cases curvilinear rather than linear. During the infancy, toddler, and preschool years, the rate of acculturation is actually more a function of the family's acculturation rate and attitude toward the new culture than the child's actual potential for acculturation. There is no question that children from very early on, because of their potential for learning and actual drive for mastery, are able to acculturate faster than adults. However, we have to consider the context for learning before school entry, which is primarily influenced by the primary caregivers (García Coll et al., 1995). Young children first learn and absorb their concepts of ethnic labels, attitudes, and behaviors from their adult caretakers (Rotherham-Borus, 1993). Thus, we might expect that the acculturation rate might be slower before school, daycare, or preschool entry, faster after entry into any one of these settings (if the settings demand acculturation), and then slower again after the formative years.

In the early years, the rate of acculturation will depend almost entirely on the level of the acculturation of the family, including the primary caregivers and significant others like substitute caregivers (e.g., grandparents) and older siblings. We have argued elsewhere that acculturation levels impact parenting styles by influencing development expectations, mother–infant interactions, and feeding and caregiving practices (García Coll et al., 1995). Aside from their own level of acculturation, the primary caregivers' and significant others' attitudes toward the new culture is another important factor. This attitude can vary from acceptance and reception to rejection and avoidance. Depending on this attitude, for example, a mother may try to teach or not to teach English to her toddler or may place her child in a primarily ethnically consonant setting. Rueschenberg and Buriel (1989) found that Mexican families' level of acculturation was positively associated with their utilization of external resources, even though the use of internal resources was not affected by their level of acculturation. Thus, a family who was very acculturated employed external resources to a higher degree than a less acculturated family, even if the two families maintained similar internal structures.

As a child grows and begins to be exposed to influences outside the family, the characteristics of these settings also affect the rate of acculturation (García Coll et al., 1995). With increasing age, there is a growing consistency between the children's understanding and the normative beliefs regarding ethnicity and society. Does the new setting affirm or celebrate diversity? Does it include instruction in the child's language and cultural background or demand complete acculturation? Are the available role models similar to those in the child's original culture or are there other attributes, values, and beliefs celebrated? What is the composition of the peer group, and, more important, what are the values of the group toward the two cultures and their interaction? As children grow into adolescents they actively determine their self-schema. Their choices, in part a reflection of their earlier socialization, are given to greater variation and independence (Rotherham-Borus, 1993). Consequently, during this period their choices are more reflective of their peer group and other institutions.

Finally, as developmentalists we are not willing to toss aside the many contexts that affect the child's development. We are aware that, as important as the individual's characteristics and developmental needs are, we must simultaneously seek an understanding of the contexts in which individuals grow and develop (Laosa, 1989; Rumbaut, 1994). These contexts include political, historical, economic, and educational circumstances of the sending and receiving communities, which play an active role in determining whether children accrue more positive or more negative outcomes from the experience of migration and the subsequent process of acculturation. For example, if unemployment is high in the receiving community, it will be difficult for the immigrant family to find work. They will suffer economically and will not feel as if they have gained a sense of mastery of their new environment. Similarly, if the receiving community's governmental policy is fiscally conservative, immigrant families might have less access to financial assistance or medical care, creating further obstacles to successful adaptation. Finally, migration in an era in which newcomers are considered a burden and therefore unwelcome by the receiving society, and in which racial and ethnic tensions are day-to-day occurrences, provides a different context for adaptation than an era in which newcomers are welcomed.

What we have yet to address is what determines whether the experience will be positive or negative, or what combination of positive and negative effects will be manifested for any one child. The answer seems to be that every child faces dialectical forces, challenges that can be positive or negative depending on the individual's characteristics, the family's characteristics, and the immediate and larger contextual forces that influence children, adolescents, and their families.

REFERENCES

Aronowitz, M. (1984). The social and emotional adjustment of immigrant children: A review of the literature. *International Review of Migration, 18,* 237–257.

Ashworth, M. (1982). The cultural adjustment of immigrant children in English Canada. In R. C. Nann (Ed.), *Uprooting and surviving* (pp. 77–83). Boston: D. Reidel.

Athey, J. L., & Ahearn, F. L. (1991). The mental health of refugee children: An overview. In J. L. Athey & F. L. Ahearn (Eds.), *Refugee children: Theory, research, and services* (pp. 1–19). Baltimore: Johns Hopkins University Press.

Baptiste, D. A. (1987). Family therapy with Spanish-heritage immigrant families in cultural transition. *Contemporary Family Therapy, 9*, 229–251.

Baptiste, D. A. (1993). Immigrant families, adolescents, and acculturation: Insights for therapists. *Marriage and Family Review, 19*, 341–363.

Beiser, M. (1988). Influences of time, ethnicity, and attachment on depression in Southeast Asian refugees. *American Journal of Psychiatry, 145*, 46–51.

Berry, J. (1990). Acculturation and adaptation: A general framework. In W. H. Holtzman & T. H. Borneman (Eds.), *The mental health of immigrants and refugees* (pp. 90–102). Austin, TX: Hogg Foundation for Mental Health, University of Texas.

Berry, J. W., Kim, U., Minde, T., & Mok, D. (1987). Comparative studies of acculturative stress. *International Migration Review, 21*, 491–511.

Biafora, F. A., Taylor, D. L., Warheit, G. J., Zimmerman, R. S., & Vega, W. A., (1993). Cultural mistrust and racial awareness among ethnically diverse Black adolescent boys. *Journal of Black Psychology, 19*, 266–281.

Brody, E. B. (1966). Cultural exclusion, character, and illness. *American Journal of Psychiatry, 122*, 852–858.

Brody, E. B. (1990). Mental health and world citizenship: Sociocultural bases for advocacy. In W. H. Holtzman & T. H. Borneman (Eds.), *The mental health of immigrants and refugees* (pp. 299–328). Austin, TX: Hogg Foundation for Mental Health, University of Texas.

Burke, A. W. (1980). Family stress and the precipitation of psychiatric disorder: A comparative study among immigrant West Indian and British patients in Birmingham. *International Journal of Social Psychiatry, 26*, 35–40.

Carlin, J. (1990). Refugee and immigrant populations at special risk: Women, children and the elderly. In W. H. Holtzman & T. H. Borneman (Eds.), *The mental health of immigrants and refugees* (pp. 224–233). Austin, TX: Hogg Foundation for Mental Health, University of Texas.

Chud, B. (1982). The threshold model: A conceptual framework for understanding and assisting children of immigrants. In R. C. Nann (Ed.), *Uprooting and surviving* (pp. 95–99). Boston: D. Reidel.

Cochrane, R. (1979). Psychological and behavioral disturbance in West Indians, Indians, and Pakistanis in Britain. *British Journal of Psychiatry, 134*, 201–210.

Cole, M., & Scribner, S. (1974). *Culture and thought.* New York: Wiley.

Compas, B. E. (1987). Coping with stress during childhood and adolescence. *Psychological Bulletin, 101*, 393–403.

Cornille, T. A., & Brotherton, W. D. (1993). Applying the developmental family therapy model to issues of migrating families. *Marriage and Family Review, 19*, 325–340.

Cropley, A. J. (1983). *The education of immigrant children.* London: Croom Helm.

Cross, W. E. (1995). Oppositional identity and African American youth: Issues and prospects. In W. D. Hawley & A. W. Jackson (Eds.), *Toward a common destiny: Improving race and ethnic relations in America* (pp. 185–204). San Francisco: Jossey-Bass.

Dasen, P. R., & Heron, A. (1981). Cross cultural test of Piaget's theory. In H. C. Triandis & A. Heron (Eds.), *Handbook of cross cultural psychology: Volume 4. Developmental psychology* (pp. 295–341). Boston: Allyn & Bacon.

Delgado-Gaitan, C. (1994). Socializing young children in Mexican-American families: An intergenerational perspective. In P. M. Greenfield & R. R. Cocking (Eds.), *Cross cultural roots of minority child development* (pp. 55–86). Hillsdale, NJ: Lawrence Erlbaum Associates.

Derbyshire, R. L. (1970). Adaptation of adolescent Mexican Americans to United States society. In E. B. Brody (Ed.), *Behavior in new environments* (pp. 275–290). Beverly Hills, CA: Sage.

Diaz, R. M. (1985). Bilingual cognitive development: Addressing three gaps in current research. *Child Development, 56,* 1376–1388.

Diaz, R. M., & Klinger, C. (1991). Towards an explanatory model of interaction between bilingualism and cognitive development. In E. Bialystok (Ed.), *Language processing in bilingual children* (pp. 167–192). New York: Cambridge University Press.

Duckitt, J. (1992). Psychology and prejudice. *American Psychologist, 47,* 1182–1193.

Eisenbruch, M. (1988). The mental health of refugee children and their cultural development. *International Migration Review, 22,* 282–300.

Ekstrand, L. H. (1976). Adjustment among immigrant pupils in Sweden. *International Review of Applied Psychology, 25,* 167–188.

El-Sheikh, M., & Klaczynski, P. A. (1993). Cultural variability in stress and control. *Journal of Cross Cultural Psychology, 24,* 81–98.

Espino, C. M. (1991). Trauma and adaptation: The case of Central American children. In J. L. Athey & F. L. Ahearn, (Eds.), *Refugee children: Theory, research, and services* (pp. 106–124). Baltimore: Johns Hopkins University Press.

Fernández-Kelly, M. P., & Schauffler, R. (1994). Divided fates: Immigrant children in a restructured US economy. *International Migration Review, 28,* 662–689.

García Coll, C. T. (1990). Developmental outcomes of minority infants: A process-oriented look into our beginnings. *Child Development, 61,* 270–289.

García Coll, C. T., Lambert, G., Jenkins, R., McAdoo, H. P., Crnic, K., Wasik, B. H., & Vázquez García, H. A. (in press). An integrative model for the study of developmental competencies in minority children. *Child Development.*

García Coll, C. T., Meyer, E. C., & Brillon, L. (1995). Ethnic and minority parenting. In M. Bornstein (Ed.), Handbook of parenting: Vol. 2. Biology and ecology of parenting (pp. 189–209). Hillsdale, NJ: Lawrence Erlbaum Associates.

Gil, A., Vega, W. A., & Dimas, J. M. (1994). Acculturative stress and personal adjustment among Hispanic adolescent boys. *Journal of Community Psychology, 22,* 43–54.

Graham, P. J., & Meadows, C. E. (1967). Psychiatric disorder in the children of West Indian immigrants. *Journal of Child Psychology and Psychiatry, 8,* 105–116.

Hakuta, K., Ferdman, B., & Diaz, R. M. (1987). Bilingualism and cognitive development: Three perspectives. In S. Rosenberg (Ed.), *Advances in applied linguistics, Volume 2* (pp. 284–319). New York: Cambridge University Press.

Hirschman, C. (1994). Problems and prospects of studying immigrant adaptation from the 1990 Population Census: From generational comparisons to the process of "becoming American." *International Migration Review, 28,* 690–713.

Inbar, M. (1977). Immigration and learning: The vulnerable age. *Canadian Review of Sociology and Anthropology, 14,* 218–234.

Jenson, G. F., White, C. S., & Galliher, J. M. (1982). Ethnic status and adolescent self-evaluations: An extension of research on minority self esteem. *Social Problems, 30,* 226–239.

Kallarackal, A. M., & Herbert, M. (1976, February 26). The happiness of immigrant children. *New Society,* 422–424.

Knight, G. P., Bernal, M. E., Garza, C. A., Cota, M. K., & Ocampo, K. A. (1993). Family socialization and the ethnic identity of Mexican-American children. *Journal of Cross-Cultural Psychology, 24,* 99–114.

Koplow, L., & Messinger, E. (1990). Developmental dilemmas of young children of immigrant parents. *Child and Adolescent Social Work, 7,* 121–134.

LaFromboise, T., Coleman, H. L. K., & Gerton, J. (1993). Psychological impact of biculturalism: Evidence and theory. *Psychological Bulletin, 114,* 395–412.

Lambert, W. E. (1977). The effects of bilingualism on the individual: Cognitive and sociocultural consequences. In P. A. Hornby (Ed.), *Bilingualism: Psychological, social, and educational implications* (pp. 15–27). New York: Academic Press.

Lambert, W. E., & Taylor, D. M. (1990). Language and culture in the lives of immigrants and refugees. In W. H. Holtzman & T. H. Borneman (Eds.), *The mental health of immigrants and refugees* (pp. 103–128). Austin, TX: Hogg Foundation for Mental Health, University of Texas.

Laosa, L. (1989). *Psychosocial stress, coping, and the development of Hispanic immigrant children.* Princeton, NJ: Educational Testing Service.

Leslie, L. A. (1993). Families fleeing war: The case of Central Americans. *Marriage and Family Review, 19*, 193–205.

Lipson, J. G., & Meleis, A. I. (1989). Methodological issues in research with immigrants. *Medical Anthropology, 12*, 103–115.

Maccoby, E. E. (1983). Socio-emotional development and response to stressors. In N. Garmezy & M. Rutter (Eds.), *Stress, coping, and development in children* (pp. 217–234). New York: McGraw-Hill.

Mendelberg. H. E. (1986). Identity conflict in Mexican American adolescents. *Adolescence, 21*, 215–224.

Nicol, A. R. (1971). Psychiatric disorder in the children of Caribbean immigrants. *Journal of Child Psychology and Psychiatry, 12*, 273–287.

Osofsky, J. D. (1995). The effect of exposure to violence on young children. *American Psychologist, 50*, 782–788.

Padilla, A. M., Cervantes, R. C., Maldonado, M., & Garcia, R. E. (1988). Coping responses to psychosocial stressors among Mexican and Central American immigrants. *Journal of Community Psychology, 16*, 418–427.

Padilla, A. M., & Lindholm, K. J. (1984). Child bilingualism: The same old issues revisited. In J. L. Martinez & R. H. Mendoza (Eds.), *Chicano psychology* (pp. 369–408). New York: Academic Press.

Paulston, C. B. (1978). Education in a bi/multicultural setting. *International Review of Education, 24*, 302–328.

Phinney, J. S. (1990). Ethnic identity in adolescents and adults: Review of research. *Psychological Bulletin, 108*, 499–514.

Phinney, J. S. (1993). A three stage model of ethnic identity development in adolescents. In M. E. Bernal & G. P. Knight (Eds.), *Ethnic identity: Formation and transmission among Hispanic and other minorities* (pp. 61–80). Albany, NY: State University of New York Press.

Phinney, J. S., Chavira, V., & Tate, J. D. (1993). The effect of ethnic threat on ethnic self concept and own-group ratings. *The Journal of Social Psychology, 133*, 469–478.

Porte, Z., & Torney-Purta, J. (1987). Depression and academic achievement among Indochinese refugee unaccompanied minors in ethnic and nonethnic placements. *American Journal of Orthopsychiatry, 57*, 536–547.

Pynoos, R. S. (1993). Traumatic stress and developmental psychopathology in children and adolescents. In J. M. Oldhams, M. B. Riba, & A. Tasman (Eds.), *American Psychiatric Press review of psychiatry (Vol. 12)*. Washington, DC: American Psychiatric Press.

Ramirez, M. (1983). *Psychology of the Americas: Mestizo perspectives on personality and mental health.* Elmsford, NY: Pergamon.

Ramirez, M. (1984). Assessing and understanding biculturalism-multiculturalism in Mexican-American adults. In J. L. Martinez & R. H. Mendoza (Eds.), *Chicano psychology* (pp. 77–93). New York: Academic Press.

Ressler, E. M., Boothby, N., Steinbock, D. J. (1988). *Unaccompanied children: Care and protection in wars, natural disasters, and refugee movements.* New York: Oxford University Press.

Rodriguez, C. (1975). A cost-benefit analysis of subjective factors affecting assimilation: Puerto Ricans. *Ethnicity, 2,* 66–80.

Rodriguez, R. (1973). Difficulties of adjustment in immigrant children in Geneva. In C. Zwingman & M. Pfister-Ammende (Eds.), *Uprooting and after...* (pp. 134–141). New York: Springer-Verlag.

Rogler, L. H., Cortes, D. E., & Malgady, R. G. (1991). Acculturation and mental health status among Hispanics: Convergence and new directions for research. *American Psychologist, 46,* 585–597.

Rosenthal, D. (1987). Ethnic identity development in adolescents. In J. Phinney & M. Rotherham (Eds.), *Children's ethnic socialization: Pluralism and development* (pp. 156–179). Beverly Hills, CA: Sage.

Rotenberg, K. J., & Cerda, C. (1994). Racially based trust expectancies of Native Americans and Caucasian children. *Journal of Social Psychology, 134,* 621–631.

Rotherham-Borus, M. J. (1989). *The impact of ethnic identity in different school settings.* Symposium on Ethnicity and Mental Health, Manhattan Children's Psychiatric Center, New York.

Rotherham-Borus, M. J. (1990). Adolescents' reference-group choices, self-esteem, and adjustment. *Journal of Personality and Social Psychology, 59,* 1075–1081.

Rotherham-Borus, M. J. (1993). Biculturalism among adolescents. In M. E. Bernal & G. P. Knight (Eds.), *Ethnic identity: Formation and transmission among Hispanic and other minorities* (pp. 81–102). Albany, NY: State University of New York Press.

Rueschenberg, E., & Buriel, R. (1989). Mexican American family functioning and acculturation: A family systems perspective. *Hispanic Journal of Behavioral Sciences, 11,* 232–244.

Rumbaut, R. G. (1988). *The adaptation of Southeast Asian refugee youth: A comparative perspective.* Paper presented at the thirteenth annual meeting of the Social Science History Association, Chicago, IL.

Rumbaut, R. G. (1991). The agony of exile: A study of the migration and adaptation of Indochinese refugee adults and children. In J. L. Athey & F. L. Ahearn (Eds.), *Refugee children: Theory, research, and services* (pp. 53–91). Baltimore: Johns Hopkins University Press.

Rumbaut, R. G. (1994). The crucible within: Ethnic identity, self esteem, and the segmented assimilation among children of immigrants. *International Migration Review, 28,* 748–794.

Rumbaut, R., & Rumbaut, R. (1976). The family in exile: Cuban expatriates in the United States. *American Journal of Psychiatry, 133,* 395–399.

Rutter, M. (1979). Protective factors in children's responses to stress and disadvantage. In M. W. Kent & J. E. Rolf (Eds.), *Primary prevention of psychopathology: Vol. III. Social competence* (pp. 49–74). Hanover, NH: University Press of New England.

Rutter, M. (1983). Stress, coping, and development: Some issues and some questions. In N. Garmezy & M. Rutter (Eds.), *Stress, coping, and development in children* (pp. 1–41). New York: McGraw-Hill.

Rutter, M., Yule, W., Berger, M., Yule, B., Morton, J., & Bagley, C. (1974). Children of West Indian immigrants–I. Rates of behavioral deviance and psychiatric disorder. *Journal of Child Psychiatry, 15,* 241–262.

Sam, D. L. (1994). The psychological adjustment of young immigrants in Norway. *Scandinavian Journal of Psychology, 35,* 240–253.

Schrader, A. (1978). The "vulnerable" age: Findings on foreign children in Germany. *Sociology of Education, 51,* 227–230.

Seifer, R., & Sameroff, A. J. (1987). Multiple determinants of risk and invulnerability. In E. J. Anthony & B. J. Cohler (Eds.), *The invulnerable child* (pp. 51–69). New York: Guilford.

Sluzki, C. E. (1979). Migration and family conflict. *Family Process, 18,* 379–390.

Spencer, M. B., Swanson, D. P., & Cunningham, M. (1991). Ethnicity, ethnic identity, and competence formation: Adolescent transition and cultural transformation. *Journal of Negro Education, 60,* 366–387.

Sung, B. L. (1985). Bicultural conflicts in Chinese immigrant children. *Journal of Comparative Family Studies, 26,* 255–269.

Szapocznik, J., Kurtines, W. M., & Fernandez, T. (1981). Bicultural involvement and adjustment in Hispanic-American youth. *International Journal of Intercultural Relations, 4,* 353–375.

Taylor, D. L., Biafora, F. A., Warheit, G. J. (1994). Racial mistrust and disposition to deviance among African American, Haitian, and other Caribbean Island adolescent boys. *Law and Human Behavior, 18,* 291–303.

Terrell, F. T., & Terrell, S. (1981). An inventory to measure cultural mistrust among Blacks. *The Western Journal of Black Studies, 5,* 180–185.

Touliatos, J., & Lindholm, B. W. (1980). Behavioral disturbance in children of native born and immigrant parents. *Journal of Community Psychology, 8,* 28–33.

Tradd, P. V., & Greenblatt, E. (1990). Psychological aspects of child stress: Development and the spectrum of coping responses. In E. Arnold (Ed.), *Childhood stress* (pp. 23–49). New York: Wiley.

Tropp, L. R., Ekrut, S., Alarcon, O., García Coll, C., & Vázquez, H. A. (1994). Toward a theoretical model of psychological acculturation. *Working Paper Series,* No. 268. Wellesley, MA: Center for Research on Women.

Vega, W. A., & Rumbaut, R. G. (1991). Ethnic minorities and mental health. *Annual Review of Sociology, 17,* 351–383.

Wagner, D. A. (1978). Memories of Morocco: The influence of age, schooling, and environment on memory. *Cognitive Psychology, 10,* 1–28.

Wagner, D. (1981). Culture and memory development. In H. C. Triandis & A. Heron (Eds.), *Handbook of cross cultural psychology, Vol. 4: Developmental psychology* (pp. 187–232). Boston: Allyn & Bacon.

Waters, M. C. (in press). The intersection of gender, race, and ethnicity in identity development of Caribbean American teens. In B. Leadbetter & N. Way (Eds.), *Urban adolescent girls: Resisting stereotypes.* New York: New York University Press.

Weinberg, A. (1979). Mental health aspects of voluntary migration. In C. Zwingman & M. Pfister-Ammende (Eds.), *Uprooting and after . . .* (pp. 110–120). New York: Springer-Verlag.

Westermeyer, J. (1989). *Mental health for refugees and other migrants: Social and preventive approaches.* Springfield, IL: Thomas.

Zambrana, R. E., & Silva-Palacios, V. (1989). Gender differences in stress among Mexican immigrant adolescents in Los Angeles, California. *Journal of Adolescent Research, 4,* 426–442.

Zavala Martinez, I. (1994a). Entremundos: Psychological processes of migration. In G. Lamberty & C. García Coll (Eds.), *Health and development of Puerto Rican women and children in the United States* (pp. 29–38). New York: Plenum.

Zavala Martinez, I. (1994b). Quién soy? Who am I? Identity issues for Puerto Rican adolescents. In E. P. Salett & D. R. Koslow (Eds.), *Race, ethnicity and self* (pp. 89–116). Washington, DC: National Multicultural Institute.

6

Research Perspectives on Constructs of Change: Intercultural Migration and Developmental Transitions

Luis M. Laosa
Educational Testing Service

IN NUMBER and complexity, the processes and other variables involved in human migration are so vast that one is soon overwhelmed when one attempts to consider more than a relatively few at a time. Further, migration is an event that can be, and is, studied by many disciplines—each one focusing on a particular aspect of the event, each one using its own distinct methodology and epistemology. Thus, migration research is simultaneously the province of demography, public policy, sociology, psychology, education, anthropology, public health, and many more specialized fields of study, each one able to illuminate only a part of the event. This characteristic makes migration an ideal focus for encouraging multidisciplinary research and interdisciplinary collaboration.[1] To this end, comprehensive conceptual models, such as the one I have elsewhere (Laosa, 1990b; see also Rogler, 1994) proposed for the study of human development in the context of intercultural migration, are best thought of as just that, *conceptual* models rather than *hypothetical* or *analytic* models. In this sense, the function of a conceptual model is to help identify and stimulate thinking about relevant domains of variables and about the

---

[1] I make a defining distinction between multidisciplinary and interdisciplinary work. A *multi*disciplinary study, investigation, or program of research (see footnote 2) approaches a particular topic or theme from the perspectives of varied disciplines. *Inter*disciplinary research, or collaboration, is conducted jointly by researchers from varied disciplines, each researcher typically representing a single discipline. The study, investigation, or program of research resulting from the collaboration may be either multidisciplinary or unidisciplinary.

plausible ways in which they may be interrelated and organized. Used in this way, a comprehensive conceptual model becomes a powerful multidisciplinary heuristic device. The process is reminiscent of how widely people differ from each other in what they perceive in a Rorschach inkblot. Thus, developmental psychologists think of migration in a manner radically different from—but complementary to—that of, say, social demographers or economists regarding the same model. Indeed, they diverge profoundly with respect to the aspects of migration they consider interesting and significant, the research questions or hypotheses they deem relevant, the variables that attract and hold their attention, the units and levels of analysis on which they concentrate, and the manner in which they analyze and interpret data. For the individual researcher, this fact is both a blessing and a daunting complication—the former because of the attendant enrichment of the topic, the latter because few people are trained in more than one discipline or specialty.

In the face of this dilemma, the proper next step is to formulate a hypothetical model by selecting realistically from the conceptual model a circumscribed set of elements (i.e., variables, research questions, hypotheses) that can be appropriately studied in a single study.[2] Finally, the need for an analytic model compels the researcher to operationalize and hone the chosen variables into precise empirical measures and effective data collection procedures and to decide how to analyze the resulting data in order to test the hypotheses, or answer the research questions, articulated in the hypothetical model. Scientific progress is largely the accretion of the advancing knowledge resulting from these individual efforts and from the corresponding restructuring of the existing body of knowledge so that, over time, more and more of the constituent elements of a comprehensive conceptual model are elucidated.

Unlike other types of event, international migration typically involves individuals' making some form of change or transition across different cultures or societies—changes that can occur at any point in the course of the individuals' development. For these reasons, international migration poses special challenges as a subject of scientific inquiry. At the same time and for the same reasons, it presents unique research opportunities. Some of these challenges and opportunities are identified and discussed in this chapter. The aim is to stimulate and help organize scientific thinking about these significant life events and transitions.

---

[2]Although the terms *study* and *investigation* are often used interchangeably, I make the following defining distinctions: An investigation is a research project that planfully comprises closely interrelated studies focused on the same specific topic or general research question. A *program of research*, a broader term, refers to a series of research projects (investigations or studies or both) expressly and systematically undertaken, typically in sequence, on the same more or less general theme.

DEVELOPMENTAL PERSPECTIVE
AND CULTURAL RELATIVITY

The study of culture change in individuals has seldom been approached from a developmental perspective. This lack is not surprising, because comprehensive conceptions of human development are typically so complex that when one attempts to superimpose them on the similarly intricate issues pertaining to migration and its sociocultural contexts, one raises to a daunting level the difficulty of the challenges the topic poses to research. The chief concern of scientists who study the development of human behavior is to provide information about the history and growth of individuals' behavior and the functions and causes of behavior—in short, *what* develops and *when, how,* and *why* (e.g., Bornstein & Lamb, 1992; Bornstein & Lerner, 1992; Hartup & van Lieshout, 1995; Parke, Ornstein, Rieser, & Zahn-Waxler, 1994). To complete this list toward a fuller account of human behavior and development, Church (1961) added information about how people feel about what they do. More broadly, the overarching goal of psychological research is to understand and explain why individuals think, feel, act, and react as they do in real life (Magnusson, 1990). To this end, models restricted to a *contemporaneous* perspective are intended to account for individuals' functioning in terms of their current psychological or biological dispositions (or both) and environmental circumstances. In contrast, *developmental* models are formulated to explain current functioning in terms of those aspects of the individual and the environment that are involved in the individual's developmental history, and how they led to the present way of functioning (Hall & Lindzey, 1978; Magnusson, 1990). The two perspectives are complementary; both are needed.

As is generally true of scientific constructs in all disciplines, development is not a straightforward empirical concept but rather a postulate; as such, there is *no* general consensus on a single conception of development. Whether development has occurred in any given instance is ascertained by whether the features of the data fit an implicit or explicit concept (e.g., metatheory, paradigm) of what development entails (see, e.g., Bornstein & Lamb, 1992; Bornstein & Lerner, 1992; Emmerich, 1968, 1977; Loevinger, 1976, 1987; Parke et al., 1994; Piaget, 1983; Wainryb, 1993; White, 1983). In addition to these within-culture, within-discipline variations in conceptions of development, there is an increasing recognition among developmental psychologists in North America that patterns and norms of human development previously thought to be universal are instead specific to their own culture, that different cultures value different developmental trajectories, and that particular trajectories arise as adaptations to environmental circumstances (e.g., Greenfield, 1993; Greenfield & Cocking, 1994; Laosa, 1979/1989, 1990a, 1990b, 1991; Rogoff, 1990;

Serpell, 1992; Valsiner, 1995). Thus, Greenfield, a leading North American developmental psychologist, recognized that "the dominant knowledge base of current developmental psychology comes from Euro-American researchers studying the development of children from their own cultural experience. Significantly, a largely unacknowledged consequence is that our developmental knowledge is primarily knowledge of the acquisition of Euro-American culture as this process transpires in the United States" (Greenfield, 1994, p. *x*). There is, as she pointed out, a need for interaction with a wider international community of researchers that can "provide perspectives on goals, conditions, and paths of development that differ from those we too often take for granted" (p. *ix*).

As an interpretive model for rendering intelligible the apparent cultural diversity in human behavior and development, cultural relativism differs from cultural universalism and cultural evolutionism. A *universalist* approach emphasizes general likenesses and overlooks specific differences. A problem with this stance is, as Shweder and Bourne (1984) cautioned, that universals can be "discovered" by moving to a level of discourse so general that the generality becomes trivial or by restricting analysis to a subset of the possible evidence. An *evolutionist* approach, on the other hand, rank orders variety into a sequence of low to high (e.g., primitive to advanced, incipient to elaborated) by locating a normative model (e.g., Piaget's cognitive stages or Kohlberg's moral development stages), by treating the normative model as the endpoint of development, and by describing the observed cultural variability as steps on a ladder progressively moving in the direction of the normative endpoint (Shweder & Bourne, 1984; Shweder, Mahapatra, & Miller, 1990).

Viewed from the perspective of cultural *relativism*, each culture is composed of unique patterns that determine and give meaning to human behavior, to its function, and to its causes (Laosa, 1979/1989; Shweder & Bourne, 1984; Spiro, 1990; Wittkower & Dubreuil, 1977). As such, for each culture there is a unique *what, when, how,* and *why* of human development. Concerning the question of whether cultural variations are susceptible to judgments regarding their relative worth, Spiro (1984) distinguished between *descriptive* and *normative* relativism. Descriptive cultural relativism does not address this question. Normative cultural relativism holds that, because there are *no* transcultural standards by which differences between cultures can be validly evaluated, there is no way by which their relative worth can be judged (Spiro, 1984, 1990).

When carried to its logical conclusion, cultural relativism poses a serious dilemma for science: The uniqueness of each culture makes comparisons between cultures difficult or impossible. On the one hand, it is important to understand a culture from its native point of view (i.e., *emic* approach). On the other hand, in order to make scientific cross-cultural comparisons possible, it is necessary that the emic approach be complemented by studies in terms of general scientific concepts (i.e., *etic* approach). When applied to the study of human development, the etic approach calls for analysis of cross-cultural variability along dimensions of development defined and calibrated by European American standards.[3] These standards have been chosen because the "mainstream" field of human development—and, indeed, science itself—has its roots in European cultures. Ideally, it should be possible to gain an understanding of any culture from both the emic and the etic points of view. This centrist aspiration is reflected, for example, in the work of psychological anthropologist R. A. LeVine (1984, 1990). In reality, however, few developmental scientists are sufficiently steeped in cultures different from their own. In any case, one can see that cultural relativism can pose knotty philosophical and methodological (and political) problems for the study of intercultural transitions. These problems revolve around the question (answers to which are beyond the scope of this discussion), Should immigrants' development be evaluated by the emic (i.e., culture of origin) approach or by the etic approach or by both?

Regardless of the differences in conceptions, however, the subject matter of research on human development is, as Wohlwill (1970) concisely described it, "behavior *change* taking place as the individual grows from birth to old age, or more particularly the properties and characteristics of these changes and the variables governing them" (p. 151). Transitional periods in an individual's life provide unique windows for viewing the organism as it undergoes change; the study of such events can lead to insights into the factors that promote the maintenance or reorganization of patterns of functioning in individuals over time (Brim & Kagan, 1980; Caspi & Bem, 1990; Connell & Furman, 1984; Rogler, 1994). In recent years, because of this recognition, the study of life transitions has attracted a growing interest in the behavioral, social, and health sciences and in education (e.g., Delgado-Gaitan, 1994; Greenfield, 1994; Hetherington & Arasteh, 1988; McCollum, 1990; Miller, 1989; Seidman, Allen, Aber, Mitchell, & Feinman, 1994; Tapia Uribe, LeVine, & LeVine, 1994; Thurber, 1995).

LIFE PASSAGES

All human societies expect or require their members to undergo some distinct forms of experience, or normative events, that mark or demand from the individual some major and lasting personal change—a transformation that alters, in a profound but typically orderly and predictable manner, the individual and the individual's relations to the other members of the society. Recognizing

---

[3]It is not the intention here to imply that the etic approach can occur only in studies conducted from perspectives with roots in European cultures. The etic approach can conceivably occur also in studies based on other cultural perspectives.

these occurrences, scholars seeking to understand human behavior have long been interested in the study of *rites of passage*—ceremonial events, existing in varied forms in all historically known societies, that mark the transition of an individual from one social status to another (Herdt, 1990; Norbeck, 1992; Whiting, 1990). Their worldwide distribution, particularly as they occur in traditional societies, has long attracted the attention of anthropologists and folklorists. In contemporary, technologically and scientifically oriented societies, passage rites tend to be secularized and appear to be less elaborately developed than those observed in many traditional societies, but they nevertheless continue to play important social, cultural, and psychological functions (Norbeck, 1992). In the United States, major normative life transitions include, for example, the child's entry into school, graduation from high school, leaving the parental residence; the college-bound student's entering higher education; the young adult's first gainful employment; forming a family; and job retirement.

Rites of passage can serve important sociological and psychological functions that pertain to group solidarity versus disorder and that allay personal anxiety over the stresses surrounding the change. Many of these passages bear a connection with a biological change of life—such as birth, weaning, maturity, reproduction, or death—but others celebrate or mark changes that are wholly cultural (Benedict, 1934). As Norbeck (1992) and others have noted, less scholarly attention has been given to the psychological than to the social or cultural aspects of passage rites, because scholars focusing on such rites have typically been anthropologists oriented toward sociocultural interpretations. Nevertheless, psychological aspects of rites enter strongly, if often implicitly, into anthropological interpretations. For example, passage rites reinforce and often create emotional ties to other members of society, personal identification with social groups and with specific statuses, and commitment to group ideology; they also serve as blueprints of social relations and of acceptable behavior (see, e.g., Herdt, 1990; Whiting, 1990). Thus, where particular social statuses have special honor and prestige, "the mere existence of these statuses offers opportunities for gaining psychological satisfaction, and the requirements for gaining these statuses serve to guide behavior in socially approved channels that offer psychological satisfaction" (Norbeck, 1992, p. 802; see also, e.g., Whiting, 1990). Considerable emotion is typically invested in these events. When anxiety is induced by the beliefs surrounding the passage rites, the rites may be said both to create and to allay anxiety. Psychological interpretations of rites have emphasized their value in allaying personal anxiety. In this regard, note has been made of the psychotherapeutic value of passage rites surrounding events in which stress may be acute (see, e.g., Laosa, 1990a, pp. 238–240; Prince, 1980, pp. 320–321, for research reviews). In short, the social and psychological value of rites appears substantial. Unfortunately, the cultural circumstances in the United States are such that passage rites seem to be declining and poorly developed compared with those of many traditional cultures.

In contrast to changes of the normative type, such as those already discussed, other forms of life transition are less prevalent but can be highly significant and profound in their impact. These transitions, which have received less research attention, are linked to events that tend to occur unpredictably and that result in uprooting, in the loss of family, friends, or possessions, and, in many cases, in intense and prolonged mental suffering. These extraordinary occurrences include international migration and its attendant life alterations. These events place extreme demands on the individual for personal change and adaptation. As such, they represent critical life changes that involve potentially stressful processes in development as well as extraordinary opportunities for personal growth.

After reading accounts and interpretations of rites of passage in various cultures, one ponders over analogous mechanisms that might exist around intercultural transitions. Over a half-century ago, anthropologist Ruth Benedict (1934) suggested that in order to understand traditions surrounding life changes, "we do not most need analyses of the necessary nature of *rites de passage;* we need rather to know what is identified in different cultures with the beginning of [the new role that the passage intends to mark] and their methods of admitting to the new status" (p. 36). In other words, her emphasis seems to have been on the need to identify the meaning of the individual's new role in the particular culture. In this regard, Benedict's point is well taken, notwithstanding the justifiable criticisms that have been directed at other implications of her overall theoretical position (i.e., that culture is personality; LeVine, 1973, p. 55). In pursuing this line of inquiry, however, it is necessary to keep in mind Church's (1961) reminder that, in any culture, "rituals and institutions lose their original meanings, or once-functional practices survive as rituals, so that it is not easy to derive the psychological life of a people directly from cultural forms" (p. 137). It is also necessary to keep in mind that, although culture influences social structure, social organization, and social behavior, culture per se does not consist of them—because the latter have noncultural (e.g., economic, political, situational) as well as cultural determinants—according to one anthropological theory of culture (Spiro, 1984). The psychologist interested in cultural factors is, as Church lamented, at a disadvantage because anthropology is not a branch of psychology and the material collected by anthropologists does not always lend itself to psychological analysis.

The foregoing discussion prompts the suggestion that one potentially worthwhile direction for future research is to focus on the *meaning* that being a member of a particular immigrant or ethnic group holds (psychological and otherwise) for both the individual and the larger society. In this regard, one cannot escape the irony in the history of shifting patterns of public opinion and of policy debates concerning new entrants to this country. Opponents of generous immigration policies traditionally charged that newcomers were mentally deficient and thus unfit for the mental rigors of a competitive economy compared with the native born (see Laosa, 1984, 1995, respectively for a historical overview and a discussion of current issues concerning the debate over intelligence testing). Whereas this argument was quickly defused by the astonishing success of certain groups, controversies over university admission quotas have subsequently been fueled in part by nativists' apprehensions that the newcomers' successes would limit the native borns' opportunities for education and financial aid if applications were rated strictly according to intellectual qualifications (Kraut, 1990).

The next section of the chapter brings forward certain conceptual issues that bear on the study of change and that have particular relevance for research on human development in the context of intercultural migration.

LIFE EVENTS, CHANGES, AND TRANSITIONS

Among the many and varied conceptions of what constitutes human development (see, e.g., Baltes & Nesselroade, 1979; Bornstein & Lamb, 1992; Brim & Kagan, 1980; Emmerich, 1968, 1977; Laosa, 1979/1989; Loevinger, 1976, 1987; Parke et al., 1994; Piaget, 1983; White, 1983; Wohlwill, 1973), one emerging view recognizes that human beings generally undergo periods of relative stability and periods of marked change or transition, that important changes occur throughout the entire life span, and that many individuals retain a great capacity for change (Brim & Kagan, 1980). Scientifically, these transitions are regarded as times when major reorganizations or discontinuities may occur; they have also been described as periods of "ceasing" and "becoming" (Connell & Furman, 1984, p. 154). In contrast, periods of relative stability are characterized by *continuities*, which broadly speaking refer to "connectedness in development, to the linkage of early behavior to later behavior" (Emde & Harmon, 1984, p. 3). Typically, however, the concept of transition has been surrounded by ambiguity; the term is used in a variety of ways and is given varied interpretations. Thus, as some writers have observed, transitions can be defined by time periods in the life span, by role changes, by internal transformations in the individual, or by external events (e.g., Bronfenbrenner & Crouter, 1983; Connell & Furman, 1984; Emmerich, 1968; Reese & Smyer, 1983).

It is helpful, therefore, to think of transitions in terms of some broad types. To this end, Connell and Furman (1984) offered a practical typology of major properties of life transitions, thus providing a useful vocabulary for considering these experiences. A *transition* thus refers to "the occurrence of relatively greater change in a characteristic or set of characteristics of an individual or of a group of individuals" (p. 154). The altered characteristic may reside at the level of overt behavior, in an underlying attribute, or in the structural or organizational properties of the person. Simple change from one age to another does not constitute sufficient evidence that a transition is occurring; instead, "the relative magnitude of change in a hypothesized transition would have to be shown to be greater than the relative magnitude of change when a transition is not underway" (p. 164). Of special significance, this conception distinguishes a *transitional event*, namely the instigation of the transition, from the *transitional period*, the duration of the transition. Simply stated, a transitional event or change initiates a period of change.

The transitional event may be *exogenous*, that is, occurrences or changes in the social ecology, such as migrating, entering school, or the death of a significant other; or *endogenous*, that is, internal events or changes in psychological or physiological processes, such as the hormonal alterations of adolescence or the discovery of a terminal disease (Connell & Furman, 1984). This distinction between endogenous and exogenous event types gains significance when transitions are considered from a developmental perspective. The distinction brings forward, for example, the consideration that the *timing* of the event— that is, the point in the course of the individual's psychological or biological development at which the transitional event occurs—may influence the characteristics of the transitional period and the consequent changes in the individual (Brim & Ryff, 1980; Laosa, 1979/1989). The other side of the coin is that the *nonoccurrence* of an event—such as an immigrant adolescent's lack of opportunity to date others from a shared cultural background, for example— too, can trigger a transition. Some events or forms of experience may be necessary for maintaining periods of stability (Connell & Furman, 1984).

The aforementioned conception of transitional events bears some similarity to the traditional idea of *life events* (Hultsch & Plemons, 1979), but the two constructs differ in important regards: If one thinks of life events as external, objective events, the two constructs differ because transitional events include endogenous events and because life events are typically thought of as occasions for change or reconstitution in an individual's characteristics. If a "relatively greater change does not occur following the event, that event would not be considered a transitional event" (Connell & Furman, 1984, p. 155). For instance, a change in school settings may or may not be followed by change in a child's pattern of functioning. There is thus some circularity in the Connell and Furman definition; theoretically, however, this apparent circularity seems warranted in light of the many factors that may give meaning to an event (see, e.g., Laosa, 1979/1989, 1990b; Reese & Smyer, 1983, concerning differences in event meaning).

The duration and timing of the transitional period are additional conceptual differentiations that contribute specificity to the framework. With regard to *duration*, the transitional period may be brief, but it is reasonable to expect the span of marked change in intercultural transitions to extend over years and in some cases indefinitely and even throughout life. Connell and Furman (1984) suggested that extended periods will most likely occur when the transitional event precipitates multiple effects or when these effects in turn initiate further changes. As to the *timing* of its manifestation, not always does the transitional period occur immediately after the event, as the cases of delayed and inhibited grief reactions illustrate (Carr, 1985; DiMatteo, 1991; Gonda, 1989). Moreover, the transitional period may begin prior to the event itself. Sociologists have named this occurrence *anticipatory socialization*, defined as the patterned but often unplanned learning of a role in advance of assuming it (Brim & Ryff, 1980; Kolker & Ahmed, 1980; Pruchno, Blow, & Smyer 1989). An illustration can be drawn from research on young children whose "school readiness" may depend on the degree of continuity between the home and the school (Laosa, 1982, 1993; Laosa & Henderson, 1991). Thus, an immigrant family, concerned about their young child's readiness to assume the role of student, may informally provide in the home the kinds of stimulation that can trigger a developmental transition in the child. One may argue that the transitional event in this case is not the school entry but rather the family's concern about the child's school readiness. Anticipatory socialization can thus facilitate role transitions. On the other hand, experiencing the world through the eyes of others can also serve as a negative instance of anticipatory socialization. For example, children born in this country to an immigrant couple may come to perceive themselves as having little control over their own lives as adult workers (a self-perception that may engender ineffectual modes of coping) as a consequence of living with parents who, because they experience anti-immigrant discrimination in the work place, realistically perceive themselves in this way. As these illustrations demonstrate, caution is warranted when attempting to pinpoint the causal events in transitions because an objective, discrete event might not be the precise marker of the occurrence, length, or timing of a transitional period (Connell & Furman, 1984; Pruchno et al., 1989; Reese & Smyer, 1983).

LEVELS OF ANALYSIS

Although development may be studied at three different foci, or levels of analysis, psychological research has tended to focus on the level of the individual, typically to the exclusion of the sociocultural and the institutional levels; conversely, other social science disciplines tend to focus largely on the last two levels. This compartmentalization may continue only at the peril of ignoring factors that can help explain significant aspects of human behavior and development.

Granted, combining more than one level or unit of analysis in a single study is difficult to accomplish. It is not surprising, therefore, that efforts in this direction have generally been limited or problematic. Instances of these problems can be seen, for example, in research on acculturation (see Rogler, Cortes, & Malgady, 1991, for a review of acculturation research). Studies of acculturation sometimes suffer from conceptual ambiguity because conceptions that pertain to the group level are applied to variables at the level of the individual. There is a need for conceptual models of human development that incorporate multiple levels of analysis—as Bronfenbrenner's (1979) ecological model does, for example—and for empirical research designed to illuminate such models.

For conceptual and hypothetical models of development that incorporate multiple levels of analysis, it is important that the corresponding analytic models (i.e., the statistical model-fitting approach) take account of the hierarchies, or nested structures, reflected by the various levels, since insufficiency in this accounting can result in inefficient and inconsistent parameter estimates. Needed for this purpose are data analytic models that take hierarchical structure into account by making it possible to incorporate variables from several levels. Until recently, fitting such quantitative multilevel models was technically impossible, although sophisticated analysts have often found ways to cope at least partially in specific instances. With recent developments in the statistical theory for estimating hierarchical linear models, an integrated set of techniques now exists that permits efficient estimation for a wider range of applications (e.g., Bock, 1989; Bryk & Raudenbush, 1992; Goldstein, 1987; Goldstein & McDonald, 1988; Mislevy, 1995; Raudenbush & Willms, 1991). In this sense, the barriers to the use of an explicit hierarchical modeling framework have now been removed. These statistical techniques make it possible to test hypotheses about relations among variables occurring at each level and relations across levels and also to assess the variation at each level. Bryk and Raudenbush (1992), who refer to this class of analytic techniques as *hierarchical linear models*, noted that they appear in diverse literatures and are variously called *multilevel linear models* (in sociological research and educational evaluation), *mixed-effects models, random-effects models* (in biometric analysis), *random-coefficient regression models* (in econometrics), and *covariance components models* (in the statistics literature). Multilevel analysis is thus an area of burgeoning interest and active development. These developments may hold promise as analytic tools for use in empirical research on human development and intercultural transitions. Hierarchical linear models are certainly *not* a solution to all the data analysis problems that investigators presently face in this research area—for this purpose they are far too limited (de Leeuw, 1992)—but they are a step toward a more realistic statistical representation of the complexities involved in human development as it occurs in its diverse and layered ecological contexts.

In sum, this chapter provides a glimpse into some of the complex and difficult challenges posed by the scientific study of international migration, particularly when this theme is approached from a developmental perspective. Transitional periods in life, such as those that surround migration, provide unique windows of opportunity for the study of individuals as they undergo change and adaptation. By facing such challenges and by drawing upon these opportunities, the behavioral and social sciences can significantly advance our knowledge and understanding of the critical life transitions and stresses that surround intercultural migration and of the extraordinary—yet too often insufficiently tapped—opportunities they present for productive personal growth. The challenges are being faced; efforts are underway.

CODA

Significantly, the basic questions that concern the field of human development represent expressions of fundamental inquiry about human existence that have engaged serious thinkers in all cultures through the ages. The theme was given eloquent expression in a one-act play by the Nobel laureate Anglo-Irish author, critic, and playwright Samuel Beckett (*Krapp's Last Tape*). The character in the play is a man of advanced age who listens to his confessions recorded on audiotape in earlier (and happier) years. This portrayal becomes an image of the mystery and wonder of individual human development: For the elderly man, the voice of his younger self is that of a total stranger.

No less accurate than Wohlwill's definition of scientific research on human development, quoted earlier in this chapter, the following lines by Latin American poet, essayist, and short-story writer Jorge Luis Borges (Sheehy, 1976, p. 1) capture in characteristic poetic fashion the essence of the question guiding this enterprise:

> What web is this
> of will be, is, and was?

ACKNOWLEDGMENTS

Portions of this chapter were presented by invitation at the National Symposium on International Migration and Family Change, held at The Pennsylvania State University, November 2–3, 1995. Parts of this chapter were written while the author was the recipient of a research grant from the William T. Grant Foundation.

REFERENCES

Baltes, P. B., & Nesselroade, J. R. (1979). History and rationale of longitudinal research. In J. R.

Nesselroade & P. B. Baltes (Eds.), *Longitudinal research in the study of behavior and development* (pp. 1–39). New York: Academic Press.

Benedict, R. (1934). *Patterns of culture*. New York: The New American Library of World Literature.

Bock, R. D. (Ed.). (1989). *Multilevel analysis of educational data*. San Diego, CA: Academic Press.

Bornstein, M. H., & Lamb, M. E. (Eds.). (1992). *Developmental psychology: An advanced textbook* (3rd ed.). Hillsdale, NJ: Lawrence Erlbaum Associates.

Bornstein, M. H., & Lerner, R. M. (1992). The development of human behaviour. *The New Encyclopaedia Britannica: Macropaedia* (15th ed., Vol. 14, pp. 712–727). Chicago: Encyclopaedia Britannica.

Brim, O. G., Jr., & Kagan, J. (Eds.). (1980). *Constancy and change in human development*. Cambridge, MA: Harvard University Press.

Brim, O. G., Jr., & Ryff, C. D. (1980). On the properties of life events. In P. B. Baltes & O. G. Brim, Jr. (Eds.), *Life-span development and behavior* (Vol. 3, pp. 367–388). New York: Academic Press.

Bronfenbrenner, U. (1979). *The ecology of human development: Experiments by nature and design*. Cambridge, MA: Harvard University Press.

Bronfenbrenner, U., & Crouter, A. C. (1983). The evolution of environmental models in developmental research. In W. Kessen (Ed.), *Handbook of child psychology. Vol. 1: History, theory, and methods* (pp. 357–414). New York: Wiley.

Bryk, A. S., & Raudenbush, S. W. (1992). *Hierarchical linear models: Applications and data analysis methods*. Newbury Park, CA: Sage.

Carr, A. C. (1985). Grief, mourning, and bereavement. In H. I. Kaplan & B. J. Sadock (Eds.), *Comprehensive textbook of psychiatry* (4th ed., pp. 1286–1293). Baltimore, MD: Williams & Wilkins.

Caspi, A., & Bem, D. J. (1990). Personality continuity and change across the life course. In L. A. Pervin (Ed.), *Handbook of personality: Theory and research* (pp. 549–575). New York: Guilford.

Church, J. (1961). *Language and the discovery of reality: A developmental psychology of cognition*. New York: Random House.

Connell, J. P., & Furman, W. (1984). The study of transitions: Conceptual and methodological issues. In R. N. Emde & R. J. Harmon (Eds.), *Continuities and discontinuities in development* (pp. 153–173). New York: Plenum.

de Leeuw, J. (1992). Series editor's introduction to hierarchical linear models. In A. S. Bryk & S. W. Raudenbush, *Hierarchical linear models: Applications and data analysis methods* (pp. *xiii–xvi*). Newbury Park, CA: Sage.

Delgado-Gaitan, C. (1994). Socializing young children in Mexican-American families: An intergenerational perspective. In P. M. Greenfield & R. R. Cocking (Eds.), *Cross-cultural roots of minority child development* (pp. 55–86). Hillsdale, NJ: Lawrence Erlbaum Associates.

DiMatteo, M. R. (1991). *The psychology of health, illness, and medical care: An individual perspective*. Pacific Grove, CA: Brooks/Cole.

Emde, R. N., & Harmon, R. J. (Eds.). (1984). *Continuities and discontinuities in development*. New York: Plenum.

Emmerich, W. (1968). Personality development and concepts of structure. *Child Development, 39*, 671–690.

Emmerich, W. (1977). Evaluating alternative models of development: An illustrative study of preschool personal-social behaviors. *Child Development, 48*, 1401–1410.

Goldstein, H. (1987). *Multilevel models in educational and social research*. New York: Oxford University Press.

Goldstein, H., & McDonald, R. P. (1988). A general model for the analysis of multilevel data. *Psychometrika, 53*, 455–467.

Gonda, T. A. (1989). Death, dying, and bereavement. In H. I. Kaplan & B. J. Sadock (Eds.), *Comprehensive textbook of psychiatry* (5th ed., pp. 1339–1351). Baltimore, MD: Williams & Wilkins.

Greenfield, P. M. (1993). International roots of minority child development. *International Journal of Behavioral Development, 16*, 385–394.

Greenfield, P. M. (1994). Preface. In P. M. Greenfield & R. R. Cocking (Eds.), *Cross-cultural roots of minority child development* (pp. *ix–xii*). Hillsdale, NJ: Lawrence Erlbaum Associates.

Greenfield, P. M., & Cocking, R. R. (Eds.). (1994). *Cross-cultural roots of minority child development.* Hillsdale, NJ: Lawrence Erlbaum Associates.

Hall, C. S., & Lindzey, G. (1978). *Theories of personality* (3rd ed.). New York: Wiley.

Hartup, W. W., & van Lieshout, C. F. M. (1995). Personality development in social context. *Annual Review of Psychology, 46*, 655–687.

Herdt, G. (1990). Sambia nosebleeding rites and male proximity to women. In J. W. Stigler, R. A. Shweder, & G. Herdt (Eds.), *Cultural psychology: Essays on comparative human development* (pp. 366–400). Cambridge, England: Cambridge University Press.

Hetherington, E. M., & Arasteh, J. D. (Eds.). (1988). *Impact of divorce, single parenting, and stepparenting on children.* Hillsdale, NJ: Lawrence Erlbaum Associates.

Hultsch, D. F., & Plemons, J. K. (1979). Life events and life-span development. In P. B. Baltes & O. G. Brim, Jr. (Eds.), *Life-span development and behavior* (Vol. 2, pp. 1–36). New York: Academic Press.

Kolker, A., & Ahmed, P. 1. (1980). Integration of immigrants: The Israeli case. In G. V. Coelho & P. I. Ahmed (Eds.), *Uprooting and development: Dilemmas of coping with modernization* (pp. 479–496). New York: Plenum.

Kraut, A. M. (1990). Historical perspective on refugee movements to North America. In W. H. Holtzman & T. H. Bornemann (Eds.), *Mental health of immigrants and refugees* (pp. 16–37). Austin, TX: Hogg Foundation for Mental Health, University of Texas.

Laosa, L. M. (1982). School, occupation, culture, and family: The impact of parental schooling on the parent-child relationship. *Journal of Educational Psychology, 74*, 791–827.

Laosa, L. M. (1984). Social policies toward children of diverse ethnic, racial, and language groups in the United States. In H. W. Stevenson & A. E. Siegel (Eds.), *Child development research and social policy* (pp. 1–109). Chicago: University of Chicago Press.

Laosa, L. M. (1989). Social competence in childhood: Toward a developmental, socioculturally relativistic paradigm. *Journal of Applied Developmental Psychology, 10*, 447–468. (Reprinted from *Primary prevention of psychopathology. Vol. 3: Social competence in children*, pp. 253–279, by M. W. Kent & J. E. Rolf, Eds., 1979, Hanover, NH: University Press of New England)

Laosa, L. M. (1990a). Population generalizability, cultural sensitivity, and ethical dilemmas. In C. B. Fisher & W. W. Tryon (Eds.), *Ethics in applied developmental psychology: Emerging issues in an emerging field* (pp. 227–251). Norwood, NJ: Ablex.

Laosa, L. M. (1990b). Psychosocial stress, coping, and development of Hispanic immigrant children. In F. C. Serafica, A. I. Schwebel, R. K. Russell, P. D. Isaac, & L. B. Myers (Eds.), *Mental health of ethnic minorities* (pp. 38–65). New York: Praeger.

Laosa, L. M. (1991). The cultural context of construct validity and the ethics of generalizability. *Early Childhood Research Quarterly, 6*, 313–321.

Laosa, L. M. (1993). *Family characteristics as predictors of individual differences in Chicano children's emergent school readiness* (Research Rep. No. 93–34). Princeton, NJ: Educational Testing Service.

Laosa, L. M. (1995). *Intelligence testing and social policy* (Research Rep. No. 95–32). Princeton, NJ: Educational Testing Service.

Laosa, L. M., & Henderson, R. W. (1991). Cognitive socialization and competence: The academic development of Chicanos. In R. R. Valencia (Ed.), *Chicano school failure and success: Research and policy agendas for the 1990s* (pp. 164–199). New York: Falmer.

LeVine, R. A. (1973). *Culture, behavior, and personality.* Chicago: Aldine.

LeVine, R. A. (1984). Properties of culture: An ethnographic view. In R. A. Shweder & R. A.

LeVine (Eds.), *Culture theory: Essays on mind, self, and emotion* (pp. 67–87). Cambridge, England: Cambridge University Press.

LeVine, R. A. (1990). Infant environment in psychoanalysis: A cross-cultural view. In J. W. Stigler, R. A. Shweder, & G. Herdt (Eds.), *Cultural psychology: Essays on comparative human development* (pp. 454–474). Cambridge, England: Cambridge University Press.

Loevinger, J. (1976). *Ego development: Conceptions and theories.* San Francisco: Jossey-Bass.

Loevinger, J. (1987). *Paradigms of personality.* New York: Freeman.

Magnusson, D. (1990). Personality development from an interactional perspective. In L. A. Pervin (Ed.), *Handbook of personality: Theory and research* (pp. 193–222). New York: Guilford.

McCollum, A. T. (1990). *The trauma of moving: Psychological issues for women.* Newbury Park, CA: Sage.

Miller, T. W. (Ed.). (1989). *Stressful life events.* Madison, WI: International University Press.

Mislevy, R. J. (1995). *What can we learn from international assessments?* (Research Rep. No. 95–12). Princeton, NJ: Educational Testing Service.

Norbeck, E. (1992). Rites of passage. *The New Encyclopaedia Britannica: Macropaedia* (15th ed., Vol. 26, pp. 798–804). Chicago: Encyclopaedia Britannica.

Parke, R. D., Ornstein, P. A., Rieser, J. J., & Zahn-Waxler, C. (Eds.). (1994). *A century of developmental psychology.* Washington, DC: American Psychological Association.

Piaget, J. (1983). Piaget's theory. In W. Kessen (Ed.), *Handbook of child psychology. Vol. 1: History, theory, and methods* (pp. 103–128). New York: Wiley.

Prince, R. (1980). Variations in psychotherapeutic procedures. In H. C. Triandis & J. G. Draguns (Eds.), *Handbook of cross-cultural psychology. Vol. 6: Psychopathology* (pp. 291–349). Boston: Allyn & Bacon.

Pruchno, R. A., Blow, F. C., & Smyer, M. A. (1989). Life events and interdependent lives: Implications for research and intervention. In T. W. Miller (Ed.), *Stressful life events* (pp. 13–29). Madison, WI: International University Press.

Raudenbush, S. W., & Willms, J. D. (Eds.). (1991). *Schools, classrooms. and pupils: International studies of schooling from a multilevel perspective.* San Diego, CA: Academic Press.

Reese, H. W., & Smyer, M. A. (1983). The dimensionalization of life events. In E. J. Callahan & K. A. McCluskey (Eds.), *Life-span developmental psychology: Nonnormative life events* (pp. 1–33). New York: Academic Press.

Rogler, L. H. (1994). International migrations: A framework for directing research. *American Psychologist, 49,* 701–708.

Rogler, L. H., Cortes, D. E., & Malgady, R. G. (1991). Acculturation and mental health status among Hispanics: Convergence and new directions for research. *American Psychologist, 46,* 585–597.

Rogoff, B. (1990). *Apprenticeship in thinking: Cognitive development in social context.* New York: Oxford University Press.

Seidman, E., Allen, L., Aber, J. L., Mitchell, C., & Feinman, J. (1994). The impact of school transitions in early adolescence on the self-system and perceived social context of poor urban youth. *Child Development, 65,* 507–522.

Serpell, R. (1992). *Cultural models of childhood in indigenous socialization, and formal schooling in Zambia.* Paper presented at the conference "Images of Childhood," Sätra Bruck, Sweden.

Sheehy, G. (1976). *Passages: Predictable crises of adult life.* New York: Bantam.

Shweder, R. A., & Bourne, E. J. (1984). Does the concept of the person vary cross-culturally? In R. A. Shweder & R. A. LeVine (Eds.), *Culture theory: Essays on mind, self, and emotion* (pp. 158–199). Cambridge, England: Cambridge University Press.

Shweder, R. A., Mahapatra, M., & Miller, J. G. (1990). Culture and moral development. In J. W. Stigler, R. A. Shweder, & G. Herdt (Eds.), *Cultural psychology: Essays on comparative human development* (pp. 130–204). Cambridge, England: Cambridge University Press.

Spiro, M. E. (1984). Some reflections on cultural determinism and relativism with special reference to emotion and reason. In R. A. Shweder & R. A. LeVine (Eds.), *Culture theory: Essays on mind, self, and emotion* (pp. 323–346). Cambridge, England: Cambridge University Press.

Spiro, M. E. (1990). On the strange and the familiar in recent anthropological thought. In J. W. Stigler, R. A. Shweder, & G. Herdt (Eds.), *Cultural psychology: Essays on comparative human development* (pp. 47–61). Cambridge, England: Cambridge University Press.

Tapia Uribe, F. M., LeVine, R. A., & LeVine, S. E. (1994). Maternal behavior in a Mexican community: The changing environments of children. In P. M. Greenfield & R. R. Cocking (Eds.), *Cross-cultural roots of minority child development* (pp. 41–54). Hillsdale, NJ: Lawrence Erlbaum Associates.

Thurber, C. A. (1995). The experience and expression of homesickness in preadolescent and adolescent boys. *Child Development, 66,* 1162–1178.

Valsiner, J. (Ed.). (1995). *Child development within culturally structured environments. Vol. 3: Comparative-cultural and constructivist perspectives.* Norwood, NJ: Ablex.

Wainryb, C. (1993). The application of moral judgments to other cultures: Relativism and universality. *Child Development, 64,* 924–933.

White, S. H. (1983). The idea of development in developmental psychology. In R. M. Lerner (Ed.), *Developmental psychology: Historical and philosophical perspectives* (pp. 55–77). Hillsdale, NJ: Lawrence Erlbaum Associates.

Whiting, J. W. M. (1990). Adolescent rituals and identity conflicts. In J. W. Stigler, R. A. Shweder, & G. Herdt (Eds.), *Cultural psychology: Essays on comparative human development* (pp. 357–365). Cambridge, England: Cambridge University Press.

Wittkower, E. D., & Dubreuil, G. (1977). Relativism, cultural, in psychiatry. In B. B. Wolman (Ed.), *International encyclopedia of psychiatry, psychology, psychoanalysis, and neurology* (Vol. 9, pp. 418–422). New York: Van Nostrand Reinhold.

Wohlwill, J. F. (1970). Methodology and research strategy in the study of developmental change. In L. R. Goulet & P. B. Baltes (Eds.), *Life-span developmental psychology: Research and theory* (pp. 149–191). New York: Academic Press.

Wohlwill, J. F. (1973). *The study of behavioral development.* New York: Academic Press.

7

Factors That Impact Developmental Outcomes of Immigrant Children

Mary Lou de Leon Siantz
Indiana University

IMMIGRANT children cannot be considered in isolation. They are part of a family. Consequently, the development and experiences of today's immigrant children cannot be understood apart from the family. Family structure, dynamics, parental mental health, and parental behavior have a direct impact on a child's well-being (Board on Children and Families, 1995; Siantz, 1990b). There is a long history of research on the negative impact of difficult life circumstances on family life. For example, stressful conditions such as poverty, large families, crowded living conditions, and unemployment are related to hostile and rejecting maternal behaviors, maternal depression, and a poor prognosis for a child's development (McLoyd & Wilson, 1991).

Conversely, parenting behavior that is sensitive to a child's personality and capabilities and to the developmental tasks they face encourages a variety of highly valued developmental outcomes which include social competence, intellectual achievement, and emotional security (Baldwin, Baldwin, & Cole, 1990; Belsky, 1984; Rutter, 1990). During the preschool years, high levels of parental nurturance and control encourage the ability to engage peers and adults in a friendly and cooperative manner (Baumrind, 1971; Belsky, 1984; Luthar & Zigler, 1991). This trend continues into the school-age period with parental use of induction or reasoning, consistent discipline, and expressions of warmth (McCall, Applebaum, & Hagarty, 1973; Garmezy, 1985).

Although longitudinal studies have investigated the effects of parental characteristics on development, none has concerned the immigrant parents and children. Generalizations from previous studies have been limited to English-

149

speaking, middle-class children. Immigrant Hispanic families, especially, value their families and prize their children, a traditional value that has helped the family survive in spite of difficult life circumstances (Zuniga, 1992). However, little is known about immigrant Hispanic families, particularly the effects of parental characteristics on developmental outcome.

Recent research on immigrants has primarily focused on adults, not children (García Coll, chapter 5, this volume). Immigrant parents are "special" adults. Their family role and its impact on their children merits the scrutiny of researchers who are investigating the adaptation of immigrant children. My response to García Coll's comprehensive discussion builds on my research and experience with the Mexican migrant parents and their children, a group that is largely immigrant.

ANALYTIC FRAMEWORK

I agree with García Coll in her identification of the need for new theoretical models that can be used to conceptualize an immigrant child's developmental outcome, particularly successful outcomes. Table 7.1 presents an analytic model of the joint influences hypothesized to predict child outcomes. It is a model that I have applied in my research with the migrant farmworker family. Represented within this table are the key concepts of resilience theory: risk factors, protective factors, and child outcomes. Much of what has been presented can fit under these categories. The model builds on Garmezy's (1985) and Laosa's framework (1989) on stress and resilience and has been extended to include concepts relevant to resilient outcomes among immigrant children. The model attempts to identify characteristics and processes that predict child outcomes. In this model, differences in environment, family stress (risk factors), and parent and child characteristics (protective factors) are expected to influence child outcomes (adaptation or maladjustment). The model emphasizes the joint importance of parent and child characteristics on child outcomes.

The concept of risk implies the identificaton of biological, psychological, social, and environmental factors that increase the probability of negative out-

TABLE 7.1
Relationship of Risk and Protective Factors to Child Outcomes

Risk Factors	Protective Factors	Child Outcomes
Environmental stress	Parent characteristics	Maladapt–Adapt
SES	Child characteristics	Academic failure–Success
		Behavior problems–Mental health
		Isolation–Bicultural

TABLE 7.2
Relationship of Risk and Parental Characteristics to Child Outcomes

Risk Factors	Parental Characterisics	Child Outcomes
Family stress	Psychological state	Successful adaptation
Social isolation	Parenting style	
Chronic problems (poverty)	Access to social support	

comes for individuals (Garmezy & Masten, 1990). García Coll discusses the multiple risk factors that can affect an immigrant child's developmental outcome. Protective factors are presumed to inhibit the expression of negative child outcomes in the presence of risk.

Protective factors are those attributes of persons, environments, and events that appear to ameliorate predictions of poor adaptation based on an individual's risk status (Rutter, 1990). Werner and Smith (1992) suggested that the interaction of risk and protective factors provides a balance between a person's power and the power of his or her physical and social environment. Far less is known about these factors than about risk factors, particularly among immigrant children. Garmezy (1985) identified three factors that protect children against risks. These include the child's dispositional attributes, such as gender, cognitive ability, temperament, perceived competence, and social acceptance; family cohesion; and availability and use of external support systems by parents and children. In addition, well-adjusted children view their environment as predictable; they can elicit positive responses from it and perceive life as a positive experience. Protection results from the ways in which children deal with life changes and the stressful or disadvantaged circumstances they experience. Longitudinal research that investigates the protective mechanisms that redirect a child from a risk to an adaptive trajectory is needed.

Research has increasingly identified the importance of focusing on competence and positive child outcomes instead of on maladjustment in the presence of risk (Garmezy, 1985; Rutter, 1990). Some Hispanic immigrant children successfully adapt to their changing environment despite difficult circumstances (Laosa, 1989). Many others are not as successful. The prevalence of mental health problems among Hispanic children appears to be negatively related to their length of stay in the United States (Baral, 1979; Borjas & Tienda, 1985). However, according to Laosa (1989), these children vary widely in their vulnerability and adaptation to events, processes associated with their immigration experiences.

As Table 7.2 illustrates, parental characteristics that have been associated with positive developmental outcome include psychological state, social support, and parenting style (Belsky, 1984; Luthar & Zigler, 1991). Environmental risk factors that affect Hispanic immigrant parents' psychological state and parental behavior include (a) family stress, including the stress from the migratory experience, (b) social isolation, and (c) chronic problematic life conditions like economic status.

FAMILY STRESS

Behavior problems in children have been found to be related to maternal everyday stressors (Belsky, 1984; Hauenstein, 1992) and stress in the family environment (Billings & Moos, 1983; Hirsch, Moos, & Reischl, 1985). Some studies have shown that such stress may contribute to decreased maternal sensitivity to children (Crinic, Greenberg, Ragozin, Robinson, & Basham, 1983; Pianta, Sroufe, & Egeland, 1989) while increasing risk for maternal depression, especially among poor mothers (Belle, 1982; Siantz, 1990a). The combination of stress and depression has been found to predict behavioral problems in children and problems in peer relationships (Hammen, Gordon, Buge, Adrian, Jaenicke, & Hiroto, 1987; Garner, Jones, & Miner, 1994). A mother's self esteem in combination with poverty has also been negatively associated with a child's academic and behavioral adjustment (Dubow & Luster, 1990).

Although the stress of the migratory experience may vary with the socioeconomic position of the immigrant, most Hispanics are economically disadvantaged, with Mexican Americans the poorest, Puerto Ricans the next poorest, and Cubans the most economically secure (Siantz, 1996). These findings are based on the first Hispanic Health and Examination Survey (H-HANES) (Siantz, 1996). The stressfulness of lower socioeconomic position is compounded by pressures stemming from fluctuations in the economy, such as changes in the inflation and employment rates, which disproportionately affect those of lower socioeconomic status, like migrant farmworkers. A common finding is that the occupations of immigrants immediately after migration represent a step down from the jobs they had in their own country. Thus, economic stress resulting from insertion at the bottom of the economic ladder is an important risk factor to consider in the migration experiences of Hispanic parents, particularly among Mexicans.

Researchers have increasingly documented that poverty and lower class status are marked by relatively punitive and coercive patterns of parenting behavior (McLoyd, 1990). Poverty is also associated with psychological distress in the parent (McLoyd & Wilson, 1991). Studies have also found that children in families undergoing economic decline suffer a variety of socioemotional problems as a result of negative changes in parenting behavior. Long term stress associated with poverty has been found to impact the behavior of parents and their children negatively (McLoyd & Wilson, 1991).

In the presence of family stress, like chronic financial problems, parents have been found to be less nurturing and less responsive to the social and emotional needs of their children and more reliant on physical control and coercion to achieve compliance (Conger, McCarty, Yang, Lahey, & Kropp, 1984). Such parental behavior has been associated with an increased risk of lower social-emotional functioning as well as behavior problems in school and with peers (Hashima & Amato, 1994; McLoyd, 1990; Schorr, 1991). However, some immigrant professionals may experience little or no socioeconomic change, or only temporary status declines. The influence of migration-induced economic stress on parental mental health and behavior should not be considered until the family's economic place has been established (Rumbaut, in press).

Another source of stress for immigrant parents is the social isolation that results from the dissolution of the immigrant's supportive interpersonal bonds as well as the cultural isolation of the host country. Interpersonal, supportive bonds left behind by the immigrant in the home country are not likely to be readily or fully restored in the host society. When networks are weakened, the probability of psychological distress increases (Hashima & Amato, 1994). Living in an unfamiliar, unpredictable world can also have an impact on parental mental health until instrumental skills like English speaking ability begins to remove the primary strain. As the unfamiliar world becomes more familiar, it becomes more controllable (Rumbaut, in press).

PARENTAL MENTAL HEALTH

Parental psychological state, which includes mastery, self-esteem, and level of depression, has been found to influence developmental outcomes in children (Colletta & Lee, 1983; Siantz, 1994). Parents who experience a strong sense of mastery are more likely to be warm and accepting with low levels of disapproval when interacting with their children (Cox, 1988). Risk for depression is highest for persons who have less than a high school education (Radloff, 1977), who lack occupational rewards (Pearlin & Schooler, 1978), who have major housing problems, or who are under severe financial strain (Makosky, 1982). Depressed mothers have been found to be less accepting, as well as hostile and indifferent to their children, with little understanding of their developmental needs. Mothers who experience even moderate levels of depression have been found to increase physical, verbal, and symbolic aggression toward their children (Zuravin, 1989). Others have reported that depressed mothers are inconsistent in their parenting (Stoneman, Brody, & Burke, 1989) and perceive their children as maladjusted (Cox, 1988; Weissman, Warner, Wickramaratne, & Prusoff, 1988).

Response to problematic life conditions such as depression, however, cannot be completely explained by investigating the nature and number of life circumstances. An individual's response to stressful conditions may be better understood by considering environmental forces that are not only stressful but supportive as well (Jennings, Stagg, & Palley, 1988; Vanfossen, 1986). Not having someone to confide in and turn to for emotional support, material aid, or child care assistance among minority and low-income mothers has been associated with maternal depression (Belle, 1982; Salgado de Snyder, 1986; Vega, Kolody, Valle, & Hough, 1986).

Social support

The importance of social support in mediating parental stress has been well documented (Belsky, 1984; Colletta & Lee, 1983; Hashima & Amato, 1994; McLoyd, 1990). Mothers who are isolated in their child rearing, and who lack others to help provide periods of relief, have been found to be harsh and rejecting of their children (Colletta, 1981; Navarro & Miranda, 1985). Conversely, among single mothers, the presence of close family members and friends and the availability of practical help have been associated with fewer behavioral problems in their children (Colletta & Lee, 1983).

Although social contact with neighbors, friends, relatives, and significant others has beneficial effects, it is the match between support wanted and needed and support received that is critical (Belle, 1982; Belsky, 1984; Siantz, 1994). For low-income mothers in particular, support provided by spouse, relatives, and friends seems to be negatively associated with maternal restrictiveness and punishment (Colletta, 1981; Crinic et al., 1983; Siantz, 1990a). Other studies have documented the general effects of social isolation on persons belonging to low socioeconomic and ethnically diverse groups. In general, such individuals are more likely to experience stress because they are unlikely to have substitute sources of support in times of need (Salgado de Snyder, 1986; Siantz, 1990a; Vega & Kolody, 1985; Vega et al., 1986). Although most studies focus on mothers, most reported effects are generalizable to fathers. To the extent that social networks mediate the negative emotional and behavioral patterns associated with economic hardship and encourage parental warmth and acceptance, they may indirectly promote positive functioning in the child. In addition, the majority of studies suggest that social networks in the context of the extended family have more indirect than direct effects on the child through their effects on the mother.

PARENTING STYLE

Parenting styles that include warmth and acceptance have been found to foster social competence in children. Social competence includes an ability to engage peers and adults in a friendly and cooperative manner and to be resourceful and achievement oriented. With less sustained positive parental interaction, the child has fewer opportunities to learn and master verbal and instrumental strategies that will facilitate the initiation and maintenance of positive peer interaction (McLoyd, 1990).

Poverty, in particular, has been associated with diminished expression of affection (Conger et al., 1984; Peterson & Peters, 1985; Portes, Dunham, & Williams, 1986). With stress from persistent financial problems, low-income parents may demonstrate less responsiveness toward the socioemotional needs of their children. Research has documented that low paternal interaction and involvement with children in combination with infrequent maternal verbal interaction has been negatively associated with peer popularity, helpfulness, leadership, involvement, and communication skills among preschool children. In the presence of a negative parenting style, preschool children are more likely to develop socially incompetent characteristics such as apprehensiveness, inability to get along with others, and unwillingness to share (Parke, MacDonald, Beitel, & Bharnagi, 1988).

PARENTAL COPING STRATEGIES

Coping responses are defined as patterns of behavior that prevent, control, or help a person to avoid distress. This concept of coping assumes that when a person faces a potentially harmful event, something must be done to satisfy the demands of the situation or a dysfunctional emotional reaction such as depression will occur (Pearlin & Schooler, 1978). Little is known about how immigrant families cope with their problems, or how their coping responses ultimately affect psychological and social well-being, parenting style, and their children's development.

Three studies (1982, 1992, ongoing) with Mexican-American migrant farm-worker parents and children have begun to support the model presented. In 1982 (Time 1), the first migrant farm-worker study, which included 100 Mexican-American migrant mothers of preschoolers who were currently registered with the Texas Migrant Council's Head Start program, investigated the effect of stress on maternal depression and the acceptance or rejection of children. In this sample, 26% had been born in Mexico, 72% in the United States, and 2% did not report their birthplace. Mothers born in the United States preferred speaking Spanish, had parents born in Mexico, and averaged 8.3 years of education. This study suggested the importance of identifying mothers who lacked social support. Isolation, in combination with chronic stressful conditions, placed the mothers at a high risk for depression (Siantz, 1990b) and placed their children at risk for maternal rejection (Siantz, 1990a). The mean score of the CES-D was 14.8, which was significantly higher than the 9.25 mean score found in the general population by Radloff (1977), and only 1.8 points below the cutoff score for depression (16). Forty-one percent of this sample scored at or above the cutoff score for depression as measured

by the CES-D, whereas in Radloff's sample only 25% of the general population scored at or above the cutoff score.

Others have documented that 18% to 20% of respondents selected from
the general population reach or exceed the cutoff point for depression. Vega et
al. (1986) established, through a survey of immigrant Mexican-American
women in San Diego county, that 40% of the sample scored at or above the
cutoff for the CES-D. These findings suggest that Mexican-American immigrant women were at risk for depression. The research on vulnerability to
depression suggests the importance of identifying those mothers who are isolated or lack access to spouse, partner, family, friends, and assistance with children. Lack of access to sources of emotional support and child care, combined
with isolation, may increase risk for depression.

In Time 1, active behavioral, active cognitive, and avoidance coping were
also examined (Colletta & Siantz, 1992). Active behavioral responses were
defined as behaviors designed to eliminate or modify the stress-producing
problem or its effects. Active cognitive responses changed the meaning of the
stressful situation in the individual's mind and included defense mechanisms
such as rationalization, denial, or projection. Avoidance removed the situation
when it was too overwhelming or when resources were considered inadequate
to allow any more active responses to emerge (Lazarus, 1966, 1985). Patterns of
coping varied by age of mother, place of birth, and length of time in the
United States. The age of migrant mothers was related to use of a range of
coping responses, with older mothers being more likely to use active cognitive, behavioral, logical analysis, information-seeking, and problem-solving
coping responses. Being born in the United States rather than in Mexico was
negatively related to active cognitive, logical analysis, and problem-solving responses. Finally, mothers who had been in the United States a shorter period
of time used more logical analysis responses. By and large, the mothers in this
sample felt unable to affect their problems: Only 10% reported feeling that
they could change or do something about the situation, 14% felt they needed
to know more before they could act, 4% had to hold themselves back from doing what they wanted to do, and 72% reported feeling that the problem had to
be accepted as is. Housing problems were most resistant and employment
problems were least resistant to change.

The authors concluded that migrant mothers have a fatalistic view of their
ability to change the problems they face. Across situations, the mothers reported that their problems must be accepted instead of changed. It is likely
that this low sense of control is based on cultural beliefs about fate and the
prevailing conditions of poverty. Researchers have long reported that, lacking
the social and financial resources necessary for controlling many areas of their
lives, poverty-level mothers often have an externalized sense of control and a
feeling that their actions will prove to be ineffective in resolving problems
(Colletta & Siantz, 1992).

Although the migrant mothers had a rather poor opinion of the efficacy of help or social support, they reported feeling that problems could be more effectively solved with help rather than by individual efforts alone. This combination of feeling personally ineffective and dependent on the assistance of others may account for the fact that social support, rather than coping responses, attenuated the negative effect of these problems on depression and on maternal warmth.

When mothers feel that they must accept the situation or that they must hold themselves back from acting on the situation they are in fact more likely to respond by dealing with their emotions (affective regulation) than by acting on the problem itself. If, on the other hand, the mothers feel that the problem is likely to be influenced by actions they are likely to use problem-solving or information-seeking coping strategies (Folkman & Lazarus, 1980). Financial and housing problems were most often addressed by active cognitive coping, logical analysis, problem solving, or affective regulation. Interpersonal problems were likely to elicit active behavioral or cognitive responses.

The data support the idea that appraisal of the situation is a crucial determinant of the focus of coping. When the mothers felt they could change or do something about the situation they responded by active information-seeking and problem-solving attempts. If, on the other hand, the mothers felt that the problem was beyond their control, they tended to deal with affect: to try to see the positive side of the situation, to try to keep attention off the problem, or to remind themselves of more cheerful topics.

In 1990 (Time 2), fathers as well as mothers were considered. The majority of the mothers (54.2%) and fathers (64.9%) had been born in Mexico and preferred speaking Spanish. Mothers were again found to be at risk for depression with a mean score of 14.74. Fathers had a mean score of 12.38, lower than the mothers but higher than the mean score found in the general population (9.25). Mothers averaged 7.59 years of education, and fathers averaged 7.46 years. Almost all the children lived in two-parent households. The numbers of children in the families ranged from one to eight.

The results of this study underlined, first, the importance of parental social support for the child's peer acceptance and school behavior. Second, migrant fathers and mothers had different sources of social support within and outside the family. Fathers, in particular, sought support outside the home. Third, mothers and teachers had contrasting views of the children's behavior, perhaps because of differences in behavior exhibited at home and at school. Feeling overlooked at home, a child may misbehave to seek maternal attention. On the other hand, he or she may behave better in school out of respect for the teacher and to comply with rules. Such behavior is expected by traditional Mexican families when children are outside the home. The finding further suggested the importance of identifying mothers and fathers who are isolated or lack access to spouse, partner, family, and friends. The problem in access to these individuals, along with the consequent isolation, could have deleterious effects on their children's behavior and achievement at home and at school (Siantz, 1994).

At Time 3 (Siantz, in press) a longitudinal study is in process with 225 Mexican-American migrant children, their mothers, fathers, and teachers. It is based on a comprehensive theoretical framework that considers the effects of multiple variables (environmental, parent, child, school) on child outcomes (social, behavioral, educational). Preliminary data analyses suggest to us that the risk for depression continues to exist among both parents, with mothers at higher risk than fathers. Parents exhibit warmth and have a moderate level of social support available. Fathers reported more social support than mothers. The preschool children seem to have few behavior problems at home and at school, as measured by the Child Behavior Checklist. Multivariate data analysis is in process.

IMPLICATIONS FOR RESEARCH

Because social support is so important to the well-being of Mexican-American immigrant and migrant parents, it is an area that needs further research. Natural support systems, in particular, need to be investigated. Such systems include family, friends, community leaders, clergy, teachers, recreation volunteers, and mutual self-help groups. These sources of support utilize the earned authority and the respect of the community to influence a person's physical, emotional, and spiritual health (U.S. Department of Health and Human Services, 1995). Natural support systems often constitute the core of social, spiritual, and economic support. Longitudinal research, in particular, will help to identify which sources of support play a protective role in the prevention of parental mental health, and parenting problems and promote positive developmental outcomes in immigrant children. Building on such knowledge, we can develop culturally sensitive preventive interventions that promote the social and developmental potential of parents and their children.

CONCLUSIONS

The immigration process itself is a stressful event that directly impacts parental psychological well-being and parenting style, as well as developmental outcomes of children. Recent research, particularly among Mexican-American immigrant and migrant farm-worker parents and their children, has suggested the importance of identifying and supporting parental characteristics that are associated with successful developmental outcomes for immigrant children. These characteristics include parental mental health and parental warmth and acceptance, as well as social support for both mothers and fathers. Parents have an important role in mediating the effects of poverty and stress on the lives of their children. Therefore, it is crucial to identify isolated mothers and fathers who are most at risk, as well as to provide them with culturally sensitive social and emotional support. This action will not only directly help parents, but will also indirectly prevent or alleviate potential behavioral and social problems their children may experience.

What is unique about our modern-day challenge is that immigration is no longer only about adults but is also about children and their families (Board on Children & Families, 1995). Research, intervention, and social policy must, therefore, consider a life-span perspective that focuses on the well-being, developmental potential, and successful integration of immigrant parents and children into American society while respecting their cultures, histories, beliefs, and migration experiences.

REFERENCES

Baldwin, A. L., Baldwin, C., & Cole, R. (1990). Stress-resistant families and stress-resistant children. In J. Rolf, A. S. Masten, D. Cicchetti, K. H. Nuechterlein, & S. Weintraub (Eds.), *Risk and protective factors in the development of psychopathology* (pp. 257–280). New York: Cambridge University Press.

Baral, D. P. (1979). Academic achievement of recent immigrants from Mexico. *Journal of the National Association of Bilingual Education, 3*(13), 1–13.

Baumrind, D. (1971). Current patterns of parental authority. *Developmental Psychology Monographs, 4*(1), 1971, 223–237.

Belle, D. (Ed.). (1982). *Lives in stress: Women and depression.* Beverly Hills, CA: Sage.

Belsky, J. (1984). The determinants of parenting: A process model. *Child Development, 55,* 83–96.

Billings, A. G., & Moos, R. H. (1983). Comparisons of children of depressed and non-depressed parents: A social environmental perspective. *Journal of Abnormal Child Psychology, 11*(4), 463–485.

Board on Children and Families, Commission on Behavioral and Social Sciences and Education, National Research Council, Institute of Medicine. (1995). Immigrant children and their families: Issues for research and policy. *The Future of Children, 5*(2), 72–89.

Borjas, G., & Tienda, M. (Eds.). (1985). *Hispanics in the U.S. economy.* New York: Academic Press.

Colletta, N. (1981). Social support and the risk of maternal rejection by adolescent mothers. *Journal of Psychology, 190,* 191–197.

Colletta, N., & Lee, D., (1983). At risk for depression: A study of young mothers. *The Journal of Psychology, 109,* 191–197.

Colletta, N., & Siantz, de Leon M. L. (1992). *Coping behavior of migrant mothers.* Poster Session presented at the biennieal conference of the Society for Research in Child Development, Seattle, WA.

Conger, R., McCarty, J., Yang, R., Lahey, B., & Kropp, J. (1984). Perception of child rearing values, and emotional distress as mediating links between environmental stressors and observed maternal behavior. *Child Development, 54,* 2234–2247.

Cox, A. (1988). Maternal depression and impact on children's development. *Archives of Disease in Childhood, 63,* 90–95.

Crinic, K., Greenberg, M., Ragozin, A., Robinson, N., & Basham, R. (1983). Effects of stress and social support on mothers and premature full term infants. *Child Development, 54,* 509–217.

Dubow, E. F., & Luster, T. (1990). Adjustment of children born to teenage mothers: The contribution of risk and protective factors. *Journal of Marriage and the Family, 52,* 393–404.

Folkman, S., & Lazarus, R. S. (1980). An analysis of coping in a middle-aged community sample. *Journal of Health and Social Behavior, 21,* 219–239.

Garmezy, N. (1985). Stress resistant children: The search for protective factors. In J. E. Stevenson (Ed.), *Recent research in developmental psychopathology* (pp. 213–233). Oxford: Pergamon Press. [Book supplemental to the *Journal of Child Psychology and Psychiatry,* No. 4.]

Garmezy, N., & Masten, A., (1990). Assessing, preventing, and reaching childhood. In L. E. Arnold (Ed.), *Childhood stress* (pp. 459–474). New York: John Wiley & Sons.

Garner, P. W., Jones, D. C., & Miner, J. C. (1994). Social competence among low-income preschoolers: Emotion socialization practices and social cognitive correlates. *Child Development, 65*(2), 622–637.

Hammen, C., Gordon, D., Buge, D., Adrian, C., Jaenicke, C., & Hiroto, D. (1987). Maternal affective disorders, illness, and stress risk for child psychopathology. *American Journal of Psychiatry, 144*(6), 736–741.

Hashima, P., & Amato, P. (1994). Poverty, social support, and parental behavior. *Child Development, 65,* 394–403.

Hauenstein, E. J. (1992). Shifting the paradigm: Toward integrative research on mothers and children. *Journal of Child and Adolescent Psychiatric and Mental Health Nursing, 5*(4), 18–29.

Hirsch, B. S., Moos, R. H., & Reischl, T. M. (1985). Psychological adjustment of adolescent children of a depressed or normal parent. *Journal of Abnormal Psychology, 94*(2), 154–164.

Jennings, R., Stagg, P., & Palley, M. (1988). Assessing support networks: Stability and evidence for convergent and divergent validity. *American Journal of Community Psychology, 16*(6), 793–809.

Laosa, L. (1989). *Psychosocial stress, coping, and the development of Hispanic immigrant children.* Princeton, NJ: Educational Testing Service.

Lazarus, R. S. (1966). *Psychological stress and the coping process.* New York: McGraw-Hill.

Lazarus, R. S. (1985). The costs and benefits of denial. In A. Monat & R. S. Lazarus (Eds.), *Stress and coping: An anthology* (pp. 154–173). New York: Columbia University Press.

Luthar, S., & Zigler, E. (1991). Vulnerability and competence: A review of research on resilience in childhood. *American Journal of Orthopsychiatry, 1*(1), 6–22.

Makosky, V. P. (1982). Sources of stress: Events or conditions? In D. Belle (Ed.), *Lives in stress: Women and depression* (pp. 35–53). Beverly Hills, CA: Sage Publication.

McCall, R. B., Appelbaum, M. I., & Hagarty, P. S. (1973). Developmental changes in mental performance. *Monographs of the Society for Research in Child Development, 38*(3, Serial No. 150).

McLoyd, V. (1990). The impact of economic hardship on Black families and children: Psychological distress, parenting, and socioemotional development. *Child Development. 61*(2), 311–346.

McLoyd V., & Wilson, L. (1991). The strain of living poor: Parenting, social support, and child mental health. In A. C. Huston (Ed.), *Children in poverty* (pp. 105–135). Cambridge: Cambridge University Press.

Navarro, S., & Miranda, M. (1985). In W. Vega & M. Miranda (Eds.), *Stress and Hispanic mental health relating research to service delivery* (pp. 239–260). Rockville, MD: U.S. Department of Health and Human Services, Public Health Service, Alcohol, Drug Abuse, and Mental Health Administration, and National Institute of Mental Health.

Parke, R., MacDonald, K., Beitel, A., & Bharnagi, N. (1988). The role of the family in the development of peer relationships. In R. D. Peters & R. McMahon (Eds.), *Social learning and approaches to marriage and the family* (pp. 17–44). New York: Brunner/Mazel.

Pearlin, L., & Schooler, C. (1978). The structure of coping. *Journal of Health and Social Behavior, 19,* 2–21.

Peterson, G., & Peters, D. (1985). The socialization values of low-income Appalachian White and rural Black mothers: A comparative study. *Journal of Comparative Family Studies, 16,* 75–91.

Pianta, R., Sroufe, L., & Egeland, B. (1989). Continuity and discontinuity in maternal sensitivity at 6, 24, and 42 months in a high risk sample. *Child Development, 60*, 481–487.

Portes, P., Dunham, R., & Williams, S. (1986). Assessing child-rearing style in ecological settings: Its relation to culture, social class, early age intervention and scholastic achievement. *Adolescence, 21*, 723–735.

Radloff, L. (1977). The CES-D scale: A self-report depression scale for research in the general population. *Journal of Applied Psychological Measurement, 1*, 385–401.

Rumbaut, R. (in press). A legacy of war: Refugees from Vietnam, Laos, and Cambodia. In S. Pedraza & R. B. Rumbaut (Eds.), *Origins and destinies: Immigration, race, and ethnicity in America.* Belmont, CA: Wadsworth Publishing Co.

Rutter, M. (1990). Psychosocial resilience and protective mechanisms. In J. Rolf, A. S. Masten, D. Cicchetti, K. H. Nuechterlein, & S. Weintraub (Eds.), *Risk and protective factors in the development of psychopathology* (pp. 181–214). Cambridge: Cambridge University Press.

Salgado de Snyder, V. (1986, September). *Acculturative stress and depressive symptomology among Mexican-American immigrant women.* Paper presented at the Sixth National Conference of the Health and Human Service Organizations (COSSMHO), New York.

Schorr, L. B. (1991). Effective programs for children in poverty. In A. Huston (Ed.), *Children in poverty: Child development and public policy* (pp. 260–281). New York: Cambridge University Press.

Siantz, d.L, M. L. (1990a). Maternal acceptance/rejection of Mexican-American migrant mothers. *Psychology of Women Quarterly, 2*(14), 245–254.

Siantz, d.L., M. L. (1990b). Correlates of maternal depression among Mexican-American migrant mothers. *Journal of Child Adolescent Psychiatric Nursing, 1*(3), 9–13.

Siantz, d.L., M. L. (1994). Parental factors correlated with developmental outcome in the migrant Head Start child. *Early Childhood Research Quarterly. 9*(3&4), 481–504.

Siantz, d.L., M. L. (1996). A profile of the Hispanic child. In S. Torres (Ed.), *Hispanic voices: Hispanic educators speak out* (pp.13–25). New York: National League for Nursing.

Siantz, d.L., M. L. (in press). *A global profile of the immigrant child.* [Monograph.] Washington, DC: American Academy of Nursing.

Stoneman, Z., Brody, G., & Burke, M. (1989). Marital quality, depression, and inconsistent parenting: Relationship with observed mother–child conflict. *American Journal of Orthopsychiatry, 59*, 105–117.

U.S. Department of Health and Human Services, Public Health Service, Substance Abuse, and Mental Health Services Administration. (1995). *CSAP Implementation Guide: Hispanic/Latino Natural Support Systems.* Rockville, MD: Center for Substance Abuse Prevention.

Vanfossen, B. (1986). Sex differences in depression: The role of spouse support. In Hobfell (Ed.), *Stress, social support, and women* (pp. 69–84). Washington, DC: Hemisphere.

Vega, W., & Kolody, B. (1985). The meaning of social support and the mediation of stress of cross cultures. In W. Vega & M. Miranda (Eds.), *Stress and Hispanic mental health: Relating research to service delivery* (pp. 18–75). Rockville, MD: National Institute of Mental Health.

Vega, W., Kolody, B., Valle, J., & Hough, R. (1986). The relationship of marital status, confidant support and depression among Mexican immigrant women. *Journal of Marriage and the Family, 48*, 597–605.

Weissman, M., Warner, V., Wickramaratne, P., & Prusoff, B. (1988). Early onset major depression in parents and their children. *Journal of Affective Disorders, 15*, 269–277.

Werner, E. E., & Smith, R. S. (1992). *Overcoming the odds: High risk children from birth to adulthood.* Ithaca, NY: Cornell University Press.

Zuravin, S. (1989). Severity of maternal depression and three types of mother to child aggression. *American Journal of Orthopsychiatry, 59*, 377–389.

Zuniga, S. (1992). Families with Latino roots. In E. L. Lynch & M. J. Hanson (Eds.), *Developing cross cultural competence* (pp. 151–179). Baltimore: Brookes.

PART III

HOW DO FAMILY STRUCTURE AND PROCESS CHANGE ACROSS SUCCEEDING GENERATIONS?

8

Immigration and Sociocultural Change in Mexican, Chinese, and Vietnamese American Families

Raymond Buriel
Pomona College

Terri De Ment
The Claremont Graduate School

FOR AT LEAST the next 50 years, immigrants and their U.S.-born children will constitute more than half of both the Asian and Latino populations in this country (Edmonston & Passel, 1994). At the same time, Asians and Latinos are the two fastest growing U.S. populations due to immigration and births in immigrant families, especially among Chinese and Mexicans. By the year 2040, it is estimated that Asians and Latinos will together make up 28% of the total U.S. population (10% and 18%, respectively; Edmonston & Passel, 1994). The relative recency and size of the Asian and Latino populations means that for the next half century these two groups will be characterized by a constant process of sociocultural change as new immigrants and their children adapt to life in the United States. The direction and nature of this change will be influenced by the sociocultural ecology of the United States, which is itself being gradually transformed by the growing numbers of Asian and Latino immigrant families. Thus, unlike European immigrants who replaced their ethnic cultures with a Euro-American culture, Asians and Latinos, by virtue of their recency and size, are creating ecological niches in this society that provide more alternatives to sociocultural change than assimilation. Prolonged immigration will sustain sociocultural links to Asia and Latin America that will make these ecological niches binational in character. Consequently, biculturalism may replace assimilation as the preferred mode of sociocultural adaptation to the United States for Asians and Latinos.

The purpose of this chapter is to document sociocultural change in Asian and Latino families that occurs as a function of length of U.S. residence,

165

generational status and acculturation. The focus is primarily on two Asian subgroups, Chinese and Vietnamese, and one Latino subgroup, Mexican Americans. Together, these three groups include both economic and political immigrants. Most Chinese and Mexican immigrants are motivated to come to the United States by a desire to improve their economic status, whereas most Vietnamese immigrants have come here to escape persecution from the political regime in Vietnam. The different motivations economic and political immigrants have for coming to the United States have implications for the rate and direction of sociocultural change that members of these groups exhibit. Political immigrants may resist change in areas of family life and cultural values due to the expectation of returning to their homelands when the political climate improves for them. A change in political climate may also decrease immigration to the United States from these countries. Economic immigrants, who are more numerous, may be more open to some forms of sociocultural change in order to fulfill their economic aspirations. Such change, however, may increasingly be more in the form of adding new cultural competencies to existing ethnic competencies (i.e., biculturalism) rather than replacing them with new ones (i.e., assimilation). The inclusion of economic and political immigrant groups in this chapter permits an examination of the possible differential adaptation of these two groups.

ENDURING PERSPECTIVES OF LATINO AND ASIAN FAMILIES

In his authoritative review of Latino family research, Vega (1990) noted that contemporary research on this topic still derives its discourse and imagery from previous work on Latino families. Thus, debate about traditional family structure and values and whether or not they are either accurate or valid has not diminished. As a result of these enduring research questions, a static and homogeneous image of Latino families has become engrained in the research literature. Thus, discussions of Mexican American families have been dominated by the themes of male superiority and female submissiveness. The family is viewed as a patriarchal structure characterized by the absolute authority of the father and the self-sacrifice of the mother (Ybarra, 1983). Within the family, children are expected to learn submission and unquestioning obedience to the father and other authority figures, including older siblings. According to Baca Zinn (1990), descriptions of Mexican American families have been normative, moralistic, and mingled with social policy implications about improving family functioning, usually through assimilation. However, the benefits of assimilation are taken for granted because few studies have actually examined the process of sociocultural change to the Euro-American mainstream and any benefits derived from this change. The image of the Mexican American family as static and homogeneous is perhaps so ingrained that most social scientists think the Mexican American family is resistant to change. As a result, change-related factors such as immigration, length of U.S. residence, generation, and women's labor force participation have received only modest attention in research with Mexican American families (Zambrana, 1995).

Although anecdotal examples are numerous, very little empirical research exists on the structure of Asian American families. Among studies in this area, most have used samples only from Chinese and Japanese American populations. In addition, the size of the sample groups selected has tended to be small (Uba, 1994). Generally, discussions about Chinese and Vietnamese American families have relied heavily on the notion of the traditional Asian family, whose structure is grounded in ancient Confucian principles, which are timeless and transcend cultural differences (Uba, 1994). Confucius developed a hierarchy defining a person's role, duties, and moral obligations within the state. This hierarchical structure was also applied to the family, with each member's role dictated by age and gender (Bond & Hwang, 1986). As a result, Chinese American and Vietnamese American families are viewed as patriarchal, with the father maintaining absolute authority and emotional distance from other members (Ho, 1992; Wong, 1988, 1995). Although considered subordinate to their husbands, mothers are still directly involved in childrearing. Meanwhile, children are expected to demonstrate filial piety in the form of unfailing obedience and loyalty to their parents (Ho, 1986; Huang, 1989). Traditionally, the family exerts strict control over all its members, who are assumed to place family needs before their own. Sons are considered to be more valuable to their families than daughters because in the event of marriage, the latter depart to live with their new husbands, whereas the former remain at home to care for their elderly parents (Shon & Ja, 1982). Because this portrayal of traditional Asian families is timeless, sociocultural change is not reflected in depictions of the family. It is therefore really an ideal composite drawn from an assortment of Asian family characteristics, and does not take into consideration differences both within and between varying groups.

Recently, the underclass model (Schorr, 1988) has emerged as a popular conceptual framework for explaining the position of ethnic minority families in the United States. According to Hurtado (1995), the underclass model is nothing more than a modern version of the culture-of-poverty thesis that contends that cultural differences explain poverty and social disorganization in minority families. The underclass model blames the problems of Mexican Americans and other ethnic minorities on their culture and implies that assimilation will resolve these problems (Hurtado, 1995).

IMMIGRANTS AND ASSIMILATIONIST IDEOLOGY

Assimilationist frameworks continue to hold wide popular support (Harrison, 1992) because they suggest the superiority of Euro-American culture over ethnic minority cultures. Appropriate sociocultural change is therefore viewed as being unidirectional in nature and aimed at replacing the ethnic culture with the mainstream Euro-American culture. The European immigrants who came to the United States at the turn of the century underwent assimilation in their transformation into "Americans." Because immigrants have historically resisted change, the assimilation process was conflictive because ethnic cultures and family processes were perceived as inferior and in need of change (Ramirez & Castaneda, 1974). Ramirez (1983) characterized the assimilation process in the United States in terms of a model of conflict and replacement: Ethnic cultures and family processes are perceived as being incompatible with the cultural mainstream, which results in conflict and eventual replacement of the pertinent sociocultural systems with those of the cultural mainstream. Ramirez (1993) cited the early work of Stonequist (1937) and Child (1943) as examples of culture conflict and replacement models that have shaped the social desirability of assimilation.

According to Stonequist (1937), the lifecycle of the immigrant followed three stages: positive feelings toward the host culture, a conscious experience of conflict, and response to the conflict, which may be prolonged and more or less successful depending on the nature of the response. Three responses to the conflict were proposed by Stonequist: nationalism, which was the organization of a collective movement to raise the status of the ethnic group; intermediation, which was an effort to accommodate the two cultures; and assimilation, which was the replacement of the ethnic culture with the mainstream culture. Because the perceived incompatibility between the ethnic and mainstream cultures was the source of conflict, assimilation was viewed as the most successful response because it completely removed the inferior culture (Ramirez, 1983). Child's (1943) research focused specifically on second-generation Italian American males whose socialization occurred in a dual cultural context, Italian and American. In describing the cultural conflict he observed in these young males, Child proposed a framework based on three types of conflict reaction: the rebel reaction, which was characterized by behaviors indicating a desire to achieve complete acceptance by the mainstream and to reject Italian associations and culture; the in-group reaction, which was marked by behaviors indicating a desire to participate only with Italians and Italian culture; and the apathetic reaction, which was a retreat from the conflict by avoiding either a strong rebel reaction or a strong in-group reaction. The apathetic reaction, according to Child (1943), could be observed in individuals making a partial approach toward both cultures in an effort to find a compromise as a solution to the conflict. It is interesting to note that Child chose to view this attempt to achieve a bicultural solution to the conflict as apathetic.

For most European immigrants, the process of assimilation was completed by the second generation. That is, the native-born children of immigrants replaced their parents' immigrant culture with a new American culture and were

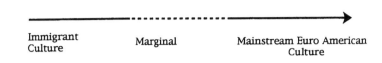

FIG. 8.1. Unidirectional model of sociocultural change.

also accepted as Americans by the larger society. Assimilation was motivated by the desire to become part of the cultural mainstream and to eliminate societal prejudice and discrimination against ethnic immigrants (Gordon, 1964; Portes & Rumbaut, 1990; Ramirez & Castaneda, 1974). Assimilation of these European immigrants was aided by the European phenotype they shared with members of the larger society, who were themselves descendants of earlier English and German immigrants.

The assimilation of European immigrants can be graphically represented as a unidirectional process of sociocultural change (see Fig. 8.1). Immigrant group members are positioned on a continuum between two cultural poles, and as they become more identified and involved with Euro-American culture, they move farther away from involvement with the immigrant culture. Immigrants were perceived as marginal when they were positioned in the middle of the continuum, away from both cultural poles (Stonequist, 1937). By the second generation, the sociocultural journey was complete as the children of immigrants became fully assimilated. Although ethnic awareness persists in varying degrees among assimilated Euro Americans, it is largely symbolic ethnicity. Alba (1990) noted that symbolic ethnicity is a vestigial attachment to a few ethnic symbols that impose little cost on everyday life.

ASSUMPTIONS ABOUT SOCIOCULTURAL CHANGE

Ethnicity and sociocultural variation from the Euro-American mainstream are enduring characteristics of American families of Mexican, Chinese, and Vietnamese descent. Although Mexican and Chinese Americans have been in contact with Euro-Americans for over a century and have acculturated to varying degrees, they have not assimilated. The non-European phenotypes of Latinos and Asians trigger stereotypes and prejudices about the "foreign" backgrounds of these groups that create social barriers to full integration into society. Nevertheless, as ethnic minority members of this society, they have had to adapt to the sociocultural context of the Euro-American majority. As a result, sociocultural diversity from the Euro-American mainstream has become an enduring aspect of ethnic minority families of non-European descent.

According to Kagitcibasi (1989), neither mainstream psychology nor cross-cultural psychology has developed a theory of the family to deal with cultural diversity. In their search for basic universal structures in the development of human relations, which turn out to be Western social constructs, psychologists have either ignored or depreciated sociocultural diversity (Kagitcibasi, 1989). Thus, the absence of a theory is a reflection of the common expectation that family diversity represents inferior sociocultural systems that are temporary and bound to decrease with modernization. As with the case of European immigrants to the United States, change is expected to be exclusively unidirectional toward the Euro-American mainstream, eventuating in complete assimilation. Sociocultural change is viewed as an aberration either when it does not take place or when it follows nonunidirectional paths. Therefore, to understand existing diversity in ethnic cultures and family processes is not of much theoretical interest to the mainstream psychologist.

ECOLOGICAL PERSPECTIVES ON THE ADAPTATION AND SOCIOCULTURAL CHANGE AMONG NON-EUROPEAN IMMIGRANTS AND U.S. ETHNIC MINORITIES

As with most children, socialization of ethnic minority children usually takes place in a family setting that includes adult caregivers. In addition to ensuring children's physical health and survival, parents attempt to inculcate values and behaviors that help children adapt to the environment as it is perceived by the parents. The parents' individual history of interaction with the larger sociocultural context, including their awareness of their ethnic group's history within the larger society, affect the manner in which they socialize their children. Harrison and her colleagues (Harrison, Wilson, Pine, Chan, & Buriel, 1990) adopted an ecological orientation to explain the diverse environmental influences that contribute to the socialization of ethnic minority children. They conceptualized the socialization of ethnic minority children in terms of the interconnectedness between the status of ethnic minority families, adaptive strategies, socialization goals, and child outcomes. Family status has to do with the socioeconomic resources available to ethnic group members, such as housing, employment, health care, and education. Despite considerable within-group diversity in socioeconomic status, a growing number of ethnic minority children live in poverty. Adaptive strategies are the cultural patterns that promote the survival and well-being of group members. Some of these cultural patterns are adaptations of the original ethnic culture to life circumstances in the United States. For instance, family extendedness expresses itself in the mobilization of extended family in response to child care needs.

Other cultural patterns may arise as a result of coping with the conflicting behavioral demands of being an ethnic minority in a predominately Euro-

American society. Thus, biculturalism, which is the simultaneous adoption of two cultural orientations, arose originally in response to conflicting cultural demands but is now part of what constitutes the ethnic minority culture. Biculturalism characterizes the lives of many Mexican Americans and other ethnic minorities.

In addition to family extendedness and biculturalism, other adaptive strategies discussed by Harrison et al. (1990) include role flexibilities and ancestral worldviews. Emerging out of the adaptive strategies of adults are the socialization goals that they endeavor to inculcate in children to help them meet the ecological challenges they will face as ethnic minorities in a class- and race-conscious society. Ethnic pride and interdependence are two important socialization goals that enable ethnic minority children to function competently as members of both their minority culture and the larger society (Harrison et al., 1990). Ethnic pride imparts a sense of self-worth in the face of societal prejudice and discrimination. Interdependence sustains effective intergroup relations that strengthen ethnic group solidarity.

From an ecological perspective, it is important to consider not only the proximal sociocultural context but also the distal or pre-immigration context for insights into the nature of sociocultural change that immigrants exhibit in the United States (Greenfield & Cocking, 1994). The economic and political motivations of potential immigrants represent one aspect of the pre-immigration context. Another aspect has to do with the self-selection factors that distinguish immigrants from those opting to remain in their native countries. Berry (1987) noted that acculturation research has paid too much attention to the contact culture as a stimulus for sociocultural change and has neglected the enduring influences of the native culture on individual development.

SELECTIVE IMMIGRATION

Contrary to popular belief, Mexican immigrants are a highly self-selected group with many psychological and cultural characteristics conducive to success in the United States. Mexican immigrants complete more years of schooling in Mexico before immigrating than the national average for that country (Portes & Bach, 1985). The vast majority come from skilled or semi-skilled occupational backgrounds that enable them to save enough money, about $550 U.S. dollars, to cross the border. This indicates they possess the psychological traits of deferred gratification and risk taking (Buriel, 1984). Psychological studies in Mexico (Fromm & Maccoby, 1970) also show that immigrants come from the most psychologically well-adjusted segments of the Mexican population. Mexican immigrants represent that segment of the Mexican population that aspires to a middle-class standing through hard work and perseverance. It is for this reason that they immigrate to the United States.

Chinese immigrants similarly possess many psychological and cultural characteristics that enable them to succeed in the United States. Originally, Chinese farmers, primarily from Guangdong province, were drawn to the west coast of the United States because of an economic boom resulting from the discovery of gold in California. It should be noted that these immigrants were sojourners who had no intention of staying very long in the United States. In fact, they sent money back home to support their wives and families still in China (Kitano & Daniels, 1988). In 1882, the United States passed the Chinese Exclusion Act, which prevented Chinese laborers from entering the country. This date marked the beginning of increasingly more discriminatory immigration laws directed specifically against Asians. However, with the passage of the Immigration Act of 1965, the nature and number of Chinese immigrants changed dramatically. During the early 1970s, a large number of professionals and their families came to the United States seeking better pay. Many were motivated to migrate by what they perceived as a large disparity between their personal aspirations and actual opportunities in their country of origin (Min, 1995). In addition, these families also had the financial and informational resources available to facilitate their move to the United States (Min, 1995). Another source of professional Chinese immigrants was the universities. Upon graduating from American colleges, many students found jobs in this country and applied for permanent residency (Min, 1995).

However, two acts were passed in 1976, which significantly decreased the number of Chinese professionals immigrating to the United States. The Eilberg Act and the Health Professionals Educational Assistance Act discouraged professionals from immigrating by requiring them to have firm job offers from American employers before coming to the United States. Consequently, after 1976, most immigrants were admitted under the family reunification category. These people had more diverse economic and educational backgrounds than the previous group. Most came from the People's Republic of China via Taiwan or Hong Kong (Min, 1995; Takaki, 1989). They also desired greater economic advantages for themselves and better educational opportunities for their children (Min, 1995; Takaki, 1989; Uba, 1994). For example, the per capita income in China for 1986 was $258, in marked contrast to the per capita income in the United States of $13,123 for 1988 (Min, 1995). Meanwhile, the potential for college admission was clearly better in the United States than in a place like Hong Kong, which had only two universities and a very limited number of openings.

REFUGEES

After the end of the Vietnam war in 1975, 130,000 refugees (first wave) found asylum in the United States. During 1977 and 1978 immigration slowed as only a small number of refugees arrived in the United States. However, in late 1978, a massive flow of Indochinese refugees (boat people or second wave) occurred before abruptly ending in 1992 (Chan, 1991; Rumbaut, 1995). Refugees are defined by the United Nations as people who have left their native countries and are unable to return because of fear of persecution or physical harm for reasons of race, religion, nationality, membership in a social group, or political opinion (United Nations High Commissioner for Refugees, 1993). In other words, refugees, unlike immigrants, leave their homeland involuntarily. Refugees also usually suffer increased psychological problems and have a more difficult time adjusting to American life than other immigrants. Furthermore, they tend to have overcome more threatening circumstances and have generally experienced more undesirable change as well as a decreasing sense of control over their lives (Rumbaut, 1991).

Nevertheless, there are some significant differences between the first and second waves of Vietnamese refugees who arrived in the United States. Members of the earlier group resided in urban areas and maintained greater contact with Americans than those from the succeeding one, who predominantly lived in rural areas. In addition, the first wave of refugees was richer and better educated than the second one (Rumbaut, 1985, 1991, 1995), who perhaps not surprisingly had more difficulty adjusting to American culture. Rumbaut (1985, 1991) characterized Vietnamese refugee adjustment as resolving both a crisis of loss (i.e., coming to terms with the past) and a crisis of load (i.e., coming to terms with the present or immediate future). Because refugees lose their homes, possessions, family, friends, social status, work, and identity, they experience a period of grieving that is sometimes accompanied by anxiety and depression (Rumbaut, 1985, 1991). At the same time that refugees are mourning their losses, they must cope with issues of survival, such as housing, work, and learning a new language. Although some refugees adapt very quickly and in the process develop a sense of self-efficacy, others experience numerous psychological problems (Rumbaut, 1991).

ACCULTURATION AND BICULTURALISM

For Latinos and Asian Americans, acculturation across generations is not a uniform process. Within each generation there is considerable diversity in terms of individuals' involvement with both the native culture and Euro-American culture. In addition, acculturation is not a unidirectional process, such that movement toward Euro-American culture is necessarily associated with a corresponding loss of the native culture. Ecological variables such as degree of societal discrimination, educational and employment opportunities, and opportunities to participate in the native culture can all contribute to variations in both the rate and direction of acculturation across generations.

Changes in any of these environmental systems (Bronfenbrenner, 1979, 1986) can affect the sociocultural nature of family ecologies and have an impact on the cultural socialization of children.

For Mexican Americans, the proximity of Mexico and the fact that the southwestern United States was once a part of Mexico create many opportunities for members of this group to participate in their ancestral culture. For Mexican and Chinese Americans, high rates of immigration result in densely populated ethnic communities that also create powerful environmental influences for retention of many aspects of ancestral cultures. Finally, for all ethnic minorities, a non-European phenotype, or physical appearance, triggers many societal stereotypes and prejudices that limit access to the larger society and its institutions (Buriel, 1994; Harrison et al., 1990). The combination of all these environmental and ethnic group influences differentially operate within and between ethnic minority groups, giving rise to adaptation strategies that do not conform to the assimilationist orientation of European immigrants and their descendants. Instead, many ethnic minority group members strive for a bicultural orientation that allows for acculturation to Euro-American culture while retaining aspects of the ancestral culture. This bidirectional adaptation strategy permits individuals to meet the dual cultural expectations that characterize the lives of ethnic minorities as they move in and out of minority and majority cultural environments. The bicultural person learns to function optimally in more than one cultural context and to switch repertoires of behavior appropriately and adaptively as called for by the situation (Harrison et al., 1990). Although all ethnic minority groups have expressed biculturalism as an important adaptive strategy (Harrison, Serafica, & McAdoo, 1984), the majority of research has focused on immigrant groups, especially Mexican Americans (Buriel, 1993a; LaFromboise, Coleman, & Gerton, 1993; Keefe & Padilla, 1987; Ramirez, 1983; Ramirez & Castaneda, 1974).

With Mexican Americans as an example, Figure 8.2 illustrates a bidirectional model of sociocultural change and cultural adaptation. This bidirectional model posits four acculturation adaptation styles for Mexican immigrants and their descendants, depending upon their involvement with Mexican immigrant culture and Euro-American culture. The four acculturation styles are the bicultural orientation, the Mexican orientation, the marginal orientation, and the Euro-American orientation. Ramirez (1983) defined biculturalism as the simultaneous adoption of the language, values, and social competencies of two cultures. Because culture is multidimensional in nature, involvement in either culture can vary along different dimensions and at different rates. Cultural involvement is represented on a scale of 1 to 5. Thus, persons expressing a bicultural orientation are those above 3 on both Mexican and Euro-American culture. The Mexican Orientation is characterized by those individuals who are primarily involved in Mexican culture. This category usually includes

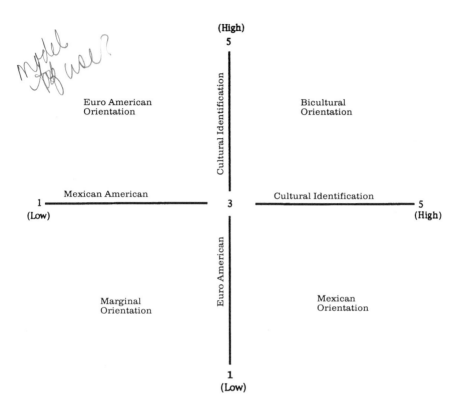

FIG. 8.2.   Bidirectional model of sociocultural change.

many adult recent immigrants as well as a few later generation persons living in rural areas. Also included in this category are the elderly parents of immigrants who are brought to this country to live with the families of their adult children after the children become financially stable. For these elderly persons, a Mexican orientation seems well suited to their life experiences, which, at their stage in life, revolve mostly around family and community rather than schooling and the labor market.

The marginal orientation includes a minority of individuals who have become deculturated (Berry, 1980; Buriel, 1984) from their ancestral culture and simultaneously alienated from the larger Euro-American society. Deculturation evolves from societal denigration of the ethnic group and the internalization of society's stereotypes of Mexican Americans (Buriel, 1984). Ogbu's (1987) description of Mexican Americans (as well as Native Americans and African Americans) as "caste-like" minorities, is probably accurate only for the minority of individuals who adopt a marginal orientation. For example, Vigil (1988) described hard-core Mexican American gang members in terms characteristic of the marginal orientation.

Individuals in the Euro-American quadrant of the bidirectional model are those who are primarily involved and identified with Euro-American culture. That is, their preference for friends, language, and social activities are those characteristic of Euro-American culture.

DECULTURATION AND MARGINALITY

With each generation, Mexican Americans lose more of their ancestral culture while becoming increasingly aware of societal prejudice and discrimination against their ethnic group (Buriel, 1994; de la Garza, DeSipio, Garcia, Garcia, & Falcon, 1995). Because the children of immigrants, the second generation, are raised by Mexican-born parents and attend school in the United States, they develop bilingual and bicultural competencies (Buriel, 1993a). However, third-generation Mexican Americans, the grandchildren of immigrants, usually grow up in households with no parental links to Mexico. As a result, much of their information about Mexican American culture comes not from their parents but from school and the media. Studies show that schools either ignore Mexican American culture in the curriculum (Carter & Segura, 1979) or present a stereotyped image of this group (U.S. Commission on Civil Rights, 1980). Studies also show that violence, deviance and illiteracy are the prevailing media themes involving Mexican Americans on TV (Greenberg & Baptista-Fernandez, 1980) and the movies (Woll, 1977). Consequently, more third-generation Mexican Americans, who rely on school and the media for information about their ethnic group, develop an image of their ethnic group consistent with the themes of violence, deviance, and illiteracy (Buriel & Vasquez, 1982). As a result, more third-generation Mexican Americans are inclined to join gangs (Buriel, Calzada, & Vasquez, 1982; Vigil, 1988) and are less successful in school than the children of immigrants (Bean, Chapa, Berg, & Sowards, 1994; Buriel, 1987; Kao & Tienda, 1995). Third-generation Mexican Americans are also less likely to attend college than the children of immigrants (Bean et al., 1994; Buriel, 1994).

Without benefit of direct parental links to Mexico and the immigrant culture that provides individuals with a salutary sense of ethnic identity, members of the third generation are at greater risk of deculturation. Berry (1980) defined deculturation as the loss of one's ancestral culture coupled with a sense of alienation from the larger society. The process of deculturation results in a state of marginality in which individuals adopt a distorted view of their ancestral culture and feel resentment toward the larger society. Thus, although marginalized individuals continue to hold a sense of identity with their ethnic group, their perception of the group is distorted through the negative group images they have internalized. Marginalized Mexican Americans are more prone to believe that members of their group are violent, deviant, and illiterate. This, in turn, becomes a self-fulfilling prophecy and may explain why the third generation is less successful in school than the children of immigrants. That is, ethnic pride motivates them to follow a cultural script of academic failure written for them by the larger society.

LIMITATIONS OF TWO-GROUP STUDIES WITH ETHNIC MINORITY FAMILIES

Research with ethnic minority families has usually relied on two-group studies to show how "culture" explains differences in family process variables between these groups and Euro-Americans. For example, a two-group study may compare Mexican American and Euro-American mothers on their use of authoritative and authoritarian parenting. Typically, these studies draw random samples of Euro- and Mexican American mothers, compare these two groups on the parenting variable, and then conclude that any difference between the two groups is the result of culture. Often, the results are discussed in terms of how Mexican American mothers are like Euro-American mothers.

However, drawing random samples of Mexican American mothers and then using group means to draw conclusions about culture is misleading because it assumes that Mexican Americans are a culturally homogeneous population. In reality, a randomly drawn sample of Mexican Americans will yield individuals who differ on a variety of culturally related characteristics such as Spanish usage and proficiency, generational status, length of U.S. residence, and ethnic identity. Because two-group studies ignore these important within-group differences, it is inappropriate to draw conclusions about the effects of culture from such studies. Moreover, by using Euro-Americans as the comparison or baseline group, two-group studies perpetuate the assumption of unidirectional assimilation by ethnic minority groups. Ethnic minority family processes therefore have meaning only in relation to their approximation to the Euro-American standard.

Especially with immigrant minority groups in transition, such as Mexicans, Chinese, and Vietnamese, it is essential to understand how family processes change in response to changing sociocultural contexts related to immigration, length of U.S. residence, generation, and acculturation. From an ecological perspective that posits that development is a response to multiple sociocultural influences across diverse settings, it is important to understand how successfully individuals adapt to their culturally diverse ecologies. The remainder of this chapter reviews literature on immigration and sociocultural change in Mexican, Chinese, and Vietnamese Americans as related to length of U.S. residence, generation, and acculturation.

FAMILY STRUCTURE

The family plays an important role in the adaptation of Latinos to life in the United States. During the first 10 years following immigration, it is not uncommon for immigrants and their children to live in extended households that include relatives and other nonfamily members (Blank, 1993). Over time, immigrants' living arrangements usually change due to economic, social, and cultural reasons. Thus, 10 years after immigration, there is very little difference in the rates of single-family households between immigrants and later generation Mexican Americans (Blank, 1993). However, as immigrants move out of extended households, they prefer to establish single households in the surrounding area, thus retaining some of the benefits of extended kin and friends, such as social support.

The longer immigrants live in the United States, the more their family networks expand. Family networks grow through marriage and birth and from continued immigration of family members. Thus even as individual family members become acculturated, the local extended family becomes larger (Keefe & Padilla, 1987). Second- and third-generation Mexican Americans have larger and more integrated extended families than immigrants (Keefe & Padilla, 1987). Griffith and Villavicencio (1985) reported that for Mexican Americans, education and income are the best predictors of contact and support from family members. In general, higher socioenomic status was associated with more social support and and contact with family members. This suggests that involvement with family is not maintained solely for socioeconomic reasons.

Involvement with family members through visits and exchange of services represent the behavioral component of familism. Another component of familism is attitudinal in nature and has to do with feelings of loyalty, solidarity, and reciprocity among family members. Unlike behavioral familism, attitudinal familism is partially susceptible to change with acculturation. Sabogal and his colleagues (Sabogal, Martin, Otero-Sabogal, VanOss Marin, & Perez-Stable, 1987) identified three dimensions of attitudinal familism: familial obligations, perceived support from family, and family as referents. They found that for Latinos, familial obligations and family as referents decreased across generations. Perceived support from family, however, remained the same despite changes in acculturation and generational status. Thus, it appears that the perception of support from family is high, even among immigrants with fewer family members, and remains high as more family members are added across generations.

Family research with Mexican Americans has often focused on how immigration and acculturation affect the adaptation of individual family members. However, the family can be viewed as an adapting entity with its own developmental processes. The family unit undergoes its own development, which transcends the development of its individual members. Rueschenberg and Buriel (1989) showed that the Mexican American family is capable of adapting to U.S. social systems while retaining many internal characteristics that are cultural in nature. Using the Family Environment Scale (Moos, Insel, & Humphrey, 1974), these researchers found that internal family attitudes such as cohesion, expressiveness, conflict, organization, and control remained unchanged from one generation to the next. Only external family variables such as independence, achievement, intellectual orientation, and recreational orientation changed across generations. Rueschenberg and Buriel (1989) concluded that, with increased exposure to Euro-American society, Mexican American families adapt to extrafamilial pressures but remain relatively stable on many important internal family orientations. In this sense, families adopt a bicultural orientation that allows them to function in mainstream Euro-American society while retaining cultural characteristics related to internal family functioning.

A recent study by Kibria (1993) found that large Vietnamese families, varying in age and gender, fared better economically than smaller nuclear families. Households with larger and more extended families stood a better chance of accessing a variety of social and economic resources. Kinship groups and neighborhood ties also provided the foundation for an expansive and complex arrangement of informal social networks within the ethnic community. In this way, households in the network could obtain various resources from their local ethnic community, such as information on public assistance and employment. Household economic cooperation can therefore be viewed as being influenced by the collectivist orientation of the family. Indeed, in Vietnamese families, the kin group is considered to be more important than the individual. This perspective has its source in Confucian principles, especially ancestor worship (Chao, 1992; Kibria, 1993). Ancestor worship for Vietnamese Americans generally consists of praying at ritually prescribed times before an altar containing pictures of deceased family members (Chao, 1992). This act affirms the sacredness, unity, and timelessness of the kin group in contrast to the transitory nature of the individual. Vietnamese family members view their kin group as an economic safety net, which is one of the factors in the creation of extended families or multiple family households.

Regarding kinship, Haines (1981) examined the question of whether migration to the United States had weakened or strengthened Vietnamese kinship. From a negative perspective, Haines (1981) noted that the exodus from Vietnam had involved the loss of relatives resulting either from separation or from death. Consequently, the size of the family was often smaller in the United States (4.5) than in Vietnam (6.5). There was also a reduction in the number of three-generation households because elderly parents often were left behind in Vietnam. Haines (1981) also found that household size, particularly regarding the number of adult workers, including women, was directly related to economic success. In fact, he found that some families pooled resources and moved toward family-owned businesses. In this manner, kinship could be used as a means of adapting to the economic demands of a new country. Kinship was also maintained and strengthened by material aid sent by relatives in the United States to family members still in Vietnam.

In contrast to cultural explanations of family structure, Glenn (1983) argued that the formation of the Chinese American family was largely determined by constantly shifting economic, legal, and political factors. Due to the immigration of Chinese males and discriminatory laws that severely limited Chinese migration to the United States, there was little or no development of the Chinese American family during the 19th and early 20th centuries. Glenn referred to families during this period as split households because the husband was in the United States working while his wife and family remained in China. Between 1920 and 1943, a second generation of Chinese Americans was born to immigrant parents (Wong, 1988). A number of these immigrants became entrepreneurs with small businesses such as laundries, grocery stores, and restaurants located in Chinatowns. All members of the small producer family worked in the business, and there was no separation of family life from work. In 1943, due to China's alignment with the United States during World War II, the exclusionary immigration acts were ended, and a quota of 105 immigrants per year was enacted. In addition to this, Chinese already in America were granted the opportunity to become citizens. The War Brides' Act in 1947 allowed Chinese women married to American citizens to enter the United States. Unlike earlier migrations consisting almost entirely of males, this new group of immigrants was predominantly female. With the ratio of males to females now nearly equal, Chinese American families began to form. According to Glenn (1983), family structures approximated Euro-American families, with a husband, wife, children, and sometimes grandparents all living together. These families survived by employing a common strategy among immigrants of pooling the incomes of the husband and wife; hence, Glenn (1983) labeled these families as dual wage earners.

SOCIALIZATION OF CHILDREN

Recent discussions of ethnic minority families (Harrison et al., 1990; Lin & Fu, 1990) suggest that parents adapt their socialization practices to meet the developmental challenges posed by changing family ecologies. In immigrant groups, acculturative pressures represent a major source of change and diversity in family ecologies. Chavez and Buriel (1986) studied the maternal reinforcement styles of immigrant and native-born Mexican American mothers and compared them to a sample of Euro-American mothers. These researchers were specifically interested in the role that success, failure, and effort played in determining mothers' allocation of rewards to children. They cited earlier work by Kagan and his associates (Kagan & Ender, 1975; Madsen & Kagan, 1973) showing that in Mexico, mothers gave almost as many rewards following failure as they did following success. In contrast, Euro- and Mexican American mothers gave half as many rewards following failure as they did following success. Kagan's conclusions were that Mexican mothers do not differentiate between children's success and failure and that Mexican American mothers were acculturating to the Euro-American pattern of reinforcement.

In Chavez and Buriel's (1986) study, mothers viewed a videotape showing a young child either succeeding or failing on a block-building task while displaying varying amounts of effort. Under conditions of high effort–failure, native-born Mexican American mothers rewarded more like Euro-American mothers, whereas under conditions of low effort–success, immigrant Mexican mothers were more like Euro-American mothers. The reward styles of Mexican-descent mothers thus did not follow a linear pattern of acculturation: In some cases, immigrant mothers were more like Euro-American mothers in their reward styles. In addition, the overall reward style of immigrant mothers was more contingent on the outcomes of children's performance (i.e., success or failure), whereas native-born Mexican American mothers rewarded more on the basis of children's effort (i.e., high or low). Chavez and Buriel (1986) interpreted these findings as casting doubt on the assumption that immigrant Mexican mothers are "just like" mothers in Mexico in their reward styles for children. The highly self-selected character of Mexican immigrants probably results in the migration of very task-oriented persons who place more value on performance outcomes than on effort. These researchers also noted that for native-born Mexican American mothers, prolonged exposure to lower societal expectations for ethnic minorities may diminish the probabilities for success and encourage parental compensation in the form of rewarding approximations to success, that is, effort.

A small number of studies suggest that despite the disruptions of immigration, immigrant family environments are less stressful than native-born family environments. Thus, McClintock and Moore (1982) found that immigrant mothers had more harmonious interactions with their children than native-born Mexican American mothers. Other studies (Casas & Ortiz, 1985; de Anda, 1984; Golding, Burnam, Timbers, Escobar, & Karno, 1985) also reported more marital satisfaction and spousal support among Mexican descent immigrant couples compared to their native-born peers. Using the 1990 PUMS data, Oropesa and Landale (1995) showed that third-generation Mexican American children are almost twice as likely to live in single-parent households (39%) compared to their first-generation (23%) and second-generation (18.9%) peers. When acculturation level is used to differentiate Mexican American families, similar results emerge. Thus, low-acculturated Mexican American parents were more likely to be low in stress and to be satisfied with family life and their spouses during the stage of raising preadolescent children than were their more acculturated counterparts (Olson, Russel, & Sprenkle, 1980). Even when chronic childhood illness is present in the family, immigrant families seem to cope better than native-born families. For example, Chavez and Buriel (1988) examined the mother–child interactions of immigrant and native-born Mexican American mothers with a child with epilepsy. The findings most pertinent to this discussion showed that native born mothers used less positive feedback and more negative feedback toward their child with epilepsy compared to the immigrant mothers with a similar child.

For a number of years, Delgado-Gaitan (1993, 1994) has been studying a small number of Mexican American families focusing on "the balance between change and constancy in socialization practices that both distinguish and unify immigrant and first-generation (native-born) Mexican-American parents" (1994, p. 59). Using ethnographic research methodology and a case study approach, she showed that childrearing is affected by generational status and participation in a grass-roots community group, organized around educational issues. Immigrant and native-born families share a common set of values including respect for elders, interdependence, and familism. Delgado-Gaitan (1994) noted that through parents' and children's participation in U.S. schools, socialization practices begin gradually to shift in an individualistic direction. A shift from Spanish to English was observed between generations. She also observed that in immigrant families children are expected to assume a great deal of responsibility by the time they are 7 years old (Delgado-Gaitan & Trueba, 1991). This greater assumption of responsibility by immigrant children is neither the result of schooling nor an indication of a shift toward individualism. She saw it instead as the other side of interdependence, which is responsibility for others.

In a recent study, Buriel (1993b) also found that early assumption of responsibility was a dominant socialization goal of Mexican immigrant parents, one that persists into adolescence. He compared the childrearing practices used by parents of first-, second-, and third-generation adolescents. Immigrant parents generally scored higher on a socialization factor called responsibility. This factor was characterized by an expectation of earlier self-reliance and an adherence to family rules within an open parent–child relationship. In contrast, native-born parents scored higher on the socialization practices making up a factor called concern. This factor was characterized by emotional support and the expectation of proper behavior at home and school. Because immigrants have smaller extended kinship networks than native-born Mexican Americans, immigrant parents may socialize children to be more self-reliant. The children of immigrants often serve as interpreters for their parents and share in the socialization of younger siblings. Consequently, a socialization style stressing self-reliance seems well adapted to the life experiences of Mexican immigrants and their children. On the other hand, native-born Mexican American parents are more acculturated and have larger extended kinship networks that reduce some of the responsibility on the children for the family's well-being. Consequently, the ecological demand to raise children to be self-reliant is not as strong among native-born Mexican American parents as it is among immigrant parents. In addition, by the second generation, and increasingly thereafter, Mexican Americans become cognizant of the socially imposed disadvantageous nature of their ethnic minority status. This awareness may motivate native born parents to be more supportive of their children and to encourage proper behavior at school as a means of overcoming their socially disadvantaged situation.

Buriel (1993b) also found greater similarity in socialization styles among immigrant mothers and fathers than among native-born mothers and fathers. Consensus in socialization styles may reflect an area of domestic interdependence conditioned by the immigrant experience. That is, because immigrants lack extended kinship networks, parents may depend more on each other for the socialization of children, which encourages agreement in parents' socialization styles. However, interdependence and consensus may be weakened in later generations through acculturation, which provides parents with different ideas and options about childrearing. Thus, acculturation may lead to greater variations in socialization styles between native-born husbands and wives.

Differences in disciplinary practices have also been noted between immigrant and native-born Mexican American mothers (Buriel, Mercado, Rodriguez, & Chavez, 1991). In responses to hypothetical situations that called for mothers to discipline their children, immigrant mothers reported they would use spanking and verbal reasoning more often than native-born mothers. However, for both groups of mothers, the most common disciplinary practice was deprivation of privileges, specifically watching TV or playing with a friend. This study also examined mothers' attitudes toward child abuse using three hypothetical vignettes of escalating violence against a child. Overall, both groups of mothers expressed a uniformly high rate of disapproval of the punitive parent and of the physical violence committed against the child in the vignettes. Immigrant mothers, however, tended to be more reticent about reporting an abusive parent to the authorities when there were no physical signs of abuse such as bleeding or burns.

There is a paucity of studies on parents and children of Chinese and Vietnamese ethnicity living in the United States. Nevertheless, general knowledge about Chinese and Vietnamese families can be gleaned from the literature, which indicates that many aspects of traditional Asian child-rearing practices were continued by Asian American families (Ho, 1986; Suzuki, 1980; Uba, 1994; Wong, 1988, 1995). Studies have generally focused on characteristics of parental control. In the case of the Chinese, it appears that parental control changes with the age of the child, with parents tending to be more lenient and indulgent to children from infancy to 6 years of age (Ho, 1986). In addition, mothers remain very close to their children, even sleeping with them during this period. However, once children enter school, they are under stricter parental control in preparation for the fulfillment of later social and filial obligations.

Differences in the child rearing attitudes of Chinese, Chinese American, and Euro-American mothers can be discerned in the areas of restriction and control as well as democratic and egalitarian perspectives. According to Chiu (1987), Chinese mothers have a tendency to endorse restrictive and controlling behavior for childrearing more often than Chinese American and Euro-American mothers. As predicted, Chiu found that Chinese American mothers were more restrictive and controlling in their childrearing attitudes than Euro-American mothers but were less so than Chinese mothers. Meanwhile, the intermediate position of Chinese American mothers suggested that the shift in their childrearing attitudes toward Euro-American ones was due to ac-culturation. In addition, Chiu also hypothesized that Euro-American mothers would probably have the most democratic and egalitarian attitudes, followed next by Chinese American mothers and then finally by Chinese mothers. However, it seems that Chinese American mothers subscribed to the most de-mocratic and egalitarian attitudes, with Chinese mothers in an intermediate position and Euro-American mothers in last place. Chiu suggested that one possible reason for higher Chinese American and Chinese scores on this scale was that parents no longer expected unquestioning obedience from their children, which seemed to indicate that families had become more democratic. However, a closer examination of the scale reveals that one item was concerned with comradeship and sharing, which are traits that would be encouraged within a family, particularly those with a collectivist perspective. Therefore, it might be possible that the Chinese and Chinese American mothers interpreted the scale from this viewpoint and not in terms of the same democratic or egalitarian attitudes held by Euro-Americans.

Lin and Fu (1990) compared Chinese, Chinese American, and Euro-American mothers and fathers in four areas of childrearing. They found cultural variations in childrearing practices among the three groups, with Chinese and Chinese American parents tending to control their children more than Euro-American parents did. This finding confirms that traditional cultural values have an important influence on childrearing practices. As in the study by Chiu (1987), Chinese mothers scored the highest on control items, followed by Chinese American mothers and then by Euro-American mothers. This suggests a shift toward Euro-American values by the Chinese American mothers due to acculturation. However, contrary to the literature on the subject, both groups of Chinese parents encouraged independence in their children more than Euro-American parents. Lin and Fu suggested that independence was promoted because it was a prerequisite for achievement. In addition, it should be noted that in Chinese tradition, a definite relationship exists between independence and achievement. According to Confucian principles, human beings apparently possess the capacity not only to change but also to control their own destinies. It should be noted that this finding is not contrary to the emphasis placed by Chinese people on interdependence. Although interdependence is stressed within the family, independence is still considered a prerequisite for success in society and a necessity in the fulfillment of filial obligations. Chinese and Chinese American parents were also not found to be any less expressive of their emotions than Euro-Americans. In contrast to what Lin and Fu expected, this result suggests that Chinese childrearing patterns are undergoing change and moving away from the traditional childrearing orientation. Although Chinese American parents can therefore be viewed as adapting to American culture, at the same time they are clearly holding on to certain traditional values. In particular, values based on Confucian principles seem to have a consistent and strong influence over childrearing attitudes.

The traditional view of Chinese parenting as authoritarian, controlling, and restrictive may also be misleading (Chao, 1994). These concepts are derived from Euro-American culture and are not necessarily relevant to Chinese childrearing. According to Chao, "The 'authoritarian' concept has evolved from an American culture and psychology that is rooted in both evangelical and Puritan religious influences" (p. 1116). Instead, Chinese parenting should be viewed as utilizing the concepts of *chiao shun* and *guan*. *Chiao shun* means training or teaching of appropriate behaviors. Parents and teachers are responsible for training children and do so by exposing them to examples of proper behavior while limiting their view of undesirable conduct. However, whereas training in the Euro-American sense is thought of in terms of rigorous discipline, for the Chinese, training is accomplished in the context of support and concern by a parent or teacher. The word *guan* means to govern, to care for, or to love, and parental care and involvement are seen as an aspect of *guan*. Thus, control and governance have positive connotations for the Chinese. Replicating Lin and Fu (1990), Chao found that immigrant Chinese mothers scored higher on standard measures of parental control and authoritarian parenting. However, they also scored higher on measures based on Chinese childrearing ideologies and on measures reflecting the concepts of *chiao shun* and *guan*. In other words, although immigrant Chinese mothers scored high on the Euro-American measure of the concept of authoritarian parenting, their parenting style could not accurately be described in terms of Euro-American concepts. Instead, the style of parenting used by immigrant Chinese mothers is best conceptualized as a type of training performed by parents who are deeply concerned and intricately involved in the lives of their children.

INTERGENERATIONAL CONFLICT

A number of studies have noted that the parent–child relationship changes with immigration and acculturation (Huang, 1989; Kibria, 1993; Rumbaut, 1995; Tran, 1988; Yao, 1985). In many cases, migration has only served to enhance intergenerational tensions. In a study of Vietnamese refugee families living in Philadelphia, Kibria (1993) found that immigration had eroded parental power and authority over children. Many parents felt that the United States had provided a cultural environment that undermined their efforts to educate and socialize their children with the appropriate values and norms of their ethnic culture. The parents attributed this to the fact that their children had been exposed to the influences of American culture on television, at school, and from peers. In addition, parents indicated that the greater economic opportunities available to their children in the United States had further weakened their control over the children. In contrast, children in Vietnam were more dependent upon their parents for financial support (Tran, 1988). However, in the United States children could easily pursue educational goals without parental help. Furthermore, parents often noticed a decline in their own social status and a corresponding increase in their children's. This was primarily because children were learning English at a faster rate than parents. Consequently, parents found themselves becoming dependent upon their children to translate for them and to deal with various institutions outside the Vietnamese community. This inevitably resulted in children holding a certain degree of power over their parents.

Nguyen and Williams (1989) examined the stability of family values among Vietnamese adolescents and their parents as a function of time spent in the United States. Adolescents and parents answered a questionnaire specifically concerned with traditional Vietnamese values and issues of adolescent independence. Vietnamese parents continued to endorse traditional values regardless of the length of time that they had been in the United States. However, Vietnamese adolescents disagreed with traditional family values, and the gap between themselves and their parents further increased with the passage of time. In addition, Vietnamese girls disagreed with traditional values more often than boys did. This finding led to the conclusion that the generation gap between parents and daughters was greater than the one between parents and sons. Nguyen and Williams suggested that the wider generational gap experienced by girls was due to the numerous changes in their roles since arriving in the United States. In Vietnam, girls were considered lower in status than boys and were not provided with the educational opportunities that were generally available to boys. In contrast, girls and boys enjoyed similar opportunities in the United States. Because girls were allowed greater freedom in this country, the frequency of conflict with their parents increased. Nguyen and Williams also noted an ambivalence on the part of Vietnamese parents regarding the rights and privileges of their children. Although parents still expected absolute obedience from their children, they did grant them certain freedoms such as dating, selecting their own marriage partners, and choosing their own careers. One attitude that appeared to be very prevalent among parents was the desire for their children to succeed in school and have successful careers. At the same time, parents did not want their children to become too Americanized.

One of the most frequently reported issues of adolescent intergenerational conflict involves autonomy (Collins & Luebker, 1994). Age expectations for autonomy consist of core values that may be resistant to acculturation in contrast to peripheral elements (such as food preference), which may change more rapidly (Feldman & Rosenthal, 1990). In a study designed to compare the differing age expectations of students from Hong Kong, first-generation Chinese Americans, second-generation Chinese Americans, Euro-Americans, first- and second-generation Chinese Australians, and Anglo Australians, Feldman and Rosenthal asked 15 through 18-year-olds to complete a time-table indicating at what age they expected to engage in certain behaviors such as attending boy–girl parties, dating, and choosing their own clothes. Overall, the students from Hong Kong had the latest age expectations for autonomy, whereas the Euro-American adolescents had the earliest age expectations. Meanwhile, second-generation Chinese Americans had later age expectations of autonomy than Euro-Americans, and the first generation of Chinese Americans had later age expectations than the second generation. In fact, first-generation Chinese Americans were closer to Hong Kong adolescents in age expectations than they were to Euro-Americans. Feldman and Rosenthal concluded that acculturation of age expectations of autonomy for Chinese Americans took place over an extended time period and that many issues of autonomy might be resistant to change. They also suggested that adolescents might be slow to change age expectations because the Chinese family was very effective in transmitting values to children due to strong ties among family members. In addition, Feldman and Rosenthal suggested that racism might also be a factor. Because of their phenotype, Chinese American adolescents might be subject to less peer pressure, as they were excluded from many Euro-American peer groups.

In describing Cuban refugee acculturation, Szapocznik and Kurtines (1980) proposed a unidirectional model of acculturation that also might account for intergenerational conflict. In this model, presented in Fig. 8.3, they conceived of acculturation as a linear function of the amount of time that an individual

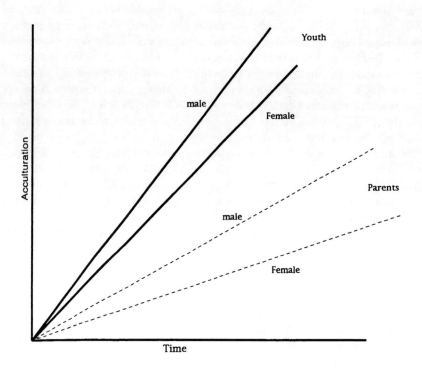

FIG. 8.3. Model of acculturation depicting intergenerational and sex differences (Szapocznik & Kurtines, 1980).

had been exposed to the host culture, with an individuals' rate of acculturation varying as a function of age and sex (Szapocznik & Kurtines, 1980). In other words, younger members of a family would acculturate more rapidly than older members. In addition, the model predicted that the most severe intergenerational conflicts due to acculturation differences would occur between young sons and their mothers.

The finding of Nguyen and Williams (1989) that Vietnamese parents have a larger generational gap with their daughters than with their sons contradicts the model proposed by Szapocznik and Kurtines (1980). In an effort to examine intergenerational conflict between immigrant and refugee children and their parents, De Ment and Buriel (1995) asked Vietnamese American adolescents and Mexican American adolescents together with their parents about age expectations for certain autonomous behaviors. Preliminary results indicate differences in age expectations between mothers and adolescents. Differences are greater between mothers and sons than between mothers and daughters, there are no differences between the age expectations of mothers of sons and mothers of daughters, and there are only slight differences between male and female adolescents. Mothers and sons seem to disagree most strongly on the age at which children should not have to tell parents where they are going. Regarding this issue, 47.1% of the mothers responded "never" (not at any age), whereas only 11.8% of the sons stated "never." In addition, boys felt that they should be able to go out on dates alone between 14 and 15 years of age (41.2%). In contrast, only 2.9% of mothers thought that their sons should date between the ages of 14 and 15. Sons also disagreed with their mothers more than daughters did on the necessity of informing their parents where they were going and on the appropriate time for returning home. These findings may conform with the theoretical model developed by Szapocznik and Kurtines (1980), who predicted that sons and mothers would have the most intergenerational conflict. The age expectation for going out on dates unchaperoned was the one area where males and females differed. On this issue, 31% of the females suggested age 16–17, whereas 41.2% of the males indicated 14–15 years of age. Overall, the greatest differences between mothers and adolescents occurred over the issues of the necessity of keeping parents informed and staying out late, as well as dating and attending boy–girl parties. The least amount of difference between mothers and adolescents appeared in age expectations for choosing a hairstyle and clothes. These differences in age expectations suggest that adolescents tend to acculturate more rapidly than their mothers. However, further analysis and evaluation of these data are necessary.

FAMILY ROLES

Immigrant and refugee families often experience changes in roles within the family upon arrival in the United States (Kibria, 1993; Uba, 1994; Yao, 1985). In some cases, husbands and wives may become separated, thus forcing one parent to take over the other's responsibilities. As a result, a child not only may lose a source of support and nurturance but may also have to assume adult responsibilities prematurely (Athey & Ahearn, 1991). In addition, because they are often the first members of their families to learn English and acquire a knowledge of American culture, children of immigrants are often required to translate and to mediate between the native culture of their families and the English-speaking community at large (Buriel & De Ment, 1993; Olsen & Chen, 1988; Tse, 1995). In a sense, a role reversal therefore occurs, with the children serving as experts in the instruction of their parents, who are novices about the complexities of daily life in the United States. For this reason, Buriel and De Ment (1993) have referred to children in this role as *children cultural brokers.* In their research with college students who had served as cultural brokers during childhood, Buriel and De Ment found that students persisted in this role even after their parents had learned English. Thus, several college students of Mexican, Chinese, and Vietnamese descent described how they were still required to make doctor appointments, translate documents, and negotiate business transactions for their parents. Even when there were other English-speaking siblings at home, these students were sought out by parents to perform brokering tasks. This sometimes created tensions between siblings who felt that the cultural broker had too much authority in family decisions. This tension was exacerbated by the fact that the cultural broker was often not the eldest child, who might be expected to hold more authority than the younger children. It appears that for some children, the role of cultural broker is a lifelong responsibility that continues even after parents have lived in the United States for many years and have learned English.

One example of a change in roles has occurred with Vietnamese refugee women, who have experienced a shift in the balance of resources between themselves and men upon arriving in the United States (Kibria, 1990, 1993). Many of the men, used to the privileged status associated with their middle-class careers in Vietnam, have now been forced to perform low-level service jobs in the United States (Kibria, 1993). On the other hand, women have experienced an expansion in their household activities, thus giving them greater access to resources and power. Not only do they continue to perform housekeeping chores and child care, but they also frequently act as liaisons between the household and outside social institutions containing resources that are essential to the family (Kibria, 1993). In fact, many Vietnamese women are responsible for interacting with large, complex bureaucracies in the utility industry as well as in public and private health care. In a real sense, women's contacts outside the home have grown, whereas men's have shrunk. These new opportunities have provided women not only with increased responsibility but also with increased control over the household's social and economic resources (Kibria, 1993). However, Kibria also found that the greater equality experienced by these women has not resulted in the restructuring of gender roles in Vietnamese American families. In fact, most Vietnamese American women continue desiring to preserve the traditional family structure.

ETHNIC IDENTITY

Ethnic identity has been defined as the manner in which individuals define themselves in terms of their ethnic group (Phinney, 1990; Uba, 1994). This definition also consists of beliefs, attitudes, values, and behavioral norms that are shared by a particular ethnic group (Rotheram & Phinney, 1987; Uba, 1994). In her review of ethnic identity in adolescents and adults, Phinney (1990) discussed it as an aspect of acculturation. Acculturation is concerned with changes in cultural attitudes, values, and behaviors that result from contact between two different cultures (Berry, 1980). In general, the group and how it relates to the dominant culture is emphasized in research. In contrast, the focus of research on ethnic identity is on individuals and how they relate to their own group's within the context of a dominant group.

An important question is how ethnic identity changes when there is contact with another group. There have been very few longitudinal studies examining this question (Phinney, 1990). However, some studies have investigated changes in ethnic identity relating to generational status. Ting-Toomey (1981, as cited in Phinney, 1990) found that ethnic identity became more important in third- and fourth-generation Chinese Americans compared to their first- and second-generation peers. In addition, Rosenthal and Feldman (1990) presented another interesting finding concerning generational changes in the ethnic identity of adolescent Chinese immigrants. They found that although knowledge of one's ethnic group and ethnic behavior decreased between the first and second generation, the second generation still maintained a positive view of their ethnicity. Rosenthal and Feldman therefore concluded that although behavioral elements of ethnic identity declined with subsequent generations, Chinese immigrants retained a commitment to their culture of origin across generations.

In his study on ethnic identity, Rumbaut (1995) identified four main types of identities: an ancestral or national origin identity, such as Mexican or Vietnamese; a hyphenated identity such as Chinese American; an assimilative or American identity; and a panethnic identity, such as Asian or Hispanic. Rumbaut concluded from an extensive survey of various ethnic minority adolescents in San Diego and Miami that ethnic identity is a gendered process. His results indicated that males were more likely to identify themselves as being American or from their country of origin. Females, on the other hand, were more inclined to assume a hyphenated identity. According to Rumbaut, these results suggested that the boundaries between ethnic identities were more fluid for girls. Ting-Toomey (1981, as cited in Phinney, 1990) also found gender differences in the ethnic identities of Chinese American college students, with female students more oriented to their ancestral culture than male students were. Rumbaut (1995) concluded that factors such as place of birth, citizenship status, language preference, and discrimination also influenced the processes of ethnic identification. For example, individuals born in the United States, had a parent born in the United States, possessed an American citizenship, or preferred to speak English, were more likely to select an American identity. On the other hand, foreign-born persons, those speaking a non-English language, and those who were not U.S. citizens were more inclined to choose an ancestral identity. Rumbaut also suggested that a panethnic identity was more probable if adolescents attended inner-city schools composed primarily of ethnic minorities. In this regard, Espiritu (1992) pointed out that panethnic identity was more likely to occur in various situations where the shifting of affiliations from smaller groups to larger ones served to protect and promote collective interests. For example, the enormous problems of poverty and crime faced by inner-city youths provided numerous reasons for their assuming a panethnic identity.

Buriel and Cardoza (1993) examined the intergenerational transmission of ethnic identity among Mexican Americans by comparing the preferred ethnic labels of parents and children. The overwhelming majority of parents preferred the label of Mexican (70% for mothers and 77% for fathers). Mexican American was the next most popular choice (15% mothers and 13% fathers), with less than 6% choosing any of the other labels. Students were fairly evenly divided between the choice of Mexican (39%) and Mexican American (40%). Chicano was chosen by 10% of the students, and Hispanic and Latino were selected by 7% and 3%, respectively. In general, students calling themselves Mexican were mostly foreign born (first generation) and had parents who were also foreign born and called themselves Mexican. Students calling themselves Mexican American were primarily second and third generation. If the students were second generation, they came from homes where parents were foreign born and very likely to call themselves Mexican. However, if the students were third generation, they were very likely to have parents who called themselves Mexican American. The greatest continuity in intrafamilial labeling therefore occurred in families of first- and third-generation students. On the other hand, the biggest discontinuity appeared in the families of second-generation students: Parents called themselves Mexican, and children referred to themselves primarily as Mexican Americans and, to a lesser extent, Chicano.

The biggest shift in ethnic labeling occurred between the first and second generation as children moved from a predominately Mexican ethnic identity to a predominately Mexican American ethnic identity. Nevertheless, the label of Mexican persisted among students even into the third generation. In fact, the label of Mexican was preferred by more third-generation students (18%) than by second-generation students (10%). Because awareness of discrimination increases across generations, some third-generation adolescents may experience disillusionment with their "American" status. As a result, they may eschew a Mexican American identity in favor of an exclusively Mexican identity.

SUMMARY

Sociocultural change is measured as a function of length of U.S. residence, generation, and level of acculturation. Length of U.S. residence is useful in marking change within a given cohort of immigrants. Generational status is helpful in documenting changes between parents and children as well as in making comparisons between same-age cohorts who are foreign or native born. A generational approach is advantageous for studying immigrant groups because it does not assume that immigrants and later generation members of their group are alike in terms of important family characteristics. Acculturation level is also an important marker of sociocultural change that is partially independent of length of U.S. residence and generation. The multidimentional nature of some acculturation scales offers the possibility of relating family changes in immigrant groups to specific cultural variables such as language or values.

Using these three approaches, sociocultural changes have been described in Mexican, Chinese, and Vietnamese American families in the areas of family structure, childrearing, intergenerational conflict, family roles, and ethnic identity. Immigrant families of these three groups seemed poised for change even before their journey to this country inasmuch as they represent very self-selected groups within their country of origin. Usually, immigrants exhibit more years of schooling than the national average for their country of origin, a strong work ethic, and favorable personality and family characteristics. These self-selected characteristics probably lead to the motivation to immigrate and also aid in the immigrants' adaptation to their new environment in the United States. Lacking extended family networks in the United States, unrelated immigrant families often share housing until they have enough resources to support a single-family dwelling. Thereafter, related families tend to live in close proximity to each other, and familism, in the form of visiting and exchange of resources, increases across generations. The initial absence of extended family support networks also encourages parents to stress self-reliance and success as socialization goals for children in order for them to develop responsibility for others in the family. Because successful adaptation depends on family members working in harmony to support each other, it is not surprising that immigrant parents are more supportive of each other and experience greater marital harmony than their U.S.-born counterparts.

Today, Mexican, Chinese, and Vietnamese American immigrant families face different social ecologies than earlier European immigrants. In the case of Mexican Americans, there is a geographical and historical connection between Mexico and the United States that diminishes the psychological and cultural distance between these two countries for members of this group. For Mexican and Chinese Americans there is also a constant flow of new immigrants that creates a perpetual first generation and a steady infusion of traditional cultural characteristics. Finally, for Mexican, Chinese, and Vietnamese Americans who exhibit a non-European phenotype or physical appearance, there is a constant reminder of their ethnicity or "otherness" within Euro-American society. These differences in social ecologies mean that these three groups will evolve adaptation strategies uniquely suited to their particular life circumstances in this country.

The studies reviewed here suggest that sociocultural change in immigrant families and their descendants do not always reflect a complete adoption or assimilation of mainstream cultural values and behaviors. Instead, change appears to assume, in many cases, an intermediate or bicultural position that incorporates aspects of both the parent culture and mainstream Euro-American culture. Thus, family member often develop cultural competencies necessary for dealing in public with Euro-Americans while interacting in culturally prescribed ways with family members and members of their ethnic group. Often, family interaction patterns and childrearing continue to reflect aspects of the parent culture into the second and third generation.

Although some traditional cultural patterns in the area of family functioning are sustained across generations, intergenerational conflicts between parents and children nevertheless arise, particularly in the realm of individual autonomy. The American core value of individualism, which is introduced through schools, the media, and cross-cultural friendships, is highly attractive to children of immigrant families. Although the findings are mixed, the greatest tensions appear to take place between immigrant mothers and their sons. As the primary socialization agent in immigrant families, mothers' efforts to transmit traditional values to boys probably meet with greater resistance because boys are typically given greater freedom than girls to explore new cultural avenues outside the home. In cases of intergenerational conflict, parents appear to compromise more on superficial cultural changes such as clothing styles and foods. On the other hand, parents appear hold the line more on core cultural values such as dating practices and family obligations. There is some evidence that refugee immigrants may experience more intergenerational conflict than economic immigrants. The anticipation of returning to the homeland when political conditions improve may motivate refugee immigrant parents to try harder to preserve traditional cultural values relative to economic immigrant parents who have voluntarily come to this country. The fact that children must often serve as interpreters or cultural brokers for immigrant parents may further exacerbate intergenerational conflict. By having to rely on children for conducting public transactions in English, parents may feel that their authority over children is undermined. Because children cultural brokers have adult responsibilities in public and then revert to a subordinate role at home, they may grow resentful of the shifting expectations parents have for them. At the same time, however, children cultural brokers may develop more insight and empathy for their parents' acculturative struggles because parents must often confide information that is personal in nature.

Despite changes in behaviors due to acculturation, an enduring ethnic identity seems characteristic of Mexican, Chinese, and Vietnamese Americans. Identity in the immigrant generation usually mirrors the national identity of the country of origin, suggesting that for members of this group the frame of reference is still the homeland. In later generations the frame of reference shifts to the United States and individuals develop identities as ethnic

Americans (e.g., Mexican American). As the frame of reference shifts, however, there may be a growing awareness of societal prejudice and discrimination against one's ethnic group. One response for smaller Asian subgroups has been to unite around a panethnic identity to strengthen group solidarity. On the other hand, due to their large numbers, most U.S.-born persons of Mexican descent express a Mexican American ethnic identity even into the third generation.

Immigrants and their children make up the majority of persons in the United States who are of Mexican, Chinese, and Vietnamese descent. Immigration projections for two of these groups, Mexicans and Chinese, suggest that immigrant families will continue to be the norm in these populations for the next half century. As a result, sociocultural change will constitute an enduring characteristic of these groups. Because these groups have often been portrayed in the literature as static and culturally homogeneous, very little research with them has focused on the nature of sociocultural change at the level of the individual or of the family. What little we know today about sociocultural change in these groups suggests that they have resisted complete assimilation and have instead developed various bicultural forms of adaptation to life in American society.

REFERENCES

Alba, R. D. (1990). *Ethnic identity.* New Haven: Yale University Press.

Athey, J. L., & Ahearn, F. L. (1991). The mental health of refugee children: An overview. In F. L. Ahearn & J. A. Garrison (Eds.), *Refugee children: Theory, research and services* (pp. 3–19). Baltimore: Johns Hopkins University Press.

Baca Zinn, M. (1990). Family, feminism, and race in America. *Gender and Society, 4,* 68–82.

Bean, F. D., Chapa, J., Berg, R. R., & Sowards, K. (1994). Educational and sociodemographic incorporation among Hispanic immigrants to the United States. In B. Edmonston & J. S. Passel (Eds.), *Immigration and ethnicity: The integration of America's newest arrivals* (pp. 73–100). Washington, DC: The Urban Institute.

Berry, J. W. (1980). Acculturation as varieties of adaptation. In A. M. Padilla (Ed.), *Acculturation: Theory, models, and some new findings* (pp. 9–25). Boulder, CO: Westview Press.

Berry, J. W. (1987, August). *Ecological analyses for acculturation research.* Paper presented at the International Association for Cross-Cultural Psychology, New Castle, Australia.

Blank, S. (1993). *Household formation and Mexican immigrants: An alternative strategy for meeting the goals of recent migration.* Paper presented at the 20th annual Center for Studies of the Family Conference, Brigham Young University, Provo, Utah.

Bond, M. H., & Hwang, K. K. (1986). The social psychology of Chinese people. In M. H. Bond (Ed.), *The psychology of the Chinese people* (pp. 171–212). New York: Oxford University Press.

Bronfenbrenner, U. (1979). *The ecology of human development.* Cambridge, MA: Harvard University Press.

Bronfenbrenner, U. (1986). Ecology of the family as a context for human development: Research perspectives. *Developmental Psychology, 22,* 723–742.

Buriel, R. (1984). Integration with traditional Mexican American culture and sociocultural adjustment. In J. L. Martinez & R. Mendoza (Eds.), *Chicano psychology* (2nd ed., pp. 95–130). New York: Academic Press.

Buriel, R. (1987). *Academic performance of foreign- and native-born Mexican Americans: A comparison of first-, second-, and third-generation students and parents.* (New Directions for Latino Public Policy Research, Working Paper No. 14.) New York: Inter-University Program for Latino Research and the Social Science Research Council.

Buriel, R. (1993a). Acculturation, respect for cultural differences, and biculturalism among three generations of Mexican American and Euro American school children. *The Journal of Genetic Psychology, 154*, 531–543.

Buriel, R. (1993b). Childrearing orientations in Mexican American families: The influence of generation and sociocultural factors. *The Journal of Marriage and the Family, 55*, 987–1000.

Buriel, R. (1994). Immigration and education of Mexican Americans. In A. Hurtado & E. E. Garcia (Eds.), *The educational achievement of Latinos: Barriers and successes* (pp. 197–226). Santa Cruz: Regents of the University of California.

Buriel, R., Calzada, S., & Vasquez, R. (1982). The relationship of traditional Mexican American culture to adjustment and delinquency among three generations of Mexican American male adolescents. *Hispanic Journal of Behavioral Sciences, 4*, 41–55.

Buriel, R., & Cardoza, D. (1993). Mexican American ethnic labeling: An intrafamilial and inter-generational analysis. In M. Bernal & G. Knight (Eds.), *Ethnic identity* (pp. 197–210). Albany, NY: State University of New York Press.

Buriel, R., & De Ment, T. (1993). *Children as cultural brokers: Recollections of college students.* Unpublished manuscript, Pomona College, Claremont, CA.

Buriel, R., Mercado, R., Rodriguez, J., & Chavez, J. M. (1991). Mexican American disciplinary practices and attitudes toward child maltreatment: A comparison of foreign- and native-born mothers. *Hispanic Journal of Behavioral Sciences, 13*, 78–94.

Buriel, R., & Vasquez, R. (1982). Stereotypes of Mexican descent persons: Attitudes of three generations of Mexican American and Anglo American adolescents. *Journal of Cross-Cultural Psychology, 13*, 59–70.

Carter, T. P., & Segura, R. D. (1979). *Mexican Americans in school: A decade of change.* New York: College Entrance Examination Board.

Casas, J. M., & Ortiz, S. (1985). Exploring the applicability of the dyadic adjustment scale for assessing level of marital adjustment with Mexican Americans. *Journal of Marriage and the Family, 47*, 1023–1027.

Chan, S. (1991). *Asian Americans: An interpretive history.* Boston: Twayne Publishers.

Chao, C. M. (1992). The inner heart: Therapy with Southeast Asian families. In L. A. Vargas & J. D. Koss-Chioino (Eds.), *Working with culture: Psychotherapeutic intervention with ethnic minority children and adolescents* (pp. 157–181). San Francisco: Jossey-Bass.

Chao, R. K. (1994). Beyond parental control and authoritarian parenting style: Understanding Chinese parenting through the cultural notion of training. *Child Development, 65*, 1111–1119.

Chavez, J. M., & Buriel, R. (1986). Reinforcing children's effort: A comparison of immigrant, native-born Mexican mothers. *Hispanic Journal of Behavioral Sciences, 8*, 127–142.

Chavez, J. M., & Buriel, R. (1988). Mother–child interactions involving a child with epilepsy: A comparison of immigrant and native-born Mexican Americans. *Journal of Pediatric Psychology, 13*, 349–361.

Child, I. L. (1943). *Italian or American: The second generation in conflict.* New Haven: Yale University Press.

Chiu, L. H. (1987). Child-rearing attitudes of Chinese, Chinese-American, and Anglo-American mothers. *International Journal of Psychology, 22*, 409–419.

Collins, A. W., & Luebker, C. (1994). Parent and adolescent expectancies: Individual and relational significance. In J. G. Smetana (Ed.), Beliefs about parenting: Origins and developmental implications (pp. 65–80). *New Directions for Child Development*, No. 66. San Francisco: Jossey-Bass.

de Anda, D. (1984). Informal support networks of Hispanic mothers: A comparison across age groups. *Journal of Social Service Research*, 7, 89–105.

de la Garza, R. O., DeSipio, L., Garcia, F. C., Garcia, J., & Falcon, A. (1995). *Latino voices: Mexican, Puerto Rican, and Cuban perspectives on American politics*. Boulder, CO: Westview Press.

De Ment, T., & Buriel, R. (1995). *Intergenerational conflict in Mexican and Vietnamese immigrant adolescents*. Unpublished manuscript, Pomona College, Claremont, CA.

Delgado-Gaitan, C. (1993). Parenting in two generations of Mexican American families. *International Journal of Behavioral Development*, 16, 409–427.

Delgado-Gaitan, C. (1994). Socializing young children in Mexican-American families: An intergenerational perspective. In P. M. Greenfield & R. R. Cocking (Eds.), *Cross-cultural roots of minority child development* (pp. 55–86). Hillsdale, NJ: Lawrence Erlbaum Associates.

Delgado-Gaitan, C., & Trueba, H. (1991). *Crossing cultural borders: The education of immigrant families in America*. London: Falmer.

Edmonston, B., & Passel, J. S. (1994). The future immigrant population of the United States. In B. Edmonston & J. S. Passel (Eds.), *Immigration and ethnicity* (pp. 317–353). Washington, DC: The Urban Institute.

Espiritu, Y. L. (1992). *Asian American panethnicity: Bridging institutions and identities*. Philadelphia: Temple University Press.

Feldman, S. S., & Rosenthal, D. A. (1990). The acculturation of autonomy expectations in Chinese highschoolers residing in two Western nations. *International Journal of Psychology*, 25, 259–281.

Fromm, E., & Maccoby, M. (1970). *Social character in a Mexican village*. Englewood Cliffs, NJ: Prentice-Hall.

Glenn, E. N. (1983). Split households, small producers and dual wage earners: An analysis of Chinese-American family strategies. *Journal of Family and Marriage*, 45, 55–46.

Golding, J. M., Burnam, M. A., Timbers, D. M., Escobar, J. I., & Karno, M. (1985, August). *Acculturation and distress: Social psychological mediators*. Paper presented at the annual meeting of the American Psychological Association, Los Angeles, CA.

Gordon, M. M. (1964). *Assimilation in American life*. New York: Oxford University Press.

Greenberg, B. S., & Baptista-Fernandez, P. (1980). Hispanic Americans: The new minority on television. In B. S. Greenberg (Ed.), *Life on television: Content analysis of U.S. TV drama* (pp. 3–12). Norwood, NJ: Ablex.

Greenfield, P. M., & Cocking, R. R. (1994). *Cross-cultural roots of minority child development*. Hillsdale, NJ: Lawrence Erlbaum Associates.

Griffith, J., & Villavicencio, S. (1985). Relationships among acculturation, sociodemographic characteristics, and social supports in Mexican American adults. *Hispanic Journal of Behavioral Sciences*, 7, 75–92.

Haines, D. (1981). Family and community among Vietnamese refugees. *International Migration Review*, 15, 310–319.

Harrison, L. E. (1992). *Who prospers: How cultural values shape economic and political success*. New York: Basic Books.

Harrison, A. O., Serafica, F., & McAdoo, H. (1984). Ethnic families of color. In R. D. Parke (Ed.), *The family: Review of child development research* (Vol. 7, pp. 329–371). Chicago: University of Chicago Press.

Harrison, A. O., Wilson, M. N., Pine, C. J., Chan, S. Q., & Buriel, R. (1990). Family ecologies of ethnic minority children. *Child Development*, 61, 347–362.

Ho, D. Y. F. (1986). Chinese patterns of socialization: A critical review. In M. H. Bond (Ed.), *The psychology of the Chinese people* (pp. 1–37). New York: Oxford University Press.

Ho, M. K. (1992). *Minority children and adolescents in therapy*. Newbury Park, CA: Sage.

Huang, L. N. (1989). Southeast Asian refugee children and adolescents. In J. J. Gibbs & K. L. Huang & Associates (Eds.), *Children of color: Psychological interventions with minority youth* (pp. 278–321). San Francisco: Jossey-Bass.

Hurtado, A. (1995). Variations, combinations, and evolutions: Latino families in the United States. In R. E. Zambrana (Ed.), *Understanding Latino families: Scholarship, policy and practice* (pp. 40–61). Newbury Park, CA: Sage.

Kagan, S., & Ender, P. B. (1975). Maternal response to success and failure of Anglo American, Mexican American, and Mexican children. *Child Development, 46*, 452–458.

Kagitcibasi, C. (1989). Family and socialization in cross-cultural perspective: A model of change. In J. J. Berman (Ed.), *Nebraska Symposium on Motivation 1989: Cross-cultural perspectives* (pp. 135–200). Lincoln, NE: University of Nebraska Press.

Kao, G., & Tienda, M. (1995). Optimism and achievement: The educational performance of immigrant youth. *Social Science Quarterly, 76*, 1–19.

Keefe, S. E., & Padilla, A. M. (1987). *Chicano ethnicity.* Albuquerque: University of New Mexico Press.

Kibria, N. (1990). Power, patriarchy, and gender conflict in the Vietnamese immigrant community. *Gender and Society, 4*, 9–24.

Kibria, N. (1993). *Family tightrope: The changing lives of Vietnamese Americans.* Princeton, NJ: Princeton University Press.

Kitano, H., & Daniels, R. (1988). *Asian American: Emerging minorities.* Englewood Cliffs, NJ: Prentice-Hall.

LaFromboise, T., Coleman, H. L. K., & Gerton, J. (1993). Psychological impact of biculturalism: Evidence and theory. *Psychological Bulletin, 114*, 395–412.

Lin, C. Y., & Fu, V. (1990). A comparison of child-rearing practices among Chinese, immigrant Chinese, and Caucasian-American parents. *Child Development, 61*, 429–433.

Madsen, M. C., & Kagan, S. (1973). Mother-directed achievement of children in two cultures. *Journal of Cross-Cultural Psychology, 4*, 221–228.

McClintock, E., & Moore, J. W. (1982). *Interactional styles of immigrant and later generation Mexican American mother–child pairs.* Paper presented at the Second Symposium on Chicano Psychology, University of California, Riverside.

Min, P. G. (1995). An overview of Asian Americans. In P. G. Min (Ed.), *Asian Americans: Contemporary trends and issues* (pp. 10–37). Newbury Park, CA: Sage.

Moos, R. H., Insel, P. M., & Humphrey, B. (1974). *Manual for the Family Environment Scale.* Palo Alto, CA: Consulting Psychologists Press.

Nguyen, N. A., & Williams, H. L. (1989). Transition from east to west: Vietnamese adolescents and their parents. *Journal of American Academy of Child and Adolescent Psychiatry, 28*, 505–515.

Ogbu, J. V. (1987). Variability in minority responses to schooling: Nonimmigrants vs. immigrants. In G. Spindler & L. Spindler (Eds.), *Interpretive ethnography of education: At home and abroad* (pp. 255–280). Hillsdale, NJ: Lawrence Erlbaum Associates.

Olsen, L., & Chen, M. T. (1988). *Crossing the schoolhouse border: Immigrant students and the California public schools.* San Francisco: California Tomorrow.

Olsen, D. H., Russell, C. S., & Sprenkle, D. H. (1980). Circumplex model of marital and family systems: II. Empirical studies and clinical interventions. In J. P. Vincent (Ed.), *Advances in family interventions, assessment, and theory* (Vol. 1, pp. 128–176). Greenwich, CT: JAI Press.

Oropesa, R. S., & Landale, N. S. (1995). *Immigrant legacies: the socioeconomic circumstances of children by ethnicity and generation in the United States.* Working Paper 95–01R, Population Research Institute, Pennsylvania State University, University Park, PA.

Phinney, J. (1990). Ethnic identity in adolescents and adults: Review of research. *Psychological Bulletin, 108*, 499–514.

Portes, A., & Bach, R. (1985). *Latin journey.* Berkeley: University of California Press.

Portes, A., & Rumbaut, R. G. (1990). *Immigrant America*. Berkeley: University of California Press.

Ramirez, M., III. (1983). *Psychology of the Americas*. Elmsford, NY: Pergamon.

Ramirez, M. III, & Castaneda, A. (1974). *Cultural democracy, bicognitive, development and education*. New York: Academic Press.

Rosenthal, D. A., & Feldman, S. (1990). The acculturation of Chinese immigrants: Perceived effects on family functioning of length of residence in two cultural contexts. *Journal of Genetic Psychology, 151*, 495–514.

Rotheram, M. J., & Phinney, J. S. (1987). Introduction: Definitions and perspectives in the study of children's ethnic socialization. In J. S. Phinney & M. J. Rotheram (Eds.), *Children's ethnic socialization: Pluralism and development* (pp. 10–28). Newbury Park, CA: Sage.

Rueschenberg, E., & Buriel, R. (1989). Mexican American family functioning and acculturation: A family systems perspective. *Hispanic Journal of Behavioral Sciences, 11*, 232–244.

Rumbaut, R. (1985). Mental health and the refugee experience: A comparative study of Southeast Asian refugees. In T. C. Owan (Ed.), *Southeast Asian mental health: Treatment, prevention, services, training, and research* (pp. 433–486). Rockville, MD: National Institute of Mental Health.

Rumbaut, R. (1991). The agony of exile: A study of migration and adaptation of Southeast Asian refugee adults and children. In F. L. Ahearn, Jr. & J. A. Garrison (Eds.), *Refugee children: Theory, research and practice* (pp. 53–91). Baltimore: Johns Hopkins University Press.

Rumbaut, R. (1995). The crucible within: Ethnic identity, self-esteem, and segmented assimilation among children of immigrants. *International Migration Review, 28*, 748–794.

Sabogal, F., Martin, G., Otero-Sabogal, R., VanOss Marin, B., & Perez-Stable, E. J. (1987). Hispanic familism and acculturation: What changes and what doesn't. *Hispanic Journal of Behavioral Sciences, 9*, 397–412.

Schorr, L. (1988). *Within our reach: Breaking the cycle of disadvantage*. Garden City, NY: Doubleday.

Shon, S. P., & Ja, D. Y. (1982). Asian families. In M. McGoldrick, J. K. Pearce, & J. Giordano (Eds.), *Ethnicity and family therapy* (pp. 208–228). New York: Guilford.

Stonequist, E. V. (1937). *The marginal man: A study in personality and culture conflict*. New York: Scribner's.

Suzuki, B. H. (1980). The Asian-American family. In M. O. Fantini & R. Cardenas (Eds.), *Parenting in a multicultural society* (pp. 74–102). New York: Longman.

Szapocznik, J., & Kurtines, W. (1980). Acculturation, biculturalism, and adjustment among Cuban Americans. In A. M. Padilla (Ed.), *Acculturation: Theory, models, and some new finding* (pp. 139–159). Boulder, CO: Westview Press.

Takaki, R. (1989). *Strangers from a different shore: A history of Asian Americans*. New York: Penguin.

Ting-Toomey, S. (1981). Ethnic identity and close friendship in Chinese-American college students. *International Journal of Intercultural Relations, 5*, 383–406.

Tran, T. V. (1988). The Vietnamese American family. In C. H. Mendel, R. W. Habenstein, & R. Wright, Jr. (Eds.), *Ethnic families in America: Patterns and variations* (3rd ed., pp. 276–299). New York: Elsevier.

Tse, L. (1995). Language brokering among Latino adolescents: Prevalence, attitudes, and school performance. *Hispanic Journal of Behavioral Sciences, 17*, 180–193.

Uba, L. (1994). *Asian Americans: Personality patterns, identity, and mental health*. New York: Guilford.

United Nations High Commissioner for Refugees. (1993). *The state of the world's refugees 1993*. New York: Penguin.

U.S. Commission on Civil Rights. (1980). *Characters in textbooks: A review of the literature* (Clearinghouse Publication 62). Washington, DC: U.S. Government Printing Office.

Vega, W. A. (1990). Hispanic families in the 1980s: A decade of research. *Journal of Marriage and the Family, 52*, 1015–1024.

Vigil, J. D. (1988). *Barrio gangs*. Austin: University of Texas Press.

Wong, M. G. (1988). The Chinese American family. In C. H. Mindel, R. W. Habenstein, & R. Wright, Jr. (Eds.), *Ethnic families in America: Patterns and variations* (3rd ed., pp. 230–257). New York: Elsevier.

Wong, M. G. (1995). Chinese Americans. In P. G. Min (Ed.), *Asian Americans: Contemporary trends and issues* (pp. 58–94). Newbury Park, CA: Sage.

Woll, A. L. (1977). *The Latin image in American film*. Los Angeles: UCLA Latin American Publications.

Yao, E. L. (1985). Adjustment needs of Asian immigrant children. *Elementary School Guidance and Counseling, 19*, 222–227.

Ybarra, L. (1983). Empirical and theoretical developments in the study of Chicano families. In A. Valdez, A. Camarillo, & T. Almaguer (Eds.), *The state of Chicano research on family, labor, and migration.* (Proceedings of the First Stanford Symposium on Chicano Research and Public Policy, pp. 91–110). Stanford, CA: Stanford Center for Chicano Research.

Zambrana, R. E. (1995). *Understanding Latino families*. Newbury Park, CA: Sage.

9

Understanding Family Change Across Generations: Problems of Conceptualization and Research Design

Charles Hirschman

University of Washington

O VER THE past quarter century, immigration has returned to center stage as a major issue in American society, politics, and academic scholarship. The percentage of immigrants in the national population is the highest since the first decade of this century, and in the cities of the West Coast, Texas, New York, Florida, and Illinois, immigrants and their children are visible in every major sector of the society and economy. Raymond Buriel and Terri De Ment addressed the question of sociocultural change for three of the most significant immigrant populations (Mexican, Chinese, and Vietnamese Americans) from the vantage point of family life and organization. The family is a strategic point from which to analyze changes in the lives of immigrants and their children. Families are the primary and most intimate units of reproduction and socialization, but they frequently also serve to mobilize labor, allocate resources, and broker communications and exchanges with other societal institutions. Moreover, change across generations in families is hypothesized to be the major mechanism of sociocultural adaptation from the origin to the host society.

Buriel and De Ment's chapter illustrates the promise and the dilemmas of research on sociocultural change among recent immigrant communities. The authors discussed a number of interesting questions, including family structure, socialization, and intergenerational conflict in light of empirical evidence from the research literature. They thoughtfully reported research findings and discussed problems of poor conceptualization and misleading interpretations.

201

The limitation of the survey, however, is that it is not clear what conclusions can or should be drawn from their broad review of the literature. The authors did not write a final summary or concluding discussion. In this brief chapter, I try to identify the problems of developing a body of cumulative research in this field.

MODELS OF SOCIOCULTURAL CHANGE
AMONG IMMIGRANTS

Buriel & De Ment reviewed some of the inadequacies of assimilation theory and suggested an alternative model of biculturalism. Their characterization of assimilation theory is of a "straight line" model of traditional country-of-origin culture among the immigrant generation being replaced by Euro-American culture among the second generation. The authors suggested that this perspective may have been appropriate for European immigrants earlier in the century (they rely heavily on the interpretations of Stonequist and Child written in the 1930s and 1940s) but is inappropriate for Latino and Asian immigrants in recent decades. Although acknowledging the validity of many of their criticisms of the assimilation model, I am not convinced that the bidirectional model of sociocultural change is an improvement. The bidirectional model posits four acculturation adaptation styles with two additional points beyond Mexican oriented (the unassimilated) and Euro-American oriented (the assimilated): bicultural orientation, which means high competencies in both cultural worlds, and marginal orientation, which seems to include persons that fit in neither world. The assimilation model with all its limitations does not preclude individuals with bicultural status; indeed, a "half-way" position was often thought to be common for the second generation. The marginal orientation in the bidirectional model does not directly specify cultural content but seems to represent social or psychological maladjustment (i.e., gang membership was the example given). This is a different dimension than those reflected in the other three categories. Recall that the traditional assimilation model offered the hypothesis that those with bicultural orientations (i.e., who had deep knowledge of both worlds) would experience status anxiety. I am skeptical that this hypothesis has empirical support, but theories should be evaluated, in part, in their ability to generate testable hypotheses.

In spite of the critique of the assimilation model in the opening section of the paper, most of Buriel and De Ment's literature review assumes (at least implicitly) a unidirectional flow from immigrant cultural orientations to some sort of American cultural orientation. The bidirectionality hypothesis is not mentioned after its initial presentation as an alternative perspective. I do not have a new and improved theoretical framework to suggest for the field. I agree that it is important to purge the assimilation model of explicit or implicit cultural biases, but I am not sure that there is an alternative theory to take its place. Most of the research literature is still organized around the expectation of cultural change in the direction of the host society. The field will be changed when a better theory is developed, but I do not see one on the horizon.

PROBLEMS OF COMPARISONS
AND RESEARCH DESIGN

Buriel and De Ment noted that most research on the Mexican American population and on Asian American populations rely on idealized and static portraits of family organization and cultural orientations at the time of immigration to the United States. In the better studies, there is some empirical comparison of characteristics between an immigrant group and a native born population of the same national origin. Cross-sectional comparisons of this type, however, are very unlikely to represent the historical process of sociocultural change across generations. Many studies have no measure of origin status, only a comparison of an ethnic population with some idealized picture of what it was like among immigrant ancestors.

The basic reality is that there are not monolithic cultures of origin and destination but rather cultural values are always in flux in both places of origin and destination. Moreover, there is always diversity within any population, and immigrants rarely represent modal types. Shifts from a "traditional" culture to an "American" sociocultural pattern can only be detected if these terms are well defined and are measured on common scales. Most important, secular changes over time may well be greater than cross-sectional comparisons between cultures or countries show. Recent Mexican immigrants are unlikely to represent the characteristics or values of the Mexican immigrants in 1900 who were the parents and grandparents of contemporary second- and third-generation Mexican Americans.

Just as Buriel and De Ment question the assumptions of homogeneous and static cultures of origin, I am dubious that there are clear modal values of American society or culture. Patterns of child rearing, socialization, and intergenerational support in American society presumably vary by geographic location, age, gender, economic position, and many other characteristics. It is difficult to know what "becoming American" means for immigrant groups. Most of the research reviewed by Buriel and De Ment did not consider comparisons with the general American population or typical findings from the general research literature on similar topics.

The review of empirical studies did not inspire great confidence about the state of knowledge in the field. Although part of the dilemma may be due to the problems of clear theory and conceptualization, the generic problems seem to be poor data and inadequate research designs. Ad hoc samples, inconsistent measurement of key concepts, and cross-sectional analyses of hypotheses of social change appear to be the norm in this field. Such studies may be useful to generate interesting questions but can not really be used to measure the stock of knowledge about social change.

10

The Concept of "Bicultural Families" and Its Implications for Research on Immigrant and Ethnic Families

Nazli Kibria
Boston University

ASSIMILATION theory today is in a largely discredited state among so-cial scientists. This is not to say that it does not continue to influence or guide research on immigration and ethnicity, but a wide-ranging critique of its fundamental assumptions has weakened its status as the dominant American paradigm on immigration and ethnicity (Kibria, 1993). Among scholars of immigrant and ethnic families there has been a movement away from questions of assimilation and toward a concern with adaptation or the ways in which such families strategize and respond to their structural circumstances (see, e.g., Glenn, 1986; Stack, 1974). However, this focus on adaptation often by-passes or at least does not deal directly with change in immigrant and ethnic families. The demise of the assimilationist framework has, I suggest, left a certain theoretical void, one that has weakened our ability and willingness to grapple with questions regarding processes of family change among immigrant and ethnic groups. If we abandon the idea that family change among ethnic groups is characterized by conflict between the ethnic and the American, with forces that pull toward the American, then how are we to think about family life?

Buriel and De Ment suggested an alternative to an assimilationist model in their review of sociocultural change in Mexican, Chinese, and Vietnamese American families. They argued that these groups do not assimilate into White mainstream U.S. society but move instead toward a bicultural pattern: Some family patterns are similar to and some are different from those of the dominant society. For example, they cited studies showing that although later generation Mexican American families do not live in the extended family households that are characteristic of Mexican immigrants, they continue to maintain a distinctly high level of involvement with family members. Buriel and De Ment's bicultural paradigm to interpret these and other findings raises important questions, both about the meaning of biculturalism and its dynamics and about consequences for immigrant and ethnic families. In the remainder of the chapter I briefly discuss some of these questions.

For researchers who study immigrant and ethnic families, the value of the bicultural paradigm may be enhanced by a more detailed elaboration of its meaning and assumptions. The concept of bicultural suggests an intermingling or mixture of two cultures. This leaves us with questions about the nature of this intermingling, or how the different cultural strands of biculturalism actually operate in relation to each other. For example, does a bicultural ethnic family compartmentalize ethnicity so that some aspects of family life remain ethnically distinctive (e.g., gender roles) whereas others (e.g., discipline of children) change in the direction of mainstream U.S. norms? Or does bicultural imply the emergence of dynamics in such areas as gender roles and the discipline of children that combine cultural elements and result in novel patterns that bear little resemblance to those of the immigrant or the dominant society? These processes are clearly neither unrelated nor mutually exclusive. The effective use of a bicultural paradigm to study families requires us to pay attention to the complex meaning of biculturalism.

A more fundamental and problematic issue in the notion of a bicultural family concerns the boundaries of the two cultural poles (i.e., the immigrant culture and the mainstream Euro-American culture) that Buriel and De Ment used to define a bicultural orientation. The contemporary social context makes it increasingly difficult to think about these two cultural poles as fixed or monolithic in character. The mainstream American family, for example, needs careful qualification given the current diversity of family forms in the United States. In an attempt to conceptually capture the complexity of U.S. family life today, Stacey (1990) argued that the current family era is a postmodern one, marked by the absence of a single dominant model of family life that has widespread legitimacy. By pointing to the complexity of the immigrant and American cultural realms, I do not mean to suggest that we should abandon the concept of bicultural family forms. Instead, I call for a more careful definition of the mainstream U.S. family, perhaps through elaboration of its specific features (e.g., nuclear family household, egalitarian parent–child relations). What we gain through such elaboration is a clearer and more precise understanding of how bicultural families incorporate elements of mainstream American family forms.

Similar questions surround the definition of the immigrant family. Once again, I urge a more specific and detailed elaboration of the relevant components of the immigrant culture. A number of variables that internally differentiate ethnic groups, including socioeconomic background, time of immigration, and nationality will shape the character of the family traditions and orientations that they bring with them to the United States. For example, the cultural orientation of an upper-middle-class family from Taiwan that emigrated in the 1970s will differ from that of a working-class family from Hong Kong that arrived in the United States in the 1980s. Further complicating the definition of the immigrant culture are globalization processes and the emergence of diaspora cultures. Both of these developments highlight the linkages of cultural systems and the fuzziness of the boundaries that distinguish them. For example, the cultural orientations of middle-class persons in Hong Kong and of people of Hong Kong origin in Britain and the United States can be seen as interconnected, operating in mutually influential ways. Technological developments in the areas of international travel and communication make such linkages more vital than ever. In a study of ethnicity among young Chinese in Britain, Parker (1995) described the emergence of a diaspora Chinese identity, centered on contemporary popular culture in Hong Kong, to which the British Chinese are continually exposed through the flow of videos and cassettes from Hong Kong to Britain.

Besides issues of definition, I also feel that it is important to consider the dynamics by which bicultural families develop or form. The very notion of biculturalism tends to privilege culture as an explanatory factor. However, as Buriel and De Ment point out, the emergence of bicultural families is clearly related to a much wider array of ecological or structural variables. These variables include the size and socioeconomic resources of the ethnic community, the character and extent of continued immigration from the sending society, and the proximity and quality of linkages between the ethnic community and the sending society. Mexican Americans and Vietnamese Americans, two of the groups that Buriel and De Ment discuss in their chapter, differ along many of these variables; thus, the dynamics by which these bicultural families develop may be different. Mexican Americans are a larger group than Vietnamese Americans, and immigration from Mexico to the United States has been more extensive and prolonged. These factors, along with the proximity of Mexico to the United States and the presence of dense and active social networks that connect communities in these two societies, are likely to enter into the development of bicultural family forms among Mexican Americans. Conditions have been different for Vietnamese Americans in many respects. Connections to Vietnam have been tenuous for Vietnamese Americans, but in recent years, liberalized economic and political policies in Vietnam, along with the normalization of diplomatic ties between the United States and Vietnam, have worked to rejuvenate ties with Vietnam among Vietnamese Americans. These renewed ties may have important implications for the extent and character of the biculturalism of Vietnamese American families. A potential development that has been mentioned to me by Vietnamese Americans is that

a growing number of Vietnamese American men who have had trouble finding marriage partners in the United States due to the high sex ratio in the Vietnamese American community are now traveling to Vietnam to find women to
marry and bring back to the United States. A similar pattern has been noted
among professional Asian Indian immigrants, many of whom return to India
to find spouses for themselves and their children (Fisher, 1980). Among the
possible consequences of such a pattern of traveling to the country of origin to
find a spouse is a reduction in rates of intermarriage for the immigrant
group—a development that has important implications for the growth of bicultural family forms.

Our understanding of the underlying dynamics of bicultural family forms
may be enhanced by analyses of these forms across ethnic groups. Such comparative analyses can address the important question of whether or not bicultural families develop or change in similar ways. Do bicultural families tend to
retain their ethnic distinctiveness in some arenas of family life rather than others? Buriel and De Ment's literature review suggested that the practice of living in an extended household tends to dissipate over time for immigrant
groups. Are there aspects of family life that are more likely to remain ethnically distinctive over time? How do socioeconomic differences compare in
their impact on family forms across groups? In general, cross-ethnic analyses
are an important alternative to the traditional two-group study in which the
ethnic family is compared to the mainstream American family.

Our understanding of bicultural family forms will also be enhanced by
studies of their consequences. How do bicultural family forms affect marital
stability and satisfaction? How do they affect the psychological and social
well-being of family members? Reflecting the influence of assimilation ideas,
the popular understanding of biculturalism is that it generates internal tur-
moil for individuals. In popular thinking, second-generation bicultural eth-
nics are caught between the conflicting dictates of two worlds. Research on
second-generation Chinese and Korean Americans suggests a very different
picture (Kibria, 1995). Although ethnic attachments and behaviors are extremely divergent among these middle-class adult children of immigrants,
all identify themselves as both Korean and American or both Chinese and
American. They define their identity in opposition primarily to two groups—
Korean or Chinese immigrants and White Americans. They feel that unlike
people in these two groups, they can claim membership in two worlds, which
enhances their individuality and provides them with an actual or potential
ability to tap into ethnic resources and networks.

The consequences of bicultural family forms for economic well-being is
another topic worth exploring. Studies show that the distinctive features of
immigrant families can enhance their ability to cope effectively with difficult
economic circumstances. For example, a collectivist familial orientation, in
contrast to the individualism of U.S. culture, facilitates the efforts of immi-

grants to engage in coping strategies such as the pooling of resources within domestic groups and networks (Kibria, 1994).

The work of Portes and Zhou (1993) on segmented assimilation also suggested some ways in which bicultural family forms can have economic implications. Portes and Zhou suggested that three different modes of cultural adaptation are apparent among the second generation today, each of which contributes to a different economic outcome. The first of these resembles the path predicted by classic assimilation theory: The second generation becomes absorbed, both economically and culturally, into mainstream U.S. society. However, shrinking economic opportunities in the United States make this path of assimilation far more tenuous for today's immigrant children than it was in the past. The second mode of adaptation involves assimilation into the economically and socially disadvantaged sectors of U.S. society, a path that has disastrous consequences for the economic well-being of the second generation. The third outcome is one whereby the second generation remains culturally oriented to the ethnic community, drawing on the economic opportunities and resources that are embedded in it. Portes and Zhou assert that this third path effectively acts as a social buffer for many who would otherwise become absorbed into the second path of downward mobility. The path of continued orientation toward the ethnic group is one that is more likely among immigrant groups that maintain bicultural family forms. It is furthermore a path that is conducive to the long-term maintenance of bicultural families. When the second generation remains ensconced in the ethnic community, they are more likely to marry endogamously and to maintain and transmit bicultural family forms to the next generation. Although bicultural family forms may also be a reality for those children of immigrants who follow the other two paths of assimilation, biculturalism is likely to differ for them in character and intensity compared to those for whom the primary reference group is the ethnic community.

In conclusion, the issue of immigrant and ethnic family forms is clearly an important one to explore. The bicultural framework suggested by Buriel and De Ment represents an attempt to conceptually grapple with the character and direction of immigrant family change. The framework opens an exciting set of research questions for those who are interested in immigrant and ethnic family change.

REFERENCES

Fisher, M. (1980). *The Indians of New York City.* New Delhi, India: Heritage.

Glenn, E. N. (1986). *Issei, nissei, war bride.* Philadelphia, PA: Temple University Press.

Kibria, N. (1995, August). *Boundary dilemmas: Conceptions of ethnicity and intermarriage among second-generation Asian Americans.* Paper presented at the annual meeting of the American Sociological Association, Washington, DC.

Kibria, N. (1994). Household structure and family ideologies: The dynamics of immigrant economic adaptation among Vietnamese refugees. *Social Problems, 41,* 301–316.

Kibria, N. (1993). *Family tightrope: The changing lives of Vietnamese Americans.* Princeton, NJ: Princeton University Press.

Parker, D. (1995). *Through different eyes: The cultural identities of young Chinese people in Britain.* Aldershot, UK: Avebury.

Portes, A., & Zhou, M. (1993). The new second generation: Segmented assimilation and its variants. *Annals of the American Academy of Political and Social Science, 530,* 74–96.

Stack, C. (1974). *All our kin.* New York: Harper & Row.

Stacey, J. (1990). *Brave new families.* New York: Basic Books.

11

Asian Immigrant Variables and Structural Models of Cross-Cultural Distress

Gargi Roysircar Sodowsky
University of Nebraska–Lincoln

Edward Wai Ming Lai
Georgia State University

THIS CHAPTER is characterized by both theoretical questions and data-based findings. An attempt is made to see the relationships among the constructs of acculturation, ethnic identity, the family, immigrant sociocultural factors, and cultural adjustment difficulties. Relationships are proposed using Asian immigrants as subjects of conceptualization and of an empirical investigation.

There are three parts to the chapter. First, the bidirectional model of acculturation is reformulated from the perspective of ethnic identity. Second, relationships between ethnic identity and the family are considered because ethnic identity and the family are at the core of the Asian collective self. Third, a data-based empirical investigation on Asian immigrants is reported; this is a study on the structural relations of some of the constructs or their related components, such as acculturation preferences for language usage and social customs, family network and support, extent of ethnic friendships, perception of prejudice, sociocultural immigrant variables, and cultural adjustment difficulties.

ACCULTURATION: FOUR ADAPTATION VARIETIES VERSUS INDIVIDUAL IDENTIFICATION PROCESSES

The bidirectional model of acculturation, originally proposed by Berry (Berry 1980, 1990; Berry, Kim, Minde, & Mok, 1987), applies to voluntary immi-

grants, sojourners, and settled ethnic groups who are the descendants of immigrants. This model shows two attitudinal conflicts interacting with each
other, with immigrant groups needing to find resolutions to both conflicts.
The first conflict is whether or not the immigrant group wishes to remain culturally as its members were in the past in terms of identity, language, and social customs. The solution to the conflict is provided by a dichotomous choice,
either yes or no. The second conflict is whether or not the group wishes to
have day-to-day interactions with members of the dominant group. The same
dichotomous resolution is available. The interactions of the answers for the
two conflicts of cultural identity and social relations result in four varieties of
acculturation: integration, assimilation, separation, and deculturation/mar-
ginalization. Figure 11.1 shows Berry's four varieties of acculturation (Berry,
1990).

Berry's (1990) first question, "Is it considered of value to maintain cultural
identity and characteristics?" (p. 216), proposes that ethnic identity is a subset
of the acculturation model. The concept of ethnic identity is important in psychology because it permits the reformulation of acculturation varieties to
psychology's paradigm of studying individual differences. In the acculturation
model, an Asian immigrant group, by interacting with the U.S. White dominant group, changes and gets modified into an ethnic group. Ethnic identity,
then, is a social or collective self-identity based on the culture of one's ancestors' national group(s), as modified by the demands of the dominant culture.

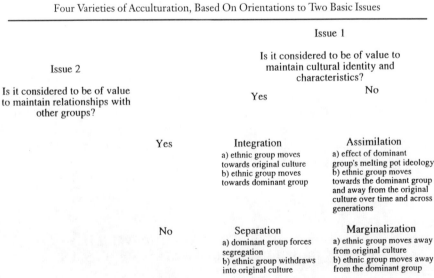

Four Varieties of Acculturation, Based On Orientations to Two Basic Issues

		Issue 1
		Is it considered to be of value to maintain cultural identity and characteristics?
Issue 2 Is it considered to be of value to maintain relationships with other groups?		Yes	No
	Yes	Integration a) ethnic group moves towards original culture b) ethnic group moves towards dominant group	Assimilation a) effect of dominant group's melting pot ideology b) ethnic group moves towards the dominant group and away from the original culture over time and across generations
	No	Separation a) dominant group forces segregation b) ethnic group withdraws into original culture	Marginalization a) ethnic group moves away from original culture b) ethnic group moves away from the dominant group

FIG. 11.1.   An understanding of John Berry's (1990) bidirectional model of acculturation.

Acculturation adaptation is a response to the dominant group, and ethnic identity is a response to one's ethnic group. To develop further the point of difference, an acculturation adaptation variety, such as separation, is the collective culture of an ethnic group, whereas ethnic identity is an individual's response to the collective culture of one's ethnic group. Thus, the construct of ethnic identity distinguishes the collective culture from a personal culture that takes place in the personality, cognitions, and emotions of the individual person, representing the internalization of one's experiences in the ethnic collective culture.

We develop Berry's first question (the value of maintaining cultural identity) from a psychological framework in order to understand the individuality of the immigrant person. Ethnic identity could be measured by assessing two dimensions: the degree of adoption of Whiteness and the degree of retention of one's Asianness (i.e., Japaneseness, Indianness, Chineseness). Sanchez and Atkinson (1983), using a bidirectional model similar to Berry's, referred to ethnic identity as a person's degree of commitment to the U.S. White culture and degree of commitment to one's ethnic culture.

First, we modify Berry's (1980) two basic acculturation issues. We propose that various ethnic identities are combinations of "yes" and "no" answers to two questions: Is my ethnic identity of value and to be retained? and Is the White identity of the U.S. dominant society to be sought? The first question measures one's identity grounded in one's ethnicity; for example, how one perceives oneself in the context of shared ethnic existence in terms of attachment, feelings of security, group organizational activities, friendships, moral obligations, values, traditions, and pride in ethnic self-image and group-image (Isajiw, 1990). Does one see oneself like or unlike others from one's ethnic origins? The second question measures one's identity grounded in the culture of the U.S. White dominant society and how one perceives oneself in the context of shared White existence, values, and attachment to the White society. Four ethnic identity orientations occur, based on four Yes or No responses to the two basic ethnic identity questions (see Fig. 11.2). Using a 2 × 2 design, the following four responses would be given: yes, yes (bicultural identity); yes, no (strong ethnic identity); no, yes (strong U.S. White identity); and no, no (identity of cultural marginalization). Second, we propose that the four ethnic identities allow for a nonlinear trend over time and across situations with an individual with one ethnic identity orientation moving to another over time or across situations, and moving back and forth among the four identities.

One's ethnic identity is dynamic because a collective culture is not held by people in the same way or to the same degree. Bicultural skills or competencies (Lafromboise, Coleman, & Gerton, 1994) have recently been praised as representing an optimum cross-cultural problem-solving style. Most U.S.-born second-generation immigrants and those who immigrated as infants manifest facile bicultural behaviors. It needs to be pointed out, however, that

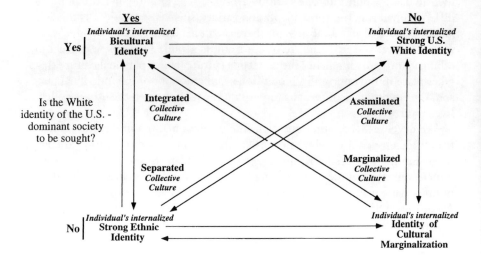

FIG. 11.2.   Nonlinear movement to different ethnic identities over time and across situations when the individual responds to two basic ethnic identity questions. *Note:* The individual has an internalized ethnic identity that is predominant. However, other potential ethnic identities become salient when the individual responds to the ethnic group's other acculturation varieties and to diverse contexts that are characterized by values.

biculturalism appears to refer to overt behaviors, whereas ethnic identity is the implicit internalization of the ethnic collective culture and collective self. Therefore one can be explicitly bicultural but implicitly have a configuration of potential ethnic identity orientations that become more salient or less salient depending on the motivational forces of the collective cultures of the ethnic group and the dominant group.

Two examples show how individual immigrants, though predominantly bicultural in their daily living, adopt variations in their ethnic identity in different contexts and time frames. Take the instance of a particular first-generation Asian Indian woman in the United States. She interacts with a strong social network of Asian Indian families in her city, feels a moral commitment to help new Asian Indian immigrants coming into her city, and visits her former hometown in India every 2 or 3 years to keep in touch with her family and relatives. Her elderly parents have also recently immigrated to live with her in the United States. Thus, she endorses an Asian Indian ethnic identity (i.e., answers "yes" to the first question). The same woman who has received her university education in the United States and is an academician in a U.S. university works cohesively with her White colleagues and becomes a concerned citizen in her White middle-class neighborhood (i.e., answers "yes" to the second question).

She also entertains in her home her White friends and colleagues. Thus, this woman has a bicultural identity in her interpersonal interactions.

In another context, this woman does not endorse a bicultural identity but rather endorses a strong ethnic identity, saying "yes" to the first question and "no" to the second question. Take, for example, her reactions to marriage and religious practices. Even though she came to the United States as a young single woman to get her university education in English language and literature, spent much time with U.S. White peers in the classroom and in research, obtained professional employment in the United States, and also sought U.S. immigration status, she chose to have an arranged marriage. Her parents and family elders chose a "suitable" bridegroom for her in India, a man she had never met prior to her wedding, and held a strongly traditional Hindu wedding for the daughter in their hometown. Although, at the time of this writing, this woman has lived in the United States for a long time, she has not sought to convert to Christianity. Rather she continues to observe Hinduism, and, in fact, meets a Hindu religion group weekly to sing Hindu hymns and chants in the classical religious language, Sanskrit. This woman is in the forefront of organizing Hindu religious ceremonies in her city.

In yet another context, the woman feels culturally marginal, without a sense of belonging to either cultural group. With regard to gender role, she does not endorse subservience to males and authority figures, which is expected in her culture of origin; thus, she says "no" to the first question. She also says "no" to the second question because she does not philosophically agree with the political agenda of U.S. White feminists and feels that White feminists do not understand and, therefore, are not sensitive to the racial and cultural issues of women of color. Thus, although in her mind and emotions the woman is engaging in ethnic identities that solve various contextual questions of belonging, to the dominant group she continues to be bicultural. An immigrant has a complex personality.

In her interpretation of the bidirectional acculturation model, Phinney (1990) conceptualized ethnic identity as the extent to which an individual acculturates to his or her native culture (e.g., Japanese, Chinese, Korean, Indian, etc). This conceptualization is illustrated by the documentary "From Hollywood to Hanoi," which is a reflection on the Vietnamese filmmaker Tiana Thi Thanh Nga's life. The filmmaker, as a child, was brought out of Vietnam to the United States by her father in 1966 and was told that she would never see Vietnam again. Her father taught her to hate the Viet Congs with threats that Ho Chi Minh would come to tear her up if she did not eat her dinner. With all neighborhood televisions tuned to the war "killing our boys there," the girl hated the "gooks" too. As a teenager, she wound up as a martial-arts "cute girl," playing in Hollywood's generic Southeast Asian types of films and also did such popular musical videos as "Karatecise," "Lust in de Jungle," and "Free as I Want 2B." She picked up a Hollywood anglicized version of her name and kept it for a long time. She tried to be everyone; she tried to tune out the Vietnam war but could not. She went to Hanoi in 1988 to seek the truth, to see for herself and not listen to rumors, even those within the Vietnamese American community. She went on a geographical, psychological, and cross-cultural journey of returning to a land that she and her family had abandoned politically, economically, and socially. Hers is a film of growing up in American suburbs and going back—back to Ho Chi Minh City and then back again to the suburbs. This person is acculturated to U.S. White society and is essentially bicultural, being a trilingual black belt, poet, songwriter, actress, professor, and now a film director and producer, who developed a sense of her ethnic identity through a process of reverse acculturation and finding her cultural self.

In conclusion, an ethnic individual, first, does not have a one-dimensional or dichotomous cultural identity, having either an ethnic identity or a White identity. Second, it is possible for a person to have different ethnic identities because an ethnic person lives in diverse social and cultural contexts. However, one ethnic identity orientation could be predominant, but not exclusive, during one period of a person's lifespan. Third, having to negotiate two ethnic identities can make an ethnic individual's life complex and difficult because many options are available for the individual, which pressure the individual to make many decisions. Such a cross-cultural life could, nonetheless, be rich, exciting, rejuvenating, and productive.

ETHNIC IDENTITY AND ASIAN FAMILIES

Root (1985) proposed that for the Asian client in psychotherapy, the family is an important aspect of one's cultural identity. Sodowsky and Carey (1987) argued that family is central for the cultural identity formation of U.S. Asian Indians. It would also appear that for many U.S. Asians, one's sense of self with reference to his or her ethnic group is uniquely tied to the family because, owing to minority status, these Asians may not be living in large ethnic communities.

A reason why the family is naturally significant in an Asian's life is that in Asian societies a person is viewed in terms of his or her relations to others. In this view of interdependence between the self and others, the self is defined in terms of interpersonal behaviors that are context specific (Markus & Kitayama, 1991). The family provides a natural context for particular person-in-relationship situations, rules of interpersonal conduct, and roles in interpersonal transactions. In the family, a person first develops a differentiated knowledge of others (as opposed to learning self-differentiation, which is encouraged in a White American family), experiences emotions that are other focused (e.g., shame and guilt), and has socially oriented motivations, such as meeting the expectations of others. This sociometric view of the person is an implicit core value of Asian identity, and because this value is first learned in the family, it is necessary to study the relationship between the family and one's ethnic identity. For many Asians, family kinship is the basic relationship and the primary socializing agent, especially for teaching obedience and discipline. Informal social friendships and peer interactions are given less priority and are considered less influential, which is not so in the case of the U.S. White social system. Owing to the preeminence of the family, it could be hypothesized that it is through the family that culture and ethnicity are transmitted to the individual. As a result, ethnicity and family are strongly intertwined (McGoldrick, 1982).

Asian Family Values

Several authors have proposed that certain family values of U.S. Asian groups are different from those of U.S. White families (Segal, 1991; Sodowsky, Kwan, & Pannu, 1995). These authors propose that most U.S. Asian groups focus on collective needs, interdependency, and conformity. In contrast, Sodowsky, Maguire, Johnson, Ngumba, and Kohles (1994) and Ihle, Sodowsky, and Kwan (1996) found in studies on world views that White Americans, relative to Chinese participants, preferred an individualistic orientation in relationships and focused on seeking harmony with personal processes. In a study on childrearing beliefs of Chinese mothers and European American mothers (Chao, 1995), Chinese mothers showed their children love for the goal of fostering a very close relationship with the child and for the continuity of this relationship as the child grew older. The European American mothers stressed love because they wanted to foster the child's self-esteem and make the child feel safe. Chinese mothers wanted to develop their children's adaptability and ability to get along with others. American mothers liked to process feelings with their children. Chinese mothers felt that getting a good education was the key to success, whereas the American mothers felt that self-esteem was the foundation for success. The Chinese mothers wanted to maintain the Chinese culture by having children involved in the Chinese community, speaking Chinese to the children in the home, and sending them to Chinese schools and back to Taiwan for vacations. The American mothers did not express a desire to maintain a specific cultural orientation but stressed the importance of a sense of community within the family as well as globally.

Many U.S.-born Asians who are acculturated to U.S. social, professional, institutional, and leisure activities maintain a strong enough ethnic identity to refuse to place their older parents and grandparents in retirement or nursing homes. Rather, they accept their elders into their homes despite the various difficulties related to family leadership, cultural generation gaps, finances, space, privacy, food and eating habits, and sharing of time—all of which they know they will need to put up with. Some U.S. Asians' sense of duty to the older generation could come into conflict with the nuclear family attitudes of U.S. Whites, who could consider extended family involvements on a daily living basis quite intrusive. This conflict could be particularly stressful to an Asian–White cross-cultural marriage. As a result of the marked contrast in certain core values, U.S. Asian families may have difficulty maintaining a strong ethnic identity in a dominant culture that is vastly different from their own.

Family identity is characterized by individual members seeking the honor and good name of the family and protecting it from shame. Reciprocal moral duties and obligations take precedence over individual desires. These obligations include those of parents to children when growing children need nurturance, education, and guidance and, later in the family's history, those of adult children to elderly parents (Sodowsky, 1991).

Social control is obtained through family demands for duty, obligations, and obedience. If these behaviors are not observed, the principal techniques of punishment employed by the family include arousing moral guilt and making the morally reprehensible person lose face through social or public shame. The family practices a collective approach to shaming and disciplining the erring person (Sodowsky, 1991).

Consider 19-year-old Dung and her family, the Le family. At the time of this writing, Dung and her 16-year-old brother, Khoi, have been in the United States for more than a decade, but her parents arrived only a few years ago, along with two more brothers and a sister. The arrival of her parents and her younger siblings, two of whom were born after Dung's departure to the United States, has left Dung torn between duty and freedom. Dung says, "I hang out with a lot of Americans, people who do not have much responsibility. But I do not want to lose the trust of my parents. I respect their wishes. This is my family, and if I don't take care of them, who will? It's my responsibility."

Dung's parents had been very unhappy with the communist regime in Vietnam and so, long ago, they decided to send Dung and her younger brother to live with their grandparents in California. Dung, at the age of 10, and her brother, then 6 years old, went by boat to Malaysia, then to the Philippines, and finally to the United States. Dung does not remember much of her journey except that she was scared, feeling that she was in the middle of nowhere. She remembers getting seasick and thinking that she would die. When Dung and her brother arrived, Dung's grandparents sent them to school in Orange County, California. Dung was nervous. She did not know English, and after the first day she did not want to go back to school. When people wanted her to do something, everyone pointed as if she were deaf.

By the sixth grade, she was speaking fluent English and had started to integrate the two cultures, but her life was uprooted again when her parents arrived in 1992 and the entire family moved to Nebraska. "It was strange," Dung says. "It felt different. All of a sudden I had two parents who wanted to tell me what to do. Vietnamese parents are very different from American parents. I'm 19, and I can't go out without permission. My parents believe that girls don't do this and don't do that. But I respect my parents. My mother is a baker in a supermarket, and my father works in a food factory, and they both work very hard. It is my responsibility to take care of my brothers and sisters. Every day I teach them English and help them with their homework. At home I'm Vietnamese, so I take care of my brothers and sister. In my culture girls do not speak with boys; they are supposed to be very quiet and not too friendly. I'm not supposed to date until after college. No problem," Dung laughs, her speech punctuated with American adolescent slang. "I have lots of friends— my parents think I have too may friends . . . and I do go out with guys—but just as friends."

Should Dung ever marry, she hopes to marry an Americanized Vietnamese. "I don't want someone who was raised in Vietnam," Dung says, "because those guys want control. I want to be equal, so that we can get together and both work, build together. I want my children to communicate with my people but also with the outside world—like Americans."

Had Dung been individualistically oriented and concerned with her personal autonomy, identity, and development, like many of her U.S. White adolescent peers, she might have expressed strong resentments against her parents. Dung hardly knows her parents, not having lived with them for 9 years, and could have found them excessively intrusive and controlling with "foreign" conventions and restrictions. She could have also viewed them as cold-hearted and rejecting parents who abandoned their 10-year-old daughter to a lone voyage to the United States, with the injunction that she also take care of her 6-year-old brother. However, when listening to Dung, one does not hear feelings of resentment to parents, opposition to familial obligations, or issues of post-traumatic stress disorder.

Studies on Asian Ethnic Families

Minimal research theoretically or empirically examines the relationship between ethnic identity and family dynamics. Phinney (1990) stated the role of context (e.g., family) needs examination with regard to ethnic identity. It is possible to categorize the Asian family studies in two ways: studies that seem to indicate familial conflict due to differences in acculturation or ethnic identity within a family and studies that indicate that visible aspects of ethnic identity may be more easily modified by U.S. Asian families than invisible aspects.

Most theoretical writings or research reviews (Matsuoka, 1990; Sodowsky & Carey, 1987; Wakil, Siddique, & Wakil, 1981) commonly focus on cultural conflict between family members due to differences in acculturation levels. They contend that parents maintain stronger ties to their Asian culture of origin, whereas children seem to have weaker ties to their cultural heritage and

stronger ties to the U.S. White-dominant culture. These differences in acculturation states within a family create conflict. Matsuoka (1990) stated that
Vietnamese American adolescents in their native culture form their identity
largely based on familial relationships. However, according to Matsuoka, once
exposed to the U.S. White culture, the independence and autonomy given to
White teenagers appeal greatly to Vietnamese youth. Consequently, they may
begin to rely increasingly on White peers for their identity development. The
diminishing use of the family as a cultural base for the formation of one's ethnic identity as well as of formal relationship ideals, code of morality, and the
collective esprit may contribute to both individual and familial difficulty. In
general, it seems that parents are afraid that children will lose a strong sense of
their ethnic identity (Segal, 1991; Wakil et al., 1981), and although the children are eager to identify with their culture of origin, they are not quite as invested as their parents (Wakil et al., 1981).

Some studies (Siddique, 1977; Wakil et al., 1981) indicate that aspects of
family functioning that are related to visible ethnic identity are more easily
modified than invisible aspects of ethnic identity. Visible aspects of ethnic
identity are overt ethnic behaviors, whereas invisible aspects are implicit cultural values or deeply ingrained culture (Sodowsky et al., 1995). Siddique
(1977) found in Asian Indian families an increase in mutual decision making
between husbands and wives and an increase in input from children regarding
their career decisions. In addition, Wakil et al. (1981) found that parents let
children participate in Western festivals. With regard to children being lis-
tened to in issues of higher education and vocational choices, there is the prag-
matic realization that the children may be better informed of the U.S. educational system and employment opportunities than the immigrant parents.
Many Asians are festival oriented, liking colorful processionals and group and
holiday celebrations. Therefore, they easily accept the gift giving and fellowship aspects of American festivals. Thus, these White acculturated behaviors
suggest that visible aspects of one's ethnic identity may be amenable to change.

However, core aspects of culture, such as relationships with the opposite
sex and dating, may not be as subject to change (Wakil et al., 1981). Similarly,
implicit aspects of certain Asian religions, beliefs about the importance of harmony, moderation, and nonconfrontation, concerns about bringing shame to
the family, and feelings of guilt when taking care of personal desires may not
be subject to change. For future research, it would be important to investigate
what invisible aspects of a U.S. Asian family's identity are core to the family
and are also troublesome to the family's adjustment to the U.S. White society.

As part of a larger study on self-esteem, Phinney and Chavira (1992) found
that participants who had progressed developmentally in terms of their ethnic
identity tended to have higher scores on a family relations measure. Thus,
Phinney and Chavira suggested that it is possible that familial support is important for minority youths, including Asians, to explore their native cultures.

Rosenthal and Feldman (1992) indicated that feelings of ethnic pride were related to families that were marked by warmth, independence, and environments that were under control.

These studies seem to suggest that certain family environments enhance one's sense of ethnic identity. Conversely, it seems equally probable that one's ethnic identity attitudes may influence one's relations with the family, because, as previously mentioned, the family is a primary representation of culture and ethnicity. For example, Sodowsky and Carey (1988) found that U.S. Asian Indian participants who self-designated their identity as Asian Indian or "mostly" Asian Indian tended to be aligned with traditional Asian Indian values. These participants also endorsed family items that were more traditional (e.g., preference for children not dating). Thus, it is possible that the extent to which one identifies with one's ethnic group influences adherence to cultural traditions that are linked to family structure or rules.

As part of a larger study, Pannu and Helms (1994) hypothesized that ethnic identity would be related to perceptions of familial acculturation and family functioning in a U.S. Asian Indian sample. Pannu and Helms felt it was possible that a strong sense of ethnic identity would enhance perceptions of family dynamics (e.g., familial cohesion) in an environment that espouses cultural values that are in marked contrast to Indian culture. Contrary to predictions, ethnic identity did not predict family functioning (i.e., cohesion and family conflict) in an Asian Indian sample. However, ethnic identity was related to perceptions of familial acculturation. Specifically, Asian Indians who had explored their ethnic identities tended to perceive their families as Asian Indian acculturated. Pannu and Helms felt that it was possible that because the family is central to the identity development of Asian Indians (Kurian, 1974, as cited in Sodowsky & Carey, 1987; Segal, 1991), participants who had actively searched for their ethnic identity may have used the family as a vehicle to explore what it meant to be Asian Indian. It may be postulated that the more people identify with their ethnic cultures, the more they may endorse cultural values and perceive their family as oriented to their ethnic culture.

Research Questions on Ethnic Identity and the Family

It seems that Phinney's (1990) developmental model can be used to generate research questions that focus on the relationship between ethnic identity and the family. Phinney described the moratorium stage as one in which the individual has begun to explore his or her ethnicity, as evidenced by confused thoughts and feelings about the implications of ethnic group membership and the achieved-identity stage as one in which the individual has completed ethnic identity exploration and emerged with a clear, secure understanding and acceptance of ethnic identity. Possible questions might be: Do individuals in the moratorium stage or achieved-identity stage use their families to explore their culture more than people in other stages? How does this cultural exploration via the family work? What role does the family play in the development of different ethnic identity stages? Are families who have numerous achieved members less vulnerable to acculturative stress?

Fernandez (1988) used the Minority Identity Development Model (MID; Atkinson, Morten, & Sue, 1993; the model was originally developed in 1979) to explore theoretically the possible influence of ethnic identity development on Southeast Asian family relationships. Fernandez outlined how each of the ethnic identity stages may be associated with different perceptions of one's family. In the conformity stage, individuals may ignore ethnic familial responsibilities because they conform to U.S. White-dominant cultural norms. In the dissonance stage, individuals face information with regard to issues of racial and cultural oppression that shakes up their previous U.S. White-conformity attitudes. They begin to feel conflict between the values of their culture of origin and the U.S. White values. Fernandez stated that in this stage, conflict between loyalty to the family and personal desire for independence (a value assumed to be preferred by U.S. Whites) may be the key issue. Conversely, Southeast Asian adolescents in the immersion stage, deeply involved in a search for their ethnic history, heritage, and heroes or heroines, may have strong familial ties and may conform to familial roles. When in the introspection stage, individuals struggle with their unequivocal bond to the ethnic group and their own personal autonomy. As a result of this struggle, individuals who retain strong ties to the family without resolving issues of personal autonomy may become self-critical. Finally, in the synergetic articulation and awareness stage, individuals may maintain a close bond with the family and may be happy with that commitment. On the other hand, it is also possible that individuals may not fulfill family commitments because of their desires for their own independence.

Fernandez's framework has not received empirical support. It might be important to examine ethnic identity from the MID framework because it takes into account the sociopolitical construct of oppression of minorities by the White-dominant group. Researchers could then begin to understand how oppression of ethnic groups, and not only of African Americans, may impact the identity attitudes and functioning of families. For instance, it is possible that the more prejudice U.S. Asians experience, the more cohesive and supportive family members may be with each other and the more segregated and traditional an Asian family may become.

VARIABLES AND STRUCTURAL MODELS OF CROSS-CULTURAL DISTRESS

Berry's (1980) basic proposition is that immigrant groups acculturate, showing one of four general types of cultural changes. These are integrating the immigrant group's original cultural ways with those of the dominant society (integration), relinquishing the former and assimilating the latter (assimilation), retaining the former and rejecting the latter (traditionalism), and being disconnected with both (deculturation/marginalization). Another proposition is that these acculturation types of changes are accompanied by adjustment-related difficulties, generically called acculturative stress (Berry & Annis, 1974). It is possible that acculturative stress is an individual's negative reactions to the tensions between two cultures quite different from each other when these societies make continuous, first-hand contact. Thus, a group acculturation phenomenon is accompanied by an individual member's stress reactions to the change dynamics of the immigrant group.

The marginalization type of acculturation provides the context for acculturative stress. A person in such a change context is out of cultural, social, and psychological contact with both his or her immigrant group and the dominant society, and is experiencing feelings of alienation toward the cultural group, a decreased sense of ethnic identity, anger against the dominant society, and personal ambivalence and confusion (Sodowsky et al., 1995). The integration context of a bicultural person creates a complex life in which one is confronted with many possibilities and decision-making dilemmas. In the context of assimilation, one is affected by the loss of one's cultural continuity; in the midst of traditional practices, one shows rigidity and interpersonal rejecting attitudes. Thus, no matter what the acculturation change type is, one experiences stress (Sodowsky & Carey, 1988).

However, this stress of the individual, just as it is societally induced, is also moderated by the immigrant characteristics of the group. Stress can vary, depending on the immigrant society's initial cultural similarity to the dominant culture and the extent of pressure on the immigrant group to show the assimilation type of acculturation. For instance, those in the United States whose cultures of origin are in Asia, Africa, and the Middle East and those who follow Islam, Hinduism, Buddhism, and Catholicism experience more acculturation-related problems than those of European and Spanish or Latin descent and who are Protestants (Sodowsky, Lai, & Plake, 1991; Sodowsky & Plake, 1992) who are culturally proximal to the White American U.S. society.

Krause, Bennett, and Tran (1989) attempted to understand the effects of acculturation changes from a life-stress model. According to this model, there are two categories of stressors: life events and chronic strains. The distinction between these two stressors is that "stressful life events involve discrete occurrences that are limited by time, whereas chronic strains are continuous and ongoing" (p. 322). In addition, chronic life strains exert a greater impact on one's health than do stressful life events. Moreover, chronic strains create pathology by engendering new (i.e., secondary) life events. Acculturation is a relatively long-term change process, even generational for units such as the family (Sodowsky et al., 1995). Thus, Krause et al. viewed acculturation as a specific type of chronic strain. This implies that immigrants will experience stresses very often, which will affect their psychological being by generating new secondary stressful life events, not all of which are necessarily cultural. For example, some Asians who may be motivated culturally as well as for survival reasons to achieve educational and career successes in White American terms may exhibit test and performance anxiety that lead to failure, which in turn, causes the cultural response of loss of face.

Acculturative stress behaviors that are pathological and disruptive to the individual, group, and family (the family being important in collectivistic societies as the transmitter of culture) include psychosomatic ailments (Nicassio, 1985; D. W. Sue & D. Sue, 1990; S. Sue, 1996), anxiety (S. Sue, 1996), depression (Draguns, 1996; S. Sue, 1996), psychosocial dysfunction (S. Sue & Zane, 1987), cultural marginality (Sodowsky et al., 1995; W. Sue & D. Sue, 1990), poor self-concept (Padilla, Wagatsuma, & Lindholm, 1985), disordered eating attitudes and behaviors (Osvold & Sodowsky, in press), and career-choice indecision (Sodowsky, 1991).

A Study of Cultural Adjustment Difficulties and Causal Immigrant Characteristics

We conducted a large cross-cultural study of Asian immigrants as well as Asian sojourners. Here we report our identification of stress symptoms of Asian immigrants and some specific immigrant variables that contributed to these stresses. The Cultural Adjustment Difficulties Checklist (CADC) was developed to understand the acculturation-induced stresses of Asians in the United States. The CADC covered majority–minority conflict-related interpersonal problems, alienation toward one's cultural reference group, and issues of self-efficacy in a White-dominant social context. Further, to understand the acculturation context, we examined the extent to which the stresses were influenced by immigrant variables, including acculturation preferences for language usage and social customs, age, age at time of immigration, years of residence in the United States, extent of ethnic friendship networks (e.g., percentage of ethnic friends and time spent with ethnic friends), family extendedness (e.g., family influence on personal decisions, members included in a family, family members that subjects felt close to), income, and perception of prejudice. Acculturation preferences for language usage and social customs were measured with the Majority–Minority Relations Scale, which has demonstrated relatively strong psychometric properties such as internal consistency, construct validity, discriminant validity, and sample generalizibility (see Sodowsky et al., 1991).

Immigrant Characteristics of the Sample. Respondents to our survey included Asian immigrant students, faculty, staff, and university-affiliated officials at the University of Nebraska–Lincoln. Two hundred subjects accounted for a 50% return rate. The largest ethnic group was Chinese Americans ($N =$ 55), followed by Asian Indians ($N = 52$), Vietnamese ($N = 32$), Koreans ($N =$ 21), Japanese Americans ($N = 18$), other Asian Americans ($N = 13$), and Filipinos ($N = 9$).

One hundred and forty-six were first generation, 37 second generation, 16 third generation, and one fourth generation. Thirty-two percent were born in the United States. Of the 68% who were born outside the United States ($n =$ 136), 53% arrived in the United States at the age of 17 or younger, 26% arrived between age 18 and 24, 20% arrived between 26 and 30, and 11% arrived at age 31 or older. Among these, 17% had lived in the United States 20 years or more, 39% had lived in the United States between 10 and 20 years, 27% between 5 and 10 years, and 16% 5 or fewer years. Half of those born outside the United States were naturalized citizens, and the other half were permanent residents (i.e., green card holders). Of those who reported their religion, 36% observed Eastern religions, such as Hinduism, Buddhism, Taoism, Islam, and Sikhism; 64% observed Protestantism and Catholicism.

Fifty-two percent were males, and 48% were females. Ages ranged from 20 to 60 years, with the median age being 27 years. Fifty-one percent were students, 29% were faculty and staff, and 19% were university-affiliated professionals. Fifty-four percent were single, and 46% were married.

Adjustment Difficulties of the Immigrant Sample.   Various exploratory factor analyses with oblique solutions indicated that 48 items with salient loadings of .30 or above loaded only on one of two factors, which had eigenvalues of 10.28 and 4.11, respectively. The two factor oblique solution seemed to be the cleanest and conceptually the most meaningful with no overlapping constructs. The internal consistency reliabilities (i.e., coefficient alphas) for the full scale and the two subscales were .92, .90, and .88, respectively. The correlation coefficient between these two factors was .35. Table 11.1 shows summarized CADC items for the Asian immigrant sample, factor loadings, and reliability and validity coefficients.

The two-factor structure for the Asian immigrant sample was compared with the two-factor structure obtained from the Asian sojourner sample. Factorial congruence (Gorsuch, 1983) of the factor structures of the two samples indicated Pearson correlations of .92 and .94. Confirmatory factor analysis (LISREL 7 program of Jöreskog & Sorbom, 1988), using the maximum likelihood estimation procedure, tested whether the data of the sojourner sample would fit the two-factor model identified for the immigrant sample. Indices of fit met the rule-of-thumb acceptance levels (see Bollen, 1989). The goodness-of-fit index (GFI) = .85; the adjusted GFI = .82; the ratio of the chi-square goodness-of-fit to its degrees of freedom = 1.85 (appropriately low); the root-mean-square residual (RMR) = .021 (appropriately low); the normed index of fit, or delta (evaluation of the fit of the proposed model relative to a logical

TABLE 11.1

CADC Summarized Items, Factor Loadings for Asian Immigrant Sample
(N = 200), and Reliability and Validity Coefficients

Items		Acculturative Distress	Intercultural Competence
	Factors	1	2
1. Having social opportunites		−.12	.62
2. Easily confronting people		−.04	.47
3. Conflicts over cultural values with members of immediate or extended family		.37	.01
4. Conflicts with people who have power		.56	−.12
5. Friendships from other ethnic groups		.01	.35
6. Comfortable in joining a group of people		−.05	.65
7. Close friendships		−.06	.40
8. White American friendships		−.07	.57
9. Confident when contradicting others		−.17	.64
10. Feeling good about abilities		−.03	.74
11. Suicidal ideation		.43	−.05
12. Feeling sadder now		.53	.05
13. Feeling good about one's looks		.06	.42
14. Suicide attempts		.30	.07
15. Lacking dating opportunities		.47	−.08
16. More guilty now		.65	−.10
17. More nervous now		.57	.07
18. Generally able to decide		.08	.57
19. More anger now		.58	.03
20. Violent behavior		.42	.10
21. Money problems		.46	−.02
22. More backaches now		.31	.06
23. More headaches now		.59	−.12
24. Upset with too much work		.52	.07
25. Happy in current job		.17	.40
26. Loss of interest in studies or work		.35	.20
27. Good performance		.17	.54
28. Able to concentrate		.12	.56
29. Major or career matches interests		.11	.59
30. High performance anxiety		.58	.03
31. Happy with major or career		.13	.56
32. Worried about not performing at the best level		.65	−.21
33. Not belonging to either the White American group or to one's ethnic group		.39	.22
34. Confused about one's gender role in one's ethnic group		.63	.07
35. Angry toward people from one's ethnic group		.42	.15
36. Experiencing conflicting feelings of two-ness in a majority–minority context		.69	.04
37. Pride in own ethnic group		−.00	.49
38. Believing that one's ethnic group is inferior		.46	.21

Continued

Table 11.1

(Continued)

Items	Acculturative Distress	Intercultural Competence
Factors	1	2
39. Feeling confused about one's gender role when with White Americans	.48	.26
40. Being certain that one is a worthy contributing member of the larger society	.03	.61
41. White Americans are better looking	.55	−.05
42. Wanting to belong to the group that has power	.55	−.11
43. Living on the margins of two cultures	.42	.23
44. Feeling accepted by people from one's ethnic group	−.04	.49
45. Being certain that one is a worthy contributing member of one's own ethnic group	.10	.42
46. Feeling accepted by White Americans	.03	.60
47. Respecting most people from one's ethnic group	.12	.44
48. Feeling caught between two cultures	.58	.05
Eigenvalues	10.28	4.11
Percentage of variance explained	21.00	8.40
Alphas of subscales	.89	.88

Alphas of full scale	.91
Interscale correlation coefficients	.34
Pearson correlation coefficients of factorial congruence	
Factor 1 on Asian Sojourner sample and Factor 1 on Asian Immigrant sample	.92
Factor 2 on Asian Sojourner sample and Factor 2 on Asian Immigrant sample	.94

Note: Italicized loadings indicate the items that are strong measures of each factor. These items have factor loadings of .30 or above. Factor 1, Acculturative Distress, has 27 items, and Factor 2, Intercultural Competence Concerns, has 21 items. The contents of the CADC items are summarized. The original items are copyrighted by the authors.

worse case, that is, the null model) = .80 (appropriately high). The standardized solution was also computed. All standardized loadings were significant according to T values (i.e., $> \pm 1.96$), with the average T value of 6.55. All but one of the terms of the modification indices were below the recommended level of 5.00. The majority of the terms in the standardized residual matrix were below the recommended threshold of 2.00, and the median was .66 (see Jöreskog & Sorbom, 1988, for these criteria).

Factor 1, called Acculturative Distress, consisted of general stress items and cultural stress items. General stress items included affective responses (i.e., anxiety, sadness, guilt, nervousness, and anger); behavioral responses (i.e., suicidal ideation and attempts, drinking, procrastination, and violence); psychosomatic symptoms (i.e., backaches, stomachaches, and headaches); and academic and career-related concerns (e.g., high performance anxiety, feeling overworked, etc.). Cultural stress items referred to experiencing cultural conflicts with White Americans, people from one's own cultural group, or one's family members; finding one's cultural group to be inferior; experiencing gender role confusion when relating to White Americans or people from one's own cultural group; feeling anger toward White Americans or people from one's own cultural group; feeling caught between two cultures; feeling distant from both cultures; and being unwilling to belong to either culture group.

Factor 2, called Intercultural Competence Concerns, referred to one's concern about social competence, academic and career competence, and cultural competence. Social competence included one's comfort level while interacting with a group of people, ability to be assertive, ability to have close friends, and ability to develop friendships with White Americans, people from one's own cultural group, and people from other cultural groups. Career and academic competence included ability to concentrate, perform, and make decisions; satisfaction with major, career, or job; and certainty regarding the appropriateness of one's major or career. Cultural Competence included pride in one's culture, perception of acceptance by White Americans or people from one's own cultural group, perception of the worthiness of one's contribution to both cultures, and perception of one's adjustment to both cultures.

Characteristics Causally Related to Acculturative Distress and Intercultural Competence Concerns.   We conceptualized two models for the Asian sample

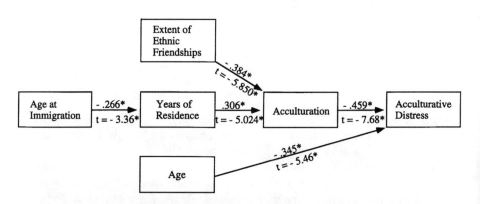

FIG. 11.3.   Structural relationships of immigrant factors and acculturation with acculturative distress for Asian immigrants ($N = 200$). *Note:* Acculturation: Subjects showed moderately low (preference for a traditional orientation) to moderately high (preference for a bicultural orientation) acculturation on a Likert scale of 1 to 6. The lower the acculturation, the more acculturative distress. The younger one is, the more acculturative distress. Immigration at a younger age, the more years of residence in the United States, the higher the acculturation. The more ethnic friendships, the lower the acculturation ($p < .05$, significant path coefficients and t scores).

on the basis of our previous empirical findings about the effects of sociocultural factors on the acculturation styles of Asians. Some of the previously discovered factors were voluntary immigration versus political refugee status, education and income, age, generational status, religion, years of residence in the United States, country of birth, and marital status (Sodowsky & Carey, 1988; Sodowsky et al., 1991; Sodowsky & Plake, 1992). We also applied to the model our social psychological understanding of Asian natural support contexts (e.g., ethnic friendship network and family loyalty) in which ethnic identification strategies of Asian immigrants take place (Sodowsky et al., 1995).

In one model, the extent of ethnic friendships, age at the time of immigration, and years of residence in the United States had structural paths to acculturation orientations for language and social customs, which, in turn, had a path to Acculturative Distress. Age was also shown to have a direct path to Acculturative Distress. In a second model, we showed that income had a structural path to perceived prejudice, which, in turn, had a path to Intercultural Competence Concerns. We also showed that both family extendedness and age had direct paths to Intercultural Competence Concerns. See Figs. 11.3 and 11.4 for the structural models of hypothesized relationships.

Structural equation modeling was employed, using LISREL 7 (Jöreskog & Sorbom, 1988) maximum likelihood estimation procedures. Strong goodness-of-fit indices were indicated for both models. Model 1: GFI = .87; AdjGFI = .85, chi-square = 1.65, p = .74 (a nonsignificant chi-square indicated that the proposed model and the actual data were not different), chi-square:df = .45,

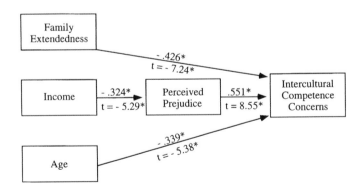

FIG. 11.4.   Structural relationships of immigrant factors and perceived prejudice with intercultural competence concerns for Asian immigrants ($N = 200$). *Note:* The greater the perception of prejudice, the more concerns with intercultural competence. With a smaller family network, the more concerns with intercultural competence. The younger one is, the more concerns with intercultural competence one has, and the lower the income, the greater the perception of prejudice ($p < .05$, significant path coefficients and t scores).

and RMR = .019. Model 2: GFI = .90; AdjGFI = .89, χ^2 = 2.10, p = < .85, χ^2:df = .43, and RMR = .017. All variables indicated significant standardized path coefficients and t scores in their respective relationships to the dependent variables.

Model 1 showed significant negative and positive relationships: the lower the acculturation scores (i.e., tending to show a more traditional than a bicultural style), the more the acculturative distress; the younger the subject, the more the acculturative distress; the greater the extent of ethnic friendships, the lower the acculturation scores; and the younger the subject was at the time of immigration, the more years the subject had lived in the United States, and the higher the subject's acculturation score.

Model 2 also showed significant positive and negative relationships: the greater the perception of prejudice, the more intercultural competence concerns; the smaller the family extendedness, the more intercultural competence concerns; the younger the subject, the more intercultural competence concerns; the lower the income, the greater the perception of prejudice.

The results of both structural models show that Asian immigrants' preferences for their native languages, customs, and social behaviors and their perception of prejudice in White American society, with the low-income subjects perceiving more prejudice, led to their experience of cultural adjustment difficulties. Younger subjects appeared to be at greater risk for cultural adjustment difficulties than older subjects. Extendedness of family network, support, and closeness led to social, academic and career, and cultural competencies (called Intercultural Competencies). Additionally, whereas the younger subjects may have had difficulties, those who immigrated at a young age and had lived in United States for a longer period of time than newly immigrating adults tended to be bicultural or U.S. society-acculturated. This, in turn, tended to reduce acculturative distress. Finally, extendedness of ethnic friendship network gave a more traditional orientation, which led to acculturative distress.

Concluding Remarks

Asian immigrants' cultural adjustment difficulties included anxious and depressed reactions, psychosomatic complaints, and cultural stress responses such as conflicts with White Americans, one's ethnic group, and one's family and gender role confusions, anger, and lowered involvement when relating to both the White American group and one's ethnic group. Immigrants living in two cultures are required to know and negotiate two different sets of cultural attitudes, knowledge, and behaviors. Smooth changes are contingent upon intercultural learning and integration of cultural abilities.

Asian immigrants indicated concerns with social, academic or career, and cultural competencies. Numerous studies have documented that Asian cultures place strong emphasis on social-restraint and -cautiousness as well as academic achievement (Givens et al., 1984; Hodgkinson, 1985; D. Sue & D. W. Sue, 1990; S. Sue & Okazaki, 1990; S. Sue, 1996). For instance, with regard to social cautiousness, Asian American students, when compared with White American students, appear to be less willing to express their impulses and feelings, more socially introverted, less assertive socially, and more comfortable in reserved and structured social situations. These attitudes are contrasted with the American emphasis on spontaneity, assertiveness, directness, and informality (Minatoya & Sedlacek, 1980; Sodowsky et al., 1995; D. W. Sue & Kirk, 1973; D. Sue & D. W. Sue, 1993). It is possible that Asian immigrants, who emphasize social cautiousness, live with two sets of opposing attitudes with regard to interpersonal behaviors. Consequently, they might be confused about how to be socially competent. One's sense of self-efficacy with regard to being socially poised may be negatively affected.

It is not surprising that Asians reported various degrees of concerns regarding academic and career competence. A number of hypotheses can be considered for the academic and career anxieties of Asians. First, in traditional Asian societies, which are strongly influenced by Hinduism, Buddhism, Taoism, Confucianism, and Islam, scholars are placed high in the social ladder. Saraswati, the goddess of learning, is accorded high status in Hindu households. Asian children are taught from an early age that academic and career achievements are crucial for one's personal development and social status. Second, Asians place high value on the collective identity and cohesiveness of the family. A high priority for most Asians is to take care of and to bring glory to their respective families. Achievement at school or at work is one of the proper means to take care of and bring glory to the family. Third, Asians in the United States have been strongly subjected to prejudice and discrimination (D. W. Sue & D. Sue, 1990). Therefore, the only avenue perceived by Asians as being available for their adaptation to and advancement in the U.S. society is education. Asians may perceive other areas as closed because of institutional racism. Thus, the sources of cultural stress may be in the White American culture as well as in the Asian immigrant cultures.

One is cautioned against overpathologizing the study's Asian sample. The Diagnostic and Statistical Manual of Mental Disorders (DSM–IV; American Psychiatric Association, 1994) states that a cultural formulation of mental health makes available a systematic review of the role of a cultural context, social stressors, and available social supports in mental health. Therefore, to prevent hasty conclusions about "Asian neuroses," we conceptualized causal models of immigrant sociocultural variables so that we could explain symptoms and start a dialogue on how to cope with these variables rather that how to cure symptoms.

From this study we have learned that the traditional orientation of one's culture of origin, young age (late adolescence and young adulthood), immigration at an older age, extensive ethnic networks that exclude White American friendships, limited family kinship and support, low income, and high levels of perceived prejudice are significantly related to acculturative distress and problems in relating to others interculturally. When assessing the difficulties of Asian immigrants it would be useful to ask about the contributions of these variables and the extent to which they can be changed or controlled. When talking about controlling causal variables, it needs to be remembered that a traditional orientation towards core values of one's ethnic identity may be a positive resolution in certain cultural conflicts, as shown in the earlier illustration of the Asian Indian woman professional. Another reminder is that not all young Asians have adjustment difficulties. The Vietnamese refugee and teenager, Dung, described earlier, makes that point. Thus, it is important to examine a configuration of immigrant variables that act as checks and balances in the etiology of disorders. Finally, cultural adjustment difficulties are not necessarily bad but rather could be a motivator for change and improvement.

REFERENCES

American Psychiatric Association. (1994). Diagnostic and statistical manual of mental disorders (4th ed.). Washington, DC: Author.

Atkinson, D. R., Morten, G., & Sue, D. W. (1993). Counseling American minorities: A cross-cultural perspective. Dubuque, IA: Brown & Benchmark.

Berry, J. W. (1980). Acculturation as varieties of adaptation. In A. M. Padilla (Ed.), Acculturation: Theory, model, and some new findings (pp. 9–25). Boulder, CO: Westview.

Berry, J. W. (1990). Psychology of acculturation. In J. J. Berman (Ed.), Cross-cultural perspectives (pp. 201–234). Lincoln, NE: University of Nebraska Press.

Berry, J. W., & Annis, R. C. (1974). Acculturative stress: The role of ecology, culture and differentiation. Journal of Cross-Cultural Psychology, 5, 382–405.

Berry, J. W., Kim, U., Minde, T., & Mok, D. (1987). Comparative studies of acculturative stress. International Migration Review, 21, 491–511.

Bollen, K. A. (1989). Structural equations with latent variables. New York: Wiley.

Chao, R. K. (1995). Chinese and European American cultural models of the self reflected in mothers' childrearing beliefs. Ethos, 23, 328–354.

Draguns, J. (1996). Multicultural and cross-cultural assessment: Dilemmas and decisions. In G. R. Sodowsky & J. Impara (Eds.), Multicultural assessment in counseling and clinical psychology (pp. 37–84). Lincoln, NE: Buros Institute of Mental Measurements.

Fernandez, M. S. (1988). Issues in counseling Southeast Asian students. Journal of Multicultural Counseling and Development, 16, 157–166.

Givens, R., Mittelback, M., Goldberg, L., Christopher, K., Genachowski, J., Reed, J., Cook, M., & Butler, D. (1984, April). Asian Americans: The drive to excel. Newsweek, 4–13.

Gorsuch, R. L. (1983). Factor analysis. Hillsdale, NJ: Lawrence Erlbaum Associates.

Hodgkinson, H. L. (1985). All one system: Demographics of education—kindergarten through graduate school. Washington, DC: Institute for Educational Leadership.

Ihle, G. M., Sodowsky, G. R., & Kwan, K.-L. K. (1996). Worldviews of women: Comparisons between White-American clients, White-American counselors, and Chinese international students. Journal of Counseling and Development, 74, 300–306.

Isajiw, W. W. (1990). Ethnic-identity retention. In R. Breton, W. W. Isajiw, W. E. Kalbach, & J. G. Reitz (Eds.), Ethnic identity and equality (pp. 34–91). Toronto: University of Toronto Press.

Jöreskog, K. G., & Sorbom, D. (1988). *LISREL 7: A guide to the program and applications.* Chicago: SPSS.

Krause, N., Bennett, J., & Tran, T. V. (1989). Age differences in the acculturation process. *Psychology and Aging, 4,* 321–332.

LaFromboise, T., Coleman, H. L. K., & Gerton, J. (1993). Psychological impact of biculturalism: Evidence and theory. *Psychological Bulletin, 114,* 395–412.

Markus, H. R., & Kitayama, S. (1991). Culture and the self: Implications for cognition, emotion, and motivation. *Psychological Review, 98,* 224–253.

Matsuoka, J. K. (1990). Differential acculturation among Vietnamese refugees. *Social Work, 35,* 341–345.

McGoldrick, M. (1982). Ethnicity and family therapy: An overview. In M. McGoldrick, J. K. Pearce, & J. Giordano (Eds.), *Ethnicity and family therapy* (pp. 3–30). New York: Guilford.

Minatoya, L. Y., & Sedlacek, W. E. (1980). *A profile of Asian American university freshmen* (Counseling Center Research Report #9-80). Counseling Center, University of Maryland, College Park.

Nicassio, P. M. (1985). The psychosocial adjustment of the Southeast Asian refugee: An overview of empirical findings and theoretical models. *Journal of Cross-Cultural Psychology, 16,* 153–173.

Osvold, L., & Sodowsky, G. R. (in press). Effects of race/ethnicity and acculturation on the eating attitudes of African American and Native American women. *Exploration in ethnic studies.*

Padilla, A. M., Wagatsuma, Y., & Lindholm, K. J. (1985). Acculturation and personality as predictors of stress in Japanese and Japanese-Americans. *Journal of Social Psychology, 125,* 295–305.

Pannu, R. K., & Helms, J. E. (1994). *Asian Indian cultural identity and perceptions of family functioning.* Unpublished manuscript, University of Maryland.

Phinney, J. S. (1990). Ethnic identity in adolescence and adulthood: A review of research. *Psychological Bulletin, 108,* 499–514.

Phinney, J. S., & Chavira, V. (1992). Ethnic identity and self-esteem: An exploratory longitudinal study. *Journal of Adolescence, 15,* 271–281.

Root, M. P. (1985). Guidelines for facilitating therapy with Asian American clients. *Psychotherapy, 22,* 349–357.

Rosenthal, D. A., & Feldman, S. S. (1992). The nature and stability of ethnic identity in Chinese youth: Effects of length of residence in two cultural contexts. *Journal of Cross-Cultural Psychology, 23,* 214–227.

Sanchez, A. R., & Atkinson, D. R. (1983). Mexican-American cultural commitment, preference for counselor ethnicity, and willingness to use counseling. *Journal of Counseling Psychology, 30,* 215–220.

Segal, U. A. (1991, April). Cultural variables in Asian Indian families. *Journal of Contemporary Human Services, 72,* 233–242.

Siddique, C. M. (1977). Structural separation and family change: An exploratory study of the immigrant Indian and Pakistani community of Saskatoon, Canada. *International Review of Modern Sociology, 7,* 13–34.

Sodowsky, G. R. (1991). Effects of culturally consistent counseling tasks on American and International student observers' perception of counselor credibility: A preliminary investigation. *Journal of Counseling and Development, 69,* 253–256.

Sodowsky, G. R., & Carey, J. C. (1987). Asian Indian immigrants in America: Factors related to adjustment. *Journal of Multicultural Counseling and Development, 15,* 129–141.

Sodowsky, G. R., & Carey, J. C. (1988). Relationships between acculturation-related demographics and cultural attitudes of an Asian-Indian immigrant group. *Journal of Multicultural Counseling and Development, 16,* 117–133.

Sodowsky, G. R., Kwan, K. L., & Pannu, R. (1995). Ethnic identity of Asians in the United States.

In J. G. Ponterotto, J. M. Casas, L. A. Suzuki, & C. M. Alexander (Eds.), *Handbook of multicultural counseling* (pp. 123–154). Newbury Park, CA: Sage.

Sodowsky, G. R., Lai, E. W. M., & Plake, B. S. (1991). Moderating effects of sociocultural variables on acculturation attitudes of Hispanics and Asian Americans. *Journal of Counseling and Development, 70,* 194–204.

Sodowsky, G. R., Maguire, K., Johnson, P., Ngumba, W., & Kohles, R. (1994). World views of White American, Mainland Chinese Taiwanese, and African students: An investigation into between-group differences. *Journal of Cross-Cultural Psychology, 29,* 309–324.

Sodowsky, G. R., & Plake, B. (1992). A study of acculturation differences among international people and suggestions for sensitvity to within group differences. *Journal of Counseling and Development, 71*(1).

Sue, D., & Sue, D. W. (1993). Ethnic identity: Cultural factors in the psychological development of Asians in America. In D. R. Atkinson, G. Morten, & D. W. Sue (Eds.), *Counseling American minorities: A cross-cultural perspective* (4th ed., pp. 199–210). Madison, WI: Brown & Benchmark.

Sue, D. W., & Kirk, B. A. (1973). Differential characteristics of Japanese-American and Chinese-American college students. *Journal of Counseling Psychology, 20,* 142–148.

Sue, D. W., & Sue, D. (1990). *Counseling the culturally different: Theory and practice* (2nd ed.). New York: Wiley.

Sue, S. (1996). Measurement, testing, and ethnic bias: Can solutions be found? In G. R. Sodowsky & J. Impara (Eds.), *Multicultural assessment in counseling and clinical psychology* (pp. 7–36). Lincoln, NE: Buros Institute of Mental Measurements.

Sue, S., & Okazaki, S. (1990). Asian American educational achievements: A phenomenon in search of an explanation. *American Psychologist, 45,* 913–920.

Sue, S., & Zane, N. (1987). The role of culture and cultural techniques in psychotherapy. *American Psychologist, 42,* 37–45.

Uba, L. (1994). *Asian Americans: Personality patterns, identity, and mental health.* New York: Guilford.

Wakil, S. P., Siddique, C. M., & Wakil, F. A. (1981). Between two cultures: A study in socialization of children of immigrants. *Journal of Marriage and the Family, 43,* 929–940.

PART IV

WHAT POLICIES
ENHANCE OR IMPEDE
IMMIGRANT FAMILY LINKS
TO U.S. INSTITUTIONS?

12

Immigrant Families and Public Policy: A Deepening Divide

Michael Fix
Wendy Zimmermann
The Urban Institute

W E BEGIN this chapter with several unremarkable observations. First, both the virtue and decline of the family are very much at the center of public debate. Second, as political scientist Francis Fukuyama wrote, immigrants—especially our newest immigrants—are thought to embody strong families and family values (Fukuyama, 1993). Immigrant families, for example, are more likely than natives to have two parents present.[1] Third, few areas of public policy have explicitly pursued family goals to the degree that immigration policies have. Indeed, family unification animates virtually all areas of immigration policy, even those like refugee policy, with which it is not conventionally associated.

In contrast to these unremarkable observations, a number of striking proposals have been advanced by the Congress that will have far-reaching impacts on both U.S. immigration and immigrant integration policies. They would reduce levels of legal immigration, restrict the admission of certain family members, and limit legal immigrants' access to public benefits. Although the family is central to both sets of reforms, Congress seems to be proceeding without taking into account the cumulative impact on the immigrant family. At the same time that these reforms are proceeding, many of the central concepts of the welfare state are being reconsidered as budgets are cut, programs are consolidated, and responsibilities are devolved to state and local govern-

---

[1] Eighty percent of families with a foreign-born head were two-parent families, compared with 73% of native-headed families, according to the 1994 Current Population Survey.

ments. These developments are likely to jeopardize further the access that immigrants and their families have to public services.

Although the backdrop against which this chapter is written is rather grand, our objectives are modest. That is, we provide a brief overview of some of the nation's immigrant and immigration policies and sketch the leading reforms that have been proposed, viewing them through the lens of the immigrant family. We then address the implications of current reforms and their potential unintended consequences. We do not, however, offer alternative proposals for reform.

For the past 30 years the United States has had a defined, inclusive immigration policy. However the nation's immigrant policies—that is, those policies that accelerate or retard the integration of newcomers—have been largely inchoate and hands-off. With no defined immigrant policy in place, legal immigrants have been eligible for public services and benefits on roughly the same terms as citizens.

However, imminent changes in welfare policy would dramatically reorder the relationship of immigrants to the social welfare state. They would effectively exclude not just illegal immigrants but also legal immigrants and, under some proposals, naturalized citizens from virtually all needs based programs, programs that range from nutrition assistance to job training. Indeed, where immigrants are concerned, the bundle of policy changes embedded in the most prominent welfare reform proposals go far beyond determining eligibility for cash transfer programs to redefining the basic terms of membership in society for immigrants and their families. If enacted, the changes would move the nation closer to an explicit immigrant policy, but it would be a policy of exclusion rather than inclusion. Further, these proposed changes fail to incorporate the insights that social science offers on the experience of adaptation and may aggravate, rather than mitigate, the adjustment problems faced by immigrant families.

At the same time that Congress may be reducing the rights and entitlements of immigrants, it is also likely to substantially revise federal immigration policy. The leading proposals would reduce overall immigration levels, restrict admissions of extended (versus nuclear) family members, require that immigrants' sponsors have substantial resources, and require that those sponsors assume full financial responsibility for the immigrants they sponsor and do so for an extended period of time.[2] These changes may lower immigration flows and mitigate immigrants' economic impacts by limiting their use of public services. At the same time, though, they may reduce the financial and social capital available to immigrant households just as public benefits are made inaccessible. As a result, they may compound the difficulties faced by immigrant

---

[2] Proposals to increase sponsors' responsibilities to immigrants appear in both the welfare and immigration reform proposals.

families. Moreover, it appears that some proposals will exclude categories of immigrant family members, most notably siblings, that have historically demonstrated rapid economic mobility.

In the first section of this chapter, we examine some of the trends that underlie current reform proposals within both immigrant and immigration policy. Second, we examine shifting policies that govern immigrant access to benefits and services, speculating on the impacts on immigrants and their families. Our focus is principally on legal rather than illegal immigrants. The third section of the chapter addresses proposed changes in the nation's immigration policies and their implications.

THE DEMOGRAPHIC AND POLICY CONTEXT

Immigration Trends

Four basic trends characterize immigration to the United States during the last decade and shed light on current debates. First, the scale of immigration to the United States throughout the 1980s and 1990s has been quite high. Indeed, the 1.1 to 1.2 million legal and illegal immigrants who enter and stay each year matches or exceeds the nation's historical peak. Immigrants and their children now account for over half of the net annual population increase. Second, the impact of these flows is magnified by its concentration. Unlike other social issues that confront the United States, immigration is essentially a 6-, not a 50-state phenomenon, because about three quarters of all immigrants live in only six states. Moreover, immigration is largely an urban phenomenon, as 93% of immigrants (versus 73% of natives) live in metropolitan areas. The impact of the new immigration has also been intensified by its pace. Almost one half of the immigrants in the United States were not here a decade ago. Thus, what might be viewed as a failure on the part of immigrants to assimilate as fast as their predecessors—to learn English, for example—can be seen as a function of the recency of their arrival rather than of their ability or their separatist inclinations. Finally, the force of the new immigration is also magnified by the diversity of recent flows. The number of countries with at least 100,000 foreign-born residents in the United States almost doubled between 1980 and 1990 alone (Fix & Passel, 1994).

Each of these dimensions of the new immigration—its scale, concentration, pace, and diversity—complicates institutional efforts to respond to immigration flows. Each has also contributed to the broad reconsideration of both immigration and immigrant policy that is being proposed today.

Concerns About Declining Quality and Rising Welfare Use

Critics of U.S. immigration policy argue that the shift to universal admissions criteria that emphasize the social goal of family unification has led to a decline in the quality of immigrants admitted.[3] Some commentators point to the low earnings of immigrants admitted on family-related grounds (Borjas, 1992). Others note that although immigrants admitted under family (versus employment) criteria have lower earnings at the time of entry, they have much higher earnings growth and eventually achieve earnings parity (Duleep & Regets, 1992). Researchers have also found that family immigrants are as likely to participate in the labor force as immigrants admitted under employment preferences (Sorensen, Bean, Ku, & Zimmermann, 1992).

One indicator of declining immigrant quality is increased use of public benefits. It is argued that higher welfare use signals not only lower skills and education but a deterioration in the character of newcomers. Our own analysis indicates that although immigrants overall have slightly higher rates of public benefits use than natives (6.6 versus 4.9%), use is heavily concentrated among two subpopulations: refugees and elderly immigrants. Welfare receipt among non-refugee working-age immigrants is about the same as for natives (5.1 versus 5.3%). However, welfare use within this population did rise between 1990 and 1993. Despite this trend, immigrants who are poor remain substantially less likely to use welfare than working-age natives who are poor (16 versus 25%) (Fix & Zimmermann, 1995).[4]

The current political controversy over immigrant use of welfare has arisen in part due to steadily rising rates of immigrant use of Supplemental Security Income (SSI). Most elderly immigrants who have turned to the SSI benefit program have not worked enough quarters to qualify for Social Security. This is either because they entered the United States when they were old or worked for employers who did not pay Social Security taxes for them. Their comparatively high use of SSI has spurred proposals to restrict their access to public benefits and to restrict the admission of the parents of U.S. citizens. It has also led to a reevaluation of the family's role in supporting the immigrants they bring in to the country.

IMMIGRANT POLICY

U.S. immigrant policy can be viewed as the investment that federal, state, and local governments choose to make in the human capital and other needs of immigrants. These integration or immigrant policies can be mapped into three broad domains. The first is express or targeted immigrant policies, those

---

[3]Quality is usually used to suggest the educational attainment, earnings, and use of public assistance on the part of immigrants (see Fix & Passel, 1994).

[4]Welfare use data are from the 1994 Current Population Survey.

aimed deliberately (and hence exclusively or largely) at newcomers. The second is the legislatively or administratively set eligibility rules for mainstream social welfare and education programs. The third is the rights of aliens as they have been defined by the courts, often interpreting Constitutional doctrine. The latter two can be viewed as the nation's de facto immigrant policies (Fix & Zimmermann, 1993).

Although the United States has had an inclusive immigration policy for the past 30 years, the federal government has had a largely laissez faire, hands-off immigrant policy. As a consequence, public responsibility for incorporating newcomers and their families has fallen, mostly by default, to state and local governments. A striking policy mismatch has emerged between the limited and declining federal expenditures devoted to immigrant-related programs and the large and growing number of immigrants admitted to the nation over the past three decades.

The lack of a deliberate integration or settlement policy like those in place in Canada, Israel, and Australia has not been a simple oversight on the part of Congress. Rather, it has been a logical correlate of the way in which most immigrants admitted for family unification or work-related reasons have been viewed historically.[5] Policy makers have viewed legal immigrants coming for family or work reasons as being either responsible for their own well-being or as the responsibility of their family, their employer, or a sponsoring non-profit agency. Most immigrants are then presumed to be self-sufficient, or at least not the responsibility of government. Hence, it has been assumed that they would impose few or no costs on the public and that government's role in their integration should be minimal.

Moreover, immigrants impose costs on state and local governments, but those costs are shared only to the extent that social expenditures are generally shared. As a result, there has been no heightened sense of federal obligation to respond to the community impacts of legal immigration.[6] However, two aspects of immigrants' fiscal impacts have led to tensions over the intergovernmental sharing of immigration's costs. First, most taxes that immigrants pay go to the federal government, whereas most services are delivered by state and local governments. Second, as we have seen, immigrants' fiscal impacts are concentrated in the handful of states and cities where large numbers of immigrants live.

---

[5]It is important to distinguish between immigrants admitted as legal permanent residents, who constitute the majority of annual admissions and whose arrival is, for the most part, planned, from immigrants admitted for humanitarian purposes: principally refugees and asylees. Because the latter are found to be escaping political persecution, their emigration is in some sense, unplanned.

[6]The federal government recently provided states with impact assistance for the costs of incarcerating illegal immigrants.

Express Immigrant Policy: Targeted Programs

A map of the express, federal immigrant policy of the United States includes at least five broad types of legislatively enacted policies. These policies consist not only of services aimed at helping immigrants and refugees adjust to life in the United States but also the provision of aid to the communities in which they live. They include:

- Targeted policies aimed at refugees and asylees that provide health, public assistance, job training, and social services.
- Policies directed at limited English proficient elementary and secondary school students and adults, principally through the Bilingual Education Act and the Adult Education Act.[7]
- Policies and resources intended to deter discrimination in employment on the basis of selected alienage and national origin characteristics. These policies have been implemented by the Equal Employment Opportunity Commission and the Department of Justice's Office of Special Counsel for Immigration Related Unfair Employment Practices.
- Resources provided to state and local governments intended to offset the fiscal impacts of specific immigrant groups. One such program is the Emergency Immigrant Education Act (EIEA),[8] a small grant program directed to states that have received recent influxes of immigrant students. Another, codified in the 1994 Violent Crime Control and Law Enforcement Act,[9] reimburses state and local costs of incarcerating criminal aliens.
- Efforts made by the federal, state and local governments to help immigrants naturalize. Most resources dedicated to naturalization pay for the processing of applications. However, the federal government and several states have begun initiatives to expand education, civics instruction, and outreach around naturalization.

Limited Number and Expenditures.   When these policies are viewed in their entirety, it is striking how few major initiatives there are, the limited number of resources that have been dedicated to them, their lack of coherent, animating policy goals, and their political fragility. However, they do address themselves to the most vulnerable population with the strongest equitable claims: refugees. Furthermore, they support spending on the most critical area of adjustment: language acquisition.[10]

---

[7] Title VII of the Elementary and Secondary Education Act, Pub. Law 90-247; Pub. Law 100-297.

[8] Pub. Law 98-511

[9] Pub. Law 103-322.

[10] Some commentators argue that the nation has a language and not an immigrant policy (Pompa, 1995).

Perhaps the only federal program that is explicitly addressed to the broad adaptation needs of immigrants and their families is the Refugee Resettlement Program. The program involves expenditures for income support, health services, job training, and social services. Moreover, the Refugee Program has developed a number of initiatives that are explicitly targeted to immigrant families, such as family-focused case management. That said, the Refugee Program is in important ways emblematic of federal immigrant policy as a whole, as we see a distinct pattern of federal fiscal retreat over the past decade. Federal funding for the Refugee Resettlement Program fell from $7,400 per refugee to $2,100 between FY 1984 and 1994.[11] At the same time, welfare reform proposals that are proceeding through the Congress would bar refugee use of public benefits beginning 5 years after admission, regardless of need.

Another example of the limited and declining character of immigrant policy can be seen in federal language acquisition programs. The federal government spends only $250 million combined on the two principal programs, bilingual education for elementary and secondary students (funded at $156 million for FY 1995) and English as a Second Language (ESL) for adults (approximately $100 million for FY 1995). Between 1984 and 1992, the number of limited English proficient children counted in the nation's schools rose 85% to about 2.5 million (Henderson, Donly, & Strang, 1994). During the same time period real increases in federal spending on bilingual education rose by only 1%.[12] Moreover, appropriation bills now before the Congress would cut in half current bilingual education spending.[13] Other proposals would repeal bilingual education outright.[14]

Federal spending on adult education over the same time period rose sharply, as did the share and total amount of spending on ESL instruction funded under the Adult Education Act. Federal spending, though, remains modest; indeed, California spends more on adult education than the federal government does.[15] The Adult Education Act programs are slated to be consolidated into education and training block grants and turned over to the states.[16] As a result, state spending on ESL services may soon have to compete against a host of ed-

---

[11]These figures represent annual Refugee Program funding and annual refugee admissions. They do not reflect actual spending or costs per refugee. The 1994 figure has been adjusted for inflation.

[12]These spending calculations are drawn from the 1984 and 1992 budgets of the United States.

[13]H.R. 2127, the FY 1996 Labor-HHS spending bill.

[14]See, for example, the Declaration of Official Language Act (H.R. 739) sponsored by Rep. Toby Roth, or the National Language Act (H.R. 1005) sponsored by Representative Peter King.

[15]In FY 1991, California spent $282 million on adult education; federal spending on adult education in that year was $201 million (Mike Dean, Office of Vocational and Adult Education, U.S. Department of Education, personal communication, October 1995).

[16]H.R. 1617 and S. 143.

ucation and training programs with more entrenched constituencies for rapidly diminishing federal support.

In sum, federal spending on language acquisition for both immigrant children and adults is likely to decline sharply, despite the importance of language resources for immigrant adjustment. Laosa (1990) noted that research studies "point to a variety of school contextual factors that are likely to affect the Hispanic child's coping and adaptation" (p. 52). These factors include "the nature of available services geared to serve foreign, limited English proficient, cultural minority students" and the linguistic composition of the schools' teaching staffs.

Beyond language acquisition, federal spending on school-related impact aid that is tied to immigration flows is negligible, amounting to about $50 million. This aid is distributed under the Emergency Immigrant Education Act (EIEA) and is intended to help offset the costs of the 700,000 students meeting the program's criteria: foreign born with less than 3 complete academic years in U.S. schools. The program spends on average less than $50 per immigrant child. Proposals now before the Congress would eliminate the EIEA. The other major impact aid program is intended to reimburse state and local governments for the costs of incarcerating criminal aliens. The program is distinctive, not only because it is new but because it is one of the most amply funded federal initiatives in immigrant policy. Spending in FY 1996 will rise to $297 million, providing over $12,000 per prisoner in impact aid.[17]

Funding to fight discrimination against immigrants has also been small in scale and narrowly targeted. The 1986 Immigration Reform and Control Act (IRCA)[18] created the Office of Special Counsel to enforce a provision of a law that prohibits employment discrimination based on national origin or citizenship status. In FY 1995, funding for this office and its activities amounted to $5.7 million, with about $1.3 million of it going to nonprofit organizations that do antidiscrimination outreach (G. Milanes, U.S. Department of Justice, personal communication, October, 1995). Funding for the EEOC is considerably higher, at about $233 million in FY 1995 (*Congressional Quarterly*, 1995), but these resources are dedicated to fighting employment discrimination more broadly, with comparatively few resources dedicated to immigrants.

The amount of federal money dedicated to naturalization has also been small, with only an estimated $29 million of direct spending by the Immigration and Naturalization Service in FY 1994. However, funding has been growing rapidly as the numbers of immigrants applying to naturalize has increased. In FY 1995, Congress approved the reprogramming of internal INS funds bringing total direct spending up to about $59 million, or double that spent in

---

[17]Although we do not know the number of criminal aliens housed in state and local prisons, we have estimated the number of illegal aliens in prisons in the seven states with the greatest number of immigrants. That number is roughly 24,000 (see Clark, Passel, Zimmermann, & Fix, 1994).

[18]Pub. Law 99-603.

FY 1994 (D. Rosenberg, Immigration and Naturalization Service, personal communication, November, 1995). In addition, several states have initiated their own programs to encourage or facilitate naturalization. For example, Illinois dedicated $1.1 million in state funds for education and application services, and Maryland allocated $100,000 for naturalization outreach (U.S. Commission on Immigration Reform, 1995). Further, some ESL training may also be geared toward preparing immigrants for passing the English language test necessary for naturalization.

Limited Reach.   The programs cited here are also notable because they fall well short of reaching the immigrant population as a whole.[19] The Refugee Program is restricted to federally designated refugees and asylees (about 10% of annual immigration levels). The limited resources made available under the Emergency Immigrant Education Act are directed only to recently arrived immigrant students. Spending under the Crime Bill offsets some costs of the small share of immigrant prisoners who are undocumented. As a result, communities that house substantial numbers of legal permanent residents—the largest segment of the entering immigrant population—do not receive any meaningful form of targeted impact assistance.

Although the immigrant policies currently in place are not organized under a coherent framework, are inadequately funded, and do not reach a large portion of the immigrant population, they can serve as building blocks for a new immigrant integration initiative. As noted in a recent report, the basic elements of a new Americanization movement could include teaching English, civics, and American history, enforcing laws against hate crimes and discrimination, and encouraging naturalization (U.S. Commission on Immigration Reform, 1995).

De Facto Immigrant Policy:
Eligibility for Mainstream Social Programs

The nation's immigrant policy is defined not only by its targeted programs but also by the degree to which immigrants are made eligible for mainstream social programs. These include two of the primary welfare programs, Aid to Families with Dependent Children (AFDC) and Supplemental Security Income (SSI), and Medicaid, publicly funded health insurance for the poor. In these programs, eligibility is determined by age, income, family composition, residential location, occupation, or some combination of these and other fac-

---

[19]Indeed, the largest single source of federal support targeted expressly to immigrants in recent memory was the $4 billion State Legalization Impact Assistance Grant program (SLIAG), which reimbursed certain costs of aliens legalizing under the 1986 Immigration Reform and Control Act. SLIAG has now lapsed.

tors. Although the fundamental purpose of the mainstream social policies has not been the integration of newcomers, they provide a safety net and help subsidize social services and human capital development for recent immigrants. Hence they constitute a key and politically controversial element of de facto national immigrant policy.

Some commentators have noted that welfare rights have been more broadly available to newcomers than political rights (Schuck & Smith, 1985), but access to benefits for aliens in the United States has been more constrained than in many Western European nations (Zimmermann & Calhoun, 1991). Since at least the 17th century, immigrants' use of benefits was checked by requiring that aliens applying for admission satisfy the public charge exclusion. That is, they had to demonstrate that they would not become paupers and go on welfare (Vialet & Eig, 1994).

One way to overcome this exclusion is to have a sponsor (usually a family member) sign an affidavit of support. The sponsor's income is then "deemed" to be available to the immigrant for the purpose of qualifying for means-tested federal benefits programs. Deeming is now applied to AFDC, SSI, and food stamps and in most cases disqualifies the immigrant for assistance. Although the process of deeming may seem punitive, in fact it plays an important, essentially inclusionary role in immigration policy by allowing the nation to admit immigrants who may be poor at the time of entry but who have the potential to work and contribute to the economy.

Immigrant eligibility for public benefits can be arrayed along a continuum. At the present time, naturalized citizens with full eligibility fall at one end of the spectrum, and undocumented immigrants with highly restricted eligibility fall at the other end. All things considered, these eligibility rules have had a generally pro-family cast.

Naturalized citizens have been eligible for benefits on the same terms as native-born citizens. Refugees, who are fleeing persecution and whose departure from their homes is unplanned, have also been eligible for public benefits on roughly the same terms as citizens. Refugees are unique among immigrants in that they can receive public benefits from the date of their arrival in the United States. Unlike natives, for whom public assistance has been largely limited to single-parent families, income support has been made available to intact refugee families for a limited period of time.

Legal permanent residents, or green-card holders, have also been able to receive most public benefits. However, most legal immigrants' eligibility for the principal federal cash and in-kind programs such as SSI, AFDC, and food stamps is restricted through deeming for a 3- or 5-year period following entry into the United States. These deeming policies strike a balance between the obligation of the family and that of the state to support immigrants.

Immigrants legalizing under the 1986 Immigration Reform and Control Act (IRCA) were barred from most federal benefit programs for 5 years following application for legalization. That bar has now lapsed for this population of more than 2.6 million.

Eligibility for certain benefit programs has been extended to groups of immigrants considered permanently residing under color of law (PRUCOL). Although not permanent residents, PRUCOL aliens have been found (mostly by the courts) to have strong claims for social welfare benefits. This owes, in part, to the fact that their presence has been known and acceded to by the government. The PRUCOL eligibility standard has allowed benefit programs to respond to the complex and constantly changing number of immigration statuses.[20]

Contrary to popular belief, undocumented immigrants are eligible for very few public benefits. Important exceptions include emergency medical assistance under Medicaid and the supplemental food program for women, infants, and children (WIC). The Supreme Court ruled in 1982 that undocumented alien children cannot be denied access to public elementary and secondary education.[21] In addition, the U.S.-born children of undocumented aliens are considered to be citizens of the United States under the 14th Amendment to the Constitution and are eligible for public benefits on the same terms as other citizens. In short, the courts and the Congress have in the past sought to extend basic protections to the children of undocumented immigrants. The passage of Proposition 187, which bars illegal immigrant children from California's public schools, obviously marks a sharp reversal of these comparatively inclusionary children's policies.[22]

CURRENT WELFARE REFORM PROPOSALS

Over the course of the past year, welfare policy has been hotly debated in the Congress, and controversial reform proposals that implicate immigrant eligibility for public benefits passed in both the House and the Senate. As this is written, reform proposals have been consolidated in a conference agreement that has, in turn, been lodged in a large budget reconciliation bill. Given the fluidity and complexity of differing proposals, we focus here on the four basic policy instruments that have consistently been advanced to restrict immigrants' access to public services: bars to the use of benefits by legal immigrants; expanded deeming of income as a means of disqualifying immigrants from using public services; changes in the pledge or affidavit of support signed by the immigrant's sponsor to make it legally enforceable in order to chill benefits

---

[20]For example, immigrants whose deportation has been suspended or who have been paroled into the United States are considered PRUCOL for purposes of AFDC and SSI eligibility.

[21]See *Plyler v. Doe*, 457 U.S. 202 (1982).

[22]Most provisions of Proposition 187 were declared unconstitutional, though the law may be revisited through court appeals.

use and establish a mechanism for government reimbursement; and expanded state and local government power to exclude immigrants from services and benefits. In reviewing the differing proposals, it is important to distinguish between the treatment accorded immigrants already in the United States (i.e., current immigrants) and those who arrive following the law's enactment (i.e., future immigrants).

Bars to Programs for Legal Immigrants

A good example of the type of bar that has been proposed is that adopted by the House and Senate Conference agreement on welfare reform. The agreement would proscribe current immigrants' use of SSI or food stamps and would extend until the immigrant naturalizes or has worked 40 qualifying quarters (i.e., at least 10 years). A qualifying quarter is one in which the immigrant earned enough to pay social security taxes and did not receive a federal means-tested benefit. Future immigrants would be barred from all other means-tested programs for 5 years after entry. There are a number of important programmatic exceptions to this bar: emergency Medicaid, immunizations, emergency disaster relief, child nutrition programs, Head Start and programs under the Elementary and Secondary Education Act of 1965 (ESEA), higher education loans and grants, and foster care. Several groups of immigrants would also be exempt from the bar: veterans and active duty service members and their immediate families, refugees and asylees for their first 5 years after entry, and those granted withholding of deportation.

Deeming for Federal Programs

Following the 5-year bar for future immigrants, the conference agreement would require deeming of the sponsor's income until citizenship on all federal means-tested programs except SSI and food stamps (and those programs named as exceptions). Though not in the conference agreement, a Senate immigration reform bill would have extended the deeming requirement for future immigrants until they had worked 40 qualifying quarters of employment, even if they became citizens.

Deeming translates into effective disqualification of most immigrants who apply for benefits. Under the law, immigrants would lose their benefits unless they have no sponsor or unless their sponsor has died or has virtually no income or resources (National Immigration Law Center, 1995).

Making Affidavits of Support Enforceable Against the Sponsor

Under current law, the affidavit of support that a sponsor signs is not enforceable by the immigrant against his sponsor. It is also not enforceable by a benefits-granting government agency against the immigrant's sponsor. Current proposals would make the affidavit enforceable by both the sponsored immigrant and by the federal, state, or local government. This means that the sponsor would be liable to any federal, state, or local agency for any benefits that the immigrant receives before attaining citizenship.

Residual State Authority to Bar Immigrants

All proposed versions of welfare reform would substantially expand state and local governments' power to restrict immigrant access to federally funded programs. The Conference Committee agreement gives states the option to bar current immigrants from Medicaid, Title XX social services, and AFDC (which would be changed to Temporary Assistance for Needy Families). States also have the option to extend the 5-year bar on these benefits for future immigrants. An earlier Senate version of the bill allowed states to restrict immigrants' access to their own programs, whereas the House version mandated that state and local governments apply deeming to programs funded with their own resources.[23]

Federal and Federally Funded Needs-Based Programs

One key to understanding the scope of these complex new proposals and their impact on immigrant families is to grasp the extraordinary range of programs that are included within the opaquely defined needs-based and means-tested programs. Some of the major programs from which legal immigrants are likely to be excluded include the following:

> Health programs
>> Non-emergency Medicaid
>> Community Health Centers
>> Migrant Health Centers
> Nutrition programs
>> Food Stamps
>> Nutrition Programs for the Elderly
> Assistance for children and their families
>> Aid to Families With Dependent Children
>> Child Care Development Block Grant
>> Child Care Programs
>> Social Services Block Grant

---

[23]These changes to eligibility for state and local programs were dropped from the conference agreement because of the bill's placement in the budget reconciliation act, which prohibits (under the Byrd rule) the inclusion of provisions that do not bear directly on federal spending.

Assistance for the elderly and disabled
   Supplemental Security Income (the proposals do not distinguish
   between aid for the elderly under SSI and aid for the disabled)
Housing
   All major general housing programs
   All programs for rural areas and farm workers
   Emergency Food and Shelter Under the McKinney Homeless
   Assistance Act.
Job training and education
   Headstart
   The Job Training Partnership Act
   Job Corps
Legal Services

Even if some of these programs are consolidated into block grants, the reconstituted programs would, presumably, exclude immigrants because they would still be needs based.

LIKELY IMPACTS OF REFORM
ON IMMIGRANTS AND FAMILIES

These massive changes in eligibility for public programs may have a number of positive effects. They may save money by reducing the direct costs of providing benefits and services. In some instances they will shift costs to families that can afford to absorb them. They will likely increase immigrants' propensity to naturalize, though they alter the incentive to naturalize in ways that may be problematic. Further, it is conceivable that by restricting access to benefits the proposals could increase employment levels and strengthen the work ethic among the immigrant population, although immigrants' workforce participation rates are comparable to those of natives. However, the proposals also raise many concerns.

In the first place, they appear likely to leave many vulnerable newcomers outside of the social safety net. These include elderly refugees who have lived in the United States more than 5 years, disabled immigrants whose eligibility for SSI payments will lapse, and others. The original version of the House welfare reform proposal, which can serve as a rough proxy for current reform proposals, would have denied some 2 million legal immigrants access to at least one of the major public assistance programs (U.S. Department of Health and Human Services and U.S. Department of Agriculture, 1995).

Another result of restricting immigrants' access to services, either through an outright bar or deeming, would be to demote the status of legal immigrants and naturalized citizens in unprecedented ways. In so doing, the proposals will advance a policy of immigrant exceptionalism, discriminating against the foreign-born in access to benefits and institutions, that has not characterized American law in the modern era.

The conference agreement would bar or deem most public benefits either until citizenship or for 5 years. The result would be to shift the bright line that has historically been drawn between illegal and legal immigrants when it comes to benefits eligibility to distinguish citizens from noncitizens. This would create an incentive to naturalize as a means to retaining eligibility for benefits and not as an expression of allegiance to the country.

The proposal to deny benefits to immigrants who have naturalized but have not worked enough quarters in qualifying employment raises similar concerns. This proposal would profoundly alter the meaning of naturalization and citizenship, literally creating second-class citizens. These citizens would be eligible to participate fully in the political system as voters and office holders but would not be eligible for public health care or an SSI disability check.[24]

This redefinition of membership raises equity concerns. Resident aliens are subject to most of the legal obligations of citizens: They must comply with conscription, tax, and criminal laws (Legomsky, 1994). Restricting access to a broad range of public services and benefits removes rights that have traditionally accompanied these obligations.

The proposal to restrict eligibility for immigrants who have not worked 40 quarters in qualifying employments is especially problematic. It is troubling because it conditions eligibility on the duration and level of taxes paid in a manner that is not applied to citizens. Further, these conditions fail to take into account the sales, property, and other taxes that immigrants pay. If adopted, the proposal would mean that immigrant participation in social welfare programs would be conditioned in the same way as participation in social insurance programs; that is, services would be made available on the basis of prior contribution, not need.[25] Once again, the distinctions drawn would translate into a policy of immigrant exceptionalism.

Other equity-related issues are also raised by the proposed legislation. For example, congressional proposals drawing sharp distinctions between native-born citizens, naturalized citizens, and legal permanent residents may be interpreted by both citizens and noncitizens as signifying that legal immigrants are not genuine members of the community in which they live. These signals could deepen social divisions between immigrants and their receiving communities.

Another result of the new restrictions will be to place greater responsibility for mutual support on immigrant versus native families. As we describe in the

---

[24]Under this proposal, an immigrant with a spouse and child earning the minimum wage, for example, would not earn enough to pay taxes and hence would never become eligible for benefits.

[25]In practice this means that many elderly immigrants who are not able to naturalize would never be eligible for SSI because they did not live in the United States long enough to work 40 quarters—the very reason they were ineligible for Social Security and needed SSI.

next section of this chapter, the families of immigrant parents may be required to purchase private health and long-term care insurance, effectively compelling them to internalize a wide range of service costs that the state subsidizes for their native counterparts. At the same time, making the affidavit of support legally enforceable forces immigrant families to assume a kind of contingent liability to reimburse any public costs incurred by their immigrant members. Moreover, this contingent liability will last indefinitely for many immigrant families, given the difficulty that some immigrants will have naturalizing (Legomsky, 1995). These heightened responsibilities would apply even when the sponsoring family in the United States is composed entirely of citizens.

The proposals also draw distinctions between and within families that may seem arbitrary from a needs-based perspective. In some cases they disadvantage particularly vulnerable populations, whereas in others they treat groups with similar needs differently. Indeed, because the programs focus exclusively on curbing immigrants' access to means-tested programs, need itself becomes a criteria of exclusion.

It might be argued that the foreign-born children of immigrant parents have distinct and in some ways greater adjustment-related needs than do U.S.-born children (García Coll, 1995). Foreign-born children have spent part of their lives in a different culture, often speaking a different language. They have endured what one scholar refers to as "an event of extraordinary intensity that involves personal uprooting, loss and separation" (Laosa, 1989, p. 38). The serial migration of some immigrant families can keep immediate family members apart for years, significantly complicating the acculturation process (Waters, 1995). Yet it is these foreign-born immigrants who will have their access to public benefits and services curtailed.

Additionally, by requiring deeming in a vast array of public assistance programs, sponsored but not unsponsored immigrants could find their access to social and health services severely restricted. (Only about one half of all immigrants are sponsored; U.S. Commission on Immigration Reform, 1994.) We presume that sponsored immigrants are poorer at time of entry than unsponsored immigrants because the latter do not raise public charge concerns in the eyes of the officers who process visas.

Refugees in the United States less than 5 years will have far broader access to services than those here 6 years. Distinctions that might be drawn on the basis of age, disability, or employability will not affect eligibility.

The current proposals impose blanket restrictions on most needs-based programs without carefully distinguishing between them. In some instances it may be reasonable to expect families to provide food, shelter, and income assistance for a temporary period. As a result, deeming for a finite period may make policy sense for cash (e.g., AFDC and SSI) and near-cash (e.g., food stamps) programs. However, the objectives of reducing social and administrative costs and promoting immigrant integration argue for a different approach in other contexts. Thus, immigrant restrictions may make less sense when the services protect the public health, the services protect the health and safety of children (who are not held accountable for the actions of their parents), the costs of administering verification and other requirements outweigh the savings, and the costs to the sponsor of providing the service are exorbitant (e.g., requiring the sponsor to pay for health care services).

This failure to draw distinctions between types of services is particularly problematic when it comes to human capital development programs. Despite the fact that job training programs, adult education, child care, and the like represent a classic "hand up" versus "hand out," they are restricted to immigrants just as cash transfer programs are.

Further, it is unclear if social insurance programs, such as unemployment compensation, would be included in the list of excluded programs. If so, this would raise additional equity concerns because eligibility and benefit levels are tied to an individual's contributions, not his or her citizenship status (Legomsky, 1995).

Regarding implementation, it should be noted that the proposals create distinct eligibility rules for natives, legal immigrants now in the United States, and those arriving after the law's enactment. The administration of these complicated, multiple regulatory regimes will fall to a host of federal, state, local, and nongovernmental organizations with quite differing levels of administrative capacity. Among other things, they will be compelled to determine the nativity and legal status of applicants, sponsorship, the sponsor's income, the number of quarters the immigrant has worked, and the wages and taxes paid during those quarters. However, the administrative problems raised by the proposals will not end with these eligibility determinations. The nation's experience with child support enforcement demonstrates that enforcing the affidavit of support will also raise difficult administrative questions, especially when the benefits provided are not expensive and hard to price and when the provider's administrative capacity is limited. One obvious danger is that some service providers will respond by discriminating against foreign-sounding and foreign-looking applicants. Finally, the rush to citizenship that has recently occurred is straining the INS's already-burdened naturalization capacity. These proposals should add to that demand and perhaps already have.

Regarding constitutional issues, there is some question whether the Congress can delegate to the states the discretion to discriminate against legal immigrants in granting access to both federal and non-federally supported public benefits and services.[26] It is not at all clear whether discriminating between

---

[26]It is, however, settled constitutional doctrine that they may not discriminate in those programs absent an express federal authorization. In *Graham v. Richardson*, the U.S. Supreme Court invalidated two state laws barring immigrants from both federal and state-funded public benefit programs, holding that the federal government had an overriding interest in matters affecting im-

naturalized and native-born citizens in the administration of federal programs would be upheld. In the past, the Supreme Court has held that the "decision to share the nation's bounty with our guests may take into account the character of the relationship between the alien and this country. . . . Congress may decide that as the alien's tie grows stronger, so does the strength of his claim to an equal share of that munificence."[27] However, does this concept of transitional alienage extend past naturalization? If so, does it amount to discrimination on the basis of national origin and run afoul of equal protection safeguards?

IMMIGRATION POLICY

Family Reunification

Although the family has not been a central focus of immigrant policy, promoting family unity has been the main imperative of U.S. immigration policy for at least the past 30 years. As such, it has strongly influenced areas of policy with which it is not conventionally associated, such as employment, diversity, and humanitarian admissions. Indeed, the goal of family unity has also shaped our policies toward providing legal status to immigrants residing illegally in the United States. Even the Immigration Act of 1990,[28] which sought to expand immigration for employment purposes, retained family reunification as the principal vehicle for admitting immigrants (Fix & Passel, 1991).

Under family reunification policies only close relatives of U.S. citizens and permanent residents are permitted entry. These close relatives have been divided into two categories: nuclear family members, including spouses and minor children, and extended family members, including siblings and adult children. Parents of U.S. residents have been viewed at different times as part of the nuclear or extended family. Most current legislative proposals would restrict admission of extended family members and include parents of U.S. residents within their scope.

The centrality of family unification is revealed by numbers. In FY 1994 about three fourths of all legal immigrants entered either as immediate relatives of U.S. citizens—who are not subject to any numerical limitations—or through the family preference system, under which a specified number of immigrants may enter.[29] The residual entered through the employment-based

---

migration and alien status, rejecting the states' argument that the restrictions were needed to conserve state resources. The court, relying in part on equal protection analysis, held that state classifications on the basis of alienage for the allocation of federal public benefits were unconstitutional.

[27] *Mathews v. Diaz*, 426 U.S. 67, (1976).

[28] Pub. Law 101-649.

[29] The total number of immigrants who entered in FY 1994 was 676,960. This figure excludes refugee and asylee adjustments and IRCA legalizations. See U.S. Department of Justice, Immigration and Naturalization Service (1995).

preferences or as diversity immigrants, a category created for people from countries that have sent few immigrants to the United States in recent years.

The share of immigrants who enter to join family members exceeds those admitted as employment immigrants because many immigrants entering under employment and diversity preferences are immediate family members of the primary beneficiaries. In FY 1993, about 45% of the 147,000 employment preference immigrants and about 40% of the 33,000 diversity immigrants were the spouses or minor children of the beneficiaries (i.e., the worker or the person who won a diversity visa; see U.S. Dept. of Justice, Immigration and Naturalization Service, 1993). Family unity also plays an important role in humanitarian admissions as refugees with relatives in the United States are given preference over those without relatives. In fact, approximately 85% of refugees enter as family reunification refugees (G. Smith, personal communication, September, 1995).

The set of policies directed at illegal immigrants also takes the family into account. Special provision has been made to permit the unification of family members of immigrants who legalized under IRCA. Most have been permitted to remain in the United States until their application for a visa is approved. These legal actions allowed thousands of otherwise undocumented immigrants to reside legally in the United States with their formerly undocumented spouse or parent.[30]

Policies directed at illegal immigrants support families in other ways. Having a family in the United States is common grounds for waiving or suspending the deportation of undocumented immigrants. Undocumented immigrants can seek a waiver of deportation when "the alien's deportation would result in extreme hardship to the U.S. citizen or lawfully resident spouse, parent or child of such alien" (Guendelsberger, 1988, p. 24). In addition, the 1994 Violence Against Women Act (VAWA)[31] includes protections for battered undocumented women and children. This legislation provides a mechanism for battered immigrant spouses and children of U.S citizens and legal residents to self-petition for legal resident status, without needing their battering relative's approval.[32] In so doing, it provides a shield from family violence that is aggravated by differences in legal status.

Although the goal of family unification has been central to U.S. immigration policy, it has not translated into an automatic or constitutional right to reunification for the nuclear family, as exists in France (Guendelsberger, 1988). Although immediate family members of U.S. citizens have been able to enter without numerical restrictions, the entry of immediate family members of legal permanent residents has been numerically capped. Because demand exceeds

---

[30]Immigration Act of 1990, Section 112.

[31]Pub. Law 103-322.

[32]One exception to the family orientation of our immigration policies is the Immigration Marriage Fraud Amendments Act, which placed greater scrutiny on the marriage of citizens and legal immigrants to foreigners.

supply for visas in this category, there is currently a waiting list of 1.1 million spouses and children of legal immigrants. A large share of those on the waiting list—about 80%—are the family members of legalizing aliens (U.S. Commission on Immigration Reform, 1995).

Proposed Changes

Two major proposals to restrict legal immigration are now proceeding through Congress.[33] The bills would reduce the overall number of immigrants entering the United States by about one third and would eliminate certain categories of family reunification immigrants. In addition to limiting the number and type of family members who can come to the United States, slated reforms would also significantly restrict the number and type of U.S. residents who can bring family members to the United States.

These far-reaching changes are intended to mitigate the impacts of immigration in several ways: by reducing the number of immigrants, by deterring those who appear likely to use public services, and by shifting greater financial responsibility to immigrants' family sponsors. An ancillary goal of the proposals is to refocus immigration policy on the reunification of nuclear families. However, these reforms may have unintended effects that could defeat some of these objectives. Further, when taken together, immigration and welfare reform proposals could have cumulative effects on the integration of immigrants and their families that have not been examined by policymakers.

Restricting Admission of Family Immigrants.   Current legislative proposals pending in Congress would restrict the immigration of several categories of family members. They would eliminate the immigration of adult brothers and sisters of citizens, eliminate the immigration of married and unmarried adult children of citizens and of legal permanent residents, and limit the immigration of parents of citizens by requiring that parents be over age 65, have health and long-term care insurance, and have the majority of their children living in the United States. These proposals would effectively restrict family reunification to the spouses and minor children of citizens and legal permanent residents and some parents of citizens. In addition, proposals have been advanced to reduce the backlog of spouses and minor children of permanent residents so that those nuclear families can reunite more quickly.

The reforms raise a number of issues that are relevant to the integration of immigrants and their families. First, they would reduce the immigration of

---

[33]These proposals are drawn from the two major immigration reform proposals under consideration by Congress. They are Rep. Lamar Smith's bill, The Immigration in the National Interest Act (H.R. 2202), and Senator Alan Simpson's bill, The Immigration Reform Act of 1995 (S. 1394).

groups that have high human capital endowments and have demonstrated rapid economic mobility. Research on immigrant men who entered as siblings indicates that they have higher initial earnings as well as higher earnings growth than immigrant groups admitted under other family and employment preferences (Duleep & Regets, 1995). To the extent that limiting their entry is aimed at mitigating immigrants' fiscal and economic impacts, these proposals may be counterproductive. By the same token, restricting the entry of parents of citizens—who have lower education, employment, and earnings levels than other family immigrants—might increase overall measures of immigrant education and earnings.

Proposed reforms could also shift the composition of the immigrant population by changing the countries of origin of the immigration flow. A large share of those economically mobile immigrants entering under the sibling preference as well as those entering under the adult children preference are Asian (Passel & Fix, 1995). Eliminating these two preferences is therefore likely to reduce the proportion of immigrants from Asia. As the proportionate share of Asian migration declines, the share of flows from Mexico and from countries where the United States has large military bases is likely to rise (Jasso, 1986).

Restricting admission of extended family members may also affect immigrant integration by reducing immigrant families' social capital. Extended family members play an important role in the high self-employment rate of certain immigrant groups (Duleep & Regets, 1995). These family members provide a pool of labor as well as the social and economic support needed to start and run a business. Extended family members, including parents of adult citizens, may also play important economic roles by providing child care and household help. This uncompensated labor may make it possible for other household members to work or pursue training or education. Family members can, however, also be the source of negative social and economic capital if they reduce productivity and consume resources or if they are a source of conflict rather than support (Rumbaut, 1995).

One unintended effect of these immigration proposals may be to reduce immigration levels beyond the anticipated one third. The largest potential pools of immigrants outside the United States are siblings and parents of U.S. citizens. Each foreign-born person has an average of over 2 siblings and .64 parents still outside the United States but only .17 children living abroad (Schulte & Wolf, 1994).[34] By eliminating the admission of extended relatives and by increasing the assets that families must have to sponsor immigrants, it is quite possible actual admissions levels will fall below those authorized by

---

[34]About 20% of the demand for family unification visas originates with naturalized citizens, some of whom entered as adult children or siblings (Jasso, 1986). The demand for unification that derives from naturalized immigrants who entered as adult children or siblings will be eliminated.

law. That is to say, the stock of U.S. citizens or legal permanent residents with immediate family members abroad could rapidly dwindle.

Finally, proposals to limit the immigration of citizens' parents may make it impossible for most families to reunite with their parents. The proposals would shrink the potential pool of parents who can immigrate by setting an age minimum of 65, requiring that most of their children live in the United States and requiring that parents have health and long term care insurance. This is a highly restrictive condition, because few private health insurers are willing to insure elderly immigrants.

Restricting Sponsorship of Family Immigrants. The current proposals would also restrict the number of U.S. residents who can reunite with a family member. They would do so by requiring that the person who petitions to bring in the relative must also be the sponsor or the person who signs the affidavit of support,[35] the petitioner or sponsor's income must be at least 200% of the poverty line for a family size that includes the potential immigrant,[36] and the sponsor must sign a legally enforceable affidavit of support.

These changes represent a significant departure from current law. Under current policy, anyone can sign an affidavit of support to sponsor an immigrant, and the affidavit of support is not legally enforceable. Perhaps most important, the income requirements for bringing in a family member are not rigid or especially onerous. The cumulative effect of these changes will be to reduce sharply the number of people in the United States who have family members who are eligible for entry, are financially able to sponsor a relative, and are willing to accept these more stringent support obligations.

Requiring that the petitioner have an income level of at least 200% of poverty (after adding an additional person to the family size) would make almost half (45%) of all families unable to sponsor a family member.[37] Further, expanded financial requirements for sponsors could undermine the goals of eliminating the backlog of immediate relatives of permanent residents and elevating the importance of the nuclear family. Fifty-eight percent of families headed by an immigrant have incomes that fall below 200% of the poverty line after the addition of another person. The restrictions, then, also reduce overall immigration.

---

[35] Under current immigration law, the petitioner must be a close family member in order for the immigrant to qualify for admission. However, the immigrant's sponsor (who signs the affidavit of support to help the immigrant overcome the public charge exclusion) need not be the petitioner, but may be someone with greater assets. The result is that the public charge exclusion can be overcome, even if the immigrant's petitioner and immediate family have comparatively few resources.

[36] Thus, a sponsoring family of four would need an income exceeding 200% of the poverty line for a family of five.

[37] These estimates are based on tabulations of the 1994 Current Population Survey.

Taken together, these two sets of restrictions on who can come in and who can bring someone in reveal a shift away from two of the three goals that have historically driven legal immigration policy: the social goal of family unification and the cultural goal of promoting diversity[38]. These reforms instead seem to focus solely on the economic goal of increasing U.S. productivity and reducing costs.

CONCLUSION

Congress is considering proposals that would dramatically change U.S. immigration and immigrant policy. Whereas each proposal raises a separate set of questions, the cumulative effect of the various provisions may have far-reaching consequences for immigrants and their families that have not been considered by policymakers or others in the current debate.

U.S. immigrant policies, which historically have been policies of benign neglect, are slated to be transformed into policies of exclusion, restricting legal immigrants' access to a wide range of public services. The restrictions would bar immigrants from public services and expand sponsorship and deeming requirements, in each case shifting responsibility for support away from the government and to the family of the immigrant. Immigrant families would be responsible for supporting the immigrant for an extended period of time and would be expected to provide a broader range of support. Restricting access to federal benefits will also shift responsibility for providing assistance to state and local governments. At the same time, U.S. immigration policies, which for the past 30 years have been aimed at unifying close family members, may now be restricted to a rather narrow conception of the nuclear family, thereby redefining who should be considered a close relative.

When viewed together, these two sets of reforms are likely to impose greater financial responsibility on immigrant families while potentially limiting the human and social capital available to those families. To illustrate, welfare reform proposals make immigrant families ineligible for publicly funded child care assistance. At the same time, immigration policy reforms will eliminate the admission of extended family members who may have provided child care.

Although the goal of reform may be to promote nuclear family reunification, the proposals may complicate it. They do so by imposing sponsorship and financial requirements strict enough to keep many citizens and immigrants from being able to reunite with their spouses and children. Further, proposed welfare reforms aimed at discouraging out-of-wedlock births and encouraging marriage are not likely to have the same effects on immigrants as

---

[38]In the simplest, most straightforward terms, the proposals do so by reducing the number of family and diversity visas.

they are intended to have on natives. Immigrants are more likely to have intact families, and immigrant welfare use is concentrated among refugees and the elderly.

Despite the centrality of devolution to current welfare reform proposals, broad federal curbs on immigrant benefit use will likely impinge state and local capacity to serve and integrate their newcomer populations. They will do so by limiting states' ability to experiment with differing strategies for moving immigrants into jobs, investing in their human capital development, or simply providing them with a safety net. To the extent that the immigrant population suffers from not being provided these services, the effects will be felt by the handful of states where immigrants are concentrated. Further, if states are provided latitude in setting eligibility rules, past experience suggests that in tough economic times and in an anti-immigrant climate they are likely to take a punitive or exclusionary approach to serving their immigrant populations (Zimmermann & Fix, 1993).

It does not appear that the current set of proposals for reform are informed by the findings of social science research. Although there is an underlying assumption that reducing family immigration will improve the "quality" or the economic integration of immigrants, research suggests that family immigrants are as likely to participate in the labor market and have faster earnings growth than do employment immigrants. Eliminating brothers and sisters would exclude a group of largely Asian immigrants associated with high self-employment, high initial earnings, and rapid earnings growth. Certainly the literature on immigrant adjustment does not suggest that limiting spending on language acquisition, reducing access to human capital programs, or singling out newcomer populations for special exclusions will accelerate their integration. More broadly, these proposals respond to political pressures to reduce the number and the perceived negative economic impacts of immigrants. However, most research suggests that, overall, legal immigration has either neutral or positive effects on the U.S. economy (Fix & Passel, 1994).

The proposals also raise a number of tough and as-yet unanswered questions. How will the proposed changes to immigration policy change the future composition and flows of immigrants? Will reduced levels of immigration make integration easier for immigrants over the long run? To what extent will the cumulative impacts of the proposals be mediated by the immigrant family, by networks, by immigrant-serving nongovernmental organizations? Finally, what impact will these unprecedented proposals have on the adjustment and economic mobility of immigrants and their families?

ACKNOWLEDGMENTS

The authors gratefully acknowledge the financial support provided by grants from the Andrew W. Mellon Foundation and the William and Flora Hewlett

Foundation. We also thank Suzanne Bianchi, Lindsay Lowell, and Joyce Vialet for their thoughtful comments and Aaron Sparrow for his research assistance.

REFERENCES

Borjas, G. (1992). National origin and the skills of immigrants." In G. J. Borjas & R. B. Freeman, (Eds.), *Immigration and the work force* (pp. 17–49). National Bureau of Economic Research. Chicago: University of Chicago Press.

Clark, R. L., Passel, J., Zimmermann, W., & Fix, M. (1994). *Fiscal impacts of undocumented aliens: Selected estimates for seven states.* Washington, DC: Office of Management and Budget and the Department of Justice.

Congressional Quarterly. (1995, September 23). Vol. 53, No. 37, p. 2917.

Duleep, H. O., & Regets, M. C. (1992). Some evidence on the effect of admission criteria on immigrant assimilation. In B. R. Chiswick (Ed.), *Immigration, language and ethnic issues: Canada and the United States* (pp. 410–440). Washington, DC: American Enterprise Institute.

Duleep, H. O., & Regets, M. C. (1995). *Family unification, siblings, and skills.* Washington, DC: The Urban Institute.

Fix, M., & Passel, J. (1991). *The door remains open: Recent immigration to the United States and a preliminary analysis of the Immigration Act of 1990.* Washington, DC: The Urban Institute.

Fix, M., & Passel, J. (1994). *Immigration and immigrants: Setting the record straight.* Washington, DC: The Urban Institute.

Fix, M., & Zimmermann, W. (1993). *After arrival: An overview of federal immigrant policy in the United States.* Washington, DC: The Urban Institute.

Fix, M., & Zimmermann, W. (1995). *When should immigrants receive public benefits?* Washington, DC: The Urban Institute.

Fukuyama, F. (1993). Immigrants and family values. *Commentary,* May, 26–32.

García Coll, C. (1995, November). *The psychological experience of immigration: A developmental perspective.* Paper presented at the 1995 National Symposium on International Migration and Family Change, Pennsylvania State University.

Guendelsberger, J. (1988). The right to family unification in French and United States immigration law. *Cornell International Law Journal, 21,* 1–102.

Henderson, A., Donly, B., & Strang, W. (1994, September). *Summary of the Bilingual Education State Educational Agency Program Survey of States' limited English proficient persons and available educational services, 1992–1993* (Final Report). Washington, DC: U.S. Department of Education.

Jasso, G. (1986). Family reunification and the immigration multiplier: U.S. immigration law, origin-country conditions, and the reproduction of immigrants. *Demography, 23,* 291–311.

Laosa, L. (1990). Psychological stress, coping and the development of Hispanic immigrant children. In F. Serafica, A. Schwebel, R. Russell, P. Isaac, & L. Myers (Eds.), *Mental Health of Ethnic Minorities.* New York: Praeger Publishers.

Legomsky, S. H. (1994). Why citizenship? *Virginia Journal of International Law, 35,* 279–300.

Legomsky, S. H. (1995). Immigration federalism and the welfare state. *UCLA Law Review, 42,* 1453–1474.

National Immigration Law Center. (1995, August 25). *Senate welfare reform bill immigrant restrictions.*

Passel, J., & Fix, M. (1995, September 13). Testimony before the U.S. Senate Subcommittee on Immigration.

Pompa, D. (1995). *The historical intersection of education policy and immigrant students.* Unpublished manuscript, Center for Applied Linguistics.

Rumbaut, R. G. (1995, November). *Ties that bind: Immigration and immigrant families in the United States.* Paper presented at the 1995 National Symposium on International Migration and Family Changes, Pennsylvania State University.

Schuck, P. H., & Smith, R. M. (1985). *Citizenship without consent: Illegal aliens in the American polity.* New Haven: Yale University Press.

Schulte, M. M., & Wolf, D. A. (1994). *Family networks of the foreign born population.* Washington, DC: The Urban Institute.

Sorensen, E., Bean, F. D., Ku, L., & Zimmermann, W. (1992). *Immigrant categories and the U.S. job market: Do they make a difference?* Washington DC: The Urban Institute.

U.S. Commission on Immigration Reform. (1994, September). *U.S. immigration policy: Restoring credibility.*

U.S. Commission on Immigration Reform. (1995, June). *Legal immigration: Setting priorities, a report to Congress.* (Legal Immigration Executive Summary)

U.S. Department of Health and Human Services, Administration for Children and Families, Office of Refugee Resettlement. (1993). *Refugee resettlement program: Annual report to the Congress.*

U.S. Department of Health and Human Services and U.S. Department of Agriculture. (1995, April 7). Preliminary impacts, summary and state-by-state analysis of H.R. 4, the Personal Responsibility Act of 1995.

U.S. Department of Justice, Immigration and Naturalization Service. (1993). *Statistical yearbook of the Immigration and Naturalization Service.* Washington, DC: U.S. Government Printing Office.

U.S. Department of Justice, Immigration and Naturalization Service. (1995, August). *INS fact book: Summary of recent immigration data.* Washington, DC: U.S. Government Printing Office.

Vialet, J., & Eig, L. (1994). *Alien eligibility for federal assistance.* Washington, DC: Congressional Research Service.

Vialet, J., & Eig, L. (1995). *Memorandum on the number of immigrants with affidavits of support.* Washington, DC: Congressional Research Service.

Waters, M. (1995, November). Remarks at the 1995 National Symposium on International Migration and Family Change, Pennsylvania State University.

Zimmermann, W., & Calhoun, C. (1991). *Immigrant policies in Western Europe.* Washington, DC: The Urban Institute.

Zimmermann, W., & Fix, M. (1993). *Immigrant policy in the States: A wavering welcome.* Washington, DC: The Urban Institute.

NOTE ADDED IN PROOF

Since this chapter was completed, legal immigration reform legislation failed to pass the Congress; stringent new restrictions on legal and other immigrants' eligibility for public benefits were enacted as part of welfare reform (P.L. 104-103); and the income requirements for immigrants' sponsors were raised to 125% of poverty under legislation that addressed illegal immigration (H.R. 2202, incorporated in P.L. 104-208).

13

Whither the 1950s?
The Family and Macroeconomic Context
of Immigration and Welfare Reform
in the 1990s

Suzanne M. Bianchi
University of Maryland

TWENTY-FIVE years ago, when the U.S. Commission on Population Growth and the American Future issued its final report to President Nixon, fertility issues dominated the recommendations. On October 27, 1995, at a 25-year retrospective on the Commission's report held on Capitol Hill in Washington DC, the issue of immigration took center stage. To the extent that the fertility behavior of American women remained of concern, the fertility of immigrant women was highlighted. The only speaker to emphasize the growth of the U.S. population as a major issue was not a demographer but rather Congressman Anthony Beilenson, Democrat from California. The congressman seemed to be aware that births in California had risen from a low of 337,000 in 1975 to over 600,000 in 1992, with more than one fourth of all births in California in 1992 to women born in Mexico (Burke, 1995). If a new commission on population were to be empowered in the mid-1990s, its mandate would be greatly influenced by recent immigration trends.

By documenting the immigration trends of the past decade, Michael Fix, Wendy Zimmermann, and others provide insight and context for the current policy debates about immigration. We cannot understand the origins of proposed legislative change without acknowledging the sheer magnitude of the immigrant flow to the United States in the past decade, without appreciating that the major destination of that flow has been only six states and a relatively small number of metropolitan areas and without realizing how non-European the flow has been, how Asian and Hispanic it has been (Chiswick & Sullivan, 1995; Fix & Passel, 1994; Fix & Zimmermann, this volume; Frey, 1995).

Fix and Zimmermann did an admirable job laying out the ways in which current proposed reforms attempt to adjust immigrant flows. They also speculated about the unanticipated consequences for families and the economy of altering the family unification preferences embodied in the current system. The picture that emerges from their discussion is clear. Proposed legislation is aimed at adjusting the immigration flows downward, adjusting the flows to focus on family unification of nuclear, preferably two-parent families, curbing immigrants' use of welfare, particularly Supplemental Security Income (SSI) use by aged immigrants who have entered under family reunification preferences in the past, and making those already in the United States more accountable, financially, for family members who may wish to immigrate in the future.

My suspicion is that the U.S. public would find much to agree with in the proposed changes, despite any misgivings social scientists might have. Many of the limitations of the squeeze on immigration, which seem to be the intent of current proposed reforms, are in keeping with the squeeze that is also underway on programs that benefit poor women and their children, be they native or immigrant, and the squeeze limits Congress would like to place on expenditures for the native-born elderly if only this group were not so politically mobilized.

To understand proposed policy changes that affect immigrant families and their connections to other institutions in American society, it seems to me that we must go beyond Fix and Zimmermann's focus on immigration and immigration policies per se. Their discussion of the program restrictions immigrants might face highlighted the interconnection between proposed immigration reforms and welfare reform. We need to understand how we arrived at our current view of "the immigration problem" or the "poverty problem" in the United States. I realize that not all immigrant families are poor, some far from it. But immigrant families, like poor families, can be categorized as "different," and, therefore, more easily viewed as "other peoples' families," not "our families," not our responsibility.

As a nation, we have convinced ourselves that we cannot afford to be as generous as we have been in the past—to our poor, to those from other nations who wish to enter our doors, indeed, to our own children and elderly. As Farley (1996) documented in the introduction to his book based on analysis of the 1980 and 1990 censuses, the thesis that America is in decline is pervasive. We hear and read that America has lost its competitive edge. Our children's future is less bright than our own. The middle class is disappearing. Families are disintegrating before our very eyes. Bad jobs, or no jobs at all, are all that are left for the majority of residents in our largest cities. Income inequality is polarizing the United States into "haves" and "have nots" and is undermining the legitimacy of our political system. We are increasingly a citizenry of "Black versus White," and a growing racial divide threatens to wrench us apart as a nation.

It is almost irrelevant that the research evidence in support of each claim is often equivocal and always more complex than these simple assertions suggest. The fact is that this is what the American public hears. It is what sells books. It is a message that can be conveyed in a short sound byte and comprehended by most American voters.

Implicit in the America-in-decline thesis (indeed, implicit in the proposed policies to redirect immigration or expenditures on the poor) is the assumption that we once had it right in America. Enter the current nostalgic view of the 1950s . . . that period before we opened our doors to all these "new" immigrants, the time before we gave women choices about marriage and family responsibilities, the last decade in which racial minorities "knew their proper place," and perhaps most important, that period in which a hard-working man could get a good job and support a family. The image is of a strong, self-contained, intact two-parent family: mothers who recognized the importance of nurturing children and stayed out of the paid workforce to do so and fathers who accepted the responsibility to support their wives and children and earned a family wage on which they could raise a family.

Implicit in the proposed immigration reforms described by Fix and Zimmermann is that the United States needs an immigration policy focused solely on unifying husbands with dependent wives and children, not extended kin. Explicit is the notion that we should deem the income of the principal wage earner, the "family breadwinner," as necessary insurance against allowing immigrants into the country who might become a drain on our already strained welfare system. (Never mind that immigrant and minority families and, increasingly, economically successful nonminority families rely on more than one family breadwinner!) If we cannot successfully encourage our native-born citizens to form families more like those of the 1950s, we can at least try to contain our current economic woes by providing a less generous, more punitive welfare system for our native-born and by curtailing the entry and access of the foreign-born.

What continues to amaze me is how unsuccessful we, as social scientists, have been in dispelling myths about the family, the economy, and the interrelationship between the two. For example, family demographers, such as Cherlin (1992), keep pointing out that if one looks at long-term trends, the family of the 1950s is more the anomaly than current families. Marriage was unusually early and unusually universal, and fertility was unusually high during that decade (McLanahan & Casper, 1995; Oppenheimer, 1994). Poor and minority families probably never relied on the income-generating capacity of one earner to sustain themselves (Goldin, 1990; Nasaw, 1985; Tilly & Scott, 1978).

As Levy (1995) pointed out, the 1950s and 1960s also make an unusual economic yardstick for measuring family well-being. The ability of working-class families to rely solely on one earner was unusual in the 1950s and 1960s. In the 1950s, the United States accounted for half the world's output. Its major potential competitors had been decimated by a world war, and there was little competitive pressure outside our borders. High productivity growth of the 1950s was also fueled by the pent-up demand for manufactured goods within our borders—demand for houses and other consumer goods that had been postponed because of World War II (Levy, 1988). Labor market dislocations occurred in that decade, but those moving off farms as agriculture mechanized could perhaps more easily convert to manufacturing jobs than those dislocated in the industrial restructuring of the 1980s. The cohort of young workers in the 1950s, born during the Depression, was also small, so demographics helped wages rise with productivity growth.

Finally, taxes were low, and there was not yet much of a welfare state in the 1950s, in part because most workers who would eventually be covered under the Social Security system begun in the mid-1930s had not yet reached retirement age. As Levy (1988) and Wilson (1987) reminded us, concern about a budget surplus rather than a budget deficit was the context in which the War on Poverty and the Great Society programs of the 1960s were launched. Given today's overriding concern with bringing down the Federal budget deficit, the notion that three decades ago we had a potential surplus seems almost a fairy tale.

The seeds of discontent, resulting in the civil rights movement and the renewed women's movement of the 1960s and 1970s, were probably sown during the surface quiet of the 1950s. Many were disadvantaged by an economic organization that tended to reserve family wage jobs for men, usually white men. Many women and minorities today would not have us return to the 1950s (Bianchi, 1995; Harrison & Bennett, 1995). However, there remains disquiet about how much things have changed.

We must understand where we have been to appreciate how we arrived at the point at which we are convinced that something is very wrong with American society and the American family, that we cannot afford more immigrants, more single-parent families, more welfare use.[1] The 1990s are a much changed context—both for the family and for the U.S. economy. Productivity growth resumed in manufacturing in the 1980s, but only after downsizing and wrenching industrial restructuring (Levy, 1995). Unlike the 1960s, when to a large extent a rising tide lifted all boats, increased income inequality meant that many

---

[1] I am thankful to Ruben Rumbaut for pointing out the importance of understanding the role of U.S. foreign policy, as well as the changing domestic economy, in fueling current immigration flows and creating pressures for proposed immigration reform. See also Teitelbaum and Weiner (1995).

boats were not lifted in the 1980s (Blank, 1991). By the end of the decade, a wide gap separated younger from older workers, the college educated from the high-school educated, those in the central cities from those in the suburbs, single mothers from dual-earning couples. There was somewhat of a hollowing out, or perhaps more accurately an end to the expansion of the middle class, leading to a middle class who felt more financially strapped and was inclined to be less generous to the poor or to those who were different. Also, the elderly came to call—the population and its entitlement to the Social Security system had matured, and health care expenses for the elderly and the poor skyrocketed. Taxes eroded earnings and caused the public to increasingly question the generosity of the welfare state.

We are a more diverse country, but perhaps more important, a more diverse labor force. Not only are immigrants at the table for a piece of the American pie, native-born women and minorities have also joined since the 1950s. We all want our fair share. It is not just the immigration context that has changed dramatically in the last three decades; the gender and racial context have also been transformed. This raises the stakes and complicates the interests in the current climate in which we have come to accept the America-in-decline thesis. We have let so many in, not only from outside our borders but from within, and they are so different!

Unfortunately, to describe where we are in the policy debates on immigration reform, as Fix and Zimmermann do, and to tie where we are currently to the larger family, social, and macroeconomic context, past and present, does not tell us what policies enhance or impede immigrant families' links to U.S. institutions, the purported topic of this part of the volume. However, many recurrent themes provide direction for needed research and policy analysis. Fix and Zimmermann and others suggested the importance of focusing on inter- and intragerational mechanisms of support to assess whether immigrants who arrive as refugees or through family unification are successfully integrated into schools and the economy in the first and subsequent generations. They also emphasized the necessity of trying to anticipate unintended consequences of policy, whether immigration reform, welfare reform, or foreign policy. However, it is important to contextualize our discussions and research on immigration and immigration policy reform. Finally, I add the need to examine the age and gender stratification within families in general and immigrant families in particular, both within and across generations, to understand fully the integration of immigrants into U.S. society and the costs and benefits of proposed reforms.

An intergenerational perspective and ethnographic research such as that by Waters (this volume) point us in the direction of schools and the need to study the school–family nexus. What happens to immigrant children in schools? Why do some groups appear to navigate the schools much more successfully than others? How will the immigrants of the 1980s do in the first, second, and third generation? Will they achieve parity with natives?

We need to follow the dictum to contextualize, perhaps nowhere moreso than in the study of labor markets and political mobilization. We must also remember what contextualizing means—one explanation doesn't fit all, and sometimes, for some places, for some labor markets, the facts may not be to our liking. For example, Fix and Zimmermann raised the question of whether restrictions on the entry of parents of immigrants has a negative childcare outcome. If immigration of extended kin is curtailed, will an unintended consequence be even more isolation, dislocation, and slower economic integration of those already here?

We must also continue to investigate seriously the interrelation between immigration, low wage, and low skill labor, and we must not assume that the effects will be uniform in all labor markets. Goldin's (1994) historical work on the great European immigration of the first decade of this century suggests that the closing of the immigrant gates in the 1920s resulted from more than xenophobic reactions after World War I. She argued that there was an important economic component to the mobilization of support for restricting immigration. Wages were depressed in certain labor markets by the availability of immigrants, and this helped turn areas from opposing to favoring restriction. In the current context, study of the mobilization of support for or against immigrant restriction probably requires systematic examination of the wage effects in certain labor markets and on certain groups (e.g., native-born minorities, less educated workers, highly educated female workers).

Finally, what are the internal dynamics of the family that change with immigration? Becoming Americanized may well entail movement away from reliance on extended kin and may ultimately entail movement away from two-parent, nuclear families, at least in the short run. For better or worse, becoming integrated into U.S. society probably also entails alterations in the gender relations within families, especially alteration in the age and gender power relations within families (as aptly demonstrated in the work of Kibria, 1993, on Vietnamese American families).

As a social demographer, as a feminist, as a mother who cares about the well-being of her own children, as a citizen who has a stake not only in the future of my own but also other people's children, and as the granddaughter of immigrants who came from Italy in the great European wave of immigration at the turn of the 20th century, I need only look to the contradictions these roles create for me to appreciate the complexity of the issues surrounding immigrant families and immigration policy. For example, I worry about the future of the American family and I, too, sometimes fall victim to the nostalgia for the 1950s, only to be chilled by some of the possibilities for "correcting" our problems. What might strengthening the two-parent family mean for women's access to labor market opportunity? It depends on how that strengthening is conceived.

One thing is certain: We cannot go back to the family, the economy, or the ethnic composition of the 1950s. Furthermore, many of us would not want to. The question then becomes which aspects of current proposals on welfare reform or immigration reform take us forward and which do not. It is healthy to have that debate. It is not healthy when, in the rush to reform, there is insufficient questioning of the implicit assumptions and potential unintended consequences of reforms. Fix and Zimmermann's chapter opens the debate on proposed immigration policy reforms. We need to head further in the direction they have pointed.

REFERENCES

Bianchi, S. M. (1995). Changing economic roles of women and men. In R. Farley (Ed.), *State of the union: America in the 1990s. Volume 1: Economic trends* (pp. 107–154). New York: Russell Sage Foundation.

Blank, R. M. (1991). Why were poverty rates so high in the 1980s? NBER Working Paper No. 3878. Cambridge, MA: National Bureau of Economic Research.

Burke, B. M. (1995). *Trends and compositional changes in fertility: California circa 1970–1990.* Paper presented at the annual meeting of the Population Association of America, San Francisco, CA.

Cherlin, A. J. (1992). *Marriage, divorce, remarriage.* Cambridge, MA: Harvard University Press.

Chiswick, B. R., & Sullivan, T. A. (1995). The new immigrants. In R. Farley (Ed.), *State of the union: America in the 1990s. Volume 2: Social trends* (pp. 211–270). New York: Russell Sage Foundation.

Farley, R. (1996). *Revealing America: Forces shaping the U.S. in the 1990s.* New York: Russell Sage Foundation.

Fix, M. I., & Passel, J. S. (1994). *Immigration and immigrants: Setting the record straight.* Washington, DC: The Urban Institute.

Frey, W. H. (1995). The new geography of population shifts. In R. Farley (Ed.), *State of the union: America in the 1990s: Vol. 2. Social trends* (pp. 271–336). New York: Russell Sage Foundation.

Goldin, C. (1990). *Understanding the gender gap: An economic history of American women.* New York: Oxford University Press.

Goldin, C. (1994). The political economy of immigration restriction in the United States, 1890 to 1921. In C. Goldin & G. D. Libecap (Eds.), *The regulated economy: A historical approach to political economy* (pp. 223–257). Chicago: University of Chicago Press.

Harrison, R. J., & Bennett, C. E. (1995). Racial and ethnic diversity. In R. Farley (Ed.), *State of the union: America in the 1990s: Vol. 2. Social trends* (pp. 141–210). New York: Russell Sage Foundation.

Kibria, N. (1993). *Family tightrope: The changing lives of Vietnamese Americans.* Princeton, NJ: Princeton University Press.

Levy, F. (1988). *Dollars and dreams: The changing American income distribution.* New York: Norton.

Levy, F. (1995). Incomes and income inequality. In R. Farley (Ed.), *State of the union: America in the 1990s: Vol. 1. Economic trends* (pp. 1–57). New York: Russell Sage Foundation.

McLanahan, S., & Casper, L. (1995). Growing diversity and inequality in the American family. In R. Farley (Ed.), *State of the union: America in the 1990s: Vol. 2. Social trends* (pp. 1–46). New York: Russell Sage Foundation.

Nasaw, D. (1985). *Children of the city: At work and at play*. New York: Oxford University Press.

Oppenheimer, V. K. (1994). Women's rising employment and the future of the family in industrial societies. *Population and Development Review, 20*, 293–342.

Teitelbaum, M. S., & Weiner, M. (Eds.) (1995). *Threatened peoples, threatened borders: World migration and U.S. policy*. New York: Norton.

Tilly, L. A., & Scott, J. W. (1978). *Women, work, and family*. New York: Routledge.

Wilson, W. J. (1987). *The truly disadvantaged: The inner city, the underclass, and public policy*. Chicago: University of Chicago Press.

14

Immigrant Integration and Pending Legislation: Observations on Empirical Projections

B. Lindsay Lowell
U.S. Commission on Immigration Reform

PROPOSALS for changing the immigration system appear certain to result in substantial changes in admissions policy in the near future. Foremost may be a shift in focus on the reunification of immediate family members away from that of siblings and married children. After a transition period, the number of immigrants permitted will return to levels characteristic of the late-1980s. Other changes, such as strengthening the legal responsibilities of U.S. sponsors or requiring citizenship for the receipt of most needs-based programs, represent an emphasis on a broader scope having to do with immigrant integration policies. The observations presented here address some key assumptions about the legacy of recent legislation, the inherent economic advantage of immigrant family members, and immigrants' use of transfer payments.

THE LEGACY OF PAST AND RECENT LEGISLATION

Gatekeeping to the United States divides into historical phases with distinct characteristics. Initially, the flow of immigrants to the United States was largely unregulated. The first restrictive elements barring illiterates and public charges were capped with the 1882 Chinese Exclusion Act. The Immigration Act of 1924 banned most Orientals and enacted limited "national origin quotas" against those not from northwestern Europe. With only minor adjustments, notably the Immigration Act of 1952, nationally selective exclusion remained in force for four decades.

The Immigration Act of 1965 marked a significant change. The old system was overhauled, yielding a complex system that permitted equal numbers of visa applicants from all sending countries under numerically limited "preference categories" based either on certain skills (i.e., occupations) or on immediate family ties (i.e., spouse, children, and siblings). Otherwise, entry was allowed for unlimited numbers of immigrants based upon immediate family relationships to U.S. citizens (spouse, children, and parents). Thus, the underlying conventions of the 1965 Act were equity for applicants from all sending countries and family reunification.

The unexpected result of the new system was a multiplier effect by which new immigrants sponsored applicants from previously underrepresented developing countries. Mexicans and other Latin Americans, who have a long history of U.S. migration, make up 40% of today's immigrants. Asians, who were either banned or restricted prior to the 1965 act, now make up another 40%. Refugee admissions has become a third pillar of the immigrant system. Refugee admissions have been most responsive to foreign policy concerns, particularly those involving people who are fleeing communist regimes, an approach that may be outmoded in the post-cold war era.

At the same time, a large number of immigrants enter off the books. The Immigration Reform and Control Act of 1986 (IRCA) sought to control and restrain illegal migration. In reality, there has been little effective reduction of unauthorized migration and, ironically, IRCA's legalization program solidifies family and community networks that may increase unauthorized flows (Bean, Edmonston, & Passel, 1990). Unfortunately, the failure to develop effective strategies to control unlawful immigration has blurred the public perception of the distinction between legal and illegal immigrants.[1]

Nevertheless, IRCA's passage cleared the way for reform of the legal system, most especially the substantial increases in immigration levels in the Immigration Act of 1990 (IMMACT90). Worldwide limited immigration numbers for family- and employment-based admissions had been set at 270,000; IMMACT90 increased those numbers 36% to 366,000. In particular, as a result of a forecasted need for skilled workers and a perceived decline in immigrant quality, the numbers allocated to the skilled categories were upped from a limit of 54,000 to a more substantial 140,000 visas per year, and both the required educational and occupational qualifications of prospective immigrants were set higher (Papademetriou, 1992). An additional 55,000 admissions were set for legalization dependents and 40,000 for diversity immigrants. The new legislation passed in the last weeks of the outgoing Congress with little national attention (Kramer & Lowell, 1992).

---

[1]The U.S. Commission on Immigration Reform's first set of recommendations addressed this ongoing predicament with proposals for improving interior and border enforcement in order to bring credibility back to immigration policy (U.S. Commission on Immigration Reform, 1994).

Overall, the levels of immigration to the United States have been increasing steadily since the 1965 act. Consider that the number of entries grew 42% between 1970 and 1980 (from 373,000 to 531,000), a more modest 24% through 1990 (656,000), but 23% in only 2 years, by 1992 (810,000; the first year IMMACT90 was in effect). These figures do not include about 2.5 million IRCA legalizations, nor do they indicate the demand for future immigration that these newly legal sponsors will generate. Did the legislation set in place a credible system that rationally regulates immigration in the interest of residents of the United States?

FAMILY ADMISSIONS AND IMMIGRANT ADAPTATION

Family reunification remains the primary goal of immigration policy, primarily due to values that rank family ties and citizen rights higher than labor market ties. Nevertheless, the reunification of family groups plays a broader economic role in the adaptation of immigrants. We know that immigrants are indeed dependent upon complex family and household relationships. Certainly, child care may be shared out to grandparents, and siblings and adult children may pool household resources. Nevertheless, we know little about the specific interactions between family admissions policy and the adaptation of the immigrant individual–family–household–community, although we might conclude that family immigrants perform remarkably well.

In fact, recent research seems to support the counterintuitive possibility that the economic performance of family-based immigrants lags only a little behind employment-based immigrants whose selection for skills should enable them to integrate more readily.[2] A longitudinal study of Koreans and Filipinos found that whereas family-based immigrants do not perform as well initially, the employment-based immigrants also experienced serious problems in transferring their skills to the U.S. labor market (Fawcett, Carino, Park, & Gardner, 1990). A study that linked INS records with Social Security earnings records as of 1980 found that the occupational and earnings advantages of employment-based individuals are not particularly sizable (Sorensen, Bean, Ku, & Zimmermann, 1992). Interestingly, employment- and family-based immigrants were equally likely to become naturalized citizens. This finding suggests a convergence to the same level of U.S. commitment and integration.

Indeed, one study using indirect measures of admission status found that the initial earnings disadvantage of family-based immigration decreases be-

---

[2]Family-based immigrants in fact generally possess lower education and skills and, in contrast to employment-based immigrants, are consequently assumed to have lower productivity and less labor market value. Some economists discern a trend toward declining average skill levels of the total immigration stream associated with third-world migration and family reunification (Borjas, 1995; Briggs, 1992).

cause of faster growth in earnings over time. In fact, family-based immigrants appear likely to catch up with the earnings of their employment-based compatriots after 11 to 18 years in the United States (Duleep & Regets, 1994). This finding apparently held over the 1980s as well (Duleep & Regets, 1995, as cited in Fix & Zimmermann, this volume). Another research team concluded that "the distinction between family-reunification immigration and immigration based on labor market 'needs' in terms of the contributions of immigrants to the economy may be less important than is commonly thought" (Jasso & Rosenzweig, 1994, p. 29).

The jobs held by employment-based and family-based immigrants do not vary on average as markedly as casual observers imagine. Only the primary immigrant must meet the requirements of the skilled visa categories, and the accompanying secondary immigrants (i.e., family members) fill lesser skilled occupations. Gallo and Bailey (1994) suggested that family-based immigrants, because they have closer ties to family and community networks, have a source of information capital not as readily available to employment-based immigrants. Furthermore, family-based immigrants are screened by sponsors, and their close ties to family and community help provide individuals places to live, places to work, support during family and job transitions, and start-up funds for purchasing homes or new businesses. According to Fix and Zimmermann (this volume), research also indicates that family members, particularly admissions under the sibling categories, tend to be entrepreneurial (Duleep & Regets, 1995).

The research on family- as compared to employment-based immigration is counterintuitive yet appears compelling when the theoretical rationale is presented. However, there are several issues that make forecasts based upon the research problematic. Few studies have been performed, and most go only through 1980. The only study on these patterns through 1990 is inferential; that is, it does not track individuals. Furthermore, the studies do not take into account changes in the demographic composition of sponsors and corresponding siblings. The last critique calls attention to the fact that persons legalized under IRCA, who have less than a seventh-grade education on average, are the largest block of sponsors for future family-based admissions. It is difficult to argue that the advantages inherent to yesterday's family-based admissions will produce the same boost to tomorrow's family and sibling immigrants.

There may be another reason why future family-based immigrants, under the current immigration system, may not perform as well. Given the backlog of applicants, the average wait for admission has increased from one year prior to IMMACT90 to about 4 years today. Variation runs from about 10 years for most countries but can run longer for oversubscribed countries—consider the 13-year wait for Mexicans or the 17-year wait for Filipinos (U.S. Commission on Immigration Reform, 1995). There are nearly 1.6 million siblings registered with the State Department for sponsored immigration, or 45% of the total family- and employment-based visa waiting list. Obviously, the lag between application and admission can only continue to lengthen, and to lengthen substantially for Latin and Asian countries that supply most immigrants.[3] In 1994 the mean age of principals admitted under family fourth preference (i.e., brother and sisters) was 46 years; this was 13 years older than the average principal immigrant, and the difference can only increase as backlogs get longer. Research clearly finds poorer wage assimilation and language acquisition of middle-age and older immigrants (Greenwood & McDowell, 1990).

Finally, the recommendation that siblings and adult children be eliminated from the system is primarily to open places for the more expedited admission of immediate family members caught in a lengthening queue (U.S. Commission on Immigration Reform, 1995). A system that makes family members wait at least 4 years and as long as 2 decades for admission is deceptive and inequitable. Elimination of the sibling and adult children categories is partly a response to problems in the system created by IMMACT90, even given its increased admission levels, and on-the-ground demand for family reunification. The balance struck in such a recommendation is to give precedence to the wives and children of U.S. residents.

HOW MANY IMMIGRANTS?
IMPACT OVER THE PAST DECADE

Much of the empirical research on the economic impact of immigration over the 1970s and much of the smaller body of studies on the 1980s leads to the same conclusion: Immigration has small impact nationwide on the earnings and employment of U.S. workers (Lowell, 1995). Most studies show very little effect, positive or negative, on native-born workers of any race or ethnicity. Still, a growing body of research suggests a more cautious appraisal of recent and future impacts on certain skill groups and on selected geographic and industrial sectors. Researchers have begun to explore the possibility that immigrants may have some adverse consequences on the labor market for advanced degrees, especially in science and engineering (North, 1995). Low-skilled workers have experienced adverse wage effects from immigration, particularly within the context of the restructuring of the U.S. economy. For example, between 1980 and 1988, "immigrant workers increased the [size of the] work force of high school dropouts by approximately 25 percent, whereas immigrant workers increased the work force of high school graduates by 6–7 per-

---

[3]Applications are dropping off, possibly because the wait is discouraging. However, there are potentially 1.4 million family members who might be sponsored by newly legalized immigrants (U.S. Commission on Immigration Reform, 1995).

cent and of college graduates by 10–11 percent" (Borjas, Freeman, & Katz, 1992, p. 232). The foreign-born comprised 20% of the labor force of high school dropouts at the end of the decade. These demographic shifts and declines in the educational levels of the most recent immigrant streams lead some to believe that immigrants have contributed to wage losses of low-skilled natives.

Due to declines in manufacturing jobs and various other causes, high school dropouts experienced a 9.5% decrease in their real wages during the 1980s. Of course, contracting demand for low-skilled workers in the overall economy, driven by economic restructuring, played a paramount role in altering outcomes. An economic simulation suggests that immigrants may have accounted for at least one fourth of this decline nationwide (Borjas et al., 1992). Other empirical studies find similar effects, mostly toward the lower end of this range, especially on the Pacific coast where various studies find low-skilled immigrants had the greatest impact on wage inequality (Jaeger, 1995).

Other research shows that, over the past decade, cities experiencing high levels of immigration have evidenced the outmigration of low-skilled natives. During the 1970s, 100 immigrants were associated with a net outmigration of 14 native blue-collar workers (Walker, Ellis, & Barff, 1992). Frey (1994) analyzed 1990 U.S. Census data and examined mobility patterns for many metropolitan areas and major states over the course of the 1980s. His general findings show that high immigration areas have high rates of native outmigration, particularly among (often white) low- and middle-income groups and non-college graduates. Although not a clear indicator of immigrant–native competition, these studies raise concern about the geographic separation of the foreign- and native-born and the concentration of localized impacts.

Concentrated immigrant flows may have very adverse impacts on resident foreign-born workers. Indeed, various theoretical strands come together around the observation that low-skilled workers compete with other low-skilled workers and that such competition can be particularly fierce in the labor-intensive industries employing immigrants. "The group most clearly and severely disadvantaged by newly arrived immigrants is other recent immigrants who are, in the final analysis, the closest substitutes for newcomers. The uniformity of research results in this area is striking" (Fix & Passel, 1994, p. 51). A long-run view might well turn from a focus on natives and give equal weight and concern to levels of immigration that can readily have the most adverse results for the already-resident foreign born.

Furthermore, a body of research suggests that the net fiscal costs of immigrants, although negligible or even favorable at the national level, may be a drain on local and state governments. Of course, there are marked differences between refugees and other legal entrants. For example, Fix and Passel (1994) found, using indirect indicators of admission status, that just 2% of non-refugees arriving during the 1980s received public assistance; 3.2% of pre-

1980 nonrefugee and 13.4% of refugee entrants during the 1980s reported public assistance income. The percentages for these nonrefugee individuals are less than the 3.7% registered by working-age natives in the 1990 Census. Another study also indicates that averaging refugees together with other immigrants hides the fact 8% of all households headed by nonrefugees receive welfare, as compared with 16% of those headed by likely refugees (Borjas, 1994).

Borjas (1994) also found that immigrant participation in welfare programs rose from 1970 through 1990. Although the use of welfare by immigrant households with less than 5 years in the United States did not increase (some of whom are ineligible for selected transfer programs), that of longer term immigrants has increased. Among immigrant households having 5 to 10 years of residence in the United States, participation rates increased from 6.5% in 1970 to 8% in 1980 and to almost 11% in 1990. Simultaneously, the average amount of welfare received by natives remained at about $4,000 between 1970 and 1990, whereas immigrant welfare receipts increased from $3,800 to $5,400 in 1989 dollars. Again, recall that marked differences occur by country of origin, immigrant status, and by state and locality.

Perhaps one of the more unfortunate trends in this regard, especially in terms of pending legislation, has been the high cost of elderly immigrants one fourth of whom receive some form of welfare (about three times the native rate). There was a tripling in the numbers of elderly immigrants receiving Supplemental Security Income (SSI) between 1986 and 1994, from 240,000 to 740,000, and costs rose from $684 million to $2.9 billion (Interpreter Releases, 1995). As of 1992, one third had applied for SSI just after their 3-year "deeming" period ended the financial responsibility of the children who sponsored them (Fix & Passel, 1994). Congress extended the deeming period to 5 years in 1993; however, the increased application rate held from 1982 through 1994. This pattern lies behind the more stringent proposals that require enforcement of affidavits of support and restricted access to retirement funds created by and for U.S. residents (U.S. Commission on Immigration Reform, 1995).[4]

CONCLUSIONS

Today's immigration system is an affirmation of the value that Americans place upon families, balanced by a concern for meeting competitive labor market

---

[4]Proposals for tougher sponsorship requirements and restricted access to welfare may permit only the wealthy to sponsor family members and reduce the number of parents admitted (Fix & Zimmermann, this volume; Interpreter Releases, 1995). Many of these proposals go beyond the kind of recommendations made by the U.S. Commission on Immigration Reform. Of course, it is possible that demand could create creative means of funding or that parent-immigrants will be younger on average.

needs. The elements of the current system represent a continuation of traditional immigrant ties as well as a rejection of the national exclusionary principles that guided the system from the turn of the century until the decade of the Great Society. Immigrants now come predominantly from developing countries, and the diversity of languages, cultures, and ethnicities are greater than any previously experienced. We remain the world's most generous immigrant nation. Legislation now being considered in Congress does not change these basic features of the U.S. immigration system.[5]

The cumulative effects of no admissions for siblings or adult children and of the restriction of access to needs-based programs are surely not known. The available research on family composition and integration may not be the best prognosticator of future outcomes, and there is a dearth of research that addresses the link between needs-based programs and integration. Clearly, in the short run some immigrant families would experience the personal loss of not being able to anticipate reunions with more extended family members, however distant such a promise might be in all likelihood. However, the loss of these more extended family members might not be a truly severe economic handicap.

Changes in sponsor responsibilities could place a strain on the budgets of immigrant families, but one should not underestimate the creative response of immigrant households and communities. The increases seen in the rates of naturalization in the past year demonstrate that it is possible for the immigrant community to become a citizen community that can restore their eligibility to needs-based programs. If access becomes more difficult, it is likely that naturalized citizens will not be singled out in a society-wide trend toward reduced transfer payments and less government for all residents. However, proposals that essentially exclude naturalized citizens from the same access to programs available to native-born persons are quite likely unconstitutional (Interpreter Releases, 1995, p. 1371) and may face the same hurdle to implementation as California's recently demised Proposition 187. Such proposals are particularly troublesome and unwelcome because they would, for the first time in U.S. history, differentiate among citizen classes.

---

[5]Many of the proposals to regulate the immigration system favor immediate family members and shorter waiting periods for admission. For the foreseeable future, the actual number of immigrants will continue at current levels until the backlog of spouses and children is reduced. It appears implausible that the number of legal immigrants will fall below levels experienced during the latter 1980s. If, as also is proposed, Congress revisits the immigration system every 3 or 5 years, there will be a mechanism that permits ongoing adjustments to the system to address problems of reunification, adjustment, or impact as they become evident.

ACKNOWLEDGMENTS

Opinions expressed in this chapter are solely those of the author and may not represent the opinions of the U.S. Commission on Immigration Reform or the U.S. Government. I extend my appreciation for their comments on this chapter to Michael Fix, Wendy Zimmermann, and Susan Martin.

REFERENCES

Bean, F. D., Edmonston, B., & Passell, J. S. (1990). *Undocumented migration to the United States: IRCA and the experience of the 1980s.* Washington, DC: Urban Institute Press.

Borjas, G. (1994). Immigration and welfare, 1970–1990. NBER Working Paper No. 4872.

Borjas, G. (1995). Assimilation and changes in cohort quality revisited: What happened to immigrant earnings in the 1980s? *Journal of Labor Economics, 13,* 201–245.

Borjas, G. J., Freeman, R. B., & Katz, L. F. (1992). On the labor market effects of immigration and trade. In G. J. Borjas & R. B. Freeman (Eds.), *Immigration and the work force* (pp. 213–244). Chicago: University of Chicago Press.

Briggs, V. M., Jr. (1992). *Mass immigration and the national interest.* Armonk, NY: M. E. Sharpe.

Duleep, H. O., & Regets, M. C. (1994). *Admission criteria and immigrant earnings profiles.* Paper presented at the meeting of the North American Economics and Finance Association/American Economics Association, Boston.

Duleep, H. O., & Regets, M. C. (1995). *Family unification, siblings, and skills.* Washington, DC: The Urban Institute.

Fawcett, J. T., Carino, B., Park, I. H., & Gardner, R. W. (1990). *Selectivity and diversity: The effect of U.S. immigration policy on immigrant characteristics.* Paper presented at the annual meeting of the Population Association of America, Toronto, Ontario, Canada.

Fix, M., & Passel, J. S. (1994). *Immigration and immigrants: Setting the record straight.* Washington, DC: The Urban Institute.

Frey, W. H. (1994). The New White Flight. *American Demographics, April,* 40–48.

Gallo, C. & Bailey, T. (1994). *Social networks and skills-based immigration policy.* Paper presented at the meeting of the North American Economics and Finance Association/American Economics Association, Boston.

Greenwood, M. J., & McDowell, J. (1990). *The labor market consequences of U.S. immigration: A survey.* (Immigration Policy and Research, Working Paper No. 1). Washington, DC: U.S. Department of Labor.

Interpreter Releases. (1995). *Senate OKs welfare bill with sweeping immigration consequences.* Washington, DC: Federal Publications.

Jaeger, D. A. (1995). *Skill differences and the effect of immigrants on the wages of natives.* Washington, DC: U.S. Bureau of Labor Statistics.

Jasso, G., & Rosenzweig, M. R. (1994, July). *Do immigrants screened for skills do better than family-reunification immigrants?* Paper presented at the 6th annual conference on Socio-Economics, Jouy en Josas.

Kramer, R. G., & Lowell, B. L. (1992). *Employment-based immigration: The rationale and politics behind the immigration act of 1990.* Paper presented at the meeting of the Population Association of America, Denver.

Lowell, B. L. (1995). *The effects of immigration on the U.S. economy and labor force.* (Immigration Policy and Research, Rep. No. 20). Washington, DC: U.S. Department of Labor.

North, D. S. (1995). *Soothing the establishment: The impact of foreign-born scientists and engineers on America*. New York: University Press.

Papademetriou, D. G. (1992). *International migration in North America: Issues, policies and implications*. (Immigration Policy and Research Working Paper No. 14). Washington, DC: U.S. Department of Labor.

Sorensen, E., Bean, F. D., Ku, L., & Zimmermann, W. (1992). *Immigrant categories and the U.S. job market*. Washington, DC: The Urban Institute.

U.S. Commission on Immigration Reform. (1994). *U.S. immigration policy: Restoring credibility*. Washington, DC: U.S. Government Printing Office.

U.S. Commission on Immigration Reform. (1995). *Legal immigration: Setting priorities*. Washington, DC: U.S. Government Printing Office.

Walker, R., Ellis, M., & Barff, R. (1992). Linked migration systems: Immigration and internal labor flows in the United States. *Economic Geography, 68*, 234–248.

15

Immigration and the Family: An Overview

Nancy S. Landale
The Pennsylvania State University

D URING the last several years, both academic and lay interest in immigration issues has skyrocketed. Attention to immigration has been fueled by a dramatic increase in the size and rate of growth of the immigrant population, the diversity of recent immigrant flows, and the failure of expectations based on traditional models of assimilation to be met for some new immigrant groups. In the public mind, the sheer number of immigrants arriving each year is cause for concern. Currently, about one million new immigrants (legal and illegal) are added to the U.S. population annually (Martin & Midgely, 1994). Most of these immigrants settle in just a handful of states in which the social and fiscal impacts of their arrival have been substantial. Although the influx of immigrants has been felt less directly in other U.S. locales, immigration issues are on the minds of many U.S. citizens in the current period.

Traditionally, academic research on both migration decisions and the experience of immigrants subsequent to resettlement approached these topics from the perspective of the lone individual. Individuals were held to make migration decisions by calculating the costs and benefits of a move to themselves (Harris & Todaro, 1970; Sjaastad, 1962; Todaro, 1969); similarly, models of assimilation focused on individual-level variables such as length of residence in the United States. Increasingly, both theoretical and empirical work on the migration decision-making process has moved beyond this atomistic perspective to a recognition of the importance of the family context of migration (e.g., Massey, Alarcon, Gonzalez, & Durand, 1987; Stark, 1984). Although research on the assimilation process has less fully incorporated the family into theories and models, the beginnings of such linkages are evident in recent work. Thus, as is noted by Rumbaut (this volume), "the family is perhaps *the* strategic research site for understanding the dynamics of immigration flows (legal and illegal) and of immigrant adaptation processes."

The role of the family in international migration is the unifying theme of the chapters in this volume. The initial chapters address a broad set of issues regarding trends in the origins and types of immigrants to the United States, with special attention to the role of marriage and family ties in shaping immigrant flows. An additional focus is the diverse family patterns of immigrants and their implications for human, social, and political capital. A second set of chapters addresses themes related to the experiences of immigrant children and families after they have settled in this country. The impact of migration on child and adolescent development as well as changes in family structure and process receive attention. The final set of chapters focuses on the critical topic of the nation's immigration and immigrant policies. A particularly important theme covered in this section is the possible effects of proposed changes in immigration policy and in welfare policy for immigrant families.

Although the majority of the chapters pertain to the lives of immigrants and their families in the years after arrival in this country, several emphasize the importance of the family to the migration process itself. The following overview therefore begins with a brief discussion of the critical role of the family in the immigration process. The focus then shifts to issues regarding the individual's and family's adjustment upon arrival to the United States.

THE FAMILY AND THE IMMIGRATION PROCESS

Understanding the role of the family in the experience of U.S. immigrants requires recognition of the importance of family ties to the migration process itself. As is argued by Rumbaut (this volume), migration flows are initiated and sustained by long-standing political and economic linkages between countries. Over time, macrolinkages increase the likelihood of social and familial ties that span national borders. To the extent that such ties are well developed, they encourage migratory flows that eventually develop a self-sustaining momentum.

Migration researchers increasingly recognize the importance of such social networks, especially family ties, to microlevel migration decisions. A major proponent of this perspective is Massey, who argued that migrant networks "bring about the cumulative causation of migration because every new migrant reduces the cost of migration for a set of nonmigrants, thereby inducing some of them to migrate, creating new network ties to the destination area for another set of people, some of whom also are induced to migrate, creating more network ties, and so on" (Massey, 1990, p. 17). Family ties form the backbone of migrant networks; each family member who migrates to a destination area reduces the costs of migration for other family members because he or she can provide information, housing, and other opportunities otherwise unavailable to the potential migrant. Thus, having family members in the United States increases greatly the likelihood of international migration to this country.

Other research points to the importance of the family as the key decision-making unit regarding migration. Most individuals live within families, and families develop strategies both to maximize their economic well-being and to minimize risk. From this point of view, the migration of individuals or families must be viewed from the perspective of the family unit rather than that of the individual. For example, in developing countries families often pursue risk-diversification strategies that entail the migration of family members to diverse labor markets, from which they remit part of their earnings to the family at home. In such situations, although we may observe the migration of a lone individual across national borders, an individual-level model of the migration decision-making process would be incorrect. In short, migration decisions are typically made within a family context in which family well-being is maximized.

U.S. immigration policies both recognize and reinforce the role of family ties in immigration. Fix and Zimmerman (this volume) emphasize that U.S. immigration policy has given high priority to the goal of promoting family unity for at least 30 years. Family reunification is the principal criterion used in determining the eligibility of potential immigrants for admission. Although recently proposed legislation would narrow the range of family members eligible for admission under the category of family reunification, the fundamental premise that at least nuclear family members have a right to be reunited remains intact. Immigration policy thus reinforces the role of the family in U.S. immigration.

THE FAMILY AND IMMIGRANT ADAPTATION

Assimilation Theory

Theoretical frameworks for understanding the role of the family in immigrant adaptation to the receiving country are less well developed than those focusing on the migration process itself. Most research on the adaptation and assimilation of immigrants examines individual-level indicators using individual-level variables. Moreover, traditional theories of immigrant assimilation have been largely discredited, and little has appeared on the horizon to replace them. Thus, the chapters in this volume that address themes related to the experience of U.S. immigrants subsequent to their arrival represent efforts to move the field into new territory.

Traditionally, studies of the experience of new immigrants were guided by what has now come to be known as straight-line assimilation theory. This perspective predicts that immigrants will become increasingly similar to the native population as they spend more time in this country (Gordon, 1964; Park, 1950). Eventually (typically after several generations), immigrants lose their cultural and socioeconomic distinctiveness, blending into the melting pot of American society. Although even the early proponents of the theory (e.g., Gordon, 1964) recognized complexities of the assimilation process (e.g., its multidimensional nature, variation in the pace with which it occurs), the theory has been under attack in recent years because of its failure to recognize the multiple pathways of assimilation and the conditions under which they are followed.

Segmented Assimilation

Several of the authors note the absence of a viable replacement for assimilation theory and the shifting orientation of the field. Indeed, major themes echoed throughout this volume are the diversity of the experience of immigrants and their families and the need to develop theories and approaches that clarify the conditions under which segmented assimilation occurs (Portes & Zhou, 1993). This theme is introduced by Rumbaut (this volume) in his discussion of the three distinct types of immigrants in the contemporary period: political refugees and asylees; highly skilled professionals, executives, and managers; and undocumented laborers. According to Rumbaut, the resources and vulnerabilities that immigrants bring to this country differ by immigrant type. In particular, there are three types of resources that are central to the outcomes of immigrants and their families: financial and human capital (i.e., social class at entry), political capital (i.e., legal status at entry), and social capital (i.e., social networks and family structure or cohesiveness). The conditions under which groups exit their origin countries and the context of their reception in the United States interact with these resources to shape the adaptation process. Accordingly, there are multiple pathways of experience among immigrant groups.

Whereas Rumbaut's analysis of the forces contributing to segmented assimilation emphasizes the global context of international migration, other authors in this volume approach the issue from somewhat different vantage points. Buriel and De Ment's discussion of biculturalism focuses on the sociocultural context of the areas in which immigrants reside. According to Buriel and De Ment, the volume and continuity of immigration from Asia and Latin America, coupled with the residential concentration of Asian and Latino immigrants, has led to the creation of ecological niches that allow for the maintenance of the ancestral culture. For example, Mexican Americans living in the Southwest often live in communities in which a substantial proportion of the residents are of Mexican origin. Spanish is widely spoken, there are widespread opportunities to participate in Mexican culture, and the distance to Mexico is relatively small. Such situations contribute to the maintenance of the ancestral culture, even though immigrants may become increasingly able to function within U.S. society over time. Kibria (this volume) places this perspective in the context of Portes and Zhou's (1993) work on the three predominant modes of incorporation of immigrants in the United States: the classic assimilation pattern, downward assimilation into the underclass, and economic advancement within the context of a strong ethnic community. Kibria argues that biculturalism is most common in the latter case, in which the immigrant is embedded in an ethnic enclave.

Although biculturalism is emphasized in Buriel and De Ment's chapter, their model of immigrant adaptation among Mexican-origin immigrants includes four acculturation styles, which they term the bicultural orientation, the Mexican orientation, the marginal orientation, and the Euro-American orientation. The marginal orientation is particularly noteworthy because it at least partially captures a phenomenon that is discussed in a number of the chapters, the increasing marginality of some immigrant groups as they gain more exposure to this country.

The forces contributing to this downward assimilation are complex and include structural factors (e.g., the employment opportunities in immigrants' areas of residence, residential segregation), family patterns, and individual-level orientations. Extending the structural perspective that is prevalent in the literature (e.g., Portes & Zhou, 1993), the authors in this volume emphasize the effects of family patterns on individual motivations and outcomes. Rumbaut provides evidence that the social capital of immigrants erodes with duration of residence in this country and second-generation status; in particular, among some groups there is a striking increase in single-parent families with increasing exposure to native norms. Rumbaut's research on the children of immigrants in San Diego and Miami indicates that this erosion of social capital has a significant effect on academic achievement and aspirations, both of which decline with additional time in this country.

Drawing on her research on West Indian immigrants, Waters (this volume) addresses the question of why this is occurring. She suggests that, in addition to structural factors (e.g., residential concentration in the central city, racial discrimination), both serial migration and lifestyle changes experienced in the United States weaken the ties between immigrant parents and their children. In particular, nuclear families are often much more isolated than they were in the origin country. At the same time, parents are less available to supervise their children because they spend long hours at work. Parental authority also is eroded by differences between American norms regarding discipline and traditional disciplinary practices. Waters argues that these and other factors weaken the immigrant ethos of high aspirations and hard work as the route to achievement, resulting in declining socioeconomic success among the children of immigrants.

Children Versus Adults

Although the children of immigrants, especially second-generation children, are increasingly regarded as central to understanding the assimilation process, neither theory nor research has systematically addressed the complexities entailed in studying immigrant children's experience. Clearly, the family plays an especially important role in structuring children's lives and in determining their success; however, as is evident in several chapters in this volume, immigrant children often play a vital role in helping their parents function within the larger society.

There is consensus in the chapters on migration and child or adolescent development that work on this topic is at an early stage. The authors point to a number of issues that are in need of attention. First, the theoretical frameworks used to understand adult experience lack a developmental perspective, which is essential to understanding the challenges faced by first- and second-generation children. García Coll and Magnuson (this volume) note that the impact of the migration experience on first-generation children varies greatly according to the age or developmental stage of the child. They propose that the ease of acculturation is a curvilinear function of age, with the youngest and oldest children acculturating less quickly than children who arrive during the middle years of childhood. This is in part because very young children have little exposure to institutions outside of the family (e.g., school), whereas older children tend to be less malleable due to both their developmental stage and the greater duration of their exposure to the origin country.

Although the importance of age or developmental stage at migration is widely recognized, there is a need for much more careful elaboration of how the capabilities and needs of children at various developmental stages intersect with the changes brought about by the migration experience. For example, García Coll and Magnuson suggest that the impact of separations from significant family members or familiar environments may vary according to age. Language acquisition and identity formation are also age-dependent processes. Research in this area would benefit from the development of conceptual models that identify the key transitions that immigrant children face and specify the ways in which developmental stage may influence children's ability to successfully make those transitions. Such work would be valuable in guiding future research toward topics that would systematically advance this field.

Another critical issue is the role of the family in shaping the outcomes of immigrant children. Sianz (this volume) argues that immigrant children cannot be considered apart from the families in which they live because children's well-being is directly affected by family structure, family dynamics, and the mental health of their parents. She presents a model of immigrant children's developmental outcomes that emphasizes the importance of family, parent, and child characteristics to children's adaptation or maladjustment. The model illustrates how family processes can be incorporated into studies of immigrant children's outcomes.

Because Siantz' research is based on the experience of Mexican-American migrant farmworkers and their children, her model is most applicable to the situation of impoverished immigrant groups facing harsh life circumstances. In brief, the chronic poverty and social isolation experienced by such immigrants are associated with high levels of family stress. All these factors place immigrant parents at risk of poor mental health (e.g., depression), although parental reactions to stress may vary according to the level of social support available to them. Parental mental health is linked to child outcomes in the model via parenting practices and parenting style. In short, the social and economic circumstances of immigrant families affect both family dynamics and parental characteristics. In combination with the attributes of the child, these factors play a major role in determining the outcomes of immigrant children.

Although the model proposed by Siantz may be more applicable to some immigrant groups than others, it exemplifies a careful treatment of the family's role as mediator between the larger environment and child outcomes. Especially in studies of children, but also in research on adults, a family perspective is a valuable addition to the individualistic orientation of the field.

Individuals Versus Families

The chapters in this volume expand the boundaries of existing research on U.S. immigrants by placing their experience in a family context. There is consensus that the family is "the strategic point from which to analyze changes in the lives of immigrants and their children" (Hirschman, this volume). Yet even these authors, who explicitly recognize family issues, tend to focus on individual-level outcomes. Although the effects of family structure and process on the outcomes of individual immigrants are in need of further study, equally important are questions concerning how the family itself changes as a result of immigration and exposure to the U.S. social context. For example, immigration may lead to changes in the subjective definition of the family (i.e., who is in my family?), family stability, and family values (i.e., what are my obligations to family members?).

Although these issues receive relatively little attention in this volume, they are addressed briefly in several chapters. For example, Rumbaut discusses studies based on census data (Jensen & Chitose, 1994; Landale & Oropesa, 1995) that show increasing rates of marital disruption and single-parenthood across succeeding generations, especially for some immigrant groups. According to Rumbaut, this pattern is indicative of a deterioration of social capital.

Buriel and De Ment (this volume) also discuss changes in household composition and the availability of nearby kin with duration of residence. They note the decline of household extension among Mexican Americans as they spend more time in this country. In contrast to Rumbaut, however, Buriel and De Ment emphasize the compensatory role of kin outside the household. Among Mexican Americans, extended kin who leave the household tend to move to residences nearby. Furthermore, extended kin networks may be richer for second- and third-generation Mexican Americans than for the immigrant generation.

These findings illustrate the potential importance of research that investigates how the immigrant family changes with exposure to the U.S. social context, both with additional years of residence for the first generation and across generations. Research on household composition, the proximity of kin outside the household, and the nature of exchanges and relations between family members is needed in order to understand temporal and generational changes in the family contexts within which immigrants shape their lives.

PUBLIC POLICY AND IMMIGRANT FAMILIES

The implications of public policy for immigrant families are addressed in additional chapters in this volume. In addition to providing an overview of both current and proposed policies regarding immigration and immigrants, the chapters emphasize possible unintended consequences of the leading immigration and welfare reforms now under consideration. Some of these reforms are targeted explicitly at immigrants; however, others must be viewed as part of a more general attempt to curb social spending and increase self-sufficiency among individuals and families.

Family reunification has been the primary goal of U.S. immigration policy in recent decades, as is evident from the fact that about three fourths of legal immigrants enter this country through family-based preference categories. Family reunification policies allow the close family members of U.S. citizens and permanent residents to enter the United States. Two categories of family members are recognized: nuclear family members (e.g., spouses and minor children) and extended family members (e.g., siblings and adult children). There are also some policies regarding illegal immigrants that take into account family ties.

Fix and Zimmerman (this volume) note that proposed legislation to restrict immigration would redefine close family members by excluding the extended family, including parents. The intended goals of this redefinition are to reduce the total number of immigrants and to allow for quicker admission of nuclear family members. According to Fix and Zimmerman, however, such a change in policy would have other, unintended consequences for immigrant families.

For example, the exclusion of parents and siblings from admission under family reunification would reduce the social capital of immigrants. Especially for immigrant groups with limited financial resources, a reduction in the availability of family members for assistance (e.g., with childcare) might reduce productivity and economic success.

Other legislation would make it more difficult for immigrants to bring acceptable types of family members to the United States by requiring a higher level of financial resources and greater financial responsibility among those who sponsor a family member. Fix and Zimmerman suggest that, although this legislation would contribute to a reduction in the level of legal immigration, it could undermine the goal of nuclear family reunification. About half of the immigrant families would not qualify to bring a nuclear family member to the United States.

Although there is consensus that these policy changes would reduce the number of legal immigrants, their effect on the total number of immigrants is less straightforward. At least some of those denied legal admission as a result of immigration reform will enter the United States illegally. This point has been forcefully made by Massey (1990) and others (e.g., Donato, Durand, & Massey, 1992; Massey & Espinosa, in press), who argue that international migration is a self-sustaining social process. Once migrant flows have become well established, it is highly unlikely that barriers to legal immigration will reduce the volume of the immigrant stream. Instead, they will increase the proportion of immigrants entering the country illegally.

The United States has had less explicit policies to address the needs of immigrants once they enter this country. The major exception pertains to refugees, who are assisted under the Refugee Resettlement Program. For most immigrants, the only available forms of assistance are mainstream public assistance programs, such as SSI, AFDC, and food stamps. The eligibility of immigrants for these programs is summarized by Fix and Zimmerman in this volume.

Welfare reform proposals currently under consideration would reduce the availability of public assistance to immigrants in unprecedented ways. For example, illegal immigrants, legal immigrants, and some naturalized citizens would be excluded from almost all needs-based programs. Other proposals call for enforcing the financial responsibilities of immigrants' sponsors more strictly, thus requiring greater responsibility for mutual support among immigrants compared to native families. Although these and other changes in welfare policy may have some positive effects, Fix and Zimmerman argue that they may also greatly increase the difficulties faced by immigrant families as they adjust to life in this country. Moreover, denying public services to legal immigrants and naturalized citizens would constitute discrimination against the foreign-born and contribute to the creation of a two-tiered society.

An important point made in these chapters is that policy-makers have failed to consider fully the cumulative impact of proposed changes in legislation on immigrant families. Fix and Zimmerman, Bianchi, and Lowell provide new insights into possible consequences of immigration and welfare reform for immigrant families. In addition, they argue that the findings of social science research should be more fully incorporated into policy discussions.

CONCLUSION

The importance of the family to international migration and immigrant adaptation processes is evident throughout this volume. Previous studies have established that the family is a key migration decision-making unit and that family and community networks affect the propensity of individuals to migrate. Less systematic attention has been devoted to understanding the ways in which family processes affect the outcomes of immigrants and how families themselves change with exposure to the U.S. social context. The chapters in this volume both assess the state of knowledge in this field and attempt to delineate a fruitful course for future studies.

Clearly, formidable challenges await future researchers. First is the challenge of transcending the straight-line assimilation theory that is increasingly viewed as unacceptable to scholars of immigration and ethnicity. Although alternative theories have been proposed (e.g., segmented assimilation), additional work on the conditions under which various pathways are taken is needed. Second, research on how the family itself changes with exposure to the U.S. social context is essential. A number of the chapters in this volume suggest that immigrant families lose some of their strengths as they spend more time in the United States. Although existing research suggests that this may be the case, studies of the changes in family structure and process that occur with duration of residence and across generations are sorely needed. Such studies are crucial for the development of models of the role of the family in immigrant adaptation. Finally, serious methodological issues add to the challenge of research on immigrant outcomes. Perhaps most serious are the problems inherent in the use of cross-sectional data to study immigrant adaptation processes. Ultimately, longitudinal data bases must be developed if we are to understand changes in immigrant families and the effect of the family on immigrants as they adjust to life in this country.

REFERENCES

Donato, K. M., Durand, J., & Massey, D. S. (1992). Stemming the tide? Assessing the deterrent effects of the Immigration Reform and Control Act. *Demography, 29*, 139–157.
Gordon, M. M. (1964). *Assimilation in American life*. New York: Oxford University Press.

Harris, J. R., & Todaro, M. P. (1970). Migration, unemployment and development: A two-sector analysis. *American Economic Review, 60,* 126–142.

Jensen, L., & Chitose, Y. (1994). Today's second generation: Evidence from the 1990 U.S. Census. *International Migration Review, 28,* 714–735.

Landale, N. S., & Oropesa, R. S. (1995). *Immigrant children and the children of immigrants: Inter- and intra-ethnic group differences in the United States.* (Population Research Group [PRG] Research Paper 95–2). East Lansing: Institute for Public Policy and Social Research, Michigan State University.

Martin, P., & Midgely, E. (1994). Immigration to the United States: Journey to an uncertain destination. *Population Bulletin, 49.*

Massey, D. S. (1990). Social structure, household strategies, and the cumulative causation of migration. *Population Index, 56,* 3–26.

Massey, D. S., Alarcon, R., Gonzalez, H., & Durand, J. (1987). *Return to Aztlan: The social process of international migration from Western Mexico.* Los Angeles, CA: University of California Press.

Massey, D. S., & Espinosa, K. (in press). What's driving Mexico–U.S. Migration? A theoretical, empirical, and policy analysis. *American Journal of Sociology.*

Park, R. E. (1950). *Race and culture.* Glencoe, IL: The Free Press.

Portes, A., & Zhou, M. (1993). The new second generation: Segmented assimilation and its variants. *Annals, AAPSS, 530,* 74–96.

Sjaastad, L. A. (1962). The costs and returns of human migration. *Journal of Political Economy, 70S,* 80–93.

Stark, O. (1984). Migration decision making: A review article. *Journal of Development Economics, 14,* 251–259.

Todaro, M. (1969). A model of labor migration and urban unemployment in less developed countries. *American Economic Review, 59,* 138–148.

Author Index

Subject Index